Oracle Database 10g Real Application Clusters Handbook

About the Author

K Gopalakrishnan (Gopal) is a senior principal consultant with the Advanced Technology Services group at Oracle Corporation, specializing exclusively in performance tuning, high availability, and disaster recovery. He is a recognized expert in Oracle RAC and Database Internals and has used his extensive expertise in solving many vexing performance issues all across the world for telecom giants, banks, financial institutions, and universities. Gopal has more than a decade of Oracle experience backed by an engineering degree in computer science and engineering from the University of Madras, India.

Gopal has previously co-authored an award-winning Oracle Press book, *Oracle Wait Interface: A Practical Guide to Performance Diagnostics and Tuning*. He was awarded an Editor's Choice award for Oracle Author of the Year by *Oracle Magazine* in 2005. Gopal was also chosen as an Oracle ACE by Oracle Technology Network (http://www.oracle.com/technology/index.html) in 2006.

Oracle Press™

Oracle Database 10g Real Application Clusters Handbook

K Gopalakrishnan

New York   Chicago   San Francisco
Lisbon   London   Madrid   Mexico City   Milan
New Delhi   San Juan   Seoul   Singapore   Sydney   Toronto

McGraw-Hill books are available at special quantity discounts to use as premiums and sales promotions, or for use in corporate training programs. For more information, please write to the Director of Special Sales, Professional Publishing, McGraw-Hill, Two Penn Plaza, New York, NY 10121-2298. Or contact your local bookstore.

Oracle Database 10g Real Application Clusters Handbook

34567890 FGR FGR 01987

ISBN-13:   978-0-07-146509-0
ISBN-10:   0-07-146509-X

Sponsoring Editor	**Technical Editors**	**Composition**
Lisa McClain	Scott Gossett and James Morle	International Typesetting and Composition
Editorial Supervisor	**Copy Editor**	
Jody McKenzie	Lisa Theobald	**Illustration**
Project Editor	**Indexer**	International Typesetting and Composition
Barbara Brodnitz	Jack Lewis	
Acquisitions Coordinator	**Production Supervisor**	**Art Director, Cover**
Mandy Canales	George Anderson	Jeff Weeks
		Cover Designer
		Pattie Lee

To my brother Dhans, my parents, and my beloved country

Contents at a Glance

PART V
Deploying RAC

Contents

PART I
High Availability Architecture and Clusters

PART III

RAC Administration and Management

PART IV
Advanced Concepts in RAC

PART V
Deploying RAC

Acknowledgments

Writing a book is not just simply about the author putting down thoughts or sharing knowledge via the printed material. It is like an orchestra. Many musicians have to come together and play their individual instruments in tune under the guidance of a good conductor to sound melodious. In the same way, a great team has to work together to help an author create a book. When a stellar team comes together this way, the result is a book that is both pleasurable to read and simple to comprehend. As the author of this book, I am greatly indebted to the team who stood behind me and helped me create this book.

First and foremost, my sincere thanks to Vijay Lunawat, who started with me as co-author of this book. Unfortunately, he could not continue for some unexpected reasons. Vijay has contributed immensely to the book, especially in the administration chapters, and helped me throughout the book in various forms. I thank Anand Rao for his constant support and for quickly helping me to get back on track. Anand has contributed to the chapters on application development, backup and recovery, and networking. The technical expertise of this pair and their practical knowledge are reflected throughout the book. Without Vijay and Anand, it would have been very tough sailing for me.

I thank my long-time friend, philosopher and guide John Kanagaraj, for his support in every project I start. John, an Oracle author himself, has been an inspiration from the very beginning. I salute him for his patience and guidance. John kept my sprits up whenever I was running low.

I wish to extend my sincere thanks to my managers Rene Foree, Jerry Rickers, and Shankar Jayaganapathy at Oracle Advanced Technology Services for supporting and encouraging me in this effort. Without their help and guidance, I am afraid that I would not have found time to work on this book. I must thank Ken Jacobs, Vivek Marla, Angelo Prucino, Sohan Demel, Erik Peterson, and Sheila Cepero, also from Oracle Corp., for their help and support at various stages.

I am thankful to everyone who contributed to this book either directly or indirectly. During the past few years, I have learned a lot from many people, and my special thanks go to Steve Adams, Jonathan Lewis, Sandesh Rao, Nandakumar, Scott Heisey, Nitin Vengurlekar, Gaja Vaidyanatha, Richard Stroupe, Sudheendra Vijayakumar, Madhavan Amruther, and Jaswinder Singh. I am thankful to Harish Kalra who was always willing to run my test scripts and Kirti Deshpande for his initial reviews.

I am truly indebted to my esteemed clients. They not only posed challenges but were also willing to implement my solutions in their systems. They played a big role in the knowledge acquisition and enhancement that I share in this book.

It was my pleasure to work with the fabulous team at McGraw-Hill: Lisa McClain, Barbara Brodnitz, Mandy Canales, Lisa Theobald, and Alexander McDonald. Thank you all very much for being so patient with me, and for making sure that this project stayed on track and on time.

Last but not least, I wish to thank my technical editors and reviewers Scott Gossett, James Morle, and Matt Sarboraria, whose great efforts are reflected in the rich content and timely completion of the book.

—K Gopalakrishnan

Introduction

Whatever is heard from whomsoever's mouth,
Wisdom will rightly discern its true meaning.

—Kural 423: Thiruvalluvar

I work as a consultant and visit many sites for Oracle RAC implementations around the globe. My regular work involves answering simple questions such as what platform to choose for RAC as well as working on very complex performance problems. Most of the customers I've met complain that there is no definite text available on the subject and many of them still treat RAC as a "black box." This is true even for seasoned database administrators who have been working on Oracle databases for many years! Customers who had previously implemented Oracle Parallel Server (OPS) also wanted to know how RAC works and how it is different from OPS.

Although a number of books on the market are devoted to Oracle RAC, I have not seen a single book that covers the complete spectrum of topics related to RAC. As a result, there is a significant gap in the public's knowledge about RAC internals and nuances. My failure to find any such book was the impetus to write this one. I was also emboldened as my other book (*Oracle Wait Interface: A Practical Guide to Performance Diagnostics and Tuning*) was a great success and even fetched me *Oracle Magazine's* Editor's Choice "Oracle Author of the Year" award in 2005.

As in my previous book, my goal in this book has been to explain implementing and using RAC in the most efficient manner rather than the theoretical overview about the grid. If you look at the contents, you will find nothing about grid technologies or grid architecture. Similarly you will not find any details about grid management, including the Enterprise Manager or Grid

Control and any of the fancy technical concepts. I have carefully avoided the topics that are not suitable for a wider audience.

I believe in the proverb, "Give a man a fish; you feed him for a day. Teach a man to fish, you feed him for life." Thus, the purpose of the book is to provide a solid background and fundamentals of Oracle Real Application Clusters rather than to provide a heap of commands and syntax that are readily available in the standard documentation and other Oracle texts. Although this book covers the spectrum of topics related to RAC, it is still by no means complete—it is more the start of a long and exciting journey. The expectation is that you can use this book as a reference and concepts guide with a long shelf life rather than using it for a specific release. I also don't intend to provide quick-fix solutions and commands. However, a few chapters contain best practice techniques and design considerations relevant to Oracle 9i and 10g.

Some of the concepts discussed here are truly complex, and I would recommend that you skip them during the first read. Once you are done reading the book, revisit these chapters a few times till you obtain a clear understanding of the concepts. Note that a few of the concepts discussed here are applicable only to current versions of Oracle unless noted otherwise.

You may also notice that some of the technical topics are treated very lightly. So, as a DBA, you just need to have a basic but solid understanding of the architecture of Oracle and the way it works. I believe that discussions about some deep technical aspects are impractical and not really required everywhere. For example, the inner workings of Cache Fusion and distributed lock managers cannot be explained in a single chapter. In my opinion, each deserves an independent book on its own. Thus, be aware that the discussions are modeled according to the context of this title.

The book is organized in five distinct parts.

Part I deals with the history and architecture of high availability clusters and compares the various clustering architecture. It also dives deep into Oracle clustering architecture, including Oracle Parallel Server and the evolution of the Oracle clustering technologies. It covers the architecture of Real Application Clusters and Oracle kernel components that make RAC a working solution.

Chapter 1 talks about high availability architecture and clusters. Here, you will learn the most common techniques used for availability and see the impact of planned and unplanned downtime for the business. The most common solutions used to achieve high availability and scalability are covered. Hardware clustering is the most commonly used method to achieve high availability and on-demand scalability.

Chapter 2 introduces the rich history of RAC with some details about the basics of clustering technologies and a discussion of the early days of Oracle Parallel Server. It also discusses the intrinsic limitations of Oracle Parallel Server and how RAC overcomes those limitations with the new techniques. You'll learn some basics about DLM locking, too.

Chapter 3 introduces Oracle RAC architecture and the components that make it work. You'll learn why global coordination is required for RAC. A brief discussion on RAID is included since RAC relies on shared storage for database operations. Version 10g–related technologies such as CRS and Automatic Storage Management (ASM) are also introduced.

Part II of this book deals with the installation of RAC software and ASM. It provides basic details of preparing the hardware for RAC and installing RAC in generic UNIX and Linux environments. The fundamentals of ASM are also introduced here.

Chapter 4 is about preparing the hardware for RAC installation. A proper and sound preparation of the hardware for the RAC installation tasks is the key to a successful deployment. Oracle Cluster Ready Services (CRS) is the Oracle Clusterware that logically binds the servers at operating system level, and installing the Oracle Clusterware is discussed.

Chapter 5 deals exclusively with installation of RAC on the cluster. Screenshots guide you through RAC and ASM software installation. The new clusterverify utility is used to validate the integrity of the Installation.

Chapter 6 is on ASM, the new database file system from Oracle. You'll learn how to manage disk groups and administer disk groups in the ASM environment, and you'll learn the command-line tools provided by ASM, including the ASMCMD and ASMFTP utility. The Oracle-provided utility asmlib is also briefly discussed in this chapter.

Part III discusses the generic administration of the RAC databases. It offers notes on the basic administration of an RAC database and lists the similarities and differences between single instance management and RAC database management. RAC Performance Management is introduced and the most common issues and wait scenarios in 10g RAC are discussed with potential solutions where applicable. Along with administration of the advanced administration, this part discusses details on service management of the RAC. Services are new in Oracle 10g.

Chapter 7 talks about administering an RAC database from a DBAs' perspective. Administering RAC is similar to administering a single instance database with slight changes. This chapter looks at the considerations for RAC database administration and covers the administration topics for Oracle CRS and voting disks.

Chapter 8 is about administering services in the RAC environment. Services are new in 10g and simplify resource management and workload distribution and provide high availability to the workload.

Chapter 9 covers backup and recovery concepts for RAC, and the concepts of instance and database recovery in RAC are discussed in more detail. Commands and syntaxes of backup and recovery procedures are not covered. This chapter delves deep into the architecture of recovery in a single instance environment, and provides good insight into the different types of recovery in an RAC database.

Chapter 10 deals with performance management in RAC. Managing and achieving good performance in any system is probably the primary objective and even more so in RAC. RAC design and performance tuning needs a few extra considerations when compared to single instance design and tuning because of the additional instances accessing the same set of the resources. Oracle RAC 10g has an additional set of wait events and those specific events are covered in detail along with advice on tuning those events

Part IV of this book is intended for advanced topics. It gets into the resource management aspect of an RAC environment and discusses how resources are shared and managed. Global cache services and global enqueue services and their inner workings are discussed, along with Cache Fusion details, including a complete overview of how things worked in the past and how Cache Fusion has changed the dynamics of data sharing between instances. Load balancing and failover topics are also discussed.

Chapter 11 is a detailed discussion of Global Resource Directory and what it does. You'll learn the different locking and serialization mechanisms and also their importance and relevance in operating an RAC database. Note that the discussions are quite deep in nature and may require that you read the chapter a few times to grasp the contents effectively. Resource mastering issues are also discussed.

Chapter 12 provides details about Cache Fusion. You'll see how Cache Fusion really works with examples and demonstration. This is the most important chapter in this book, and understanding Cache Fusion will help you appreciate the intelligence built in to this component. It will also help you design a scalable RAC solution. Here you will learn some of the exciting and internal techniques of how RAC works in Oracle 10g as well as 9i. A well documented example helps you understand the facts easily.

Chapter 13 introduces workload management from Oracle's perspective. You'll learn about Transparent Application Failover (TAF) and how to implement it. Oracle 10g introduced Fast Application Notification (FAN) and service-based management. This chapter talks about all these and their usage.

Chapter 14 deals with RAC troubleshooting, one of the least known topics. This chapter attempts to provide you with some of the methods that can be used quickly to troubleshoot a misbehaving RAC instance. This chapter discusses troubleshooting from an operational perspective and introduces performance diagnosis as well troubleshooting instance recovery.

Part V talks about deploying RAC, including extending RAC to a geocluster environment and common application development best practices. The most common RAC application development techniques are discussed here.

Chapter 15 discusses extending RAC in a WAN environment. Oracle RAC is most commonly used as a scalability and availability solution. However, in specific cases, it could also be used as a disaster recovery solution.

Chapter 16 introduces some of the best practices in application development for RAC. It covers some of the most commonly found issues in an RAC environment and provides some best practice methods for overcoming those challenges.

Most useful and commonly used V$ views are explained in Appendix A. The dynamic performance views are grouped together based on their use. Appendix B discusses adding nodes to and removing nodes from a cluster. Appendix C lists the texts used as references during the writing of this book.

By no means have we attempted to cover all the aspects of RAC. This is just the beginning.

As an author, I would like to hear from you about how you liked the book and what could be done to improve it. Please feel free to contact me at kaygopal@yahoo.com with any comments you have regarding this book.

PART I

High Availability
Architecture and Clusters

CHAPTER
1

Introduction to High Availability and Scalability

n today's super-fast world, data and application *availability* can make or break a business. With access to these businesses granted via the ubiquitous and "always-on" Internet, data availability is an extremely important component in any business function.

Database systems are growing at an enormous rate in terms of both the number of simultaneously connected and active users as well as the volume of data they handle. Even though the servers used to store huge, active databases have also improved in performance and capacity, a single server, powerful though it may be, may not be able to handle the database load and capacity requirements, making it necessary to scale the processing load or scale the hardware or software to accommodate these requirements.

High Availability

When availability is everything for a business, extremely high levels of disaster tolerance must allow the business to continue in the face of a disaster, without the end-users or customers noticing any adverse consequences. The effects of global businesses across time zones spanning $24 \times 7 \times$ forever operations, e-commerce, and the risks associated with the modern world drive businesses to achieve a level of disaster tolerance capable of ensuring continuous survival and profitability.

Different businesses require different levels of risk with regard to loss of data and potential downtime. A variety of technical solutions can be used to provide various levels of protection with respect to these business needs. The ideal solutions would have no downtime and allow no data to be lost. Such solutions do exist, but they are expensive, and their costs must be weighed against the potential impact to the business of a disaster and its effects.

Computers are working faster and faster, and the businesses that depend on them are placing more and more demands on them. The various interconnections and dependencies in the computing fabric consisting of different components and technologies is becoming more complex every day. The availability of worldwide access via the Internet is placing extremely high demands on businesses and the IT departments and administrators that run and maintain these computers in the background.

Adding to this complexity is the globalization of businesses, which ensures that there is no "quiet time" or "out of office hours" so essential to the maintenance requirements of these computer systems. Hence, businesses' computer systems—the life blood of the organization—must be available at all times: day or night, weekday or weekend, local holiday or workday. The term $24 \times 7 \times$ *forever* effectively describes business computer system availability and is so popular that this term is being used in everyday language to describe non-computer–based entities such as 9-1-1 call centers and other emergency services.

The dictionary defines the word *available* as follows: 1) Present and ready for use; at hand; accessible. 2) Capable of being gotten; obtainable. 3) Qualified and willing to be of service or assistance. When applied to computer systems, the word's meaning is a combination of all these factors. Thus, access to an application should be present and ready for use, capable of being accessed, and qualified and willing to be of service. In other words, an application should be available easily for use at any time and should perform at a level that is both acceptable and useful. Although this is a broad, sweeping statement, a lot of complexity and different factors come into play when availability is present.

HA Terminology

The term *high availability* (*HA*), when applied to computer systems, means that the application or service in question is available all the time, regardless of time of day, location, and other factors that can influence the availability of such an application. In general, it is the ability to continue a service for extremely long durations without any interruptions. Typical technologies for HA include redundant power supplies and fans for servers, RAID (Redundant Array of Inexpensive/Independent Disks) configuration for disks, clusters for servers, multiple network interface cards, and redundant routers for networks.

Fault Tolerance

A *fault-tolerant* computer system or component is designed so that, in the event of component failure, a backup component or procedure can immediately take its place with no loss of service. Fault tolerance can be provided with software, embedded in hardware, or provided by some combination of the two. It goes one step further than HA to provide the highest possible availability within a single data center.

Disaster Recovery

Disaster recovery (DR) is the ability to resume operations after a disaster—including destruction of an entire data center site and everything in it. In a typical DR scenario, significant time elapses before a data center can resume IT functions, and some amount of data typically needs to be re-entered to bring the system data back up to date.

Disaster Tolerance

The term *disaster tolerance* (DT) is the art and science of preparing for disaster so that a business is able to continue operation after a disaster. The term is sometimes used incorrectly in the industry, particularly by vendors who can't really achieve it. Disaster tolerance is much more difficult to achieve than DR, as it involves designing systems that enable a business to continue in the face of a disaster, without the end users or customers noticing any adverse effects. The ideal DT solution would result in no downtime and no lost data, even during a disaster. Such solutions do exist, but they cost more than solutions that have some amount of downtime or data loss associated with a disaster.

Planned and Unplanned Outages

So what happens when an application stops working or stops behaving as expected, due to the failure of even one of the crucial components? Such an application is deemed *down* and the event is called an *outage*. This outage can be planned for—for example, consider the outage that occurs when a component is being upgraded or worked on for maintenance reasons.

While planned outages are a necessary evil, an unplanned outage can be a nightmare for a business. Depending on the business in question and the duration of the downtime, an unplanned outage can result in such overwhelming losses that the business is forced to close. Regardless of the nature, outages are something that businesses usually do not tolerate. There is always pressure on IT to eliminate unplanned downtime totally and drastically reduce, if not eliminate, planned downtime. We will see later how these two requirements can be effectively met for at least the Oracle database component.

Note that an application or computer system does not have to be totally down for an outage to occur. It is possible that the performance of an application degrades to such a degree that it is unusable. In this case, although the application is accessible, it does not meet the third and final qualification of being willing to serve in an adequately acceptable fashion. As far as the business or end user is concerned, this application is down, although it is available. We will see later in this book how Oracle Real Application Clusters (RAC) can provide the horizontal scalability that can significantly reduce the risk of an application not providing adequate performance.

An End-to-End Perspective

From the start, you should be clear that high availability is not just dependent on the availability of physical components such as hardware, system software (operating system and database), environment, network, and application software. It is also dependent on other "soft" resources such as experienced and capable administrators (system, network, database, and application specialists), programmers, users, and even known, repeatable business processes. It is entirely possible that a business installs and configures highly available "hard" components but does not employ competent administrators who are able to maintain these systems properly. Even if the administrators are competent, availability can be adversely affected when a business process, such as change control, is not followed properly, and incorrect, untested changes are made that could bring such a system down. High availability thus needs to be seen with an end-to-end perspective that covers all aspects.

Having said this, we should now define the *single point of failure* (SPOF)—any single component that can bring down the entire system as a result of failure. For example, when a computer system has a single controller that interfaces to the disk subsystem, a hardware failure of this controller will bring the whole system down. Although the other components are working, this single component has caused a failure. Identification of and protection against SPOFs are crucial tasks of providing HA.

It is not possible to cover all aspects of HA in an Oracle-specific book such as this. We will cover only how HA can be achieved specifically in the area of the Oracle RDBMS, which is an important component of the HA picture. We will also equip you—the database administrator, programmer, or architect—with techniques that will enable you to achieve HA in these areas.

As well, HA is not something that can be achieved simply by installing HA-aware hardware and software components, employing competent administrators, creating proper procedures, and walking away from it all. The HA process needs continual adjustment, evolution, and adaptation to changing circumstances and environments. Sometimes, this uphill battle occurs on a continual basis—so be prepared!

Cost of Downtime

As hinted at earlier, there is a cost to downtime, just as there is a cost to ensuring that downtime is drastically reduced or even completely eliminated. The trick is to build your systems so that they never go down, even though you *know* that they *will* go down at some time or another. Making downtime the last option will ensure HA. Of course, most companies cannot continue to throw large sums of money at this issue. At some point in time, the additional money spent will return only marginal benefits. Thus, it is essential to price out your downtime and then use that figure to determine how much you can afford to spend to protect against these problems. With some effort and experience, this expense can be determined, and you might want to use this information while providing various options and scenarios to management.

The cost of being down usually amounts to lost user productivity, and the actual cost is mostly dependent on what work the users perform when accessing the affected systems. For example, if your development server went down for one hour during prime office time, and 10 developers sat

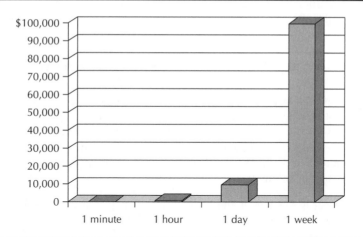

FIGURE 1-1. *Cost of downtime*

idle for that hour waiting for the server to come up, and each developer costs $100 per hour, then the downtime has effectively cost $100 × 10 × 1 = $1,000. However, if the server that went down served a major shopping site on the Internet during a holiday gift-buying season, you might count the losses in millions of dollars, even if the downtime was brief, as shoppers may move away to a competing site rather than wait for yours to become usable. Figure 1-1 shows an example chart comparing downtime to cost.

The potential cost of downtime is also dependent on various factors such as time of day and duration of the downtime. For example, an online stock brokerage firm cannot afford to be down even for seconds during business hours. On the other hand, it could go down for hours during non-trading hours without any consequences. Cost of downtime is not linearly dependent on the duration of the downtime. For example, a two-hour outage may not necessarily cost the same as two one-hour downtime periods.

One helpful trick used with balancing cost of downtime versus cost of ensuring no downtime is an "availability curve." The more you spend on HA components, the higher you move up the curve. However, the incremental costs of moving from one level to the next increase as you move up the curve.

Four distinct levels of system availability components on the curve are as follows:

- **Basic systems**   These are systems with no protection or those that employ no special measures to protect their data and accessibility. Normal backups occur, and administrators work to restore the system if and when it breaks. There is no extra cost for HA.

- **Redundant data**   Some level of disk redundancy is built into the system to protect against loss of data due to disk failures. At the most basic level, this is provided by RAID 5 or RAID 1–based disk subsystems. At the other end of the scale, redundancy is provided by storage area networks (SANs) that have built-in disk protecting mechanisms such as various RAID levels, hot swappable disks, "phone-home" type maintenance, and multiple paths to the SAN. The cost of such protection includes procurement of the SAN, attendant SAN fabric and controllers, as well as extra sets of disks to provide RAID protection.

■ **System failover** In this case, two or more systems are employed to do the work of one. When the primary system fails, the other, usually called the secondary system, takes over and performs the work of the primary. A brief loss of service occurs, but everything quickly works as it did before the failure. The cost of this solution is more than double that of the basic systems. Usually, a SAN needs to be employed to make sure that the disks are protected and to provide multiple paths to the disks from these servers.

■ **Disaster recovery** In this case, in addition to the systems at the main site (which in themselves may incorporate the previous highest level of protection), all or part of these systems are duplicated at a backup site that is usually physically remote from the main site. You must develop ways of replicating the data and keeping it up to date. The costs are more than double that of the previous level, as you will also have to duplicate an entire site including data centers, real estate facilities, and so on.

As you can easily see, higher and higher levels of availability equate to escalating costs. When faced with even a rough estimate of cost, business leaders (and especially accounting staff) are quick to adjust their levels of expectancy.

Underpinning every aspect, of course, is the fact that you are monitoring, measuring, and recording all this uptime (or downtime as the case may be). It is a given that you cannot quantify what you do not measure. Nevertheless, many organizations that demand 100 percent uptime do not even have basic measurement tools in place.

Five Nines

The phrase *five nines* is usually thrown about during discussions of high availability, and you need to understand what this means before agreeing (as an administrator or system architect) to provide such a level of availability. A user or project leader will invariably say that 100 percent availability is a necessity, and barring that, at least five nines availability must be maintained—that is, 99.999 percent availability.

To make this concept a bit clearer, the following table compares uptime and downtime percentages to real time figures. As you study this table, keep in mind that the cost of providing higher and higher levels of uptime become successively (and sometimes prohibitively) expensive. As you work with management, understanding this can help you provide a clear explanation of these terms and what they mean when translated to actual downtime and attendant costs.

Percent Uptime	Percent Downtime	Downtime per Year	Downtime per Week
98	2	7.3 days	3 hours, 22 minutes
99	1	3.65 days	1 hour, 41 minutes
99.8	0.2	17 hours, 30 minutes	20 minutes, 10 seconds
99.9	0.1	8 hours, 45 minutes	10 minutes, 5 seconds
99.99	0.01	52.5 minutes	1 minute
99.999	0.001	5.25 minutes	6 seconds

Building Redundant Components

High availability is made possible by providing availability in multiple layers of the technical stack. Key to this is the inclusion of redundant components that reduce or eliminate SPOFs. For example, more than one host bus adaptor (HBA), a controller for communicating with remote disks, is usually present in each server that connects to a SAN. These HBAs in turn are able to connect into two or more network adaptor switches to which the SANs are themselves connected. This way, the failure of one HBA or even one network switch will not bring down the server and the application hosted on that server. *Multi-hosting* (the ability to attach multiple hosts to a single set of disks) and *multi-pathing* (the ability to attach a single host to its set of disks via more than one path) are common ways of introducing redundancy in such HA systems.

Redundant components exist in the software layers as well. For example, multiple web servers can be front-ended by a load balancer that will direct all web requests to a bank of web servers. In this case, when one web server fails, existing connections migrate over to surviving web servers, and the load balancer connects new requests to these surviving web servers.

Redundancy is not restricted to hardware and software, however. Redundancy also includes building physical, environmental, and other elements into the framework. Most of the major Internet data centers or Internet exchange points now have complete redundancy in terms of power, air conditioning, and other factors, so that the failure in any one of the provider's resources won't affect the operation.

In New York City, for example, two telecommunication systems were strategically placed one in each tower of the erstwhile World Trade Center complex, with the assumption that the probability of both buildings collapsing was close to zero. However, unfortunately, that assumption was proved wrong. Now, companies are building redundant data centers that are geographically separated across state or even country boundaries to avoid natural or other catastrophic events. Availability of dark fibers and the improvements in technology such as dense wavelength division multiplexers (DWDMs) make this possible.

Redundancy in the network layer is achieved through the redundant hardware engines in a chassis, a redundant network through multiple chassis, or a combination of the two. Host protocols such as ICMP Route Discovery Protocol (IRDP), Cisco's Hot Standby Routing Protocol (HSRP), and Virtual Router Redundancy Protocol (VRRP) help choose the best next-hop router to reach if one of the routers is unavailable from the server's perspective. In the routing level, Non-Stop Forwarding (NSF) protocol suites combined with millisecond timers reduce the failure or switchover time in case of primary hardware switching engine failure.

In the transport level, physical layer redundancy can be achieved by SDH/SONET self healing that restores the traffic in an alternative path in case of fiber link failure. During early 2000, a major transport provider experienced fiber cut in its long-haul, coast-to-coast transport network in the United States and rerouted the traffic through Europe without most of the end users knowing that the rerouting even took place.

As well, it is now possible to provide redundant database services via use of the Oracle RAC, and you will see this in detail in subsequent chapters. Suffice it to say at this time that redundancy in database services is an important part of providing HA in the organization, and Oracle RAC enables such a provision.

Of course, adding redundancy into the system also increases its cost and complexity. We hope that the information contained in this book can help you understand that complexity and ease your fears about managing such a complex environment.

Common Solutions for HA

Depending on your budget, you can arrive at a number of solutions for providing high availability. Clustering servers has been a common way to build a highly available and scalable solution. You can provide increasing levels of HA by adopting one of the higher levels of protection described earlier. In most current data centers, RAID disks, usually in SANs, provide at least a basic level of disk protection. Failover servers at the third level provide some protection from server failure. At the highest level, the disaster recovery site protects against drastic site failure.

Oracle technology can be used to provide all these levels of protection. For example, you can use Automatic Storage Management (ASM) to provide protection at the disk level, Oracle RAC to provide failover protection at the database level (in addition to database level load balancing), and Oracle standby and Oracle replication to provide site protection failure. Of course, all this requires varying levels of support at the hardware, network, and software layers.

Cluster, Cold Failover, and Hot Failover

Although we will be dealing with clustering in detail in subsequent chapters, we will define it here. A *cluster* is a set of two or more similar servers that are closely connected to one another and usually share the same set of disks. The theory is that in case of failure of one of the servers, the other surviving server (or servers) can take up the work of the failed server. These servers are physically located close to one another and connected via a "heartbeat" system. In other words, they check one another's heartbeats or live presence at closely defined intervals and are able to detect whether the other node is "dead" within a short period of time. When one of the nodes is deemed nonresponsive to a number of parameters, a failover event is initiated and the service of the nonresponsive node is taken over by other node(s). Additional software may also allow a quick takeover of one another's functions.

Clusters can be configured in many fashions. When one or more servers in a cluster sits idle, and takeover from another server (or servers) occurs only in the case of a failure, a *cold failover* occurs. When all servers in a cluster are working, and the load is taken on by the surviving server (or servers), this is called a *hot failover*. Assuming that all the servers in the cluster are similar in configuration, in a cold failover, the load carried by the surviving server is the same. In case of a hot failover, however, the load taken on by the surviving server may be more than it can handle, and thus you will need to design both the servers and the load carefully.

There are three general approaches to system failover. In order of increasing availability, they are *no failover*, *cold failover*, and *hot failover*. Each strategy has varying recovery time, expense, and user impact, as outlined in the following table.

Approach	Recovery Time	Expense	User Impact
No failover	Unpredictable	No to low cost	High
Cold failover	Minutes	Moderate	Moderate
Hot failover	Immediate or in seconds	Moderate to high	None

(To be precise, saying there is no user impact in a hot failover scenario is inaccurate. Very few systems are truly "hot" to the point of no user impact; most are somewhat "lukewarm," with a transient brownout.)

Variations on these strategies do exist: for example, many large enterprise clients have implemented hot failover and also use cold failover for disaster recovery. It is important to differentiate between *failover* and *disaster recovery*. *Failover* is a methodology used to resume system availability in an acceptable period of time, while *disaster recovery* is a methodology used to resume system availability when all failover strategies have failed.

No Failover

If a production system failure occurs, such as a hardware failure, the database and application are generally unaffected. Disk degradation, of course, is an exception. Disk redundancy and good backup procedures are vital to mitigate problems arising from disk failure.

With no failover strategy in place, system failures can result in significant downtime, depending on the cause and your ability to isolate and resolve it. If a CPU has failed, you replace it and restart, while application users wait for the system to become available. For many applications that are not business-critical, this risk may be acceptable.

Cold Failover

A common and often inexpensive approach to recovery after failure is to maintain a standby system to assume the production workload in the event of a production system failure. A typical configuration has two identical computers with shared access to a remote disk subsystem.

After a failure, the standby system takes over the applications formerly running on the failed system. In a cold failover, the standby system senses a heartbeat from the production system on a frequent and regular basis. If the heartbeat consistently stops for a period of time, the standby system assumes the IP address and the disk formerly associated with the failed system. The standby can then run any applications that were on the failed system. In this scenario, when the standby system takes over the application, it executes a preconfigured start script to bring the databases online. Users can then reconnect to the databases that are now running on the standby server.

Customers generally configure the failover server to mirror the main server with an identical CPU and memory capacity to sustain production workloads for an extended period of time. Figure 1-2 depicts server connections before and after a failover.

Hot Failover

The hot failover approach can be complicated and expensive, but it comes closest to ensuring 100 percent uptime. It requires the same degree of failover used for a cold failover but also requires that the state of a running user process be preserved to allow the process to resume on a failover server. One approach, for example, uses a three-tiered configuration of clients and servers. Hot failover clusters are normally capable of client load balancing, Oracle RAC supports hot failover configuration.

The following table shows load distribution of a 3,000-user work load in a 3-node cluster. During normal operation, all nodes share approximately an equal number of connections; and after failover, the work load from the failed node will be distributed to surviving nodes.

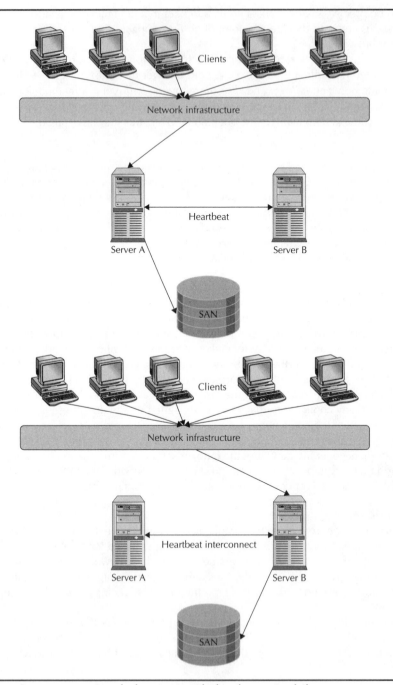

FIGURE 1-2. *Server connections before (top) and after (bottom) a failover*

State	A	B	C
Normal	1,000 users	1,000 users	1,000 users
B fails	1,000 users	0 users	1,000 users
B users log on again	1,500 users	0 users	1,500 users

The 1,000 users on servers A and C are unaware of server B's failure, but the 1,000 users that were on the failed server are affected.

The most common aspects of cold failover versus hot failover are summarized in the following table.

Aspects	Cold Failover	Hot Failover
Scalability/number of nodes	Scalability limited to the capacity of the single node.	As nodes can be added on demand, it provides infinite scalability. High number of nodes supported.
User interruption required	Required up to a minimal extent. The failover operation can be scripted or automated to a certain extent.	Not required. Failover is automatic.
Transparent failover of applications	Not possible.	Transparent application failover will be available where the sessions can be transferred to another node without user interruption.
Load balancing	Not possible; only one server will be used.	Incoming load can be balanced between both nodes.
Usage of resources	Only one server at a time; the other server will be kept idle.	Both the servers will be used.
Failover time	More than minutes as the other system must be cold started.	Less than a minute; typically in a few seconds.

HA Option Pros and Cons

Each HA option has its own advantages and disadvantages. Costs of setup and running the service are important to consider when deciding which HA option to use. At the end of the day, as an administrator or system architect, you are responsible for costing out the various options and helping management decide what is best. As well, you will need to figure in the additional complexity of maintaining various configurations, remembering that as you add more redundancy into the system, you are also increasing the options for failure when handling these now complex configurations. In addition, employing consultants to set up these complex configurations, deploy additional hardware and software, and maintain these systems can also quickly add to the basic costs.

Scalability

As mentioned at the beginning of the chapter, even powerful servers cannot always handle database load and capacity requirements. Server scalability can be improved using one or more of the following methods:

- Increase the processor count on the system, or *scale-up* the computing resources.
- Increase the amount of work done in a given time via application tuning or *speed-up* processing.

The most common view of scaling is that of hardware scaling, which has at least as much to do with the software components as with the hardware. But what do you do when you cannot increase the processor count as you have reached the maximum capacity for that line of servers, or when you have tuned all the workloads as best you can and no more tuning opportunities exist?

Initial solutions to these problems include the use of multiple application copies and databases, but this results in data sync problems and other process issues. The best solution, of course, is the use of clustered servers that can collectively perform much better than a single server for many applications. This is exactly where Oracle RAC excels.

Oracle Real Application Cluster Solution

Oracle Corporation introduced database clustering with Oracle version 6.2 exclusively on the DEC VAX/VMS. We will deal with many details of RAC in later chapters and see how RAC provides for high availability and scalability. Keep in mind that application scalability is based on how good the application scales in a single instance. You might compare RAC to a stereo amplifier: if the quality of the recording, whether on an audio tape or a digital device, is bad, placing even the best amplifier in front of it will not solve the problem. Instead, it will amplify it and make the situation unbearable. This is also applicable for RAC or any other scalability solution.

Oracle RAC-based systems can be configured to eliminate SPOF as far as the database layer is concerned. When database servers fail, applications based on Oracle RAC systems simply keep running. When designed and coded properly, this application failover is mostly transparent to users.

When combined with Oracle Data Guard, Oracle RAC is protected from major site failures. Oracle RAC enables horizontal scalability and thus the ability to support large, global single instance computing that hosts thousands of users. When protected via various HA options, such single global instances significantly reduce costs via consolidation in terms of servers, data centers, software licenses, and skilled staff to maintain them.

In a Nutshell

Modern business requirements have great impact on database and application availability. The key to designing highly available systems relies on eliminating single point failures in all critical components. Clusters provide an enterprise with uninterrupted access to their business-critical information, enabling the nonstop functions of the business. Clusters can be configured with various failover modes, depending on the requirements of the business. When designed and implemented judiciously, clusters also provide infinite scalability to business applications.

CHAPTER
2

Clustering Basics
and History

s defined in Chapter 1, a cluster is a group of interconnected nodes that acts like a single server. In other words, clustering can be viewed logically as a method for enabling multiple standalone servers to work together as a coordinated unit called a *cluster*. The servers participating in the cluster must be *homogenous*—that is, they must use the same platform architecture, operating system, and almost identical hardware architecture and software patch levels—and independent machines that respond to the same requests from a pool of client requests.

Traditionally, clustering has been used to *scale up* systems, to *speed up* systems, and to *survive failures.*

Scaling is achieved by adding extra nodes to the cluster group, enabling the cluster to handle progressively larger workloads. Clustering provides horizontal on-demand scalability without incurring any downtime for reconfiguration.

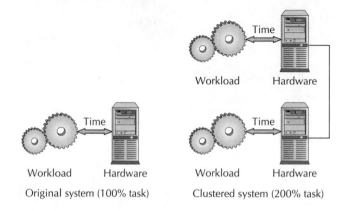

Original system (100% task)   Clustered system (200% task)

Speeding up is accomplished by splitting a large workload into multiple smaller workloads and running them in parallel in the available CPUs. Parallel processing provides massive improvement in performance for jobs that can be run in parallel. The simple "divide and capture" approach is applied to the large workloads, and parallel processing uses the power of all the resources to get work done faster.

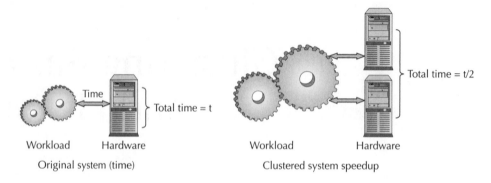

Original system (time)   Clustered system speedup

Because a cluster is a group of independent hardware nodes, failure in one node does not halt the application from functioning on the other nodes. The application and the services are seamlessly transferred to the surviving nodes and the application continues to function normally as it was functioning before the node failure. In some cases, the application or the user process may not even be aware of such failures, as the failover to the other node is transparent to the application.

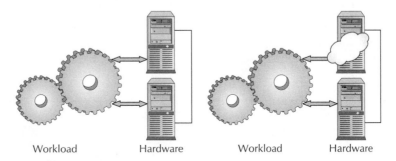

| Workload | Hardware | Workload | Hardware |

When a uniprocessor system reaches its processing limit, it imposes a big threat to scalability. Symmetric multiprocessing (SMP)—the use of multiple processors (CPUs) sharing memory (RAM) within a single computer to provide increased processing capability—solves this problem. SMP machines achieve high performance by *parallelism*, in which the processing job is split up and run on the available CPUs. Higher scalability is achieved by adding more CPUs and memory.

Figure 2-1 compares the basic architectural similarities between symmetric multiprocessing and clustering. However, the two architectures maintain cache coherency at totally different levels and latencies.

Grid Computing with Clusters

Clustering is part of Oracle's grid computing methodology, by which several low-cost commodity hardware components are networked together to achieve increased computing capacity. On-demand scalability is provided by supplying additional nodes and distributing the workload to available machines.

Performance improvement of an application can be done via three methods:

- By working harder
- By working smarter
- By getting help

Working harder means adding more CPUs and more memory so that the processing power increases to handle any amount of workload. This is the usual approach and often helps as additional CPUs address the workload problems. However, this approach is not quite economical, as the average cost of the computing power does not always increase in a linear manner. Adding computing power for a single SMP box increases the cost and complexity at a logarithmic scale.

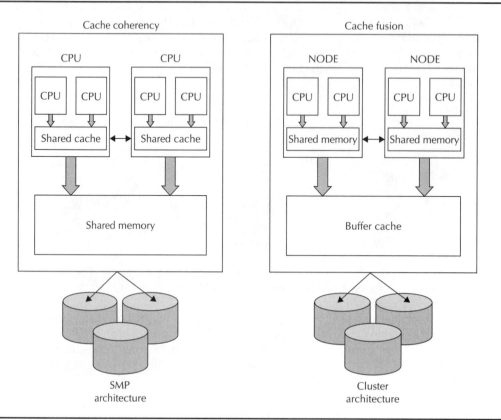

FIGURE 2-1. *SMP vs. clusters*

Working smarter is accomplished by employing intelligent and efficient algorithms. These reduce the total amount of work to be done to achieve the desired results. Working smarter often requires rewriting the application or changing the way it works (or sometimes changing the application design itself), which is quite impossible for a running application and requires unacceptable downtime. This option sometimes becomes almost impossible for a third-party vendor and packaged applications, as getting everyone onboard can become a tedious and time-consuming task.

Getting help can be as simple as using other machines' computing power to do the work. In other words, getting help is simply clustering the hardware, using the spare processing capacity of the idle nodes, and combining the processing transaction results at the end. More importantly, this approach does not require any changes to the application because it is transparent to the application. Another advantage to using this approach is that it allows on-demand scalability—you can choose to get help whenever required, and you do not need to invest in massive hardware.

Shared Storage in Clustering

One of the key components in clustering is *shared storage*. Storage is accessible to all nodes, and all nodes can parallelly read and write to the shared storage depending on the configuration of the cluster. Some configurations allow the storage to be accessible by all the nodes at all times; some allow sharing only during failovers.

More importantly, the application will see the cluster as a single system image and not as multiple connected machines. The cluster manager does not expose the system to the application, and the cluster is transparent to the application. Sharing the data among the available nodes is a key concept in scaling and is achieved using several types of architectures.

Types of Clustering Architectures

Clustering architecture can be broadly categorized in three types based on how storage is shared among the nodes:

- Shared nothing architecture
- Shared disk architecture
- Shared everything architecture

Table 2-1 compares the most common functionalities across the types of clustering architectures and their pros and cons along with implementation details with examples. Shared disks and shared everything architecture slightly differ in the number of nodes and storage sharing.

Shared Nothing Architecture

Shared nothing architecture is built using a group of independent servers, with each server taking a predefined workload (see Figure 2-2). If, for example, a number of servers are in the cluster, the total workload is divided by the number of servers, and each server caters to a specific workload. The biggest disadvantage of shared nothing architecture is that it requires careful application partitioning, and no dynamic addition of nodes is possible. Adding a node would require complete redeployment, so it is not a scalable solution. Oracle does not support the shared nothing architecture.

In shared nothing clusters, data is typically divided across separate nodes. The nodes have little need to coordinate their activity, since each is responsible for different subsets of the overall database. But in strict shared nothing clusters, if one node is down, its fraction of the overall data is unavailable.

The clustered servers neither share disks nor mirror data—each has its own resources. Servers transfer ownership of their respective disks from one server to another in the event of a failure. A shared nothing cluster uses software to accomplish these transfers. This architecture avoids the distributed lock manager (DLM) bottleneck issue associated with shared disks while offering comparable availability and scalability. Examples of shared nothing clustering solutions include Tandem NonStop, Informix OnLine Extended Parallel Server (XPS), and Microsoft Cluster Server.

The biggest advantage of shared nothing clusters is that they provide linear scalability for data warehouse applications, as they are ideally suited for that. However, they are unsuitable for online transaction processing (OLTP) workloads, and they are not totally redundant, so failure of one node will make the application running on that node unavailable. Still, most major databases, such as IBM DB2 Enterprise Edition, Informix XPS, and NCR Teradata, do implement shared nothing clusters.

Function	Shared Nothing	Shared Disks	Shared Everything
Disk ownership/ sharing	Disks are owned by individual nodes and are not shared among any of the nodes at any time.	Disks are usually owned by active nodes and the ownership is transferred to the surviving node during failure of the active node—i.e., disks are shared only during failures.	Disks are always shared and all instances have equal rights to the disk. Any instance can read/ write data to any of the disks as no disk is owned by any nodes. (Basically JBOD shared between all the nodes.)
Number of nodes	Typically very high number.	Normally two nodes, with only one node active at any time.	Two or more depending on the configuration. Number of nodes sometimes limited by the cluster manager or distributed lock manager (DLM) capacity when vendor supplied clusterware is used.
Data partitioning	Strictly partitioned as one node cannot access the data from the other nodes. Local nodes can access data local to that node.	Data partitioning not required as only one instance will access the complete set of data.	No data partitioning required as the data can be accessed from any nodes of the cluster.
Client coordinator	External server or any group member.	No coordinator required as the other node is used only during failover.	Not required. Any node can be accessed for any set of data.
Performance overhead	No overhead.	No overhead.	No overhead after three nodes. Less overhead up to three nodes.
Lock manager	Not required.	Not required.	DLM required to manage the resources.
Initial/on-demand scalability	Initially highly scalable, but limited to capacity of the individual node for local access. On-demand scalability not possible.	Not very scalable. Scalability limited to the computing capacity of the single node.	Infinitely scalable as nodes can be added on demand.

TABLE 2-1. *Functionalities of Clustering Architectures*

Function	Shared Nothing	Shared Disks	Shared Everything
Write access	Each node can write but only to its own disks. One instance cannot write to the disks owned by another instance.	Only one node at a time. One node can write to all the disks.	All nodes can write to all disks as the lock manager controls the writes.
Load balancing	Not possible.	Not possible.	Near perfect load balancing.
Application partitioning	Strictly required.	Not required as only one node is active at any time.	Not required.
Dynamic node addition	Not possible.	Possible, but does not make any sense as only one node will be active at any time.	Very possible. A key strength of this architecture.
Failover capacity	No failover as the nodes/disks are not accessible by other nodes.	Can be failed over to other nodes.	Very capable. Often it is transparent.
I/O fencing	Not required.	Not required.	Provided by the DLM and cluster manager.
Failure of one node	Makes a subset of data inaccessible momentarily: $100/N$% of the data is inaccessible, with N being the number of nodes in the cluster. Then the ownership is transferred to the surviving nodes.	Data access momentarily disrupted, until the applications are failed over to the other node.	As connections spread across all the nodes, a subset of sessions may have to reconnect to the other node and total data is accessible to all the nodes. No data loss due to node failures.
Addition of nodes	Requires complete reorganization as redeployment of the architecture.	Not possible as addition of nodes does not help anything.	Can be added and removed on the fly. Load balancing is done automatically during reconfiguration.
Example	IBM SP2, Teradata, Tandem NonStop, Informix OnLine XPS, Microsoft Cluster Server	HP M/C ServiceGuard, Veritas Cluster Servers	Oracle Parallel Server/RAC, IBM HACMP

TABLE 2-1. *Functionalities of Clustering Architectures* (continued)

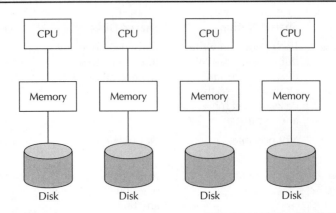

FIGURE 2-2. *Shared nothing clusters*

Shared Disk Architecture

For high availability, some shared access to the data disks is needed (see Figure 2-3). In shared disk storage clusters, at the low end, one node can take over the storage (and applications) if another node fails. In higher-level solutions, simultaneous access to data by applications running on more than one node at a time is possible, but typically a single node at a time is responsible for coordinating all access to a given data disk and serving that storage to the rest of the nodes. That single node can become a bottleneck for access to the data in busier configurations.

In simple failover clusters, one node runs an application and updates the data; another node stands idle until needed, and then takes over completely. In more sophisticated clusters, multiple nodes may access data, but typically one node at a time serves a file system to the rest of the nodes and performs all coordination for that file system.

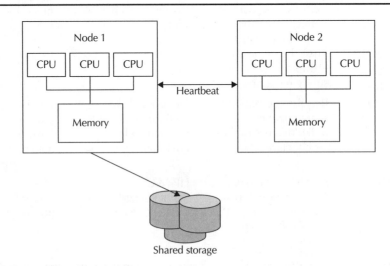

FIGURE 2-3. *Shared disk cluster*

Shared Everything Architecture

Shared everything clustering utilizes the disks accessible to all computers (nodes) within the cluster. These are often called shared disk clusters because the I/O involved is typically disk storage for normal files and/or databases. These clusters rely on a common channel for disk access as all nodes may concurrently write or read data from the central disks. Because all nodes have equal access to the centralized shared disk subsystem, a synchronization mechanism must be used to preserve coherence of the system. An independent piece of cluster software, the DLM, assumes this role.

In a shared everything cluster, all nodes can access all the data disks simultaneously, without one node having to go through a separate peer node to get access to the data (see Figure 2-4). Clusters with such capability employ a cluster-wide file system (CFS), so all the nodes view the file system(s) identically, and they provide a DLM to allow the nodes to coordinate the sharing and updating of files, records, and databases.

A CFS provides the same view of disk data from every node in the cluster. This means the environment on each node can appear identical to both the users and the application programs, so it doesn't matter on which node the application or user happens to be running at any given time.

Shared everything clusters support higher levels of system availability: If one node fails, other nodes need not be affected. However, higher availability comes at a cost of somewhat reduced performance in these systems because of overhead in using a DLM and the potential bottlenecks that can occur in sharing hardware. Shared everything clusters make up for this shortcoming with relatively good scaling properties.

Oracle RAC and IBM HACMP (High Availability Cluster Multiprocessing) are classic examples of the shared everything architecture. RAC is a special configuration of the Oracle database that leverages hardware clustering technology and extends the clustering to the application level. The database files are stored in the shared disk storage so that all the nodes can simultaneously read and write to them. The shared storage is typically networked storage, such as Fibre Channel SAN or IP-based Ethernet NAS, which is either physically or logically connected to all the nodes.

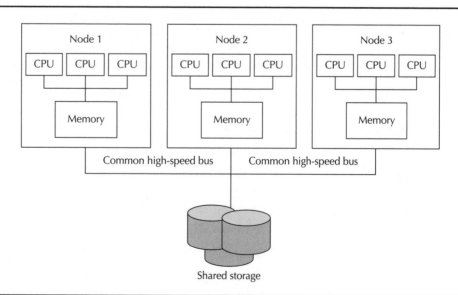

FIGURE 2-4. *Shared everything cluster*

History of Oracle RAC

The ever-hungry vagabonds of the Silicon Valley pioneered the concept of *massive parallel processing* (MPP) and christened the same as *clustering*. Digital, IBM, and Cray were some of the pioneers in the field of clustering. The first success toward creating a clustering product, ARCnet, was developed by DataPoint in 1977.

ARCnet, though a good product in the research labs and a darling in the academic world (for university-based research groups, departments, and computer cluster resources for an entire university), was not a commercial success and clustering didn't really take off until Digital Equipment Corporation (DEC) released its VAX cluster product in the 1980s for the VAX/VMS operating system. The ARCnet and VAX cluster products not only supported parallel computing, but they also shared file systems and peripheral devices. They were intended to provide the advantage of parallel processing while maintaining data atomicity.

Oracle's cluster database was introduced with Oracle 6 for the Digital VAX cluster product and on nCUBE machines, and Oracle was the first commercial database that supported clustering at the database level. Oracle created the lock manager for VAX/VMS clusters, as the original lock manager from Digital was not very scalable for database applications, and a database requires fine-grained locking at the block level. Oracle 6.2 gave birth to Oracle Parallel Server (OPS), which used Oracle's own DLM and worked very well with Digital's VAX clusters. Oracle was the first database to run the parallel server.

In the early '90s, when open systems dominated the computer industry, many UNIX vendors started clustering technology, mostly based on Oracle's DLM implementation. Oracle 7 Parallel Server (OPS) used vendor-supplied clusterware. OPS was available with almost all UNIX flavors and worked well, but it was complex to set up and manage as multiple layers were involved in the process.

When Oracle introduced a generic lock manager in version 8, it was a clear indication of the direction for Oracle's own clusterware and lock manager for future versions. Oracle's lock manager is integrated with Oracle code with an additional layer called OSD (Operating System Dependent). Oracle's lock manager soon integrated with the kernel and became known as the IDLM (Integrated Distributed Lock Manager) in later versions of Oracle.

Oracle Real Application Clusters version 9i used the same IDLM and relied on external clusterware. The following table lists the most common clusterware for various operating systems. Oracle provided its own clusterware for Linux and Windows in Oracle 9i and for all operating systems starting from 10g.

Operating System	Clusterware
Solaris	Sun Cluster, Veritas Cluster Services
HP-UX	HP MC/ServiceGuard, Veritas
HP Tru64	TruCluster
Windows	Microsoft Cluster Services
LinuxX86	Oracle Clusterware
IBM AIX	HACMP (High Availability Cluster Multiprocessing)

Oracle Parallel Server Architecture

An Oracle parallel or cluster database consists of two or more physical servers (nodes) that host their own Oracle instances and share a disk array. Each node's instance of Oracle has its own System Global Area (SGA) and its own redolog files, but the data files and control files are common to all instances. Data files and control files are concurrently read and written by all instances; however, redologs can be read by any instance but written to only by the owning instance. Some parameters, such as db_block_buffers and log_buffer, can be configured differently in each instance, but other parameters must be consistent across all instances. Each cluster node has its own set of background processes, just as a single instance would. Additionally, OPS-specific processes are also started on each instance to handle cross-instance communication, lock management, and block transfers.

Figure 2-5 shows the architecture of OPS.

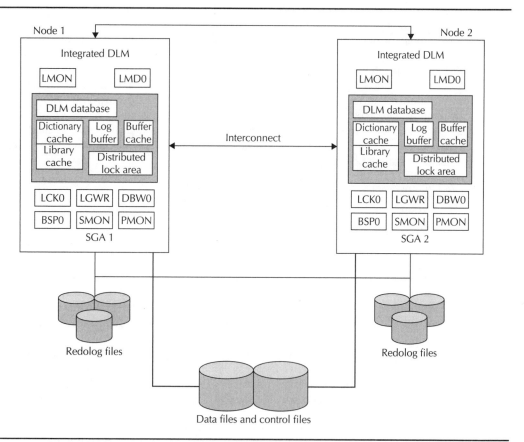

FIGURE 2-5. *OPS architecture*

Components of an OPS Database

On every instance of an Oracle 8i Parallel Server database, the following components can be found:

- Cluster manager—OS vendor specific (except Windows), including node monitoring facility and failure detection mechanism
- Distributed Lock Manager (DLM), including deadlock detection and resource mastering
- Cluster interconnect
- Shared disk array

NOTE
Vendor-specific cluster manager software is not discussed here and mentioned only for completeness. The vendor product is the basic cluster software that is mandatory before installing and configuring OPS. This is generally termed as the cluster manager *(CM), which has its own group membership services, node monitor, and other core layers.*

Cluster Group Services (CGS)

One of the key "hidden" or lesser known components of OPS is the CGS, which was formally known as the Group Membership Services (GMS) in Oracle 8. CGS has some OSD components (node monitor interface), and the rest of it is the GMS part that is built into the Oracle kernel. CGS holds a key repository used by the DLM for communication and network-related activities. This layer in the Oracle 8i kernel (and beyond) provides some key facilities without which an OPS database cannot operate:

- Internode messaging
- Group membership consistency
- Cluster synchronization
- Process grouping, registration, and deregistration

Some cluster components were still OS specific, so an OSD layer had to be developed and implemented. Certain low-level cluster communication can be done only by this OSD layer, which communicates with the Oracle kernel using Oracle-specified application programming interfaces (APIs). These OSD components are included with the Node Monitor (NM) that is part of the CGS.

A whole set of cluster communication interfaces and APIs became an internal part of the Oracle code in OPS 8i. GMS provided many services such as member status, node evictions, and so on, which was external in Oracle 8 but was made internal within Oracle 8i. GMS, now CGS in Oracle 8i (8.1.6), basically includes the GMS as well as the NM component of cluster management. Below this layer is the cluster monitor, or the cluster software provided by an OS vendor (such as TruCluster, Veritas Cluster Services, HP MC/ServiceGuard, and so on).

Oracle 8i also introduced network redundancy, in which problems or breakdowns of the network path were communicated up to the cluster monitor level (part of CGS) and allowed for the instance to be shut down or to provide for a failover of the network path using redundant network hardware. Until OPS version 8i, network problems would cause an indefinite hang of the instance.

Distributed Lock Manager (DLM)

The DLM is an integral part of OPS and the RAC stack. As mentioned, earlier Oracle versions relied on OS vendors to provide this component, which coordinated resources globally and kept the system in sync. Data consistency and integrity are maintained by this layer in all versions of Oracle OPS from 7 to 10g. Any reference to DLM from Oracle 8/8i onward pertains to the Integrated DLM (IDLM), which was introduced with Oracle 8 and integrated into the Oracle OPS kernel. The terms *DLM* and *IDLM* are used to describe a single entity and are one and the same.

In versions prior to version 8, the DLM API module had to rely on external OS routines to check the status of a lock (since DLM functions were provided by the OS vendor). This communication was done using UNIX sockets and pipes. With IDLM, the required data is in the SGA of each instance and requires only a serialized lookup using latches and/or enqueues (see the next section) and may require global coordination, the algorithm for which was built into Oracle kernel code.

With OPS 8i, the IDLM has undergone significant development and stabilization. IDLM holds an inventory of all the locks and global enqueues that are held by all the instances in the OPS database. Its job is to track every lock granted to a resource. The coordination of requests from various instances for lock acquisition and release is done by the DLM. The memory structures required by DLM to operate are allocated out of the shared pool. The lock resources, messages buffers, and so on are all in the shared pool of each instance. DLM is designed such that it can survive node failures in all but one node of the cluster.

The DLM is always aware of the current holders or requestors of locks and the grantee. In case locks are not available, the DLM queues the lock requests and informs the requestor when a lock resource becomes available. Some of the resources that the DLM manages are data blocks and rollback segments. Oracle resources are associated with the DLM locks by instance, using a complex hashing algorithm. The lock and enqueue functionality in OPS is the same as in a single instance RDBMS server, except that OPS takes a global view.

DLM relies on the core RDBMS kernel for locking and enqueues services. These established and already proven techniques and functionalities need not be rewritten again in the DLM layer. The DLM coordinates locking at the global level, and this is a service that the core layers don't provide. To make things simpler, the locking and enqueues kernel services in Oracle 8i OPS, Oracle 9i RAC, and Oracle 10g RAC are kept separate from the DLM functionality.

Locking Concepts in Oracle Parallel Server

In an OPS database, a user must acquire a lock before he can operate on any resource. This is also applicable in a single instance scenario. In pure DLM terminology, a *resource* is any object accessed by users, and a *lock* is a client operational request of certain type or mode on that resource.

A new concept in OPS called *Parallel Cache Management* (PCM) means that coordination and maintenance of data blocks exists within each data buffer cache (of an instance) so that the data viewed or requested by users is never inconsistent or incoherent. The access to data is controlled using the PCM framework using data blocks with global coordinated locks. In simple terms, PCM ensures that only one instance in a cluster can modify a block at any given time. Other instances have to wait.

Broadly speaking, locks in OPS are either PCM locks or non-PCM locks. PCM locks almost exclusively protect the data blocks, and non-PCM locks control access to data files, control files, data dictionary, and so on. PCM locks are static in OPS, and non-PCM locks are dynamically set using the init.ora settings of certain parameters. Locks on PCM resources are referred to as *lock elements* and non-PCM locks are called *enqueues*. DLM locks are acquired on a resource and are typically granted to a process. PCM locks and row level locks operate independently.

PCM Lock and Row Lock Independence   PCM locks and row locks operate independently. An instance can disown a PCM lock without affecting row locks held in the set of blocks covered by the PCM lock. A row lock is acquired during a transaction. A database resource such as a data block acquires a PCM lock when it is read for update by an instance. During a transaction, a PCM lock can therefore be disowned and owned many times if the blocks are needed by other instances.

In contrast, transactions do not release row locks until changes to the rows are either committed or rolled back. Oracle uses internal mechanisms for concurrency control to isolate transactions so modifications to data made by one transaction are not visible to other transactions until the transaction modifying the data commits. The row lock concurrency control mechanisms are independent of parallel cache management: concurrency control does not require PCM locks, and PCM lock operations do not depend on individual transactions committing or rolling back.

IDLM lock modes and Oracle lock modes are not identical, though they are similar. In OPS, locks can be local or global depending on the type of request and operations. Just as in a single instance, locks take this form:

   <Type, ID1, ID2>

where *Type* consists of two characters and *ID1* and *ID2* are values dependant on the lock type. The ID is a 4-byte, positive integer.

Local locks can be divided into latches and enqueues. These could be required for local instance-based operations. A shared pool latch is a simple example of a local latch, irrespective of whether OPS is present or not. Enqueues can be local or global. They take on a global role in an OPS environment and remain local in a single instance. A TX (transaction) enqueue, control file enqueue (CF), DFS (Distributed File System) enqueue lock, or a DML/table lock are examples of a global enqueues in an OPS database. The same enqueue is local in a single instance database. Similarly, data dictionary and library cache locks are global in an OPS environment.

Local locks provide transaction isolation or row-level locking. Instance locks provide for cache coherency while accessing shared resources. GV$LOCK and GV$LOCK_ELEMENT are important views that provide information on global enqueues and instance locks.

In Oracle 8i, the DLM is implemented by two background processes, Lock Manager Daemon (LMD) and Lock Monitor (LMON) (see Figure 2-5). Each instance has its own set of these two processes. The DLM database stores information on resources, locks, and processes. In Oracle 9i, the DLM has been renamed Global Cache Services (GCS) and Global Enqueue Services (GES). While some of the code has changed, the basic functionality of GES and GCS remain the same as the prior versions of DLM.

DLM Lock Compatibility Matrix   Every resource is identified by its unique resource name. Each resource can potentially have a list of locks currently granted to users. This list is called the *Grant Q*. Locks that are in the process of converting or waiting to be converted from one mode to another are placed on *Convert Q* of that resource. For each lock, a resource structure exists in the memory that maintains a list of owners and converters. Each owner, waiter, or converter has a lock structure, as shown in the following table.

Lock	NL	CR	CW	PR	PW	EX
NL	Grant	Grant	Grant	Grant	Grant	Grant
CR	Grant	Grant	Grant	Grant	Grant	Queue
CW	Grant	Grant	Grant	Queue	Queue	Queue
PR	Grant	Grant	Queue	Grant	Queue	Queue
PW	Grant	Grant	Queue	Queue	Queue	Queue
EX	Grant	Queue	Queue	Queue	Queue	Queue

Every node has directory information for a set of resources it manages. To locate a resource, the DLM uses a hashing algorithm based on the name of the resource to find out which node holds the directory information for that resource. Once this is done, a lock request is done directly to this "master" node. The directory area is nothing but a DLM memory structure that stores information on which node masters which blocks.

The traditional lock naming convention (such as SS, SX, X) are provided in the following table along with the DLM mode:

Conventional naming	NL	CR	CW	PR	PW	EX
DLM naming	NL	SS	SX	S	SSX	X

Note that in this table, NL means null mode; CR/SS means concurrent read mode; CW/SX means concurrent write mode; PR/S means protected read mode; PW/SSX means protected writemode; and EX/X means exclusive mode.

Lock Acquisition and Conversion   Locks granted on resources are in the *Grant Q* (as discussed previously). Locks are placed on a resource when a process acquires a lock on the Grant Q of that resource. It is only then that a process owns a lock on that resource in a compatible mode.

A lock can be acquired if there are no converters and the mode the Oracle kernel requires is compatible with the modes already held by others. Otherwise, it waits on the Convert Q till the resource becomes available. When a lock is released or converted, the converters run the check algorithm to see if they can be acquired.

Converting a lock from one mode to another occurs when a new request arrives for a resource that already has a lock on it. *Conversion* is the process of changing a lock from the mode currently held to a different mode. Even if the mode is NULL, it is considered as holding a lock. Conversion takes place only if the mode required is a subset of the mode held or the lock mode is compatible with the modes already held by others and according to a conversion matrix within the IDLM.

Processes and Group-Based Locking   When lock structures are allocated in the DLM memory area, the operating system Process ID (PID) of the requesting process is the key identifier for the requestor of the lock. Mapping a process to a session is easier inside Oracle, and the information is available in V$SESSION. However, in certain clients, such as Oracle multithreaded servers (MTS) or

Oracle XA, a single process may own many transactions. Sessions migrate across many processes to make up a single transaction. This would disable identification of the transaction and the origin of the same. Hence, lock identifiers had to be designed to have session-based information where the transaction ID (XID) is provided by the client when lock requests are made to the DLM.

Groups are used when group-based locking is used. This is preferred particularly when MTS is involved, and when MTS is used the shared services are implicitly unavailable to other sessions when locks are held. From Oracle 9i onward, process-based locking no longer exists. Oracle 8i OPS (and later) uses group-based locking irrespective of the kind of transactions. As mentioned, a process within a group identifies itself with the XID before asking Oracle for any transaction locks.

Lock Mastering   The DLM maintains information about the locks on all nodes that are interested in a given resource. The DLM nominates one node to manage all relevant lock information for a resource; this node is referred to as the *master node*. Lock mastering is distributed among all nodes.

Using the Interprocess Communications (IPC) layer, the distributed component of the DLM permits it to share the load of mastering (administering) resources. As a result, a user can lock a resource on one node but actually end up communicating with the LMD processes on another node. Fault tolerance requires that no vital information about locked resources is lost irrespective of how many DLM instances fail.

Asynchronous Traps   Communication between the DLM processes (LMON, LMD) across instances is done using the IPC layer using the high-speed interconnect. To convey the status of a lock resource, the DLM uses *asynchronous traps* (AST), which are implemented as interrupts in the OS handler routines. Purists may differ on the exact meaning of AST and the way it is implemented (interrupts or other blocking mechanism), but as far as OPS or RAC is concerned, it is an interrupt. AST can be a *blocking AST* or an *acquisition AST*.

When a process requests a lock on a resource, the DLM sends a blocking asynchronous trap (BAST) to all processes that currently own a lock on that same resource. If possible and necessary, the holder(s) of the lock may relinquish the lock and allow the requester to gain access to the resource. An acquisition AST (AAST) is sent by DLM to the requestor to inform him that the resource (and the lock) is now owned by him. An AAST is generally regarded as a "wakeup call" for a process.

How Locks Are Granted in DLM   To illustrate how locking works in OPS's DLM, consider an example two-node cluster with a shared disk array:

1. Process p1 needs to modify a data block on instance 1. Before the block can read into the buffer cache on instance 1, p1 needs to check whether a lock exists on that block.

2. A lock may or may not exist on this data block, and hence the LCK process checks the SGA structures to validate the buffer lock status. If a lock exists, LCK has to request that the DLM downgrade the lock.

3. If a lock does not exist, a lock element (LE) has to be created by LCK in the local instance and the role is local.

4. LCK must request the DLM for the LE in exclusive mode. If the resource is mastered by instance 1, DLM continues processing. Otherwise, the request must be sent to the master DLM in the cluster.

5. Assuming the lock is mastered on instance 1, the DLM on this instance does a local cache lookup in its DLM database and finds that a process on instance 2 already has an exclusive (EX) lock on the same data block.

6. DLM on instance 1 sends out a BAST to DLM on instance 2 requesting a downgrade of the lock. DLM on instance 2 sends another BAST to LCK on the same instance to downgrade the lock from EX to NULL.

7. The process on instance 2 may have updated the block and may not have committed the changes. Dirty Buffer Writer (DBWR) is signaled to write out the block to disk. After the write confirmation, the LCK on instance 2 downgrades the lock to NULL and sends an AAST to DLM on the same instance.

8. DLM on instance 2 updates its local DLM database about the change in lock status and sends a AAST to DLM on instance 1.

9. The master DLM on instance 1 updates the master DLM database about the new status of the lock (EX) that can now be granted to the process on its instance. DLM itself upgrades the lock to EX.

10. DLM on instance 1 now sends another AAST to the local LCK process informing it about the lock grant and that the block can be read from disk.

Cache Fusion Stage 1, CR Server

OPS 8i introduced Cache Fusion Stage 1. Until version 8.1, cache coherency was maintained using the disk (ping mechanism). Cache Fusion introduced a new background process called the *Block Server Process* (BSP). The major use or responsibility of BSP was to ship consistent read (CR) version(s) of a block(s) across instances in a read/write contention scenario. The shipping was done using the high-speed interconnect and not the disk. This was called Cache Fusion Stage 1 because it was not possible to transfer all types of blocks to the requesting instance, especially with the write/write contention scenario.

Cache Fusion Stage 1 laid the foundation for Oracle 9i and 10g for Cache Fusion Stage 2, in which both types of blocks (CR and CUR) can be transferred using the interconnect, although a disk ping is still required in some circumstances.

Oracle 8i also introduced the GV$ views, or "global views." With the help of GV$ views, DBAs could view cluster-wide database and other statistics sitting on any node/instance of the cluster. This was of enormous help to DBAs as they earlier had to club or join data collected on multiple nodes to analyze all the statistics. GV$ views have the instance_number column to support this functionality.

Block Contention   Block contention occurs where processes on different instances need access to the same block. If a block is being read by instance 1 or is in the buffer cache of instance 1 in read mode, and another process on instance 2 requests the same block in read mode, *read/read contention* results. This situation is the simplest of all cases and can easily be overcome since there are no modifications to the block. A copy of the block is shipped across by BSP from instance 1 to instance 2 or read from the disk by instance 2 without having to worry about applying an undo to get a consistent version. In fact, PCM coordination is not required in this situation.

Read/write contention occurs when instance 1 has modified a block in its local cache, and instance 2 requests the same block for a read. In Oracle 8i, using the Cache Fusion Stage 1, instance locks are downgraded, and the BSP process builds a CR copy of the block using the undo data stored in its own cache and ships the CR copy across to the requesting instance. This is done in coordination with DLM processes (LMD and LMON).

If the requesting instance (instance 2) needs to modify the block that instance 1 has already modified, instance 1 has to downgrade the lock, flush the log entries (if not done before), and then send the data block to disk. This is called a *ping*. Data blocks are pinged only when more than one instance need to modify the same block, causing the holding instance to write the block to disk before the requesting instance can read it into its own cache for modification. Disk ping can be expensive for applications in terms of performance.

A *false ping* occurs each time a block is written to disk, even if the block itself is not being requested by a different instance, but another block managed by the same lock element is being requested by a different instance.

A *soft ping* occurs when a lock element needs to be down converted due to a request of the lock element by another instance, and the blocks covered by the lock are already written to disk.

Write/Write Contention   This situation occurs when both instances have to modify the same block. As explained, a disk ping mechanism results where the locks are downgraded on instance 1 and the block is written to disk. Instance 2 acquired the exclusive lock on the buffer and modifies it.

Limitations of Oracle Parallel Server

OPS's scalability is limited on transactional systems that perform a lot of modifications on multiple nodes. Its scalability is also limited to I/O bandwidth and storage performance.

OPS requires careful and clear application partitioning. For example, if two different applications require two logical sets of data, the application should be configured in such a way that one node is dedicated to one application type, and no overlapping of the connections occurs on the other node. Hence the scalability is also restricted to the computing capacity of the node. Because of this "application partitioning" limitation, OPS is of limited suitability for packaged applications.

On-demand scalability is also limited, as we cannot dynamically add the nodes in an OPS cluster. Sometimes adding nodes will require careful analysis of the application partitioning and sometimes application repartitioning. This greatly limits true scalability.

OPS does require careful setup and administration, as a third-party cluster manager is necessary for clustering, requiring additional cost to the total application deployment. In other words, OPS is not cheap in any context.

Lock Configuration

OPS requires a highly skilled database architect for tuning and initial configuration. OPS supports many types of locks, and each needs to be carefully analyzed; the number of locks is also limited by physical memory. DLM requires additional memory for lock management, and careful analysis is necessary before configuring fixed/releasable/hash locks.

OPS lacks diagnosable capacity. Operating systems, the cluster manager, and the database are integrated, and diagnosing the errors in this stack is quite complex, even for experienced support staff. Deadlock detection, lock tracing, and cluster-wide statistics are inadequate in OPS. These features or functionalities are difficult to implement or expensive to run, and customers are usually not cooperative enough to understand the complexities involved in dealing with the technical challenges, difficulties, or requirements.

For example, to diagnose an application locking problem or a deep-rooted OPS issue, a cluster system state dump of all the instances is required. In a four-node OPS cluster, this task *will consume time*. This is not a limitation but a requirement. Dumping the contents of the entire SGA, all its lock structures, and so on, is an expensive task. Oracle 9i RAC has come a long way in its diagnostics capability and Oracle 10g RAC has improved on those capabilities.

Manageability

OPS requires RAW partitions for almost all operating systems. RAW devices are complex to set up and manage for novice DBAs. A RAW device does not support dynamic file extensions, and there are some limitations in the number of RAW partitions an operating system can support. RAW device backup and recovery is different from normal file system backup, and extra care should be taken for RAW device management. Reconfiguration of a DLM takes a lot of time, and cluster availability (as well as database availability) is compromised due to the enormously heavy OSD-level API calls when a node crash is noticed by OPS. The RDBMS kernel has to make calls to many APIs to communicate with the OS cluster software, and the DLM has to wait for OS clusterware to finish its job before doing its own configuration. In Oracle 9i, tightly integrated code in the kernel for cluster communication has reduced this time lag.

The Oracle RAC Solution

Oracle RAC is a natural evolution of OPS. The limitations of the OPS are addressed through improvements in the code, the extension of Cache Fusion (discussed in detail later in the book), and dynamic lock remastering. Oracle 10g RAC also comes with an integrated clusterware and storage management framework, removing the dependency of the vendor clusterware and providing ultimate scalability and availability for database applications.

Availability

Oracle RAC systems can be configured to have no single point of failure, even when running on low-cost, commodity hardware and storage. With Oracle RAC, if database servers fail, applications simply keep running. Failover is frequently transparent to applications and occurs in seconds.

Scalability

Oracle RAC allows multiple servers in a cluster to manage a single database transparently. Oracle RAC allows database systems to scale out rather than scale up. This means that the previous ceilings on scalability have been removed. Collections of servers can work together transparently to manage a single database with linear scalability.

Reliability

Oracle RAC has proven time and again in all "near death" situations that it can hold the honor of the hour with its controlled reliability. The paradigm has shifted from reliability to maximum reliability. Analyzing and identifying the subsystem and system failure rates in accordance with the appropriate standard ensures reliability, which is a key component in the RAC technology.

Affordability

Oracle RAC allows organizations to use collections of low-cost computers to manage large databases rather than needing to purchase a single large, expensive computer. Clusters of small, commodity-class servers can now satisfy any database workload. For example, a customer needing to manage a large Oracle database might choose to purchase a cluster of 8 industry-standard servers with 4 CPUs each, rather than buying a single server with 32 CPUs.

Transparency

Oracle RAC requires no changes to existing database applications. A clustered Oracle RAC database appears to applications just like a traditional single-instance database environment. As a result, customers can easily migrate from single-instance configurations to Oracle RAC without needing to change their applications. Oracle RAC also requires no changes to existing database schemas.

Commoditization

Oracle RAC allows clusters of low-cost, industry-standard servers running Linux to scale to meet workloads that previously demanded the use of a single, larger, more expensive computer. In the scale-up model of computing, sophisticated hardware and operating systems are needed to deliver scalability and availability to business applications. But with Oracle RAC, scalability and availability are achieved through functionality delivered by Oracle above the operating system.

In a Nutshell

On demand scalability and uninterrupted availability can be achieved by the right clustering technology. Oracle database has a good history on clusters with the OPS and its successor RAC. The previous limitations of OPS are addressed in the current versions of RAC, with the introduction of the Cache Fusion framework. Oracle RAC 10g provides enormous scalability, availability, and flexibility at low cost. It makes the consolidation of databases affordable and reliable by leveraging scale across architecture.

CHAPTER
3

RAC Architecture

racle Real Application Clusters allows multiple instances to access a single database. Instances running on multiple server nodes access the common set of data files comprising a single database. In a single instance environment, one Oracle database is used by only one instance running on a server machine; thus users accessing the database can connect to the database via that single server only. The processing resources (CPU memory and so on) available for the database work are limited to the single server's processing resources. In an RAC environment, more than one instance can use the same database. This scenario presents multiple processing resources for database users.

NOTE
An instance *is a set of memory structures in a machine associated with the data files. A* database *is a collection of physical files. Database and instance share one to many relationships. A database can be mounted by more than one instance in RAC, and at any point, one instance will be part of only one database.*

The nonvolatile storage for data files comprising the database is equally available to all the nodes for read and write access. Oracle RAC needs to coordinate and regulate simultaneous data access from multiple server nodes. Hence an efficient, reliable, and high-speed private network must exist among the nodes of the cluster for sending and receiving data. Figure 3-1 shows the configuration of a single instance database and an RAC database.

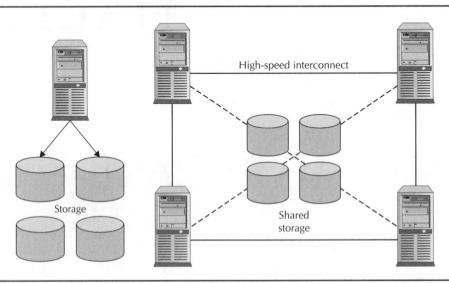

FIGURE 3-1. *Single instance database and an RAC setup*

Single Instance vs. RAC Environment

Similar to a single instance environment, each instance in an RAC environment has its own System Global Area (SGA) and background processes. However, all the data files and control files are equally accessible to all the nodes, so these files must be placed on a shared disk subsystem. Each instance also has its own dedicated set of online redolog files. The online redolog files can be written to only by the instance to which they belong. However, these files can be read by other instances during instance crash recovery. This requires that online redolog files reside on a shared disk subsystem and not on a node's local storage, because the files would be lost if the node crashed. Table 3-1 compares single instance components to components of an instance in an RAC environment.

Instances in an RAC environment share the data, as the same set of data might be needed by multiple instances simultaneously. There is no danger in multiple instances reading the same data simultaneously; however, data integrity issues may arise if one instance modifies (via insert or update),

Component	Single Instance Environment	RAC Environment
SGA	Instance has its own SGA.	Each instance has its own SGA.
Background processes	Instance has its own set of background processes.	Each instance has its own set of background processes.
Datafiles	Accessed by only one instance.	Shared by all instances, so must be placed on shared storage.
Control files	Accessed by only one instance.	Shared by all instances, so must be placed on shared storage.
Online redolog file	Dedicated for write and read to only one instance.	Only one instance can write, but other instances can read during recovery and archiving. If an instance is shut down, log switches by other instances can force the idle instance redologs to be archived.
Archived redolog	Dedicated to the instance.	Private to the instance, but other instance will need access to all required archive logs during media recovery.
Flash recovery log	Accessed by only one instance.	Shared by all the instances, so must be placed on shared storage.
Alert log and other trace files	Dedicated to the instance.	Private to each instance; other instances never read or write to those files.
ORACLE_HOME	Multiple instances on the same machine accessing different database can use the same executable files.	Same as single instance, plus can be placed on shared file system, allowing a common ORACLE_HOME for all instances in an RAC environment.

TABLE 3-1. *Components of Single Instance vs. RAC*

and another instance(s) reads or multiple instances modify the same data concurrently. This concurrent read/write or write/write behavior, if not coordinated correctly, might lead to data corruption or inconsistent representation of data. Single instance Oracle already ensures that readers never block writers and that "dirty" reads are never allowed. RAC ensures that all the instances across the clusters see a consistent image of the database. The Distributed Lock Manager (or DLM, called the Global Resource Directory, or GRD, beginning with version 9i) coordinates resource sharing among the instances.

RAC Components

The RAC stack is slightly different from versions previous to Oracle10*g* because the clustering software is totally integrated into the RDBMS kernel in the latest version. The clustering software was provided by third-party vendors in previous versions, except for the Linux and Windows versions.

The major components of Oracle RAC are

- Shared disk system
- Oracle clusterware
- Cluster interconnects
- Oracle kernel components

Figure 3-2 shows the basic architecture.

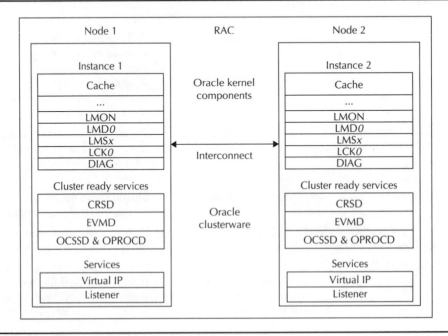

FIGURE 3-2. *Oracle 10g architecture*

Shared Disk System

Shared storage is a critical component of an RAC environment. Traditionally, storage was attached to each individual server. Today, more flexible storage that is accessible over storage area networks (SANs) or regular Ethernet networks is popular. These new storage options enable multiple servers to access the same set of disks through a network, simplifying provisioning of storage in any distributed environment. SANs represent the evolution of data storage technology to this point.

Traditionally, in single instance client/server systems, data was stored on devices either inside or directly attached to the server. Next in the evolutionary scale came network attached storage (NAS) that removed the storage devices from the server and connected them to the network. SANs take the principle a step further by allowing storage devices to exist on their own separate networks and communicate with each other over very fast media, such as a high-speed Fibre Channel network. Users can gain access to these storage devices through server systems that are connected to the local area network (LAN) and SAN.

In shared storage, database files should be equally accessible to all the nodes concurrently. Generic file systems do not allow disks to be mounted in more than one system. Generic UNIX file systems (UFS) do not allow the files to be shared among the nodes because of the obvious file locking (inode locks) issues and unavailability of a coherent file system cache. One option is to use the Network File System (NFS), but it is unsuitable as it relies on a single host (which mounts the file systems) and for performance reasons. Since the disks in such an implementation are attached to one node, all the write requests must go through that particular node, thus limiting the scalability and fault tolerance. The total available I/O bandwidth is dependent on the bandwidth provided by that single host through which all I/O can be serviced. Because that node may become a single point of failure (SPOF), it is another threat for the high availability (HA) architecture.

The choice of file system is critical for RAC deployment. Traditional file systems do not support simultaneous mounting by more than one system. Therefore, you must store files in either raw volumes without any file system or on a file system that supports concurrent access by multiple systems.

Thus, three major approaches exist for providing the shared storage needed by RAC:

- **Raw volumes** These raw devices require storage that operate in block mode such as Fiber Channel SANs or Internet SCSI (iSCSI). This was the preferred and only available options in releases previous to Oracle 9i.

- **Cluster File System** One or more cluster file systems can be used to hold all RAC data files. Oracle provides the Oracle Cluster File System (OCFS) for RAC for Microsoft Windows and Linux operating systems. It is not most widely used, and we will not be discussing it in great detail.

- **Automatic Storage Management** (ASM) A portable, dedicated, and optimized cluster file system for Oracle database files, introduced in Oracle 10g. ASM is the only supported storage if you use Oracle 10g Standard Edition with RAC. ASM is discussed in Chapter 6.

Use of raw devices has been the traditional approach for sharing files across nodes. Some experts even recommend the use of raw devices for single instance systems for performance reasons. The RAW partition avoids the double buffering in the file system cache, and data is read

Performance Benefits of RAW Partitions

Oracle's database cache algorithms, based on the touch count of the buffers, are more sophisticated than the traditional operating system algorithms. Most OSs just keep the *most recently used* buffers rather than *most frequently used* buffers. Buffering the data blocks in the file system cache wastes precious main memory, and two versions of the blocks are cached in two different places. Leaving the unwanted file system cache to the OS will provide additional memory to Oracle or OSs and may improve performance, as the OS can resort to paging of non-database files under memory pressure.

Avoiding double buffering greatly increases the I/O performance, as data doesn't need to be written in two locations. Oracle's log writer process writes small pieces of change records to the file system cache, and then the cache writes back to the redolog files. In RAW partitions, the log writer directly writes the change records to the log files, which dramatically increases the performance of the online transaction processing (OLTP) systems.

Of course, additional administrative overhead is necessary if RAW partitions are used, as normal RAW partitions cannot be grown on demand, like file systems, without third-party volume management software. Limitations on the number of RAW partitions on a few operating systems limits the use of raw devices for the packaged applications, which requires numerous datafiles and tablespaces. Another limitation in the raw device is that because they are not visible to the operating systems, a rookie system administrator may ruin the RAW partitions, thinking that they are unused partitions.

into the Oracle database buffer cache, thus avoiding the operating system buffer cache altogether. A lot of storage vendors these days offer file systems whose performance comes close to that of raw devices.

RAID

Any discussion about storage choices would be incomplete without including RAID, which is a common concept in highly available storage systems, as uninterrupted access to storage is one of the key aspects in a highly available solution. Redundant Array of Independent (or Inexpensive) Disks, affectionately known as RAID, is key in high performance storage systems.

Numerous varieties of RAID implementation mechanisms are available, depending on the standards, and few vendor-specific implementations are also on hand, such as Auto RAID from HP. We will discuss common RAID concepts and most common RAID implementations and pros and cons of each of them.

Conceptually, RAID uses two or more physical disks to create a single logical disk, where the physical disks operate in tandem to provide greater size and more bandwidth. Before delving deeper into RAID, you need to be clear about terminology, especially the terms *striping*, *mirroring*, and *parity*. Striping yields better I/O performance, mirroring provides protection, and parity (when applicable) is a way to check the work. Using these three aspects of RAID, you can achieve scalable, protected, and highly available I/O performance.

Striping is the process of breaking down data into pieces and distributing it across multiple disks that support a logical volume. This often results in a logical volume that is larger and has greater I/O bandwidth than a single disk. Most volume managers stripe the data across all of the devices (either RAID or disks) based on a stripe width. The stripe width is generally set to a value based on the number of streams of I/O and the I/O request size such that all of the devices can be in use. The goal is to keep all of the disks busy to achieve parallelism on all the devices.

By creating a single volume from pieces of data on several disks, you can increase the capacity to handle I/O requests in a linear fashion, by combining each disk's I/O bandwidth. When multiple I/O requests for a file on a striped volume are processed, they can be serviced by multiple drives in the volume, as the requests are subdivided across several disks. This way, all drives in the striped volume can engage and service multiple I/O requests in a more efficient manner.

Mirroring is the process of writing the same data simultaneously to another member of the same volume. Mirroring provides protection for data by writing exactly the same information to every member in the volume. Additionally, mirroring can provide enhanced read operations because the read requests can be serviced from either member of the volume.

Parity is error checking. Some implementations of RAID (such as RAID 5) perform calculations when reading and writing data. The calculations primarily occur on write operations. However, if one or more disks in a volume is unavailable, then depending on the level of RAID, even read operations would require parity operations to rebuild the pieces on the failed disks. Parity is used to determine the write location and validity of each stripe that is written in a striped volume.

Parity is implemented on those levels of RAID that do not support mirroring. Parity algorithms contain error correction code (ECC) capabilities, which calculate parity for a given stripe or chunk of data within a RAID volume. The size of a chunk is OS and hardware specific. The codes generated by the parity algorithm are used to recreate data in the event of disk failure(s). Because the algorithm can reverse this parity calculation, it can rebuild data lost as a result of disk failures.

Types of RAID   RAID can be software-based, where the control software is usually bundled with the OS or in the form of an add-on, such as Veritas Volume Manager. This type of RAID, also known as *host-based* RAID, imposes a small overhead, as it consumes memory, I/O bandwidth, and CPU space on the host where it is implemented. Normally, this overhead is not alarming, but it should be factored into the resource capacity plans of the host.

RAID implemented by hardware is in the form of micro-code present in dedicated disk controller modules that connect to the host. These controllers are internal to the host where RAID is implemented. This type of RAID is also known as *embedded controller–based RAID*.

RAID can also be implemented using controllers that are external to the host where it is implemented. This implementation is called *bridge-based* and is not preferred, as it can incur longer service times for I/O requests due to the longer I/O paths from the disks to the host. This type of implementation is usually typical of I/O subsystems that are half fiber and half SCSI. It is also common to see this implementation on storage systems that support multiple hosts running multiple operating systems. The "bridges" also have a tendency to become saturated when the system is busy with I/O requests. Hardware-based RAID should be preferred over software-based or host-based RAID, which is preferred over bridge-based RAID.

RAID Levels   Initially, RAID was a simple method of logically joining two or more disks, but like all things in our industry, more choices were needed to meet different requirements. Today, RAID levels usually range from 0 to 7, and because of the peculiar way that we count in our world, this offers us more than eight choices. The differences among the various levels are based on varying I/O patterns across the disks. These patterns by their inherent nature offer different levels and types of protection and performance characteristics.

- **RAID 0**   A "normal" file system with striping, in which data loss is imminent with any disk failure(s). Simply put, it is data striped across a bunch of disks. This level provides good read/write performance but no recoverability.

- **RAID 1**   Provides mirroring and thus full data redundancy; often called a *mirrored disk*. In most cases, the volume the operating system sees is made up of two or more disks. However, this is presented to an application or a database as a single volume. As the system writes to this volume, it writes an exact copy of the data to all members in the volume. This level requires twice the amount disk storage as compared to RAID 0. Additionally, some performance gains can be reaped from parallel reading of the two mirror members. RAID 1 doubles the capacity of processing read requests from the volume when compared to not having mirrored members. There are no parity calculations involved in this level of RAID.

- **RAID 0 + 1**   Stripe first, and then mirror what you just striped. This level combines levels 0 and 1 (striping and mirroring) and provides good write and read performance and redundancy without the overhead of parity calculations. On disk failure(s), no reconstruction of data is required, as the data is read from the surviving mirror. This level is the most common RAID implementation for write-intensive applications and is widely used. The most common complaint is the cost, since it requires twice as much space. To justify this, you will have to spend some time understanding the performance requirements and availability needs of your systems. Note that if one of the pieces becomes unavailable due to a disk failure, the entire mirror member becomes unavailable. This is a very important consideration as the loss of an entire mirror member reduces the I/O servicing capacity of the volume by 50 percent.

- **RAID 1 + 0**   Mirror first, then stripe over what you mirrored. This level has the same functionality as RAID 0 + 1 but is better suited for high availability. This is because on the loss of one disk in a mirror member, the entire member of a mirrored volume does not become unavailable. Note that the loss of one disk of a mirrored member does not reduce the I/O servicing capacity of the volume by 50 percent. This is the preferred method for configurations that combine striping and mirroring, subject to hardware limitations.

- **RAID 2**   Incorporates striping and redundancy/protection provided through parity. This method requires less disk space compared to RAID 1, but the need to calculate and write parity will make writes slower. This level was one of the early implementations of "striping with parity" using the famous hamming code technique but was later replaced by RAID 3, 5, and 7. This level of RAID is rarely implemented.

- **RAID 3**   The error correction code (ECC) algorithm calculates parity to provide data redundancy as in RAID 2, but all of the parity is stored on one disk. The parity for this level is stored at the bit/byte-level as opposed to the block/chunk level. RAID 3 is slowly gaining popularity but is still not widely used. It is best suited for data mart/data warehouse applications that support a few users but require sequential bulk I/O performance (data-transfer intensive). When full table scans and/or index range scans are the norm for a given application and the user population is small, RAID 3 may be the ticket.

- **RAID 4**   The same as RAID 3 but with block level parity—rarely implemented.

- **RAID 5**   In by far one of the most common RAID implementations today, data redundancy is provided via parity calculations as in RAID 2, 3, 4, and 7, but the parity is stored along with the data. Hence, the parity is distributed across the number of drives configured in the volume. RAID 5 is attractive for many environments, because it results in minimal loss of disk space to parity values, and it provides good performance on random read operations and light write operations. RAID 5 caters better to Input Output Per Second (IOPS) with its support for concurrently servicing many I/O requests. It should not be implemented for write-intensive applications, since the continuous process of reading a stripe, calculating the new parity, and writing the stripe back to disk (with the new parity) will make writes significantly slower.

- **RAID 6**   Parity is calculated using a more complex algorithm and redundancy is provided using an advanced multidimensional parity method. RAID 6 stores two sets of parity for each block of data and thus makes writes even slower than RAID 5. However, on disk failures, RAID 6 facilitates quicker availability of the drives in the volume (after a disk failure), without incurring the negative performance impact of re-syncing the drives in the volume. This level of RAID is rarely implemented.

- **RAID 7**   A better implementation of RAID 3. Since read and write operations on RAID 3 are performed in a synchronous fashion, the parity disk can bottleneck during writes; RAID 7 allows asynchronous reads and writes, which inherently improves overall I/O performance. RAID 7 has the same characteristics as RAID 3, where all of the parity is stored on a dedicated drive. RAID 7 is relatively new in the market and has potential to be a great candidate for implementations that historically have chosen RAID 3. With RAID 7, you can "have your cake and eat it too," as you can reap the data-transfer benefits of RAID 3 and not lose the transactional I/O features that RAID 7 offers.

- **RAID-S**   If you are using EMC storage arrays, this is your version of RAID 3/5. It is well suited to data mart/data warehouse applications. This level of RAID should be avoided for write intensive or high-volume transactional applications for the same reasons as any RAID 5 implementation. EMC storage solutions are usually configured with large write caches, but generally speaking, these write caches are not large enough to overcome the additional overhead of the parity calculations during writes.

- **Auto RAID**   As implemented by HP, the controller along with the intelligence built within the I/O subsystem dynamically modifies the level of RAID on a given disk block either to RAID 0 + 1 or RAID 5, depending on the near historical nature of the I/O requests on that block. The recent history of I/O patterns on the disk block is maintained using the concept of a *working set* (a set of disk blocks). For obvious reasons, there is one working set each for reads and writes, and blocks keep migrating back and forth between the two sets, based on the type activity. A disk block in this context is 64K in size.

Said in a different way, a RAID 5 block can be dynamically converted into a RAID 0 + 1 block, if the "intelligence" determines and predicts that the block will be accessed primarily for writes. The controller can also perform the converse of the previous operation, namely converting a RAID 0 + 1 block into a RAID 5 block, if it determines and predicts that the block will be primarily accessed for reads. To support this configuration, all the drives in the array are used for all

Level	Description	Comments
RAID 0	Plain striping	No recoverability, provides read/write performance without recoverability
RAID 1	Plain mirroring	Recoverability, excellent write performance as writes can go parallel
RAID 0 + 1/1 + 0	Combination of 0 and 1—stripe and then mirror or mirror and then stripe	Recoverability, provides read and write performance, very widely used; 1 + 0 is better than 0 + 1 for availability
RAID 2	Early implementation of striping with parity	Uses the hamming code technique for parity calculations, was replaced by RAID 3, 5, and 7; rarely implemented
RAID 3	Striping with bit/byte-level parity, dedicated parity disk	Recoverability, good read performance for bulk sequential reads, not widely used but gaining popularity
RAID 4	Striping with block-level parity	Dedicated parity disk, recoverability, rarely implemented
RAID 5	Striping with block-level parity, distributed parity across the number of disks in the volume	Recoverability, provides better read performance for random reads that are small in nature, widely used
RAID 6	Striping with block-level multidimensional parity	Recoverability, slower writes than RAID 5, rarely implemented
RAID 7	Same as RAID 3, but with better asynchronous capability for reads and writes	Significantly better overall I/O performance when compared to RAID 3, significantly more expensive than RAID 3
RAID-S	EMC's implementation of RAID 3/5	Provides better write performance when used with cache at storage array level
Auto RAID	HP's automatic RAID technology	Automatically configures the I/O system based on the nature and type of I/O performed on the disk blocks within the RAID array

TABLE 3-2. *Levels of RAID*

RAID volumes that are configured on that array. This means that physical drive-independence across volumes cannot be achieved.

Table 3-2 summarizes the various levels of RAID with their descriptions and implementation issues.

Oracle Clusterware

Beginning with Oracle version 10*g*, Oracle software ships with Oracle Clusterware, the portable software required to run the RAC options. It provides the basic clustering support at the OS level and enables Oracle software to run in clustering mode. It supports up to 64 nodes, which helps to achieve higher levels of scalability. Oracle Clusterware can run as a standalone cluster service or with a vendor-supplied clusterware such as Sun Cluster or TruCluster, though care should be taken when Oracle Clusterware is installed on top of a vendor clusterware, as discussed a bit later in this chapter.

Oracle Clusterware Components

Oracle Clusterware software enables nodes to communicate with each other and forms the cluster that makes the nodes work as single logical server. Oracle Clusterware is run by Cluster Ready Services (CRS) using the Oracle Cluster Registry (OCR) that records and maintains the cluster and node membership information, and the voting disk, which acts a tiebreaker during communication failures. Consistent heartbeat information from all the nodes is sent to the voting disk when the cluster is running.

CRS has four components—namely Process Monitor daemon (OPROCd), the CRS daemon (CRSd), Oracle Cluster Synchronization Service daemon (OCSSd), and Event Volume Manager daemon (EVMd)—and each handles a variety of functions. Failure or death of the CRSd can cause node failure, and it automatically reboots the nodes to avoid data corruption because of possible communication failure among the nodes. The CRSd runs as the superuser *root* in the UNIX platforms and runs as a service in Windows platforms.

The following functionalities are covered by Oracle CRS:

- CRS is installed and run from a different Oracle home known as ORA_CRS_HOME, which is independent from ORACLE_HOME.

- CRSd manages resources such as starting and stopping the services and failovers of the application resources. It spawns separate processes to manage application resources.

- CRSd has two modes of running during startup and after a shutdown. During a planned clusterware startup it is started in reboot mode, and it is started in restart mode after an unplanned shutdown. In reboot mode, CRSd starts all the resources under its management. In restart mode, it prevails the previous state and returns the resources to their previous states before shutdown.

- CRS manages the OCR and stores the current known state in the OCR.

- CRS runs as root on UNIX and LocalSystem on Windows and automatically restarts in case of failure.

- CRS requires a public interface, private interface, and the virtual IP (VIP) for operation; all these interfaces should be up and running and should be pingable to each other before starting CRS installation. Without this network infrastructure CRS cannot be installed.

OCSSd provides synchronization services among the nodes. It provides the access to the node membership and enables basic cluster services, including cluster group services and cluster locking. It can also run without integrating with vendor clusterware. Failure of OCSSd causes the machine to reboot to avoid a "split-brain" situation (when all the links of the private interconnect fail to respond to each other, but the instances are still up and running; each instance thinks that the other instance is dead and tries to take over ownership). This is also required in a single instance if Automatic Storage Management (ASM) is used. (ASM is a new feature in Oracle 10g and discussed in detail in Chapter 6.) OCSSd runs as the *oracle* user.

The following functionalities are covered by OCSSd:

- CSS provides basic Group Services support. Group Services is a distributed group membership system that allows applications to coordinate activities to archive a common result.

- Group Services use vendor clusterware group services when it is available. But it is capable of working independently if no vendor clusterware group services are available.

- Lock Services provide the basic cluster-wide serialization locking functions. It uses the First In, First Out (FIFO) mechanism to manage locking.

- Node Services uses OCR to store data and updates the information during reconfiguration. It also manages the OCR data, which is otherwise static.

The third component in OCS is called the Event Management Logger, which runs the daemon process EVMd. The daemon process spawns a permanent child process called *evmlogger* and generates the events when things happen. The evmlogger spawns new children processes on demand and scans the callout directory to invoke callouts. It will restart automatically on failures and death if the EVMd process does not halt the instance. EVMd runs as *oracle* user.

OPROCd provides the I/O fencing solution for the Oracle Clusterware. It is the process monitor for Oracle Clusterware and uses the hangcheck timer or watchdog timer (depending on the implementation) for the cluster integrity. OPROCd is locked in memory and runs as a real-time process. This sleeps for a fixed time and runs as *root* user. Failure of the OPROCd process causes the node to restart.

IO Fencing

Fencing is an important operation that protects processes from other nodes modifying the resources during node failures. When a node fails, it needs to be isolated from the other active nodes. Fencing is required because it is impossible to distinguish between a real failure and a temporary hang. Therefore, we assume the worst and always fence. (If the node is really down, it cannot do any damage; in theory, nothing is required. We could just bring it back into the cluster with the usual join process.) Fencing, in general, insures that I/O can no longer occur from the failed node. Raw devices using a fencing method called STOMITH (Shoot The Other Machine In The Head) automatically power off the server.

Other techniques can be used to perform fencing. The most popular are reserve/release (R/R) or persistent reservation (SCSI3). SAN Fabric fencing is also widely used both by Red Hat Global File System (GFS) and Polyserv. Reserve/release by its nature works only with two nodes. (That is, one of the two nodes in the cluster upon detecting that the other node has failed will issue the reserve and grab all the disks for itself. The other node will commit suicide if it tries to do I/O in case it was temporarily hung. The I/O failure triggers some code to kill the node.)

In general, in the two nodes case, R/R is sufficient to address the split-brain issue. For more than two nodes, the SAN Fabric fencing technique does not work well because it would cause all the nodes but one to commit suicide. In those cases, persistent reservation, essentially a match on a key, is used. In persistent reservation, if you have the right key, you can do I/O; otherwise, your I/O fails. Therefore, it is sufficient to change the key on a failure to ensure the right behavior during failure.

CRS Process	Functionality	Failure of the Process	Runs as
Process Monitor (OPROCd)	Provides basic cluster integrity services	Node restart	root
Event Management (EVMd)	Spawns a child process event logger and generates callouts	Automatically restarted, does not cause node reboot	oracle
Cluster Synchronization Services (CSSd)	Basic node membership, Group Services, and basic locking	Node restart	oracle
Cluster Ready Services (CRSd)	Resource monitoring, resource failover, and node recovery	Process restarted automatically, does not cause node restart	root

TABLE 3-3. *CRS Processes and Functionality*

Table 3-3 summarizes the details of the various CRS processes and their functionalities.

Cluster-Ready Services

Oracle Clusterware uses CRS for interaction between the OS and the database. CRS is a new component in Oracle 10g RAC and is the background engine for the 10g RAC high availability framework, which provides the standard cluster interface for all platforms. The functionality was previously handled by vendor clusterware based on the platform.

CRS must be installed in a separate Oracle home before the standard RAC installation. This separate Oracle home is known as ORA_CRS_HOME. CRS is a mandatory component for 10g RAC and can run either alone or on top of vendor-supplied clusterware such as Veritas Cluster Server, Sun Cluster, or HP Serviceguard. However, if third-party clusterware is used for OS clustering, Oracle Clusterware should be integrated on top of them.

When CRS is installed on the cluster where a third-party clusterware is integrated, CRS relies on the vendor clusterware for the node membership functionality and just manages Oracle services and resources. If CRS is the only clusterware in the cluster, it manages the node membership functionality along with managing regular RAC-related resources and services.

Cluster Membership Decisions   Oracle Clusterware contains logic for determining the health of other nodes of the cluster and whether they are alive. After a certain period of inactivity of a node, Oracle Clusterware declares the node dead and evicts it. If a new node needs to be added, it is allowed to join immediately.

In the presence of vendor clusterware, Oracle Clusterware limits its view of the cluster to those nodes that the vendor also sees. Oracle Clusterware allows new nodes to join as soon as the vendor clusterware reports that the new node is up and waits to evict a node until vendor clusterware is certain that the remote node is dead. However, if Oracle Clusterware cannot communicate with a node for 10 minutes, and vendor clusterware maintains that the node is still alive, Oracle Clusterware will forcibly evict the remote node to prevent an indefinite hang at the Oracle layer.

This delay is set so that if vendor clusterware is taking a long time to resolve network splits, Oracle does not end up killing the nodes on the wrong side of the split. This dueling clusterware scenario can otherwise yield a full cluster outage if this timeout is too low.

Resource Management Frameworks Resources represent applications or system components (both local and remote to the cluster) whose behavior is wrapped and monitored by a cluster framework. Thus, the application or system component becomes highly available. Correct modeling of resources stipulates that they must be managed by only one cluster framework. Having multiple frameworks managing the same resource can produce undesirable side effects, including race conditions in start/stop semantics.

Consider an example in which two cluster frameworks manage the same shared storage, such as a raw disk volume or cluster file system. In the event that the storage component goes down, both frameworks may compete in trying to bring it back up and may decide to apply totally different recovery methods (for example, restart vs. notification for human intervention, wait before restarting vs. retrying in a tight loop).

In the case of single application resources, both frameworks may even decide to failover the component to a totally different node. In general, clusterware software systems are not prepared to handle resources that are managed by multiple HA frameworks.

Starting and Stopping Oracle Clusterware

When a node fails, Oracle Clusterware is brought up at boot time via the init daemon (on UNIX) or Windows Service Management (on Windows). Therefore, if the init process fails to run on the node, the OS is broken and Oracle Clusterware does not start.

The Oracle Clusterware can be manually started, stopped, enabled, and disabled using the following commands (which must be run as the superuser).

In 10.1.0.4:

```
/etc/init.d/init.crs start      # starts Oracle Clusterware
/etc/init.d/init.crs stop       # stops Oracle Clusterware
/etc/init.d/init.crs enable     # enables Clusterware at boot
/etc/init.d/init.crs disable    # disables Clusterware at boot
```

(The location of these scripts is platform dependent: for HP, the scripts are in /sbin/init.d; for AIX, the scripts are in /etc; for Solaris and Linux, the scripts are in /etc/init.d.)

In 10.2:

```
crsctl stop crs      # stops Oracle Clusterware
crsctl start crs     # starts Oracle Clusterware
crsctl enable crs    # enables Oracle Clusterware
crsctl disable crs   # disables Oracle Clusterware
```

The commands to start and stop Oracle Clusterware are asynchronous, but while stopping it, a small wait time may occur before returning control. Only one set of CRSs can be run on one cluster.

In Oracle Database 10g Release 2, the Oracle Clusterware APIs are documented. Customers are free to use these programmatic interfaces in their custom or non-Oracle software to operate and maintain a coherent cluster environment. To start and stop Oracle resources named with *ora.*, you must use SRVCTL. Oracle does not support third-party applications that check Oracle resources and take corrective actions on those resources. Best practice is to leave Oracle resources controlled by

Cluster Repositories

The cluster repository on Microsoft Cluster Service (MSCS) is called the Cluster Configuration Database (CCD), where the cluster bootstrap information resides. The CCD contains information about the physical and logical entities in a cluster. MSCS exposes a registry-like interface (API) that can be used by cluster-aware applications to retrieve and store data from the CCD. A Configuration Database Manager (CDM) resides on every node, which is responsible for keeping the CCD consistent.

The cluster repository for Sun Cluster 3.0 is called the Cluster Configuration Repository (CCR) and is a distributed database for storing cluster configuration and state information. Information is stored in flat ASCII files. Each node maintains its own independent copy of this database and uses two-phase commit to ensure consistency of contents of CCR. One or more files on the CFS act as the cluster repository.

Oracle Clusterware. For any other resource, either Oracle or the vendor clusterware (not both) can manage the resource directly.

Oracle Cluster Registry

Oracle Cluster Ready Services (CRS) uses the cluster registry to keep the configuration information. This should be a shared storage and should be accessible to all the nodes in the clusters simultaneously. This shared storage is called Oracle Cluster Registry (OCR), and OCR is the integral component on RAC architecture. This component is automatically backed by the daemons, and manual backups are also available for OCR. OCSSd uses the OCR extensively and writes the changes to the registry.

OCR is the central repository for the CRS and keeps the details of the services and status of the resources. OCR is the registry equivalent of Microsoft Windows, which stores name value pairs of information such as resources that are used to manage the resource equivalents by the CRS stack. Resources with the CRS stack are components, which are managed by CRS and need to store some basic demographic information about the resources—the good, the bad state, and the callout scripts. All such information makes it into the OCR. The OCR is also used to bootstrap CSS for the port information, nodes in the cluster, and similar information. This is a binary file and cannot be edited by any other Oracle tools.

Oracle Universal Installer (OUI) uses OCR during the installation time. All the CSS daemons have read-only access during startup. OCR information is also cached at node level and this acts as a distributed cache for CRS daemons. Only one of the nodes is the master for the OCR and handles all of the writes to the registry. Other nodes pass their changes to and read the OCR information from the cache of the master node. OCR cache is also used by other Oracle tools such as Enterprise Manager. It is recommended that at least 100MB is used for the OCR repository.

The Cluster Synchronization daemon (CSSd) updates OCR during the cluster setup. Once the cluster is set up, OCR will be used by read-only operations. During node addition or deletion, CSS updates the OCR with the new information. The CRS daemon will update the OCR about the status of the nodes during failures and reconfiguration. Other management tools such as NetCA or DBCA and SRVCTL update the services information in the OCR as they are executed. OCR information is also cached in all nodes, and more of the read-only operations will be benefited by the OCR cache.

OCR data is automatically backed up in the OCR location every four hours. These backups are stored for a week and circularly overwritten. The last three successful backups of OCR, a day old, and a week old, are available in the directory $ORA_CRS_HOME/cdata/<*cluster name*>. The OCR backup location can also be changed using the ocrconfig command line utility. OCR information can be exported and imported by this utility. Similarly, OCR can also be upgraded during database upgrades and can also be downgraded if required. Since OCR is a key component in RAC, it is recommended that the OCR disk be mirrored, or use the OCR mirroring feature available from Oracle 10g Release 2.

Voting Disk

The *voting disk* is a shared disk that will be accessed by all the member nodes in the cluster during the operation. The voting disk is used as a central reference for all the nodes and keeps the heartbeat information between the nodes. If any of the nodes is unable to ping the voting disk, the cluster immediately recognizes the communication failure and evicts the node from the cluster group to prevent data corruptions. The voting disk is sometimes called a "quorum device" as the split-brain resolution is decided based on the ownership of the quorum device.

The voting disk manages the cluster membership and arbitrates the cluster ownership during communication failures between the nodes. RAC uses the voting disk to determine the active instances of the cluster and inactive instances are evicted from the cluster. Since the voting disk plays a vital role, you should mirror the voting disk. If Oracle mirroring is not used for the voting disk, external mirroring should be used.

Voting is perhaps the most universally accepted method of arbitration. It has been used for centuries in many forms for contests, for selecting members of government, and so forth. One problem with voting is plurality—the leading candidate gains more votes than the other candidates, but not more than half of the total votes cast. Other problems with voting are that ties can occur and the process can be time consuming. This may not scale well for large populations.

Occasionally, voting is confused with a quorum. They are similar but distinct. A vote is usually a formal expression of opinion or will in response to a proposed decision. A quorum is defined as the number, usually a majority of officers or members of a body, that, when duly assembled, is legally competent to transact business. Both concepts are important; the only vote that should ratify a decision is the vote of a quorum of members. For clusters, the quorum defines a viable cluster. If a node or group of nodes cannot achieve a quorum, they should not start services because they risk conflicting with an established quorum.

Oracle Virtual IP

Virtual IP is required to ensure that applications can be designed to be highly available. A system needs to eliminate SPOFs. In Oracle, clients connected to an RAC database must be able to survive a node failure. Client applications connect to the Oracle instance and access the database through the instance. So a node failure will bring down the instance to which the client might have connected.

The first design available from Oracle was Transparent Application Failover (TAF). With TAF, a session can failover to the surviving instances and continue processing. Various limitations existed with TAF; for instance only query failover is supported. Also, to achieve less latency in failing over to the surviving node, Oracle tweaked the TCP timeout (platform dependent, defaults to 10 minutes in most UNIX ports). It wouldn't be a good idea to design a system in which a client takes 10 minutes to detect that there is no response from the node to which it has connected.

To address this, Oracle version 10g introduced a new feature called *cluster VIPs*—a cluster virtual IP address that would be used by the outside world to connect to the database. This IP address needs to be different from the set of IP addresses within the cluster. Traditionally, listeners would be listening on the public IP of the box and clients would contact the listener on this IP. If the node dies, the client would take the TCP timeout value to detect the death of the node. In 10g, each node of the cluster has a VIP configured in the same subnet of the public IP. A VIP name and address must be registered in the DNS in addition to the standard static IP information. Listeners would be configured to listen on VIPs instead of the public IP.

When a node is down, the VIP is automatically failed over to one of the other nodes. During the failover, the node that gets the VIP will "re-ARP" to the world, indicating the new MAC address of the VIP. Clients who have connected to this VIP will immediately get a reset packet sent. This results in clients getting errors immediately rather than waiting for the TCP timeout value. When one node goes down in a cluster and a client is connecting to same node, the client connection will be refused by the down node, and the client application will choose the next available node from the descriptor list to get a connection. Applications need to be written so that they catch the reset errors and handle them. Typically for queries, applications should see an ORA-3113 error.

NOTE
In computer networking, the Address Resolution Protocol (ARP) is the method of finding the host's hardware address (MAC address) when only the IP address is known. ARP is used by the hosts when they want to communicate with each other in the same network. It is also used by routers to forward a packet from one host through another router. In cluster VIP failovers, the new node that gets the VIP advertises the new ARP address to the world. This is typically known as gracious-ARP, *and during this operation, the old hardware address is invalidated in the ARP cache, and all the new connections will get the new hardware address.*

Cluster Interconnect

Cluster interconnect is another important component in the RAC. It is a communication path used by the cluster for the synchronization of resources and is also used in some cases for the transfer of data from one instance to another. Typically, the interconnect is a network connection that is dedicated to the server nodes of a cluster (and thus is sometimes referred to as a *private* interconnect) and has a high bandwidth and low latency. Different hardware platforms and different clustering software have different protocol implementations for the high-speed interconnect.

Table 3-4 lists the various interconnects used by the implementations based on the clusterware used and network hardware.

At the network level, a failure in a NIC can cause an outage to the cluster, especially if the failure occurs at the interface on which the interconnect is configured. To achieve high availability at this layer, network teaming/bonding can be used.

Bonding allows a node to see multiple physical NICs as a single logical unit. The Linux kernel includes a bonding module that can be used to achieve software-level NIC teaming. The kernel-bonding module can be used to team multiple physical interfaces to a single logical interface, which is used to achieve fault tolerance and load balancing. The bonding driver is available as part of the Linux kernel version 2.4 or later. Since the bonding module is delivered as

Operating System	Clusterware	Network Hardware	RAC Protocol
HP OpenVMS	HP OpenVMS	Memory Channel	TCP
HP OpenVMS	HP OpenVMS	Gigabit Ethernet	TCP
HP Tru64	HP TruCluster	Memory Channel	RDG
HP Tru64	HP TruCluster	Memory Channel	UDP
HP Tru64	HP TruCluster	Gigabit Ethernet	RDG
HP Tru64	HP TruCluster	Gigabit Ethernet	UDP
HP-UX	Oracle Clusterware	Hyper fabric	UDP
HP-UX	Oracle Clusterware	Gigabit Ethernet	UDP
HP-UX	HP Serviceguard	Hyper fabric	UDP
HP-UX	HP Serviceguard	Gigabit Ethernet	UDP
HP-UX	Veritas Cluster Server	Gigabit Ethernet	LLT
HP-UX	Veritas Cluster Server	Gigabit Ethernet	UDP
IBM AIX	Oracle Clusterware	Gigabit Ethernet (FDDI)	UDP
IBM AIX	HACMP	Gigabit Ethernet (FDDI)	UDP
Linux	Oracle Clusterware	Gigabit Ethernet	UDP
MS Windows	Oracle Clusterware	Gigabit Ethernet	TCP
Sun Solaris	Oracle Clusterware	Gigabit Ethernet	UDP
Sun Solaris	Fujitsu Primecluster	Gigabit Ethernet	ICF
Sun Solaris	Sun Cluster	SCI Interconnect	RSM
Sun Solaris	Sun Cluster	Firelink interconnect	RSM
Sun Solaris	Sun Cluster	Gigabit Ethernet	UDP
Sun Solaris	Veritas Cluster Server	Gigabit Ethernet	LLT
Sun Solaris	Veritas Cluster Server	Gigabit Ethernet	UDP

TABLE 3-4. *Interconnects Based on Clusterware and Hardware*

part of the Linux kernel, it can be configured independently from the interface driver vendor (different interfaces can constitute a single logical interface).

Various hardware vendors provide different types of NIC bonding solutions for the network interconnect resiliency. Typically, bonding offers the following benefits:

- **Bandwidth scalability** Adding a network card doubles the network bandwidth. It can be used to improve aggregate throughput.

- **High availability** Provides redundancy or link aggregation of computer ports.

- **Load balancing** HP Auto Port Aggregation (APA) supports true load balancing and failure recovery capabilities and distributes traffic evenly across the aggregated links.

■ **Single MAC address**   Because ports aggregated with HP APA share a single, logical MAC address, there is no need to assign individual addresses to aggregated ports.

■ **Flexibility**   Ports can be aggregated to achieve higher performance whenever network congestion occurs.

Interconnect Switch

The basic requirement of an interconnect is to provide reliable communication between nodes, but this cannot be achieved by a crossover cable between the nodes. However, using a crossover cable as interconnect may be appropriate for development or demonstration purposes. Substituting a normal crossover cable is not officially supported in production RAC implementations for the following reasons:

■ Crossover cables do not provide complete electrical insulation between nodes. Failure of one node because of a short circuit or because of an electrical interferences will bring the down the surviving node.

■ Using crossover cables instead of a high-speed switch greatly limits the scalability of the clusters as only two nodes can be clustered using a crossover cable.

■ Failure of one node brings down the entire cluster as the cluster manager cannot exactly detect the failed/surviving node. Had there been a switch during split-brain resolution, the surviving node can easily deduct the heartbeat and take the ownership of the quorum device and node failures can be easily detected.

■ Crossover cables do not detect split-brain situations as effectively as communication interface through switches. Split-brain resolution is the effective part in cluster management during communication failures.

Split-Brain Resolution

In the RAC environment, server nodes communicate with each other using high-speed private interconnects. The high-speed interconnect is a redundant network that is exclusively used for interinstance communication and some data block traffic. A *split-brain* situation occurs when all the links of the private interconnect fail to respond to each other, but the instances are still up and running. So each instance thinks that the other instance(s) is/are dead, and that it should take over the ownership.

In a split-brain situation, instances independently access the data and modify the same blocks and the database will end up with changed data blocks overwritten, which could lead to data corruption. To avoid this, various algorithms have been implemented.

In the RAC environment, the Instance Membership Recovery (IMR) service is one of the efficient algorithms used to detect and resolve the split-brain syndrome. When one instance fails to communicate with the other instance, or when one instance becomes inactive for some reason and is unable to issue the control file heartbeat, the split brain is detected and the detecting instance will evict the failed instance from the database. This process is called *node eviction*. Detailed information is written in alert log and trace files, and this is also discussed in detail in Chapter 14.

Oracle Kernel Components

The Oracle Kernel components in the RAC environment are the set of additional background processes in each instance. The buffer cache and shared pool become global in the RAC environment, and managing the resources without conflicts and corruptions requires special handling. The new background processes in the RAC environment, along with those normal background processes which usually exist in single instances, manage the Global resources effectively.

Global Cache and Global Enqueue Services

In RAC, as more than one instance is accessing the resource, the instances require better coordination at the resource management level. Otherwise, data corruption may occur. Each instance will have its own set of buffers but will be able to request and receive data blocks currently held in another instance's cache. Buffer manipulation in the RAC environment is quite different from a single instance environment because at any time only one set of processes may be accessing the buffer. In RAC, the buffer cache of one node may contain data that is requested by another node. The management of data sharing and exchange in this environment is done by the Global Cache Services (GCS).

Global Resource Directory

All the resources in the cluster group form a central repository of resources called the Global Resource Directory (GRD), which is integrated and distributed. Each instance masters some set of resources and together all instances form the GRD. The resources in the cluster group are equally distributed among the nodes based on their weight. The GRD is managed by two services called Global Cache Services (GCS) and Global Enqueue Services (GES). GCS and GES together form and manage the GRD (called the DLM in prior cluster releases such as Oracle Parallel Server, and often still referred to as such in some Oracle documentation).

When one instance departs the cluster, the GRD portion of that instance needs to be redistributed to the surviving nodes. Similarly, when a new instance enters the cluster, the GRD portions of the existing instances must be redistributed to create the GRD portion of the new instance. The components of the GRD and management issues are discussed in Chapter 11.

RAC Background Processes

RAC databases have two or more instances with their own memory structures and background processes. Other than the normal single instance background processes, some additional processes are started to manage the shared resources. Thus the RAC database has the same structure of the single instance Oracle database plus additional processes and memory structures that are specific to RAC. These processes maintain cache coherency across the nodes.

Maintaining cache coherency is an important part of an RAC. *Cache coherency* is the technique of keeping multiple copies of a buffer consistent between different Oracle instances (or disjoint caches) on different nodes. Global cache management ensures that access to a master copy of a data block in one buffer cache is coordinated with the copy of the block in another buffer cache. This ensures the most recent copy of a block in a buffer cache contains all changes that are made to

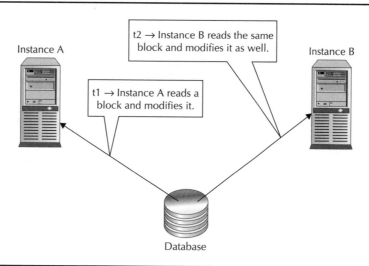

FIGURE 3-3. *Instances read block without any coordination*

that block by any instance in the system, regardless of whether those changes have been committed on the transaction level.

The Importance of Coordination

You must understand why interinstance cache coordination is necessary in an RAC environment. Consider a two-instance environment without any cache coordination and communication among the instances, as shown in Figure 3-3.

1. Referring to Figure 3-3, consider at time t1, instance A reads a block in its buffer cache and modifies row 1 in it. The modified block is still in its buffer cache and has not yet been written to the disk.

2. Sometime later at time t2, instance B reads the same block in its buffer cache and modifies another row in that block. Instance B also has not written the block to disk, thus the disk still contains the old version of the block.

3. Now at time t3, instance A writes the block to disk. At this stage, modifications from instance A are written on disk (Figure 3-4).

4. Some time later at time t4, instance B writes the block to disk. It overwrites the block written by instance A in step 3. As you can easily infer, the changes made to the block by instance A are lost (Figure 3-5).

This scenario and many other similar situations require that when data is simultaneously accessed by multiple machines, the read and especially the write activities must be coordinated among these machines or else data integrity problems will result, which may manifest as data corruption.

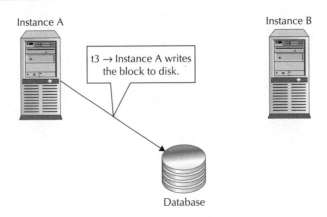

FIGURE 3-4. *Instance A writes block without coordination*

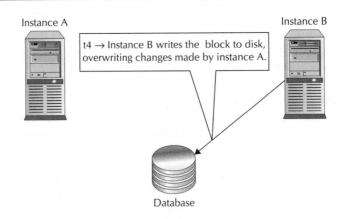

FIGURE 3-5. *Instance B overwrites the changes made by instance A*

Now let's repeat the above sequence of operation in the presence of coordination (more details later in this chapter):

1. At time t1, when instance A needs a data block with an intent to modify, it reads the block from disk. However, before reading, it must inform the GCS (DLM) of its intention to do so. GCS keeps track of the lock status of the block being modified by instance A by keeping an exclusive lock against the block on behalf of instance A.

2. At time t2, instance B wants to modify the same block. Before doing so, it must inform the GCS of its intention to modify the block. When GCS receives the request from instance B, it asks the current lock holder instance A to release the lock. Thus GCS ensures that instance B gets the latest version of the block and also passes on the write privilege to it (exclusive lock).

   3. At time t3, instance B gets the latest (current) version of the block that has the changes
   made by instance A and modifies it.

   4. At any point in time, only one instance has the current copy of the block. Only that
   instance can write the block to disk, thereby ensuring that all the changes to the block
   are preserved and written to the disk when needed.

   The GCS thus maintains data coherency and coordination by keeping track of the lock status
of each block that is read and/or modified by the server nodes in the cluster. GCS guarantees that
only one copy of the block in memory can be modified and that all the modifications are written
to disk at the appropriate time. It maintains the cache coherence among the nodes and guarantees
the integrity of the data. GCS is an in-memory database that contains information about the current
locks on blocks and also keeps track of instances that are waiting to acquire locks on blocks. This
is known as *Parallel Cache Management* (PCM) and has been a central feature of Oracle clustered
databases since the introduction of Oracle Parallel Server (OPS) in the early 1990s.

   PCM uses distributed locks on the resources to coordinate access to resources by different
instances of an RAC environment. The GRM helps to coordinate and communicate the lock
requests from Oracle processes between instances in the RAC environment.

   Each instance has a buffer cache in its SGA. To ensure that each RAC database instance
obtains the block that it needs to satisfy a query or transaction, RAC instances use two processes,
the GCS and the GES. The GCS and GES maintain records of the lock status of each data file and
each cached block using a GRD. The GRD contents are distributed across all of the active
instances.

   Hence, it is good to increase the SGA size by a factor but not more than 5 percent of the total
SGA size. Tests have found that the larger your block size, the lower the memory overheads for
the extra GCS, GES, and GRD components in the SGA. For large SGAs that exceed 20GB, it has
been noted that the overhead is dependent on the block size used and could be around 600 to
700MB for a 16KB block–sized database.

   The *cost* (or overhead) of cache coherency is defined as the need to check with other instances if
a particular access is permitted before granting any access to a specific shared resource. Algorithms
optimize the need to coordinate on each and every access, but some overhead is incurred. Cache
coherency means that the contents of the caches in different nodes are in a well-defined state with
respect to each other. Cache coherency identifies the most up-to-date copy of a resource, also called
the master copy. In case of node failure, no vital information is lost (such as committed transaction
state) and atomicity is maintained. This requires additional logging or copying of data but is not part
of the locking system.

   A *resource* is an identifiable entity—that is, it has a name or reference. The entity referred to
is usually a memory region, a disk file, or an abstract entity. A resource can be owned or locked
in various states, such as exclusive or shared. By definition, any shared resource is lockable. If it
is not shared, no access conflict will occur. If it is shared, access conflicts must be resolved,
typically with a lock. Although the terms *lock* and *resource* refer to entirely separate objects, the
terms are sometimes (unfortunately) used interchangeably.

   A *global resource* is visible and used throughout the cluster. A *local resource* is used by only
one instance. It may still have locks to control access by the multiple processes of the instance,
but no access to it occurs from outside the instance. Data buffer cache blocks are the most
obvious and most heavily used global resource. Other data item resources are also global in the
cluster, such as transaction enqueues and database data structures. The data buffer cache blocks
are handled by the Global Cache Service (GCS), also called Parallel Cache Management (PCM).

The nondata block resources are handled by Global Enqueue Services (GES), also called Non-Parallel Cache Management (non-PCM). The Global Resource Manager (GRM), also called the Distributed Lock Manager (DLM), keeps the lock information valid and correct across the cluster.

All caches in the SGA are either global and must be coherent across all instances, or they are local. The library, row (also called dictionary), and buffer caches are global. The large and Java pool buffers are local. For RAC, the GRD is global in itself and also used to control the coherency.

After one instance caches data, in some cases other instances within the same cluster database can acquire a block image from another instance in the same database faster than by reading the block from disk. Therefore, Cache Fusion moves current copies of blocks between instances rather than re-reading the blocks from disk under certain conditions. When a consistent block is needed or a changed block is required on another instance, Cache Fusion can transfer the block image between the affected instances. RAC uses the private interconnect for inter-instance communication and block transfers. GCS manages the block transfers between the instances.

The GRD manages the locking or ownership of all resources that are not limited to a single instance in RAC. The GRD comprises GCS, which handles the data blocks, and GES, which handles the enqueues and other global resources.

Each process has a set of roles, and we will study them in detail in the following sections. In RAC, the library cache and shared pool are globally coordinated. All the resources are managed by locks and the key background process also manage the locks. GCS and GES use the following processes to manage the resources. These RAC-specific processes and the GRD collaborate to enable Cache Fusion.

- **LMS**   Global Cache Services process
- **LMON**   Global Enqueue Services Monitor
- **LMD**   Global Enqueue Services daemon
- **LCK0**   Instance Enqueue process
- **DIAG**   Diagnostic daemon

The LMON and LMD processes communicate with their partner processes on the remote nodes. Other processes may have message exchanges with peer processes on the other nodes (for example, PQ). The LMS process, for example, may directly receive lock requests from remote foreground processes.

LMS: Global Cache Services Process

LMS is a process used in Cache Fusion. The acronym is derived from the Lock Manager Server process. It enables consistent copies of blocks to be transferred from a holding instance's buffer cache to a requesting instance's buffer cache without a disk write under certain conditions. It also retrieves requests from the server queue queued by LMD to perform requested lock operations.

It also rolls back any uncommitted transactions for any blocks that are being requested for consistent read by the remote instance. LMS processes also control the flow of messages between instances. Each instance can have up to 10 LMSn processes, though the actual number of LMSn processes varies according to the amount of messaging traffic between nodes. The hidden parameter _lm_lms can also be used manually to control the number of LMSn processes. If this parameter is not set manually, the number of LMS processes automatically started during instance startup is a function of the CPU_COUNT of that node and is usually adequate for most types of applications. It is only under special circumstances that you may need to tweak this parameter to increase the default number of LMSn processes.

LMS processes can also be started dynamically by the system based on demand and is controlled by the parameter _lm_dynamic_lms. By default, this parameter is set to FALSE. In addition, LMS processes manage lock manager service requests for GCS resources and send them to a service queue to be handled by the LMSn process. It also handles global lock deadlock detection and monitors for lock conversion timeouts.

LMON: Global Enqueue Services Monitor

LMON is the Lock Monitor process and is responsible for managing the Global Enqueue Services (GES). It maintains consistency of GCS memory in case of process death. LMON is also responsible for the cluster reconfiguration and locks reconfiguration when an instance joins or leaves the cluster. It also checks the instance death and listens for local messages. The LMON process also generates a detailed trace file that tracks instance reconfigurations.

The background LMON process monitors the entire cluster to manage global resources. LMON manages instance deaths and the associated recovery for any failed instance. In particular, LMON handles the part of recovery associated with global resources. LMON-provided services are also known as Cluster Group Services (CGS).

LMD: Global Enqueue Services Daemon

LMD is the daemon process that manages enqueue manager service requests for the GCS. The acronym *LMD* refers literally to the Lock Manager Daemon, the term used for the process in OPS. The resource agent process manages requests for resources to control access to blocks. The LMD process also handles deadlock detection and remote resource requests. Remote resource requests originate from another instance.

LCK0: Instance Enqueue Process

The Lock (LCK) process manages instance resource requests and cross-instance call operations for shared resources. It also builds a list of invalid lock elements and validates lock elements during recovery. An instance can use only a single LCK process since primary functionality is handled by the LMSn process.

DIAG Process

DIAG is a lightweight daemon process for all the diagnostic needs of an instance in an RAC environment. Although several debugging and diagnostic tools are available, they do not provide a single interface for a cluster environment and are not cluster-ready, making diagnosis across multiple instances difficult.

To solve the cluster-related debugging, the DIAG framework was introduced with the DIAG daemon. This framework does not interfere with or affect the normal operation of the system. DIAG works independently from an instance and relies only on services provided by the underlying operating system. This is integrated with the RDBMS kernel for startup and shutdown and its need to access the SGA for trace buffers. This framework implements Clusterwide debuging using the oradebug utility.

Process Monitor (PMON) restarts a new DIAG process to continue its service if the DIAG process dies. The DIAG daemon also monitors the health of the local RAC instance. On failure of an essential process, DIAG can capture the system state and other useful information for later diagnosis, and notify DIAG on the other instances to capture similar information. This provides a snapshot view of the entire cluster environment. DIAG will be responsible for monitoring the liveliness of operations of the local RAC instance and performing any necessary recovery, if an operational hang is detected.

In a Nutshell

This chapter introduced the various building blocks of the RAC. It looked into the different options available for storage and interconnects, which are key to the systems to support scalability and availability. You should understand the importance of resource coordination and the kernel components involved in the clusterwide operations. With this background in mind, we will begin preparing the hardware to install RAC in the next chapter.

PART
II

Installation, Configuration, and Storage

CHAPTER
4

RAC Preinstallation

his chapter focuses on preparing the hardware for installation of RAC. This includes configuring additional network interface cards (NICs) and the Oracle Clusterware installation before installing the RDBMS software. Figure 4-1 shows the installation process for the Oracle 10g RAC.

The first step is configuring the operating system for the clusterware and RAC software. Each server in the cluster will have one public network interface and one private network interface. The *public network interface* is the standard network connection that connects the server to all of the other computers in your network. The *private network interface* is a private network connection shared by only the servers in the cluster. The private network interface is used by the Oracle Clusterware and RAC software to communicate with the servers in the clusters.

Another important step is the decision about shared storage. The *shared storage* for datafiles marks an important step in hardware preparation. As a fundamental requirement for high availability, all the database files in the cluster will be stored on shared storage that is separate from the server nodes in the cluster. The shared storage allows multiple database instances, running on different servers, to access the same database information and ensures that if one or more server nodes fail, all remaining nodes will continue to have access to all database files.

After the shared storage for the datafiles is defined, the next step is installing the Oracle Clusterware, which logically binds multiple servers into a cluster. During the Clusterware install, you specify the location at which to create two clusterware components: a voting disk to record node membership information and the Oracle Cluster Registry (OCR) to record cluster configuration information. The Clusterware install is performed on one server and will be automatically installed on the other servers in the cluster.

At the end of the Clusterware install, you configure the virtual IP (VIP) addresses for the servers in the cluster. A VIP address is an alternate public address that client connections use

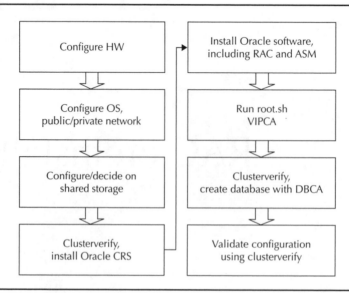

FIGURE 4-1. *RAC installation flowchart*

instead of the standard public IP address. If a node fails, the node's VIP fails over to another node on which the VIP can accept connections. Clients that attempt to connect to the VIP receive a rapid connection refused error instead of waiting for TCP connect timeout messages.

After the Clusterware is installed, you will install the Oracle Database 10g RAC binaries and create the database. The installer will recognize that the Clusterware has already been installed. Like the Clusterware install, the database and RAC install is performed on one server, and the software is automatically installed on the other servers in the cluster.

After the database software is installed, you will create a database using the Database Configuration Assistant. The last step will be installing the Enterprise Manager Agent. The Enterprise Manager Agent connects to the Enterprise Manager Grid Control, where you administer the RAC environment. Like the previous installs, the agent install is performed on one node in the cluster and automatically installed on the other nodes.

In this chapter, Linux is assumed to be the operating system in use and Oracle Database 10g Release 2 the installation. Port-specific documentations and installation guides should be consulted during installation. This chapter does *not* intend to replace the Oracle installation guide. However, it can be used in parallel with the installation manuals.

Preinstallation Tasks

The preinstallation tasks start with configuring the network configuration files. The /etc/hosts file contains the Internet Protocol (IP) host names and addresses for the local host and other hosts in the Internet network. This file is used to resolve a name to an address (that is, to translate a host name into its Internet address). When your system is using a domain name server (DNS) for address resolution, this file is accessed only if the name server cannot resolve the host name.

Following is an example hosts file. The command `ping` (which stands for Packet Internet Grouping) can be used to verify the configuration. Except for the VIP interface, all other interfaces should be up and running at this time.

```
127.0.0.1        localhost.localdomain   localhost
152.69.170.41    i3dl041e.idc.oracle.com  i3dl041e
152.69.170.45    i3dl045e.idc.oracle.com  i3dl045e
1.1.1.2          i3dl041i
1.1.1.6          i3dl045i
152.69.171.24    i3dlvip24.us.oracle.com  i3dlvip24
152.69.171.25    i3dlvip24.us.oracle.com  i3dlvip25
```

In this entry, the IP address is specified in either dotted decimal or octal format, and the host name is specified in either relative or absolute domain name format. If you specify the absolute domain name, the portion of the name preceding the first period (.) has a maximum length of 63 characters and cannot contain blank spaces. For both formats of the name, the total number of characters cannot exceed 255 characters, and each entry must be contained on one line. Multiple host names (or aliases) can be specified.

After the hosts file is configured properly on one of the nodes, copy it to the other nodes so that they are exactly the same. The hosts file on each node needs to contain the private, public, and virtual IP (VIP) addresses and node names of each node in the cluster.

Set up the Groups and Users

In typical installations, the UNIX user *oracle* will own the RDBMS binaries and all Oracle-related files. Normally this user will be the part of the *dba* group. Any user who is part of the DBA group and has sysoper/sysdba privileges can connect to the *oracle* instance without supplying a password. This is called *operating system authentication*. This privileged user can also start up and shut down instances. These users and groups should be configured before starting the installation.

Verify that the attributes (uid and gid) of the user *oracle* are identical on both nodes. Internally to the operating systems and cluster layer, the uids are compared to the uids while authorizations and permissions occur. So it is important to keep the user IDs and group IDs consistent across the nodes.

```
id oracle
uid=500(oracle) gid=500(dba) groups=500(dba),500(oinstall)
```

Configure Raw Devices

If you decide to use Automatic Storage Management (ASM) as storage for data files, raw partitions should be configured. ASM requires raw disks for storage, as file systems cannot be used as ASM devices. Raw devices are disk partitions without any file systems and initially owned by root. They are accessed by the application, bypassing the file system buffer cache. The /etc/sysconfig/rawdevices file should be configured as root as follows. The same file can also be transferred to the other nodes using scp or rcp.

```
# raw device bindings
# format:   <rawdev> <major> <minor>
#           <rawdev> <blockdev>
# example: /dev/raw/raw1 /dev/sda1
#          /dev/raw/raw2 8 5
/dev/raw/raw1    /dev/sdb1
/dev/raw/raw2    /dev/sdb2
/dev/raw/raw3    /dev/sdb3
/dev/raw/raw4    /dev/sdb4
```

The ownership of the raw devices should be transferred to the user *oracle* upon configuration. All raw partitions should be owned by *oracle* with the group permission set to *dba*. The command /etc/init.d/rawdevices restart restarts the raw devices and should be executed from both the nodes to have the proper bindings to all the nodes.

```
[root@i3dl041e raw]# /etc/init.d/rawdevices restart
Assigning devices:
           /dev/raw/raw1  -->   /dev/sdb1
/dev/raw/raw1:  bound to major 8, minor 17
           /dev/raw/raw2  -->   /dev/sdb2
/dev/raw/raw2:  bound to major 8, minor 18
           /dev/raw/raw3  -->   /dev/sdb3
/dev/raw/raw3:  bound to major 8, minor 19
           /dev/raw/raw4  -->   /dev/sdb4
/dev/raw/raw4:  bound to major 8, minor 20
done
```

The following command will show the current raw device bindings. The information should be identical in all the nodes.

```
[root@i3dl041e raw]# raw -qa
/dev/raw/raw1:  bound to major 8, minor 17
/dev/raw/raw2:  bound to major 8, minor 18
/dev/raw/raw3:  bound to major 8, minor 19
/dev/raw/raw4:  bound to major 8, minor 20
[root@i3dl045e raw]# raw -qa
/dev/raw/raw1:  bound to major 8, minor 17
/dev/raw/raw2:  bound to major 8, minor 18
/dev/raw/raw3:  bound to major 8, minor 19
/dev/raw/raw4:  bound to major 8, minor 20
```

Secure Shell Configuration

Oracle Universal Installer (OUI) installs the binaries in one node and then propagates the files to the other nodes. The installer uses the ssh and scp commands in the background during installation to run remote commands and copy files to the other cluster nodes. This requires noninteractive file copying across the nodes. You must configure ssh so that these commands do not prompt for a password. Setting up scp or rcp can enable this across the nodes. You also need to turn off the banner for ssh.

The following process sets up password-less file copying across nodes. This includes creating the public keys and private keys and transferring data to the nodes. You must create either RSA or DSA type public and private keys on both nodes. You can accept the default location for the key file.

Secure Shell Algorithms

Secure Shell (SSH) is a program as well as a network protocol that provides strong authentication and secure encrypted communications between two machines over an insecure network. It is designed for logging into and executing commands on a remote machine, as well as moving files back and forth between the two machines.

SSH has various authentication mechanisms and the most secure is based on keys rather than passwords. Using keys, SSH can authenticate you to all your computer accounts securely without your needing to memorize many passwords or enter them repeatedly. SSH generates a private and a public key. The public key can be stored on the machines with which you want to communicate. SSH will then connect to those machines with keys instead of with a standard account password.

The Digital Signature Algorithm (DSA) was developed by the U.S. National Security Agency (NSA) and promulgated by the U.S. National Institute of Standards and Technology (NIST) as part of the Digital Signature Standard (DSS). DSA can be used only to provide digital signatures and cannot be used for encryption. The Rivest-Shamir-Adleman (RSA) public-key algorithm is the most widely used asymmetric cipher. RSA can be used for both encryption and digital signatures. It is currently difficult to obtain the private key from the public key.

Leave the Pass Phrase blank. This command writes the public key to the /home/oracle/.ssh/id_rsa.pub file and the private key to the /home/oracle/.ssh/id_rsa file. You can do one or the other depending on security policy. You do not have to generate keys for both rsa and dsa. Just make sure to use the same one on all servers. Use one of the two following commands on each server in the cluster:

```
$ usr/bin/ssh-keygen -t rsa
$ /usr/bin/ssh-keygen -t dsa
```

You can accept the default location for the key file and leave the Pass Phrase blank. This command writes the public key to the /home/oracle/.ssh/id_dsa.pub file and the private key to the /home/oracle/.ssh/id_dsa file. You can copy the public key files /home/oracle/.ssh/id_rsa.pub and /home/oracle/.ssh/id_rsa from node 1 to node 2.

```
$ cd /home/oracle/.ssh
$ scp id_rsa.pub  i3dl045e:/home/oracle/.ssh/.
$ scp id_rsa      i3dl045e:/home/oracle/.ssh/.
$ cd /home/oracle/.ssh
$ scp i3dl045e:/home/oracle/.ssh/id_rsa.pub  id_rsa.pub2
$ scp i3dl045e:/home/oracle/.ssh/id_dsa.pub  id_dsa.pub2
```

Once the keys are generated, you must concatenate the rsa and dsa public keys of both nodes into one file called *authorized_keys*. This file should be propagated to all the participating nodes.

```
$ cat id_rsa.pub id_rsa.pub2 id_dsa.pub  id_dsa.pub2 > authorized_keys
$ scp authorized_keys   i3dl045e:/home/oracle/.ssh/
```

The first time you ssh from one node to another, it will prompt you to indicate a yes or no to continue connecting. It updates the key database during the first login and on subsequent logins will not prompt to continue connecting. A node must be able to ssh to itself without being prompted. Each node must be able to ssh to the public and private IP addresses for each node in the cluster. Normal RAC operations do not require ssh and rsh commands. They are used only during installation.

Configure the Kernel Parameters

As *root*, update the kernel parameters in the /etc/sysctl.conf file on *both* nodes. If these settings are already configured, make sure that they are at least set to the following values (it is OK if the values are set higher):

```
kernel.shmall = 2097152
kernel.shmmax = 2147483648
kernel.shmmni = 4096
kernel.sem = 250 32000 100 128
fs.file-max = 65536
net.ipv4.ip_local_port_range = 1024 65000
net.core.rmem_default = 262144
net.core.rmem_max = 262144
net.core.wmem_default = 262144
net.core.wmem_max = 262144
```

NOTE
X11 forwarding must be disabled during the installation and database creation with the Database Configuration Assistant. To disable X11 forwarding, set or comment out the following parameter X11Forwarding no *in the /etc/ssh/sshd_config file as* root.

Configure the Hangcheck-Timer Module

The hangcheck-timer module monitors the Linux kernel for extended operating system hangs that could affect the reliability of an RAC node and cause database corruption. If a hang occurs, the module restarts the node in seconds. To determine whether the hangcheck-timer is running, use the /sbin/lsmod | grep hang command. If nothing is returned, the hangcheck-timer is not running. It can be enabled by adding the following command to /etc/rc.d/rc.local as *root* to start the hangcheck-timer automatically on system startup:

```
/sbin/insmod hangcheck-timer hangcheck_tick=30 hangcheck_margin=180
```

Run the Cluster Verification Utility

Deploying RAC is a multistage operation, and components can malfunction at any stage due to the various dependencies at each layer. Testing and verification are required at each stage before proceeding to the next stage. Oracle provides a tool you can use to verify the cluster setup at every stage: the Cluster Verification Utility, clusterverify.

Clusterverify is a standalone utility used to verify a well-formed RAC cluster. It can be used at any stage—preinstallation, configuration, and operation—as it verifies the entire cluster stack and does not perform any configuration changes on cluster or RAC operations. It can be used to verify the stage-by-stage progress during RAC installation as each stage comprises of a set of operations during RAC deployment. Each stage has its own set of entry (prechecks) and/or exit (postchecks) criteria.

Clusterverify Stages

Following are the seven stages in the RAC deployment at which clusterverify can be run. Note that the utility automatically checks all nodes that are specified, so it is necessary to run the utility from only one node.

```
$> ./runcluvfy stage -list
      -post hwos      :  post-check for hardware & operating system
      -pre  cfs       :  pre-check for CFS setup
      -post cfs       :  post-check for CFS setup
      -pre  crsinst   :  pre-check for CRS installation
      -post crsinst   :  post-check for CRS installation
      -pre  dbinst    :  pre-check for database installation
      -pre  dbcfg     :  pre-check for database configuration
```

At the first stage in preparing the hardware for RAC installation, you can use clusterverify to check the hardware for basic network connectivity and most common operating system requirements. And it also checks the *oracle* user privileges and access to shared storage from both the nodes. It can be invoked by using the following command-line option. The output text (edited for clarity and simplicity) will be similar to the following:

```
$ ./runcluvfy.sh stage -post hwos -n i3dl041e,i3dl045e -verbose

Performing post-checks for hardware and operating system setup
Checking node reachability...
Check: Node reachability from node "i3dl041e"
Result: Node reachability check passed from node "i3dl041e".
Check: User equivalence for user "oracle"
Result: User equivalence check passed for user "oracle".
Checking user equivalence...
Checking node connectivity...
Interface information for node "i3dl041e"
  Interface Name                    IP Address                     Subnet
  ----------------------------      ----------------------------   ----------------
    eth0                            152.69.170.41                  152.69.168.0
    eth1                            1.1.1.2                        1.1.1.0
Interface information for node "i3dl045e"
  Interface Name                    IP Address                     Subnet
  ----------------------------      ----------------------------   ----------------
    eth0                            152.69.170.45                  152.69.168.0
    eth1                            1.1.1.6                        1.1.1.0
Check: Node connectivity of subnet "152.69.168.0"
  Source                            Destination                    Connected?
  ----------------------------      ----------------------------   ----------------
    i3dl041e:eth0                   i3dl045e:eth0                  yes
Result: Node connectivity check passed for subnet "152.69.168.0" with node(s)
i3dl041e,i3dl045e.
Check: Node connectivity of subnet "1.1.1.0"
  Source                            Destination                    Connected?
  ----------------------------      ----------------------------   ----------------
    i3dl041e:eth1                   i3dl045e:eth1                  yes
Result: Node connectivity check passed for subnet "1.1.1.0" with node(s)
i3dl041e,i3dl045e.
Suitable interfaces for VIP on subnet "152.69.168.0":
i3dl041e eth0:152.69.170.41
i3dl045e eth0:152.69.170.45
Suitable interfaces for VIP on subnet "1.1.1.0":
i3dl041e eth1:1.1.1.2
i3dl045e eth1:1.1.1.6
Result: Node connectivity check passed.
Checking shared storage accessibility...
  Disk                                       Sharing Nodes (2 in count)
  ----------------------------------         ------------------------
    /dev/sda                                 i3dl041e i3dl045e
    /dev/sdb                                 i3dl041e i3dl045e
Shared storage check was successful on nodes "i3dl041e,i3dl045e".
Post-check for hardware and operating system setup was successful.
```

Note that clusterverify can also be used to verify the components level. An individual subsystem or a module of the RAC cluster is known as a *component* in the utility. Availability, integrity, liveliness, sanity, or any other specific behavior of a cluster component can be verified. Components could be simple like a specific storage device, or complex like the CRS stack, involving a number of subcomponents such as CRSD, EVMD, CSSD, and OCR.

The following components are listed in the clusterverify utility:

```
$./runcluvfy comp -list
```

```
nodereach    : checks reachability between nodes
nodecon      : checks node connectivity
cfs          : checks CFS integrity
ssa          : checks shared storage accessibility
space        : checks space availability
sys          : checks minimum system requirements
clu          : checks cluster integrity
clumgr       : checks cluster manager integrity
ocr          : checks OCR integrity
crs          : checks CRS integrity
nodeapp      : checks node applications existence
admprv       : checks administrative privileges
peer         : compares properties with peers
```

Once the hardware, operating system, and network are verified, the cluster is ready for Oracle Clusterware installation. Oracle Cluster Ready Services (CRS) is the foundation for the Oracle Clusterware and the readiness for the CRS installation can be checked by using the following option in the clusterverify utility. It should be invoked as the OS user *oracle* and the nodes should be listed as command-line parameter arguments. The resulting output is edited for clarity.

```
$ ./runcluvfy.sh stage -pre crsinst -n i3dl041e,i3dl045e -orainv dba
```

```
Performing pre-checks for cluster services setup
Checking node reachability...
Node reachability check passed from node "i3dl041e".
Checking user equivalence...
User equivalence check passed for user "oracle".
Checking administrative privileges...
User existence check passed for "oracle".
Group existence check passed for "dba".
Membership check for user "oracle" in group "dba" [as Primary] passed.
Administrative privileges check passed.
Checking node connectivity...
Node connectivity check passed for subnet "152.69.168.0" with node(s)
i3dl041e,i3dl045e.
Node connectivity check passed for subnet "1.1.1.0" with node(s)
i3dl041e,i3dl045e.
Suitable interfaces for VIP on subnet "152.69.168.0":
i3dl041e eth0:152.69.170.41
i3dl045e eth0:152.69.170.45
Suitable interfaces for VIP on subnet "1.1.1.0":
i3dl041e eth1:1.1.1.2
i3dl045e eth1:1.1.1.6
Node connectivity check passed.
```

```
Checking system requirements for 'crs'...
Total memory check passed.
Free disk space check passed.
Swap space check passed.
System architecture check passed.
Kernel version check passed.
Package existence check passed for "make-3.79".
Package existence check passed for "binutils-2.14".
Package existence check passed for "gcc-3.2".
Package existence check passed for "glibc-2.3.2-95.27".
Package existence check passed for "compat-db-4.0.14-5".
Package existence check passed for "compat-gcc-7.3-2.96.128".
Package existence check passed for "compat-gcc-c++-7.3-2.96.128".
Package existence check passed for "compat-libstdc++-7.3-2.96.128".
Package existence check passed for "compat-libstdc++-devel-7.3-2.96.128".
Package existence check passed for "openmotif-2.2.3".
Package existence check passed for "setarch-1.3-1".
Group existence check passed for "dba".
Group existence check passed for "dba".
User existence check passed for "nobody".
System requirement passed for 'crs'
Pre-check for cluster services setup was successful.
```

When clusterverify does not report any errors, you have successfully set up the cluster for Oracle CRS installation. If errors are reported, you must fix them before starting the CRS installation. If clusterverify is successful, the next step will be installing CRS on the nodes. CRS installation uses OUI and the steps are common across all the operating systems.

CRS Installation

CRS installation is the foundation for the RAC database installation. CRS is the backbone of the remainder of the installation, as more than one database can share the same CRS foundation. OUI is run from one node in the cluster under an *X* environment, and the files will be propagated to the other nodes using the scp commands. The installer works in the background and appears to be hanging in the foreground. For those who are interested in knowing the undercover operations of the installer, we will trace the installer using the following options.

Tracing the Universal Installer

OUI is a simple Java program that copies the files from the staging area and relinks with the operating system libraries to create and update the Oracle inventory. The staging area can be the CD-ROM/DVD or a local mount point in the file system.

OUI puts minimum details about the installations options and progress in the installactions_timestamp.log. This log file will be typically stored in the $ORACLE_HOME/orainventory directory. However, this log does not contain detailed level of operations to debug the installation issues.

Starting from Oracle 10*g*, OUI can be invoked using the DTRACING, or Java tracing, option in the command line. The following invokes the installer with tracing:

```
$ runInstaller  -j -dtracing.enabled=true  -j-dtracing.level=2
```

Optionally, you can redirect the tracing output to a file. (I always start the installer with tracing on so that I don't need to restart the installer if any failures occur.) This tracing option is useful during installation of RAC, where the files are copied to the remote nodes using the `scp` or `rcp` command.

Tracing tells you what the installer is doing at any point of time by providing detailed traces to the install actions. However, the limited information is also written to the trace file, installactions_date_time.log. This information is very "high level" and does not get into the actual problems faced by the installer.

Tracing DBCA/VIPCA   Since OUI is invoked from the command line, you can easily set the tracing to that program. But in Windows, the platform installer is called by another program, setup.exe, and this program calls most of the other programs such as dbca and VIPCA/NetCA. To trace these programs, you need to add the tracing codes inside the respective batch files. For example, the dbca utility invokes the dbca.jar and we should add the tracing information in the JAR file to get the tracing of the other packaged programs.

The following procedure illustrates dbca tracing in Windows environment. Here you need to customize the dbca.bat (under the $ORACLE_HOME/bin directory). You need to add the tracing option inside the batch file and save the batch file with a different name; let's change dbca to cdbca (customized dbca).

Simply add the `-DTRACING.ENABLED=TRUE   -DTRACING.LEVEL=2` line before the `-classpath` argument. (I always customize the required batch files before any installation and use the customized startup files for the installation.)

```
**dbca.bat file** after customization . cdbca.bat
if "%args%"=="" goto with_no_args
"C:\oracle\product\10.1.0\db_1\jdk\jre\BIN\JAVA"   -Dsun.java2d.noddraw=true  -DORACLE_
HOME="%OH%" -DJDBC_PROTOCOL=thin -mx64m -DTRACING.ENABLED=TRUE -DTRACING.LEVEL=2
-classpath "%JRE_CLASSPATH%;%I18N_CLASSPATH%;%DBCA_CLASSPATH%;%ASSISTANTS_COMMON_
CLASSPATH%;%EWT_CLASSPATH%;%BALISHARE_CLASSPATH%;%SWING_CLASSPATH%;%ICE_BROWSER_CLASSPATH%;%HELP_
CLASSPATH%;%KODIAK_CLASSPATH%;%XMLPARSER_CLASSPATH%;%GSS_CLASSPATH%;%EM_CLASSPATH%;%SRVM_CLASSPATH%;%NETCFG_
CLASSPATH%;%JDBC_CLASSPATH%;%ORB_CLASSPATH%;%ORACLE_OEM_CLASSPATH%;%INSTALLER_CLASSPATH%"
oracle.sysman.assistants.dbca.Dbca   %args%
goto end
:with_no_args
"C:\oracle\product\10.1.0\db_1\jdk\jre\BIN\JAVA" -Dsun.java2d.noddraw=true -DORACLE_
HOME="%OH%" -DJDBC_PROTOCOL=thin -mx64m -DTRACING.ENABLED=TRUE -DTRACING.LEVEL=2
-classpath "%JRE_CLASSPATH%;%I18N_CLASSPATH%;%DBCA_CLASSPATH%;%ASSISTANTS_COMMON_
CLASSPATH%;%EWT_CLASSPATH%;%BALISHARE_CLASSPATH%;%SWING_CLASSPATH%;%ICE_BROWSER_CLASSPATH%;%HELP_
CLASSPATH%;%KODIAK_CLASSPATH%;%XMLPARSER_CLASSPATH%;%GSS_CLASSPATH%;%EM_CLASSPATH%;%SRVM_CLASSPATH%;%NETCFG_
CLASSPATH%;%JDBC_CLASSPATH%;%ORB_CLASSPATH%;%ORACLE_OEM_CLASSPATH%;%INSTALLER_CLASSPATH%"
oracle.sysman.assistants.dbca.Dbca
**dbca.bat** file after customization
```

When you involve the dbca after customization, it will show all the tracing information on the screen. Optionally, you can redirect the output to a trace file and use it for offline diagnosis, as in the following example, in which the output is moved to a new trace file called cdbca.out:

```
C:> cdbca >cdbca.out
Sample Tracing output:
[main] [1:4:45:401] [NetworkUtils.getOneLocalListenerProtocolAddress:2594]
returning bestSoFar=(ADDRESS=(PROTOCOL=IPC)(KEY=EXTPROC))
[main] [1:4:45:401] [NetworkUtils.getOneLocalListenerProtocolAddress:2461]
bestSoFar=(ADDRESS=(PROTOCOL=IPC)(KEY=EXTPROC))
```

```
[main] [1:4:45:401] [NetworkUtils.getOneLocalListenerProtocolAddress:2461]
bestSoFar=(ADDRESS=(PROTOCOL=IPC)(KEY=EXTPROC))
[main] [1:4:45:401] [NetworkUtils.getOneLocalListenerProtocolAddress:2474]
host=null hostParam=IBM-0B84C585AB2
[main] [1:4:45:401] [NetworkUtils.getOneLocalListenerProtocolAddress:2534]
returning bestAddrSoFar=(ADDRESS=(PROTOCOL=TCP)(HOST=IBM-0B84C585AB2)(PORT=1521))
[main] [1:4:45:401] [NetworkUtils.getOneLocalListenerProtocolAddress:2594]
returning bestSoFar=(ADDRESS=(PROTOCOL=TCP)(HOST=IBM-0B84C585AB2)(PORT=1521))
[main] [1:4:45:401] [NetworkUtils.getOneLocalListenerProtocolAddress:2594]
returning bestSoFar=(ADDRESS=(PROTOCOL=TCP)(HOST=IBM-0B84C585AB2)(PORT=1521))
[main] [1:4:45:401] [NetworkUtils.getOneLocalListenerProtocolAddress:2594]
returning bestSoFar=(ADDRESS=(PROTOCOL=TCP)(HOST=IBM-0B84C585AB2)(PORT=1521))
[main] [1:4:45:401] [NetworkUtils.getLocalListenerAddresses:881]
listener[0]=LISTENER address=null
[main] [1:4:45:851] [DBCAWizard.removePageFromList:1238]   DBCAWizard-
>removePageFromList: The page to be removed = NetworkConfPage
[main] [1:4:45:851] [DBCAWizard.removePageFromList:1238]   DBCAWizard-
>removePageFromList: The page to be removed = NetworkConfPage
```

From this trace file, you can see that tracing is enabled for the customized dbca and it puts detailed information about the activities at every millisecond. This detailed tracing is quite enough to find and diagnose the most common problems expected during the runtime of the database configuration utility.

Cloning Process and OUI   OUI uses the parameter file called oraparam.ini, which is included in the directory where the setup.exe or runinstaller.sh is located. For example, in Solaris systems, the file is under /Disk1/install/solaris/OraParam.ini, and in Windows, it's under \Disk1\install\win32\OraParam.ini.

OUI verifies that all the conditions are set in the oraparam.ini file and begins the installation. Most of the prerequirement checks are specified in the installer parameter file, and you normally don't need to modify the contents. Under certain conditions, you can modify the parameter file to install the components or to skip certain conditions for testing purposes.

OUI also supports a few command-line parameters during the installation. The following is the output from the `runInstaller -help` command, which shows the full list of command-line options and their descriptions, as well as command-line variables usage:

```
runInstaller [-options] [(<CommandLineVariable=Value>)*]
Where options include:
-help  Displays above usage.
-silent  For silent mode operations, the inputs can be a response file or a list of
command line variable value pairs.
-responseFile <Path>  Specifies the response file and path to use.
-formCluster  To install the Oracle clusterware in order to form the cluster.
-remoteShell <Path>  Used only for cluster installs, specifies the path to the remote
shell program on the local cluster node.
-remoteCopy <Path>  Used only for cluster installs, specifies the path to the remote
copy program on the local cluster.
-record -destinationFile <Path>  For record mode operation, information is recorded in
the destination file path.
-deinstall  For deinstall operations.
-debug  For getting the debug information from OUI.
-ignoreSysPrereqs  For ignoring the results of the system pre-requisite checks.
```

```
-executeSysPrereqs  Execute system pre-requisite checks and exit.
-paramFile  Specify location of oraparam.ini file to be used by OUI.
-clone  For making an Oracle Home copy match its current environment.
-force  Allowing silent mode installation into a non-empty directory.
-noconsole  For suppressing display of messages to console. Console is not allocated.
-addNode  For adding node(s) to the installation.
-removeHome  For removing homes from the OUI inventory.
```

OUI also sends the exit codes after the installation. This can be used in an unattended installation. The following table summarizes the OUI exit codes and relevant descriptions.

Code	Description
0	All installations were successful.
1	All installations were successful, but some optional configuration tools failed.
−1	At least one installation failed.

OUI and Cloning   OUI can also be used to recreate the oraInventory for the cloned installations. The following command creates the regular oraInventory for the cloned installations:

```
./runInstaller -clone ORACLE_HOME="<target location>"
ORACLE_HOME_NAME="<unique name on node>"
```

After the cloning process has completed, you can run oraInstRoot.sh to move the oraInventory to the desired location. Cloned installations can also be patched and upgraded, as they also have a valid oraInventory.

Installing CRS

Oracle CRS installation is simple and straightforward once the prerequisites are cleared. It can be installed from the installation media (CD-ROM or DVD) or from the staging directory if the software is dumped to the disk. CRS can be installed by a user other than *oracle*, but the new user should belong to the *oinstall* group.

Run the following steps in an X client on only the first node in the cluster:

```
$ cd /u01/stage/10gR2/clusterware
$ ./runInstaller
```

The OUI will display a Welcome screen (Figure 4-2), where you can click About Oracle Universal Installer to see the version details about the OUI. You can click Installed Products to check the previously installed components. And if you want to uninstall some components, you can click Deinstall Products.

Click Next in the Welcome screen to open the Specify Inventory Directory and Credentials screen (Figure 4-3), where you specify the Oracle Inventory. Oracle keeps the details about the installed components in the oraInventory directory. This can be roughly compared to the Windows registry that keeps the details about the installed software components. Here you also need to specify the operating system group, which has the write permissions on that directory. If you don't specify anything, only the superuser will have write access to the Oracle Inventory.

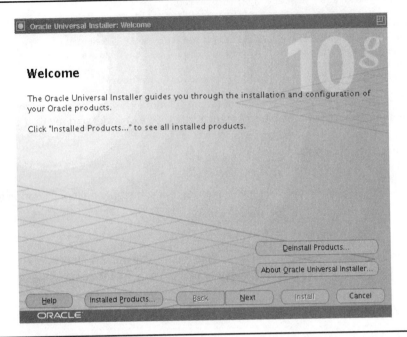

FIGURE 4-2. *The Oracle Universal Installer Welcome screen*

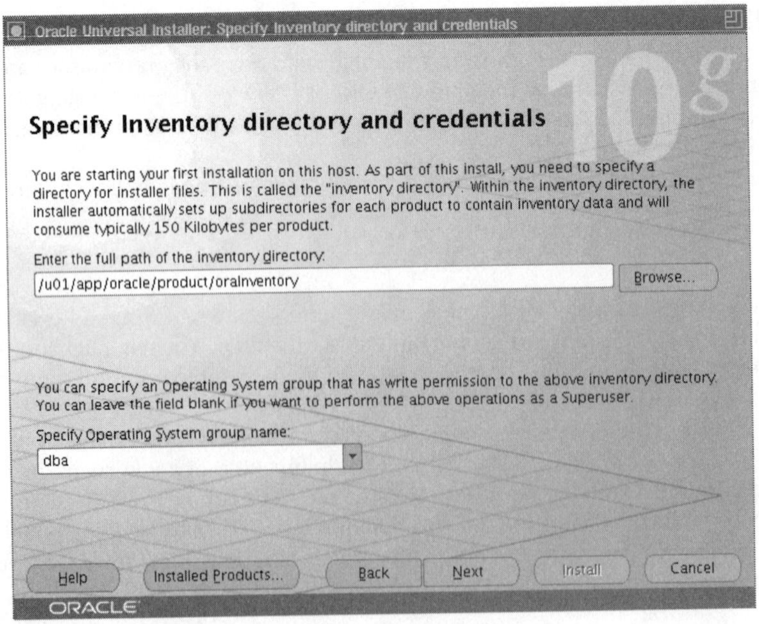

FIGURE 4-3. *Specify Inventory Directory and Credentials screen*

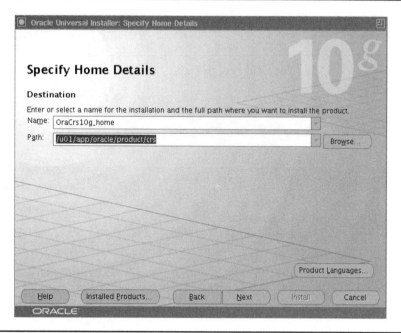

FIGURE 4-4. *Specify Home Details screen*

After specifying oraInventory and the operating system group name for the Oracle Inventory, click Next. In the Specify Home Details screen (Figure 4-4), specify the CRS home directory. CRS home is the Oracle product home and is filled in by default. You can optionally select the product languages here. If you don't specify any languages, the operating system settings are taken for the National Language Support (NLS) languages. Specify the CRS home directory and click Next.

You will see Product-Specific Prerequisite Checks screen (Figure 4-5), where the installer verifies the minimum requirements for installing the selected components. Details appear at the bottom of the screen as the installer verification process progresses. Once the installer verifies the required prerequisites, it will display the message "Check Complete: The overall result of this check is: Passed." This completes the product-specific prerequisite checking by the installer. Click Next to continue.

Now you will see the Specify Cluster Configuration screen (Figure 4-6), where you can specify the names of the cluster and the participating nodes. For each node, you must specify the name of the public IP address, private IP address, and the virtual IP address. Optionally, you can use the cluster configuration file with the same information. The cluster configuration file is useful when you have to specify many nodes. Click Next to continue.

In the Specify Network Interface Usage screen (Figure 4-7), you can mention the planned usage of each network interface. If many network cards are in the nodes, you can instruct the CRS about which one to use for public traffic and which one to reserve for private network traffic. Here you also specify the interface name and the IP address. You will also specify the public and private networks and VIP interface must be selected as Do Not Use. If you don't want Oracle to

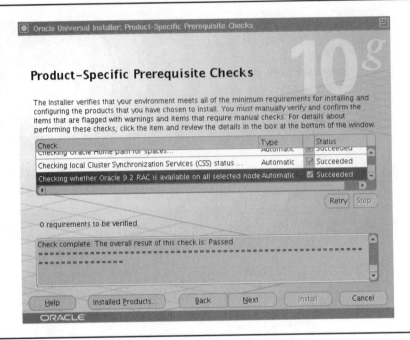

FIGURE 4-5. *Product-Specific Prerequisite screen*

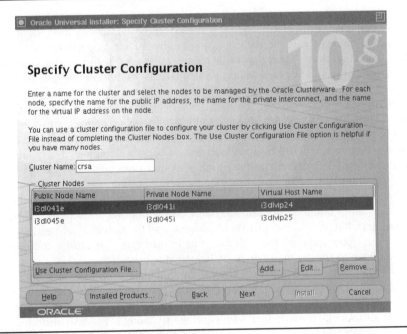

FIGURE 4-6. *Specify Cluster Configuration screen*

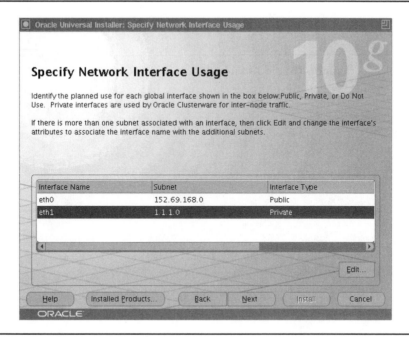

FIGURE 4-7. *Specify Network Interface Usage screen*

use a specific network interface, you can select Do Not Use. If the network IP address starts with *10.x* or *192.x*, it is assumed to be a private network by default. Once the correct network is selected, click Next.

You'll see the Specify Oracle Cluster Registry Location screen (Figure 4-8). The OCR contains critical information about the cluster configuration, including the public and private network configuration details. The OCR location is a shared file system or a raw device at least 100MB in size—a 100MB partition is recommended, as reconfiguration of OCR may affect the entire cluster, though the actual information in OCR is relatively small. Beginning with Oracle Database 10g Release 2, the OCR can be mirrored. If you decide to choose mirroring, select Normal Redundancy and provide the location of the mirror device. Otherwise, choose External Redundancy. The OCR location can be either a clustered file system or RAW partitions. ASM cannot be used to host the OCR information. Click Next after entering the OCR location.

In the next screen (Figure 4-9), you specify the location of the voting disk, one of the critical files for Oracle Clusterware. The voting disk is generally a file of approximately 20MB on a shared storage. It can be either a cluster-wide file system (CFS) or a RAW device. The voting disk is used by the Cluster Synchronization Service (CSS) to resolve network splits, commonly referred to as *split-brains*. It is used as the final arbiter on the status of configured nodes, either up or down, and to deliver eviction notices. It contains the kill block, which is formatted by the other node during the node eviction. Starting with Oracle Clusterware 10g Release 2, a cluster can have multiple

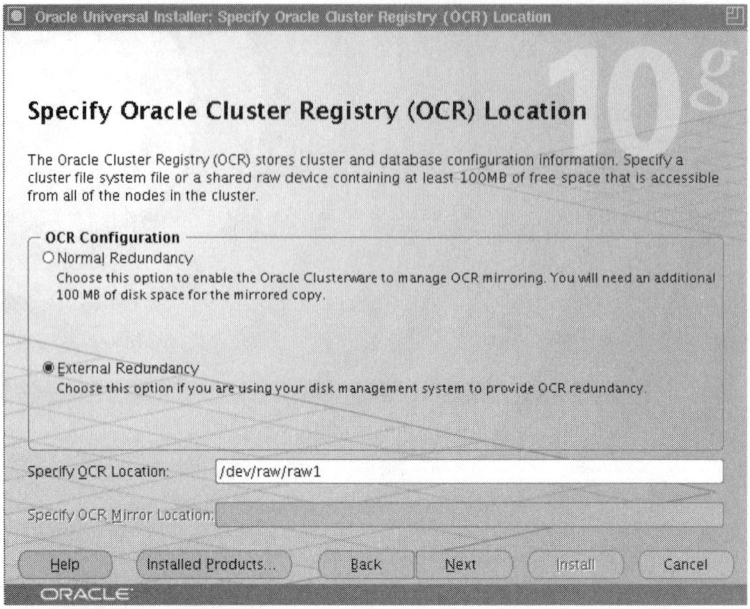

FIGURE 4-8. *Specify Oracle Cluster Registry Location screen*

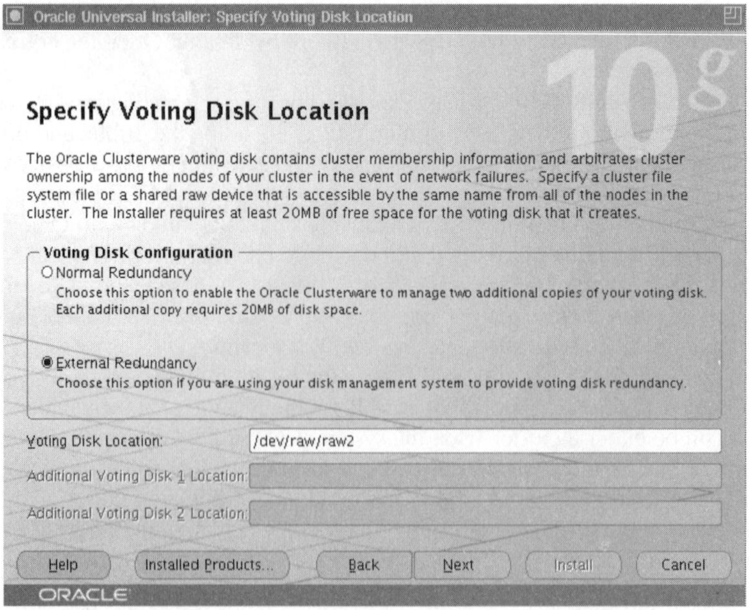

FIGURE 4-9. *Specify Voting Disk Location screen*

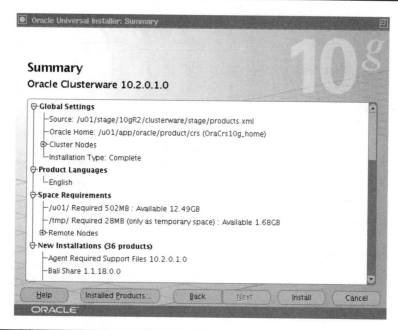

FIGURE 4-10.   *Summary screen*

voting disks to provide redundancy against disk failures. Specify the location(s) of the voting disk depending on the redundancy chosen and click Next.

Now the Summary page (Figure 4-10) appears, which contains all the information about the cluster. You can verify the information and make changes by clicking the Back button and returning to the required screen. If you are satisfied with the summary and no changes are required, click the Install button to install the CRS components.

Installation of CRS will take about 10 to 15 minutes, depending on the hardware configuration. The installer will copy all the required files to the Oracle CRS home directory and link the files with the operating system libraries. Once the installation and linking is done at the local node, it will copy the files to the remote node. During the entire process, you can see the status in the progress bar (Figure 4-11), which shows the percentage completion. When the installation and linking is done, click Next.

You will be instructed to run the installation scripts as the superuser *root*. You need to open a new terminal window and run the orainstRoot.sh and root.sh as the superuser. The first script, orainstRoot.sh, sets the inventory settings. The second script, root.sh, assigns the default hostnames for the participating nodes and populates the necessary OCR keys. At this time, you can run root.sh on the remaining nodes. This script creates the /etc/oracle directory and oratab file entries. These entries are used by the run control scripts in /etc/init.d, which are executed during startup and shutdown of the operating system. Once the scripts are run, click Next to see the End of Installation screen (Figure 4-12).

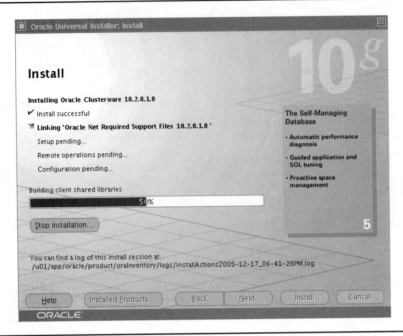

FIGURE 4-11. *Oracle CRS installation progress*

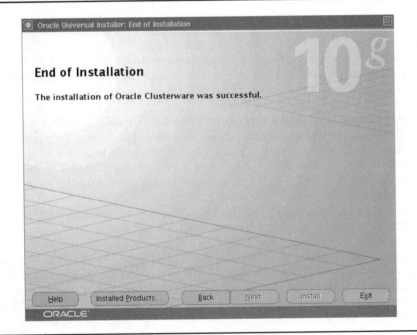

FIGURE 4-12. *End of Installation screen*

```
[root@i3dl041e oraInventory]# sh orainstRoot.sh
Changing permissions of /u01/app/oracle/product/oraInventory to 770.
Changing groupname of /u01/app/oracle/product/oraInventory to dba.
The execution of the script is complete

[root@i3dl045e oraInventory]# sh orainstRoot.sh
Changing permissions of /u01/app/oracle/product/oraInventory to 770.
Changing groupname of /u01/app/oracle/product/oraInventory to dba.
The execution of the script is complete
[root@i3dl045e oraInventory]#

[root@i3dl041e crs]# sh root.sh
WARNING: directory '/u01/app/oracle/product' is not owned by root
WARNING: directory '/u01/app/oracle' is not owned by root
WARNING: directory '/u01/app' is not owned by root
WARNING: directory '/u01' is not owned by root
Checking to see if Oracle CRS stack is already configured
/etc/oracle does not exist. Creating it now.

Setting the permissions on OCR backup directory
Setting up NS directories
Oracle Cluster Registry configuration upgraded successfully
WARNING: directory '/u01/app/oracle/product' is not owned by root
WARNING: directory '/u01/app/oracle' is not owned by root
WARNING: directory '/u01/app' is not owned by root
WARNING: directory '/u01' is not owned by root
assigning default hostname i3dl041e for node 1.
assigning default hostname i3dl045e for node 2.
Successfully accumulated necessary OCR keys.
Using ports: CSS=49895 CRS=49896 EVMC=49898 and EVMR=49897.
node <nodenumber>: <nodename> <private interconnect name> <hostname>
node 1: i3dl041e i3dl041i i3dl041e
node 2: i3dl045e i3dl045i i3dl045e
Creating OCR keys for user 'root', privgrp 'root'..
Operation successful.
Now formatting voting device: /dev/raw/raw2
Format of 1 voting devices complete.
Startup will be queued to init within 90 seconds.
Adding daemons to inittab
Expecting the CRS daemons to be up within 600 seconds.
CSS is active on these nodes.
        i3dl041e
CSS is inactive on these nodes.
        i3dl045e
Local node checking complete.
Run root.sh on remaining nodes to start CRS daemons.
```

Running root.sh in the other nodes will start the CRS daemons in the other node and at the end it will start up all the resources.

```
[root@i3dl045e crs]# sh root.sh
WARNING: directory '/u01/app/oracle/product' is not owned by root
WARNING: directory '/u01/app/oracle' is not owned by root
WARNING: directory '/u01/app' is not owned by root
WARNING: directory '/u01' is not owned by root
Checking to see if Oracle CRS stack is already configured
/etc/oracle does not exist. Creating it now.

Setting the permissions on OCR backup directory
Setting up NS directories
Oracle Cluster Registry configuration upgraded successfully
WARNING: directory '/u01/app/oracle/product' is not owned by root
WARNING: directory '/u01/app/oracle' is not owned by root
WARNING: directory '/u01/app' is not owned by root
WARNING: directory '/u01' is not owned by root
clscfg: EXISTING configuration version 3 detected.
clscfg: version 3 is 10G Release 2.
assigning default hostname i3dl041e for node 1.
assigning default hostname i3dl045e for node 2.
Successfully accumulated necessary OCR keys.
Using ports: CSS=49895 CRS=49896 EVMC=49898 and EVMR=49897.
node <nodenumber>: <nodename> <private interconnect name> <hostname>
node 1: i3dl041e i3dl041i i3dl041e
node 2: i3dl045e i3dl045i i3dl045e
clscfg: Arguments check out successfully.

NO KEYS WERE WRITTEN. Supply -force parameter to override.
-force is destructive and will destroy any previous cluster
configuration.
Oracle Cluster Registry for cluster has already been initialized
Startup will be queued to init within 90 seconds.
Adding daemons to inittab
Expecting the CRS daemons to be up within 600 seconds.
CSS is active on these nodes.
        i3dl041e
        i3dl045e
CSS is active on all nodes.
Waiting for the Oracle CRSD and EVMD to start
Oracle CRS stack installed and running under init(1M)
Running vipca(silent) for configuring nodeapps

Creating VIP application resource on (2) nodes...
Creating GSD application resource on (2) nodes...
Creating ONS application resource on (2) nodes...
Starting VIP application resource on (2) nodes...
Starting GSD application resource on (2) nodes...
Starting ONS application resource on (2) nodes...
Done.
```

You can exit the installer and look for the installActions.log in the oraInventory home. If you had enabled installer tracing you will also get more information on the installer actions with finer details.

Verifying the CRS Installation

After the installation, exit the installer. Optionally, the clusterverify utility can be used to verify the CRS installation. This stage is automated starting from version 10.2, as the installer runs clusterverify at both the start and the end of the install.

```
$ ./runcluvfy.sh stage -post crsinst -n i3dl041e,i3dl045e
Performing post-checks for cluster services setup
Checking node reachability...
Node reachability check passed from node "i3dl041e".
Checking user equivalence...
User equivalence check passed for user "oracle".
Checking Cluster manager integrity...
Checking CSS daemon...
Daemon status check passed for "CSS daemon".
Cluster manager integrity check passed.
Checking cluster integrity...
Cluster integrity check passed
Checking OCR integrity...
Checking the absence of a non-clustered configuration...
All nodes free of non-clustered, local-only configurations.
Uniqueness check for OCR device passed.
Checking the version of OCR...
OCR of correct Version "2" exists.
Checking data integrity of OCR...
Data integrity check for OCR passed.
OCR integrity check passed.
Checking CRS integrity...
Checking daemon liveness...
Liveness check passed for "CRS daemon".
Checking daemon liveness...
Liveness check passed for "CSS daemon".
Checking daemon liveness...
Liveness check passed for "EVM daemon".
Checking CRS health...
CRS health check passed.
CRS integrity check passed.
Checking node application existence...
Checking existence of VIP node application (required)
Check passed.
Checking existence of ONS node application (optional)
Check passed.
Checking existence of GSD node application (optional)
Check passed.
Post-check for cluster services setup was successful.
```

CSS Lock File CRS daemons are stopped during the graceful shutdown by the run control scripts. If the node is not shut down cleanly, either due to node failure, running shutdown without stopping cluster services, starting a node without cluster services, running `/etc/init.crs stop`, or for any other reasons including system crash, the CRS daemons may not start on reboot. A lock file, `/etc/oracle/scls_scr/<hostname>/root/cssnorun`, will stop the daemons from starting. This is checked in `/etc/init.cssd`. This is to ensure CRS daemons are only started at boot time. If you encounter this problem, you may want to delete the file before manually starting the CRS daemons.

In a Nutshell

Oracle 10g has made significant improvements in the installation and configurations with the new clusterverify utility. Each stage of installation can be verified before and after installation. The tracing option with the universal installer is handy while debugging the installation issues. In the next chapter we will be installing Oracle 10g with the RAC option.

CHAPTER
5

RAC Installation

n this chapter we will walk through the Oracle Database 10g RAC installation process in detail. Because most of the required groundwork for installation was completed in the preinstallation stages in previous chapters, installing the Oracle RAC software will be similar to performing a single instance installation. Even internally, the Oracle Universal Installer (OUI) installs the binaries in a single node and uses the underlying file transfer mechanisms to propagate the files to other nodes, relinking them with the respective operating system binaries.

The Cluster Verification Utility (clusterverify) can also be used for the pre-database installation check. You can run the Cluster Verification Utility in preinstallation mode to verify the basic node reachability to the cluster manager and integrity of Cluster Ready Services (CRS). This will also check the basic kernel parameters and required operating system libraries. At the end, the utility checks the status of the CRS daemons and the network infrastructure issues. To confirm the install readiness on the hardware, run clusterverify as shown here:

```
$ ./runcluvfy.sh stage -pre dbinst -n i3dl041e,i3dl045e -osdba dba
Performing pre-checks for database installation
Checking node reachability...
Node reachability check passed from node "i3dl041e".
Checking user equivalence...
User equivalence check passed for user "oracle".
Checking administrative privileges...
User existence check passed for "oracle".
Group existence check passed for "dba".
Membership check for user "oracle" in group "dba" [as Primary] passed.
Administrative privileges check passed.
Checking node connectivity...
Node connectivity check passed for subnet "152.69.168.0" with node(s)
i3dl041e,i3dl045e.
Node connectivity check passed for subnet "1.1.1.0" with node(s)
i3dl041e,i3dl045e.
Suitable interfaces for VIP on subnet "152.69.168.0":
i3dl041e eth0:152.69.170.41 eth0:152.69.171.24
i3dl045e eth0:152.69.170.45 eth0:152.69.171.25
Suitable interfaces for VIP on subnet "1.1.1.0":
i3dl041e eth1:1.1.1.2
i3dl045e eth1:1.1.1.6
WARNING:
Could not find a suitable set of interfaces for the private interconnect.
Node connectivity check passed.
Checking system requirements for 'database'...
Total memory check passed.
Free disk space check passed.
Swap space check passed.
System architecture check passed.
Kernel version check passed.
Package existence check passed for "make-3.79".
Package existence check passed for "binutils-2.14".
Package existence check passed for "gcc-3.2".
Package existence check passed for "compat-db-4.0.14-5".
```

```
Package existence check passed for "compat-gcc-7.3-2.96.128".
Package existence check passed for "compat-gcc-c++-7.3-2.96.128".
Package existence check passed for "compat-libstdc++-7.3-2.96.128".
Package existence check passed for "compat-libstdc++-devel-7.3-2.96.128".
Package existence check passed for "glibc-2.3.2-95.27".
Package existence check passed for "openmotif-2.2.3".
Package existence check passed for "setarch-1.3-1".
Kernel parameter check passed for "semmsl".
Kernel parameter check passed for "semmns".
Kernel parameter check passed for "semopm".
Kernel parameter check passed for "semmni".
Kernel parameter check passed for "shmall".
Kernel parameter check passed for "shmmni".
Kernel parameter check passed for "file-max".
Kernel parameter check passed for "rmem_default".
Kernel parameter check passed for "rmem_max".
Kernel parameter check passed for "wmem_default".
Kernel parameter check passed for "wmem_max".
Group existence check passed for "dba".
User existence check passed for "nobody".
System requirement passed for 'database'
Checking CRS integrity...
Checking daemon liveness...
Liveness check passed for "CRS daemon".
Checking daemon liveness...
Liveness check passed for "CSS daemon".
Checking daemon liveness...
Liveness check passed for "EVM daemon".
Checking CRS health...
CRS health check passed.
CRS integrity check passed.
Checking node application existence...
Checking existence of VIP node application (required)
Check passed.
Checking existence of ONS node application (optional)
Check passed.
Checking existence of GSD node application (optional)
Check passed.
Pre-check for database installation was successful.
```

That is it! Now you are ready to start the installation of RAC after choosing the storage location for the datafiles. If you are going to use the RAW partitions, you can slice the disks before starting the RAC installation. If you decide to use Automatic Storage Management (ASM), your next step will be to install the ASM instance.

Before installation, you can adjust the environment settings for your favorite shell and start the installer with the tracing option turned on. Tracing will help you get the current stage of the installer and debug the installation in case of failures and/or hang.

Automatic Storage Management

ASM is a new option for managing storage beginning with Oracle Database 10g. ASM is designed for storage of RDBMS database files, and its self-tuning and self-managing framework helps DBAs managing huge database storage systems. More details on ASM are included in Chapter 6; we will look at its basic installation in this chapter.

As ASM is integrated into the database server, you use the OUI and the Database Configuration Assistant (DBCA) for installation and configuration. The OUI allows you either to install and configure a database that uses ASM for storage management or install and configure an ASM instance by itself, without creating a database instance. OUI calls DBCA to perform either or both of these tasks.

Like any other Oracle server components, ASM needs an Oracle home. This Oracle home is different from the Cluster Ready Services (CRS) home or RDBMS Oracle homes. Though this is an optional requirement, by using separate Oracle homes, you can upgrade and patch the ASM environment and database environments independently. It also helps to uninstall database software without impacting the ASM instance.

Once you have set up the environment variables, you invoke the OUI to install the ASM instance in the new Oracle home directory. First, you'll see the Welcome screen.

Click Next. In the next screen, you specify the installation type. ASM is part of the Oracle Enterprise Edition in this case. However, ASM can also be used with Oracle Standard Edition when RAC is enabled. ASM is the only choice for storage when using RAC in the Standard Edition. Select Enterprise Edition.

The installer will prompt for the installation directories (Figure 5-1). They will be under the newly created Oracle home directory, OraAsm10g_Home1; normally, this directory will be

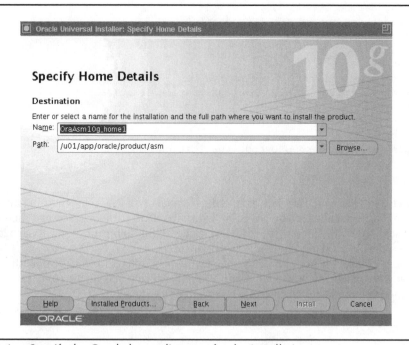

FIGURE 5-1. *Specify the Oracle home directory for the installation*

Optimal Flexible Architecture

OFA is set of guidelines for administering and managing (Oracle part number A19308-1) Oracle database environments. OFA makes specific configuration recommendations based on actual field experience from the Oracle System Performance Group. OFA is the world's most popular specification for configuring high-performance, low-maintenance Oracle database systems.

OFA defines the standards for the Oracle database installations starting from the directory structure of the alert log and trace files to the disk layouts for the tablespaces. However, with the introduction of ASM storage for datafiles, OFA guidelines are no longer used for datafiles. However, all other specifications are still valid for current configurations. The detailed document on OFA can be downloaded from Oracle MetaLink.

/u01/app/oracle/product/asm or any of the Optimal Flexible Architecture (OFA)-compliant structures. Once the Oracle home is specified, click Next.

OUI will automatically detect the cluster option if the Oracle Clusterware services are installed and CRS daemons are running. In this case, OUI will populate the nodes in the installer. The local node from where you are running the installer is automatically selected for the ASM installation (Figure 5-2).

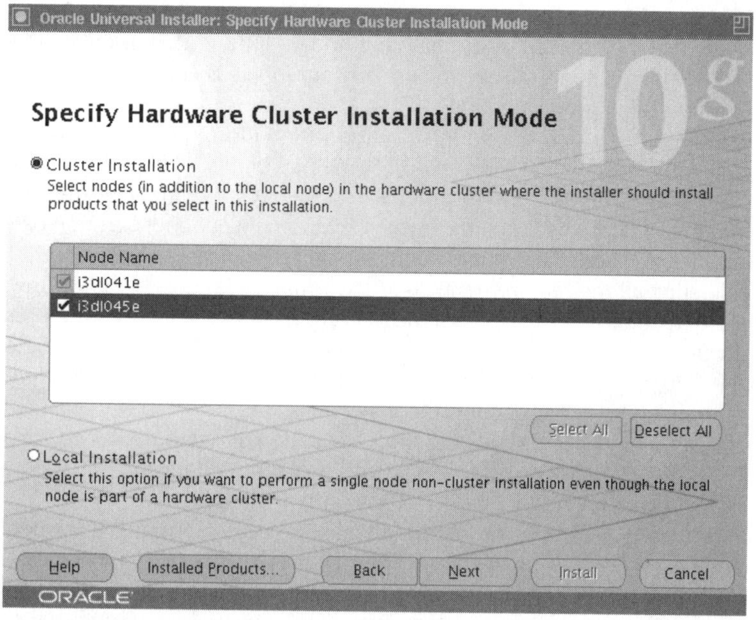

FIGURE 5-2. *Specify Hardware Cluster Installation Mode screen*

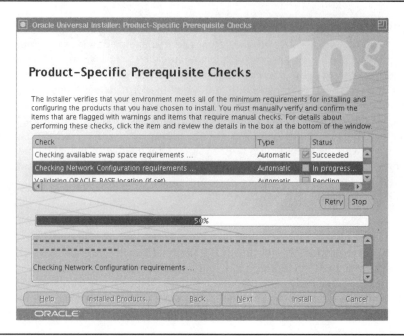

FIGURE 5-3. *Product-Specific Prerequisite Checks screen*

The ASM instance can also be running under cluster mode, thus eliminating storage as a single point of failure (SPOF). You can select the other node(s) for the ASM installation. Optionally, you can run the ASM in a single node, though the underlying storage is connected to the cluster. However, this configuration is not recommended.

Once you have selected the node(s) for the installation, the installer will again check the prerequisites for the installation (Figure 5-3). Some part of this verification framework is externalized in the clusterverify utility, but the installer will still check the prerequisites before proceeding to installation—this includes verifying the swap size and network configuration details.

The installer will verify all the product-specific prerequisites, and you will be able to proceed only after meeting all the requirements. If any warning or failures occur during this phase, you can optionally fix them and retry the same operation. After completing the prerequisite checks, the installer displays "Check complete: The overall result of this check is: Passed."

Click Next to open the Select Configuration Option screen (Figure 5-4). Here you can specify the type of configuration. You can install the ASM instance or database. Optionally, you can choose to install the binaries alone and use the tools to create the database. Since we are interested in installing ASM, select the ASM option. You will be prompted for the SYS password for the ASM instance. After specifying the password in this screen, click Next.

In the Configure Automatic Storage Management screen (Figure 5-5), specify the disk group name and the associated disk partitions. You can also select the redundancy level for the disk groups. If the disks are not discovered, you can optionally provide the disk discovery string to select all the partitions beginning with that string. You can also select the disk partitions or ask ASM to use all the available disks.

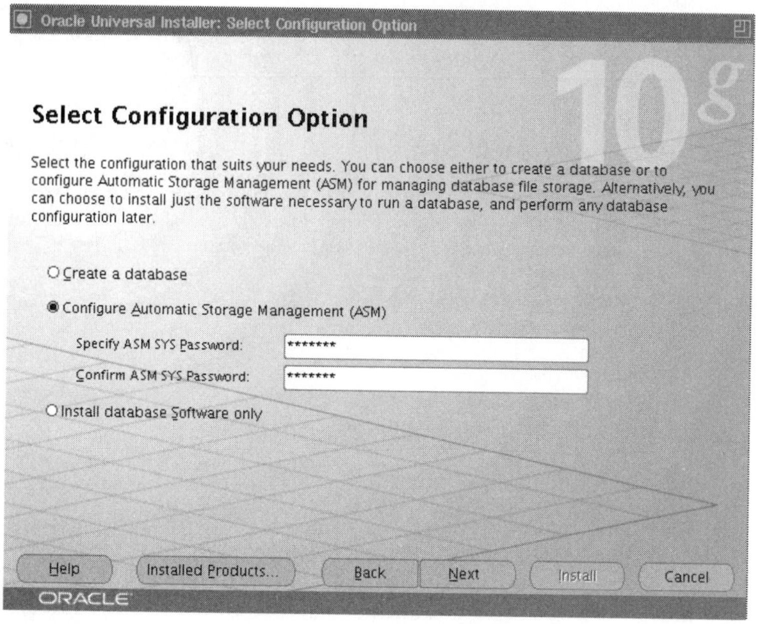

FIGURE 5-4. *Select Configuration Option screen*

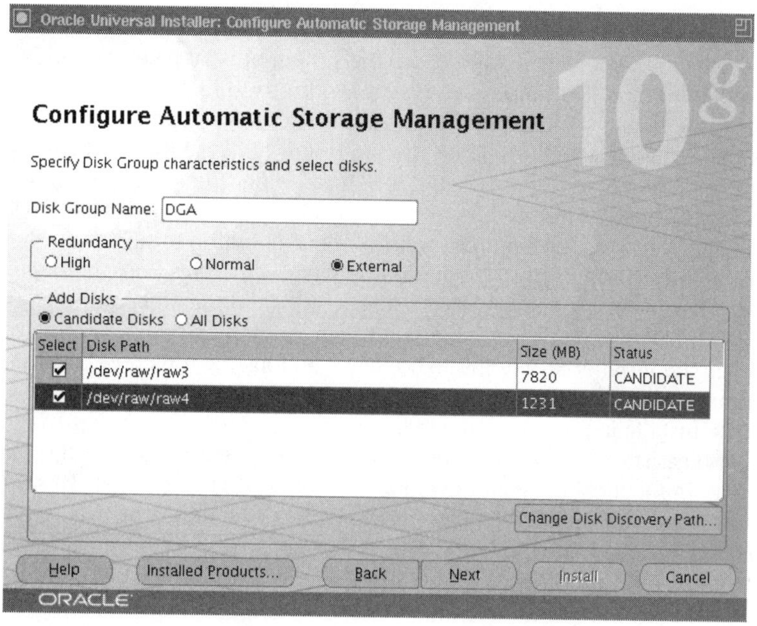

FIGURE 5-5. *Configure Automatic Storage Management screen*

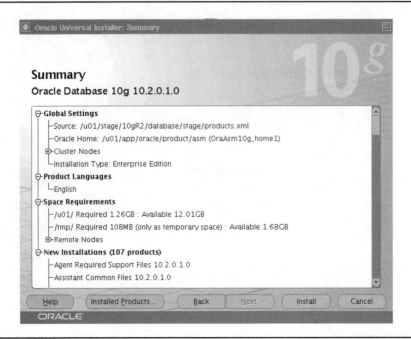

FIGURE 5-6. *Summary screen*

By default, the External redundancy option is selected. External redundancy does not provide any redundancy at Oracle level, and operating system or SAN level redundancy is assumed. Normal redundancy is like simple two-way mirroring, and high redundancy is like three-way mirroring. More details about redundancy and disk groups are included in Chapter 6.

After making your selections, click Next to install ASM binaries and create an ASM instance. You will see the Summary screen (Figure 5-6) that verifies the installation options, including the path and Oracle home. This screen also lists space required and available in the Oracle home locations. After verifying the summary, click the Install button to start the installation.

Now the installation begins. The installer will copy the files from the staging area to disk and relink with OS binaries. It first installs the files to a local node and copies the files to a remote node. If you have invoked the installer with tracing turned on, you can monitor the progress from the console. The installer also writes to the installactions.log file under $ORAINVENTORY/logs/installActionsTIMESTAMP.log.

After the installation is completed in the local node and files are copied in the remote nodes, configuration assistants will be invoked. During this time the installer will prompt you to run the root.sh script in the local node and then to all other nodes (Figure 5-7). This script creates the oraenv and oratab files under /etc and sets the Oracle executable permissions to the owner and group levels. The location of the file for the oratab entry is platform specific and normally found in either the /etc or /var/opt/oracle directory. This root.sh script should be run as the superuser *root*.

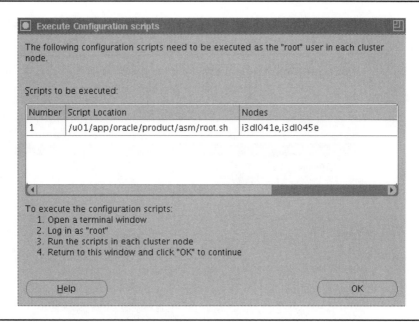

FIGURE 5-7.   *Execute configuration scripts*

```
[root@i3dl041e asm]# sh root.sh
Running Oracle10 root.sh script...
The following environment variables are set as:
    ORACLE_OWNER= oracle
    ORACLE_HOME=  /u01/app/oracle/product/asm
Enter the full pathname of the local bin directory: [/usr/local/bin]:
The file "dbhome" already exists in /usr/local/bin.  Overwrite it? (y/n)
[n]: y
    Copying dbhome to /usr/local/bin ...
The file "oraenv" already exists in /usr/local/bin.  Overwrite it? (y/n)
[n]: y
    Copying oraenv to /usr/local/bin ...
The file "coraenv" already exists in /usr/local/bin.  Overwrite it? (y/n)
[n]: y
    Copying coraenv to /usr/local/bin ...
Creating /etc/oratab file...
Entries will be added to the /etc/oratab file as needed by
Database Configuration Assistant when a database is created
Finished running generic part of root.sh script.
Now product-specific root actions will be performed.
```

After root.sh is run, go back to the installer and click the OK button. The installer will invoke
the scripts to configure the Net Configuration Assistant (Figure 5-8). The $ORACLE_HOME/
cfgtoollogs/ConfigToolAllCommands script contains all commands executed by the configuration
assistants.

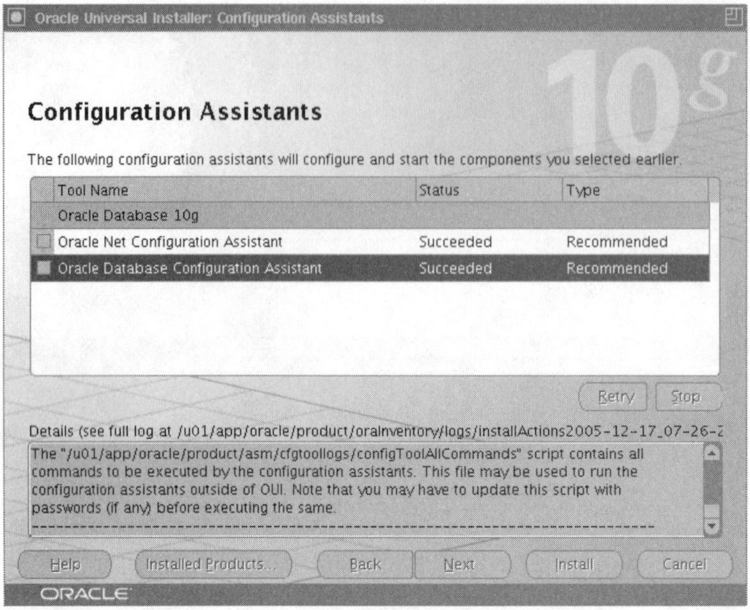

FIGURE 5-8. *Configuration Assistants screen*

Click Next after the scripts' completion, and you'll see the End of Installation screen (Figure 5-9) that displays the iSQL*Plus URL and other J2EE (Java 2 Platform Enterprise Edition) application URLs. Once you have noted the paths, click the Exit button to confirm the exit and close the installer. Optionally, you can verify the installation using the clusterverify utility.

Real Application Clusters Installation
Once the ASM is installed and configured, you can install Oracle Database 10g with Real Application Clusters. Installing RAC binaries is similar to installing the ASM with a few differences (select the Install Database Software Only option in the Select Configuration Type screen).

The clusterverify utility can be used for the pre-database configuration check. You must run the utility as the user *oracle*.

```
$./runcluvfy.sh stage -pre dbcfg -n i3dl041e,i3dl045e -d
/u01/app/oracle/product/10g
Performing pre-checks for database configuration
Checking node reachability...
Node reachability check passed from node "i3dl041e".
Checking user equivalence...
User equivalence check passed for user "oracle".
Checking administrative privileges...
User existence check passed for "oracle".
Group existence check passed for "dba".
```

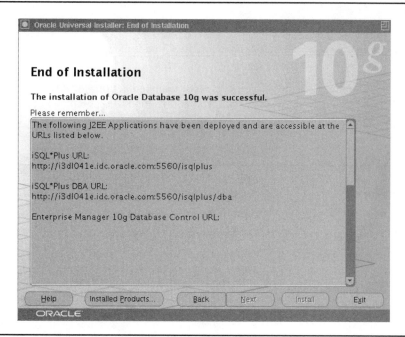

FIGURE 5-9. *End of Installation screen*

```
Membership check for user "oracle" in group "dba" [as Primary] passed.
Administrative privileges check passed.
Checking node connectivity...
Node connectivity check passed for subnet "152.69.168.0" with node(s)
i3dl041e,i3dl045e.
Node connectivity check passed for subnet "1.1.1.0" with node(s)
i3dl041e,i3dl045e.
Suitable interfaces for VIP on subnet "152.69.168.0":
i3dl041e eth0:152.69.170.41 eth0:152.69.171.24
i3dl045e eth0:152.69.170.45 eth0:152.69.171.25
Suitable interfaces for VIP on subnet "1.1.1.0":
i3dl041e eth1:1.1.1.2
i3dl045e eth1:1.1.1.6
WARNING:
Could not find a suitable set of interfaces for the private interconnect.
Node connectivity check passed.
Checking CRS integrity...
Checking daemon liveness...
Liveness check passed for "CRS daemon".
Checking daemon liveness...
Liveness check passed for "CSS daemon".
Checking daemon liveness...
Liveness check passed for "EVM daemon".
```

```
Checking CRS health...
CRS health check passed.
CRS integrity check passed.
Pre-check for database configuration was successful.
$
```

Table 5-1 summarizes the screens and recommended actions for RAC database installation. These steps are common for most of the installations done using OUI and common across all platforms.

Screen Name	Suggested Action
Welcome	Start of the installation. Click Next.
Select Installation Type	Select Enterprise Edition and click Next.
Specify Home Details	Enter name of the Oracle home and path of the Oracle home where you want to install the product. This must be different from the ASM Oracle home. Click Next.
Specify Hardware Cluster Installation Mode	Select Cluster Installation. Select all the node names. Click Next.
Product-Specific Prerequisite Checks	OUI checks the system to verify that it is configured correctly to run Oracle software. If you have completed all of the reinstallation steps in this guide, all the checks should pass. If a check fails, review the cause of the failure listed for that check on the screen. If possible, rectify the problem and rerun the check. Alternatively, if you are satisfied that your system meets the requirements, you can select the checkbox for the failed check to verify the requirement manually. Verify that all of the prerequisite checks succeed, and then click Next.
Select Configuration	Select Install Database Software Only and click Next.
Summary	The installer displays the summary for the installation. Review the information displayed on the screen and click Next.
Execute Configuration Scripts	Run the configuration scripts when prompted. Click OK to continue.
End of Installation	The configuration assistants configure several Web-based applications, including Oracle Enterprise Manager Database Control. This screen displays the URLs configured for these applications. Make a note of the URLs used. The port numbers used in these URLs are also recorded in the file *oracle_home*/install/portlist.ini. To exit from OUI, click Exit and then click Yes.

TABLE 5-1. *RAC Database Installation Process*

Creating the RAC Database

Creating the RAC database in an RAC environment is as simple as creating the database in a single instance environment. The only change in the creation process using DBCA is to select the nodes in the Node Selection screen. Optionally, you can generate the scripts using DBCA and run them later.

To create a database using ASM for datafiles, walk through the following steps. (The number of steps may vary a bit if different storage choices are used. However, the database creation process is the same as creating the database in the ASM environment.)

1. Start the Database Configuration Assistant (DBCA) as the user *oracle*. If you want to enable tracing, you need to customize the Java runtime environment as discussed in Chapter 4 to get the trace information.

   ```
   $ ./dbca
   ```

   DBCA enables you to create, configure, or delete a cluster database and manage database templates. In the Welcome screen, select the Oracle Real Application Clusters Database option to create a RAC database using DBCA. Click Next.

2. In creating an RAC database, you'll select the participating nodes, whereas in a single instance environment, the node from where DBCA is invoked is the default node for database creation. In the next screen (Figure 5-10), choose Create a Database. In this screen, you can also configure the ASM instance. Click Next.

3. If the Oracle Cluster Ready Services (CRS) stack is up and running, the Database Configuration Assistant will automatically detect the cluster and the number of nodes in the cluster and populate the node names in the next screen (Figure 5-11). The local node is selected by default. Click Select All and then click Next.

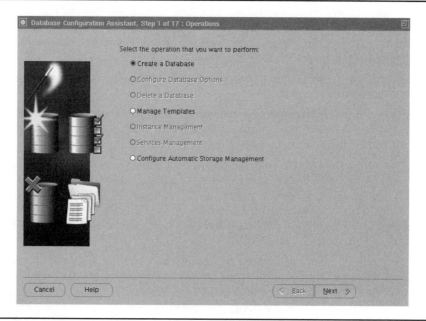

FIGURE 5-10. *Operations screen*

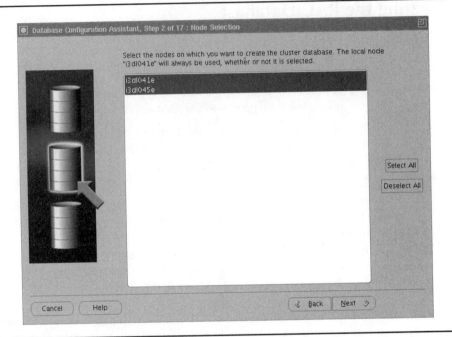

FIGURE 5-11 *Node Selection screen*

4. Predefined database configuration templates are available to make the process easier. Three types of configurations, namely Data Warehouse, General Purpose, and Transaction Processing, have predefined datafiles. You can also create a custom database that does not have preconfigured datafiles. In the next screen (Figure 5-12), choose the General Purpose template and click Next.

5. In the next screen, enter a database name that uniquely identifies the database. Then click Next.

6. You can use Oracle Enterprise Manager to manage the database. In the next screen (Figure 5-13), if you would like to use the Grid Control, uncheck Configure the Database with Enterprise Manager. Then click Next.

7. Next, you are asked to enter the passwords for the SYS and SYSTEM accounts. In earlier Oracle versions, the SYS and SYSTEM accounts used a default password (for SYS, it was *change_on_install*, and for system, it was *manager*). As no default passwords for the SYS and SYSTEM accounts exist, select the Use the Same Password for All Accounts option, enter and confirm the password, and click Next. Optionally, you can use different passwords for SYS and SYSTEM by choosing the Use Different Passwords option.

8. In the next screen, specify the storage mechanism for the database. The available options are Cluster File System, Automatic Storage Management, and Raw Devices. If raw devices are used, the mapping filename can be entered here. The raw device mapping file is a text file where you specify the device name and the equivalent filename for Oracle Database. Choose Automatic Storage Management and click Next.

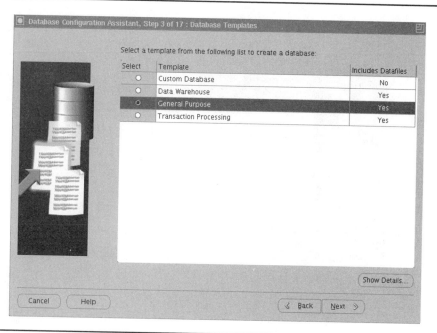

FIGURE 5-12 *Database Templates screen*

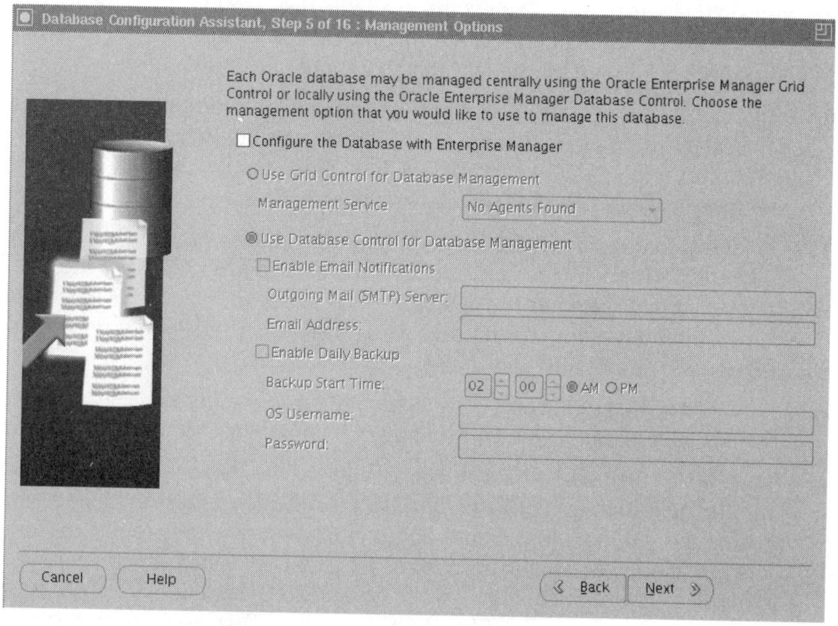

FIGURE 5-13 *Management Options screen*

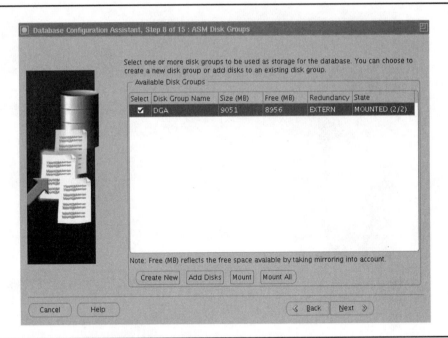

FIGURE 5-14 *ASM Disk Groups screen*

9. In the next screen (Figure 5-14), you select a disk group, which is a set of disks managed as a single logical group. Select the available disk group for the database. More details about ASM, including creating and managing disk groups, are included in Chapter 6. Select the disk group for the RAC database and click Next.

10. In the next screen (Figure 5-15), choose the Use Oracle-Managed Files option for the database files. You can also optionally specify the file location variables for the data files (for example, +DGA for the datafiles). You can also use the same screen to do the multiplexing of the online redologs and control files.

11. Click Next to open the Recovery Configuration screen (Figure 5-16). You can enable archiving and specify the Flash Recovery Area and flash recovery file size. The Flash Recovery Area is used as the default for all the backup and recovery operations and is also required for automatic backup while using the Oracle Enterprise Manager. Specify the required details and click Next.

12. In the next screen, you can choose to create *sample schemas*, a set of schemas that can be used for training purposes. They include the infamous EMP and DEPT tables. Click Next.

13. In the next screen (Figure 5-17), you can set up the database services. Services allow you granular definition of workload, and the DBA can dynamically define which instances provide the service. More details about managing services are discussed in Chapter 8. Connection Load Balancing needs to be set up to allow the user connections to be balanced across all instances providing a service. Workload Distribution and Connection Management are discussed in Chapter 13. Click Add to create the first instance, and name it *HR*. Designate the first instance (dba1) as Preferred and the second instance (dba2) as Available.

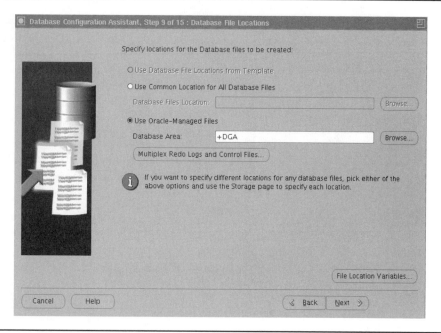

FIGURE 5-15 *Database File Locations screen*

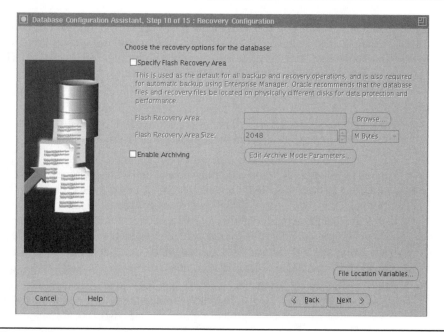

FIGURE 5-16 *Recovery Configuration screen*

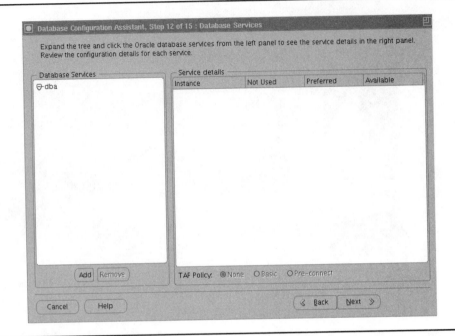

FIGURE 5-17   *Database Services screen*

14. To add another service, click Add (Figure 5-18), and name the second service *CRM*. Designate the first instance as Available and the second instance as Preferred. Click Add and name the third service WEBSITE. Select Basic for the TAF Policy. TAF (Transparent Application Failover) is discussed in detail in Chapter 13. Click Next.

15. You can specify the initialization parameters for memory (Figure 5-19). Most of the tuning parameters can be changed later. The only important thing you must be aware of at this stage is the character set for the database. Choose the appropriate character set and leave the rest of the initialization parameters set to the defaults. You can refine these later.

16. Click Next to open the Database Storage screen. Here you can specify the locations for the datafiles, control files, and redolog groups. File location variables for datafiles and redologs can also be specified. Once you have specified the locations for the datafiles, control files, and redolog groups, you are ready to create the database (Figure 5-20). You can create a database immediately or generate scripts for database creation. If you create the database immediately, it is a good practice to generate the scripts to be able to see what is being run and to have the scripts available if something happens.

17. Click Finish to view the Summary screen (Figure 5-21) that contains the selected options for the installation. Click OK. The Java user interface may respond slowly; do not click OK a second time. After the database is created, click Exit to start the database instances.

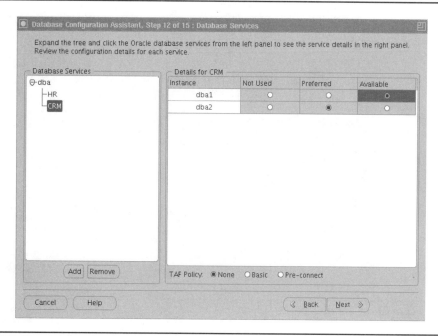

FIGURE 5-18   *Adding database services*

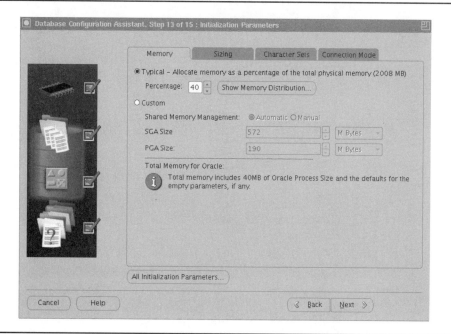

FIGURE 5-19   *Initialization Parameters screen*

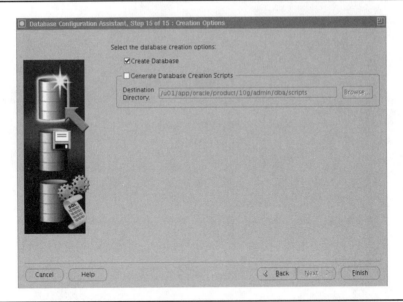

FIGURE 5-20   *Creation Options screen*

FIGURE 5-21   *Summary screen*

In a Nutshell

This chapter covered the installation process of Oracle Database 10g RAC in detail. The number of steps in the installation may vary slightly depending on the options and configurations selected. We also walked through the ASM installation process. In the next chapter, we will discuss ASM architecture and explore its functionalities in detail.

CHAPTER
6

Automatic Storage
Management

anaging storage is one of the most complex and time-consuming tasks of a DBA. Data growth occurs at an exponential pace due to consolidation of databases and high velocity business growth. Business requirements demand the continuous availability of database storage systems, and the maintenance window for storage is shrinking from hours to minutes. Legal requirements add even more baggage, as data has to be retained for an extended period of time. (I know some sites that store terabytes of active data for seven years or more!) The average storage size managed by a DBA has grown from a few gigabytes to few terabytes. Figure 6-1 shows the management gap between disk capacities to management capacity per DBA.

Other than the challenge posed by the external entities, storage management always involves many internal operational organizations. It involves participation of system administrators, network administrators, and storage (or SAN) administrators, along with the DBA. To eliminate complexities and interdependence with various entities, all this data is required to be stored in one place.

New technologies help the DBA easily manage huge volumes of data without a considerable amount of administrative overhead. New tools are being developed that work closely with the RDBMS kernel to make data management and data consolidation easier. Automatic Storage Management (affectionately called *Awesome Storage Management*) is one of those revolutionary solutions from Oracle that helps the database storage administration and management manage databases.

Facts about Automatic Storage Management

ASM is a database file system that provides a cluster file system and volume manager capabilities for Oracle datafiles that are integrated into the Oracle Database 10g kernel. The ASM environment provides the performance of raw I/O with the easy management of a file system. It simplifies database administration by eliminating the need to manage potentially thousands of Oracle database files in a direct manner.

The number of datafiles per database has consistently increased since Oracle version 7, in which only 1,022 datafiles per database could be used. Current Oracle versions support 65,533 datafiles—managing thousands of files in a multidatabase environment is a challenge. ASM

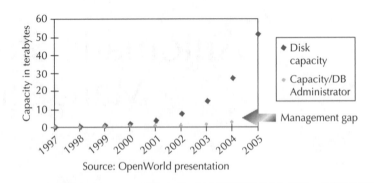

Source: OpenWorld presentation

FIGURE 6-1. *Storage growth and management gap*

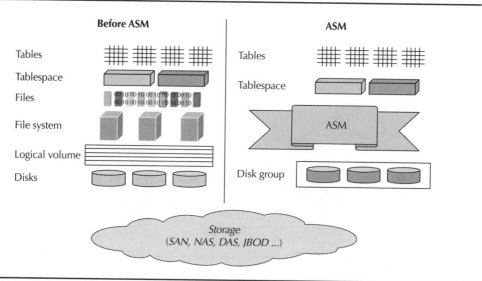

FIGURE 6-2. *Traditional framework vs. ASM*

simplifies storage management by enabling you to divide all available storage into disk groups. You manage a small set of disk groups, and ASM automates the placement of the database files within those disk groups. Figure 6-2 compares the traditional data storage framework to that of ASM.

ASM divides a file into pieces and spreads them evenly across all the disks. This is the key difference from the traditional striping techniques that used mathematical functions to stripe complete logical volumes independent of files or directories. Striping requires careful capacity planning at the beginning, as adding new volumes requires rebalancing and downtime.

With ASM, whenever new storage is added or removed, ASM does not restripe all the data. It just moves an amount of data proportional to the amount of storage added or removed to redistribute the files evenly and maintain a balanced I/O load across the disks. This occurs while the database is active and is totally transparent to the database and end user applications.

ASM supports datafiles, log files, control files, archive logs, Recovery Manager (RMAN) backup sets, and other Oracle database file types, including Flash recovery files. ASM also supports Real Application Clusters (RAC) and eliminates the need for a cluster Logical Volume Manager or a cluster file system. ASM does not show up as a separate option in the custom tree installation, and it is available in both the Enterprise Edition and Standard Edition installations.

SQL is the interface to the database, and ASM provides the SQL interface for creating database structures such as tablespaces, control files, and redolog and archive log files; you specify file location in terms of disk groups. ASM then creates and manages the associated underlying files for you. Internally, ASM uses the Stripe and Mirror Everything (SAME) architecture.

ASM Building Blocks

ASM is implemented as a special kind of Oracle instance with the same structure and its own System Global Area (SGA) and background processes. Additional background processes in ASM manage storage and disk rebalancing operations. The components discussed next can be considered the building blocks of ASM.

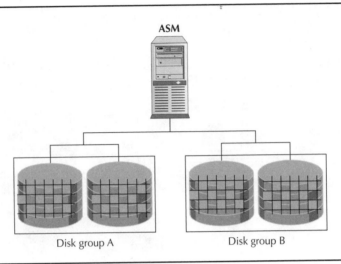

FIGURE 6-3. *Disk groups in ASM*

Disk Groups

A *disk group* is a group of disks that are managed together as a single unit of storage. The primary component of ASM, this collection of ASM disks is self describing, independent of the associated media names. Oracle provides SQL statements that create and manage disk groups, their contents, and their metadata. Disk groups are integrated with Oracle managed files and support three types of redundancy: external, normal, and high. Figure 6-3 shows the architecture of the disk groups.

The disks in a disk group are referred to as *ASM disks*. In ASM, a disk is the unit of persistent storage for a disk group. The disk group in a typical database cluster is part of a remote shared-disk subsystem, such as a SAN or network-attached storage (NAS). It can be accessed via the normal operating system interface and must be accessible to all nodes. Oracle must have read and write access to all the disks, even if one or more servers in the cluster fails. The disk group cannot be a local or networked file system file in a supported configuration. On Windows operating systems, an ASM disk is always a partition. On all other platforms, an ASM disk can be a partition of a logical unit number (LUN) or any NAS device.

Allocation Unit

ASM disks are divided into a number of units or storage blocks that are small enough not to be hot. The allocation unit of storage is large enough for efficient sequential access. The allocation unit defaults to 1MB in size and is sufficient for most configurations. ASM allows you to change the allocation unit size, but that is not normally required unless the ASM hosts a very large database (VLDB).

Failure Groups

Failure groups define ASM disks that share a common potential failure mechanism. A failure group is a subset of disks in a disk group dependent on a common hardware resource whose failure must be tolerated. It is important only for normal or high redundancy configurations. Redundant copies

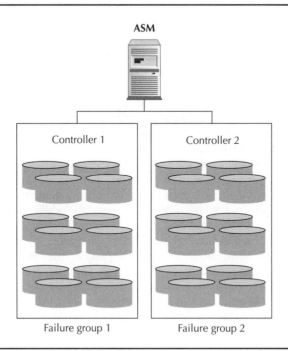

FIGURE 6-4. *Failure groups*

of the same data are placed in different failure groups. An example might be a member in a stripe set or a set of SCSI disks sharing the same SCSI controller. Failure groups are used to determine which ASM disks should be used for storing redundant copies of data. By default, each disk is an individual failure group. Figure 6-4 illustrates the concept of a failure group.

For example, if two-way mirroring is specified for a file, ASM automatically stores redundant copies of file extents in separate failure groups. Failure groups apply only to normal and high redundancy disk groups and are not applicable for external redundancy disk groups. You define the failure groups in a disk group when you create or alter the disk group.

ASM Files

Files written on ASM disks are called *ASM files*. ASM file names normally start with a plus sign (+). Although the names are automatically generated by ASM, you can specify a meaningful, user-friendly alias name (or alias) for ASM files. Each ASM file is completely contained within a single disk group and evenly divided throughout all of the ASM disks in the group. At present, ASM supports only Oracle file types. Current versions do not support trace files, alert logs, or executables.

Disk Partners

Disk partners limit the possibility of two independent disk failures losing both copies of a virtual extent. Each disk has a limited number of partners and redundant copies are allocated on partners. The disk partner is automatically chosen by ASM and partners are placed in different failure groups. Partner disks should be the same in size, capacity, and performance characteristics.

ASM Instance

An *ASM instance* is an Oracle instance that manages the metadata for disk groups. All metadata modifications are done by an ASM instance to isolate failures. Database instances connect to an ASM instance to create, delete, resize, open, or close files, and database instances read/write directly to disks managed by the ASM instance. Only one ASM instance is possible per node in a cluster. This can be a disadvantage for a large RAC cluster (such as an eight-node RAC, where eight separate instances need to be maintained for ASM in addition to eight "user" instances). An ASM instance failure kills attached database instances.

ASM Striping and Mirroring

ASM does not require external volume managers or external cluster file systems for disk management; these are not recommended because the functionalities provided by the ASM will conflict with the external volume managers. ASM extends the power of Oracle-managed files that are created and managed automatically for you, but with ASM you get the additional benefits of features such as mirroring and striping.

Striping is a technique used for spreading data among multiple disk drives. A big data segment is broken into smaller units, and these units are spead across the available devices. The unit at which the data is broken is called the *data unit size* or *stripe size*. Stripe size is also sometimes referred to as *block size*, referring to the size of the stripes written to each disk. The number of parallel stripes that can be written to or read from simultaneously is known as the *stripe width*. Striping can speed up operations that retrieve data from disk storage as it extends the power of the total I/O bandwidth. This optimizes performance and disk utilization, making manual I/O performance tuning unnecessary.

ASM supports two levels of striping: *fine striping* and *coarse striping*. Fine striping uses 128K as the stripe width, and coarse striping uses 1MB as the stripe width. Fine striping can be used for files that usually do smaller reads and writes. For example, online redologs and controlfiles are the best candidates for fine striping when the reads or writes are small in nature. Current Oracle versions do not support other striping options.

ASM mirroring is more flexible than operating-system mirrored disks because ASM mirroring enables the redundancy level to be specified on a per-file basis rather than on a volume basis. Internally mirroring takes place at the extent level. If a file is mirrored, depending on the redundancy level set for the file, each extent has one or more mirrored copies, and mirrored copies are always kept on different disks in the disk group.

The following table describes the available mirroring options that ASM supports on a per-file basis:

ASM Redundancy	Mirroring Level	Description
External	No mirroring	No mirroring from ASM. Can be used when mirroring is implemented at storage or disk level.
Normal	Two-way mirroring	Each extent has one mirrored copy.
High	Three-way mirroring	Each extent has two mirrored copies.

Stripe and Mirror Everything (SAME)   ASM implements the Oracle SAME methodology, in which all types of data are striped and mirrored across all available drives. This helps the I/O load be evenly distributed and balanced across all disks within the disk group. Mirroring provides the much required fault tolerance for the database servers, and striping provides performance and scalability to the database.

Character Devices and Block Devices

Any direct attached or networked storage device can be classified as a *character device* or a *block device*. A character device holds only one file. Normally, raw files are placed on character devices. The location of the raw devices is platform-dependent and they are not visible in the file system directory. A block device is a type of character device, but it holds an entire file system. ASM uses character devices, as only raw files are supported as ASM disks. If ASMLib is used as a disk API, ASM supports block devices.

Storage Area Network

A *storage area network* is the networked storage device connected via uniquely identified host bus adapters (HBAs). The storage is divided in to LUNs, and each LUN is logically represented as a single disk to the operating system.

In automatic storage management, the ASM disks are either LUNs or disk partitions. They are logically represented as a raw device to the ASM. The name and path of the raw device is dependent on the operating system. For example, in the Sun operating system, the raw device has the name *cNtNdNsN*, where

> *cN* is the controller number;
>
> *tN* is the target ID (SCSI ID);
>
> *dN* is the disk number, which is the LUN descriptor; and
>
> *sN* is the slice number or partition number.

So when you see a RAW partition in Sun listed as *c0t0d2s3*, you'll know that the device is the third partition in the second disk connected to first controller's first SCSI port. HP UX does not expose the slice number in the raw device.

HP uses the *cNtNdN* format for the raw partitions. Note that there is no concept of slice designation, as HP/UX does not support slices. (HP/UX Itanium does have slice support, but the use of this feature is not supported by HP.) The entire disk must be provided to ASM.

A typical Linux configuration uses *straight disks*. RAW functionality was an afterthought. However, Linux imposes a limit of 255 possible RAW files, and this limitation is one of the reasons for the development of Oracle Cluster File System (OCFS) and the use ASMLib. Raw devices are typically stored in /dev/raw and are named raw1 to raw255. ASMLib is discussed later in the chapter.

RAW Device Bindings in Linux

The `raw` command is used to bind a raw device to a block device. RAW bindings are not persistent and need to be done each time the system is rebooted by placing the raw device mapping entries in **/etc/sysconfig/rawdevices** or updating the run control script to do the bindings. The following `raw` command binds the device /dev/sda1 as /dev/raw/raw1:

```
device raw /dev/raw/raw1 /dev/sda1
```

ASM Administration and Management

Administering an ASM instance is similar to managing a database instance but with fewer tasks. An ASM instance does not require a database instance to be running for you to administer it. An ASM instance does not have a data dictionary, as metadata is not stored in a dictionary. ASM metadata is small and stored in the disk headers. SQL *Plus can be used to perform all ASM administration tasks in the same way you work with a normal RDBMS instance.

NOTE
*To administer ASM with SQL *Plus, you must set the* ORACLE_SID *environment variable to the ASM SID before you start SQL *Plus. The default ASM SID for a single instance database is* +ASM, *and the default SID for ASM on RAC nodes is* +ASMnode#. *ASM instances do not have a data dictionary, so you must use operating system authentication and connect as SYSDBA. When connecting remotely through Oracle Net Services, you must use a password file for authentication.*

ASM Instance Management

An ASM instance is designed and built as a logical extension of the database instances; they share the same mechanism of instance management. Similar to the database instance parameter file, an ASM parameter file name is suffixed by the SID of the instance. The SID for ASM defaults to *+ASM* for a single-instance database and *+ASMnode#* for RAC nodes. The same rules for file names, default locations, and search orders that apply to the database initialization parameter files apply to the ASM initialization parameter files. But they have a separate set of initializaiton parameters, which cannot be set in the database instance.

Adminstering the ASM Instance

ASM instances are started similarly to Oracle database instances; as with connecting to the instance with SQL *Plus, you must set the ORACLE_SID environment variable to the ASM SID. The initialization parameter file, which can be a server parameter file, must contain the parameter INSTANCE_TYPE = ASM to signal the Oracle executable that an ASM instance is starting and not a database instance.

The STARTUP command does start the instance with the set of memory structures and it mounts the disk groups specified by the initialization parameter ASM_DISKGROUPS. If ASM_DISKGROUPS is blank, the ASM instance starts and warns that no disk groups were mounted. You can then mount disk groups with the ALTER DISKGROUP (similar to ALTER DATBASE) MOUNT command.

The following table describes the various startup modes of the ASM instance:

Startup Mode	Description
NOMOUNT	Starts up the ASM instance without mounting any disk groups.
MOUNT	Starts up the ASM instance and mounts the disk groups.
OPEN	Mounts the disk groups and allows connections from database. This is the default startup mode.
FORCE	Starts up MOUNT after a SHUTDOWN ABORT.

Other startup clauses have comparable interpretation for ASM instances as they do for database instances. For example, RESTRICT prevents database instances from connecting to this ASM instance. OPEN is invalid for an ASM instance. NOMOUNT starts up an ASM instance without mounting any disk group.

An ASM instance does not have any data dictionary, and you can connect to the ASM instance only as SYSDBA. You can use SQLPlus to connect to the instance and run simple SQL commands like show sga and show parameter <parameter name>.

```
$ sqlplus '/as sysdba'
SQL*Plus: Release 10.2.0.1.0 - Production on Sat Feb 4 01:03:55 2006
Copyright (c) 1982, 2005, Oracle.  All rights reserved.

Connected to:
Oracle Database 10g Enterprise Edition Release 10.2.0.1.0 - Production
With the Partitioning, Real Application Clusters, OLAP and Data Mining
options

SQL> show sga
Total System Global Area    92274688 bytes
Fixed Size                   1217884 bytes
Variable Size               65890980 bytes
ASM Cache                   25165824 bytes
```

An ASM instance shutdown is similar to a database instance shutdown. The database instances using the ASM instance must be shut down before shutting down the ASM instance. When using a NORMAL, IMMEDIATE, or TRANSACTIONAL shutdown, ASM waits for any in-progress SQL to complete. Once all the ASM SQLs are completed, it dismounts all disk groups and shuts down the ASM instance in an orderly fashion. If any database instances are connected to the ASM instance, the SHUTDOWN command returns an error and leaves the ASM instance running.

When SHUTDOWN ABORT is used, the ASM instance is immediately terminated. It does not dismount the disk groups in an orderly fashion. The next startup requires recovery of ASM. If any database instance is connected to the ASM instance, the database instance aborts as it does not get access to the storage system that is managed by the ASM instance.

ASM Background Processes

As ASM is built using the RDBMS framework, the software architecture is similar to that of Oracle RDBMS processes. The ASM instance is built using various background processes, and a few of these processes specific to the ASM instance manage the disk groups in the ASM. The following listing shows the background processes of the ASM instance having an SID of ASM.

```
oracle    30420    1    0 Feb01 ?        00:01:13 asm_pmon_+ASM1
oracle    30434    1    0 Feb01 ?        00:02:50 asm_diag_+ASM1
oracle    30436    1    0 Feb01 ?        00:00:09 asm_psp0_+ASM1
oracle    30438    1    0 Feb01 ?        00:05:03 asm_lmon_+ASM1
oracle    30440    1    0 Feb01 ?        00:05:05 asm_lmd0_+ASM1
oracle    30442    1    0 Feb01 ?        00:06:18 asm_lms0_+ASM1
oracle    30448    1    0 Feb01 ?        00:00:10 asm_mman_+ASM1
oracle    30450    1    0 Feb01 ?        00:00:10 asm_dbw0_+ASM1
```

```
oracle    30452    1   0 Feb01 ?        00:00:10 asm_lgwr_+ASM1
oracle    30454    1   0 Feb01 ?        00:00:15 asm_ckpt_+ASM1
oracle    30467    1   0 Feb01 ?        00:00:31 asm_smon_+ASM1
oracle    30483    1   0 Feb01 ?        00:00:10 asm_rbal_+ASM1
oracle    30485    1   0 Feb01 ?        00:00:48 asm_gmon_+ASM1
oracle    30538    1   0 Feb01 ?        00:00:29 asm_lck0_+ASM1
oracle    14373    1   0 Feb01 ?        00:00:00 asm_o000_+ASM1
oracle     9364    1   0 00:59 ?        00:00:00 asm_pz99_+ASM1
oracle     9391    1   0 00:59 ?        00:00:00 asm_pz98_+ASM1
```

Look at the background processes closely, and you will see that the background processes used in RDBMS instance management are similar to smon and pmon. However, there are additional processes, such as rbal and gmon, which are specific to ASM instances. Let's take a closer look at the ASM-specific processes.

ASM Processes in the Database Instance

Each database instance using ASM has two background processes called ASMB and RBAL. The ASMB background process runs in a database instance and connects to a foreground process in an ASM instance. Over this connection, periodic messages are exchanged to update statistics and to verify that both instances are healthy. All extent maps describing open files are sent to the database instance via ASMB. If an extent of an open file is relocated or the status of a disk is changed, messages are received by the ASMB process in the affected database instances.

During operations that require ASM intervention, such as a file creation by a database foreground, the database foreground connects directly to the ASM instance to perform the operation. Each database instance maintains a pool of connections to its ASM instance to avoid the overhead of reconnecting for every file operation.

A group of slave processes in O001 to O010 establishes a connection to the ASM instance, and these slave processes are used as a connection pool for database process. Database processes can send messages to the ASM instance using the slave processes. For example, opening a file sends the open request to the ASM instance via a slave. However, slaves are not used for long running operations, such as those for creating a file. The slave connections eliminate the overhead of logging into the ASM instances for short requests. These slaves are automatically shut down when not in use.

Initialization Parameters

The following initialization parameters can be set in the ASM instance. The usual trace and dump directory parameters used in database instances can also be set in the ASM instance. Parameters that start with *ASM_* cannot be used in database instances.

- INSTANCE_TYPE   This parameter instructs the Oracle executables about the instance type. By default, the Oracle executables assume the instance type is a database instance. This is the only mandatory parameter in an ASM instance. All other parameters have suitable default parameters when not specified.

- ASM_POWER_LIMIT   Sets the power limits for disk rebalancing. This parameter defaults to 1. Valid values are 0 through 11. This parameter is not dynamic. More details on rebalancing are discussed later in the chapter.

- `ASM_DISKSTRING`   A comma-separated list of strings that limits the set of disks that ASM discovers. This parameter accepts wildcard characters. Only disks that match one of the strings are discovered. String format depends on the ASM library in use and the operating system. The standard system library for ASM supports glob pattern matching.

- `ASM_DISKGROUPS`   A list of the names of disk groups to be mounted by an ASM instance at startup, or when the `ALTER DISKGROUP ALL MOUNT` statement is used. If this parameter is not specified, no disk groups are mounted. This parameter is dynamic, and when using a server parameter file (SPFILE), altering this value is not required.

The internal packages used by ASM instances are executed from the large pool, and therefore you should set the value of the initialization parameter `LARGE_POOL_SIZE` to a value greater than 8MB. Regarding other buffer parameters, you can use their default values.

Creating a Disk Group Manually

The `CREATE DISKGROUP` command is used to create a disk group in an ASM instance. Before creating a disk group, the ASM instance will check that the disk/RAW partition being added in a disk group is addressable. If the disk/RAW partition is addressable and not being used by any other group, ASM writes specific information in the first block of the disk or RAW partition being used to create the disk group.

ASM mounts the disk group automatically when the `CREATE DISKGROUP` command is executed, and a disk group name is also added in the `ASM_DISKGROUPS` parameter in the SPFILE so that whenever the ASM instance is restarted later only this newly created disk group will be mounted.

If you want ASM to mirror files, define the redundancy level while creating the ASM disk group. Oracle provides two redundancy levels: normal redundancy and high redundancy. In normal redundancy, each extent has one mirrored copy; in high redundancy, each extent has two mirrored copies in different disk groups.

Disks in a disk group should be of a similar size with similar performance characteristics. It's always advisable to create different disk groups for different types of disks. Disks in disk groups should be of the same size to avoid wasting disk space in failure groups. All disks that will be used to create disk groups must be in line with the `ASM_DISKSTRING` parameter to avoid disk discovery issues.

Creating a Disk Group

In the following example, we create disk group named DGA with two failure groups named FLGRP1 and FLGRP2 using four raw partitions—namely /dev/raw/raw3, /dev/raw/raw4, /dev/raw/raw5, and /dev/raw/raw6.

```
SQL> CREATE DISKGROUP DGA NORMAL REDUNDANCY
  2   FAILGROUP FLGRP1 DISK
  3  '/dev/raw/raw3',
  4  '/dev/raw/raw4',
  5   FAILGROUP FLGRP2 DISK
  6  '/dev/raw/raw5',
  7  '/dev/raw/raw6',
```

After creating a disk group, you may need to alter the disk group depending upon your business requirements. Oracle allows you to perform create, drop/undrop, resize, rebalance, and mount/dismount operations on disk groups after they've been created.

Adding Disks to a Disk Group

Whenever disks are added into a disk group, Oracle internally rebalances the I/O load. The following example shows you how to add disks to an existing disk group. Oracle uses the ADD clause to add disks or a failure group to an existing disk group. In this example, raw partition /dev/raw/raw7 is being added to the existing group DGA:

```
ALTER DISKGROUP DGA ADD DISK
      '/dev/raw/raw7' NAME disk5;
```

No failure group is defined in the statement, so the disk will be assigned to its own failure group.

Dropping Disks in a Disk Group

Oracle provides the DROP DISK clause in conjunction with the CREATE DISK GROUP command to drop a disk within a disk group. Oracle internally rebalances the files during this operation. Oracle fails the DROP operation if other disks in the disk group don't have enough space. If you are adding and dropping disks from a disk group, it is advisable that you add first and then drop, and both operations should be performed in single ALTER DISKGROUP statement, as this reduces time spent on rebalancing. Oracle also provides force options to drop a disk within a disk group even if ASM can't read or write to those disks. This option can't be used with external redundancy disk groups.

In this example, we drop /dev/raw/raw7 from the DGA disk group:

```
ALTER DISKGROUP DGA DROP DISK '/dev/raw/raw7';
```

Resizing the Disks

Oracle provides a RESIZE clause that can be used in conjunction with the ALTER DISKGROUP command to resize the disk, resize any specific disk, or to resize the disks within a specific failure group.

Resizing is useful for reclaiming the disk space. For example, if a SIZE defined for the disks was less than the disk size while creating the disk group and later on you want to claim the full size of disk, this option can be used without giving any SIZE so that Oracle will take SIZE as returned by the operating system.

```
ALTER DISKGROUP DGA RESIZE DISK '/dev/raw/raw6' SIZE 500M;
```

ASM Rebalancing

ASM does not require any downtime during storage configuration and reconfiguration—that is, you can change the storage configuration without having to take the database offline. ASM automatically redistributes file data evenly across all the disks of the disk group after you add or drop disks from a group. This operation is called *disk rebalancing* and is transparent to the database.

A rebalancing operation evenly spreads the contents of every file across all available disks in that disk group. The operation is driven by space usage in the disks and not based on the I/O statistics on those disks. It is invoked automatically when needed and no manual intervention is required during the operation. You can also choose to run the operation manually or change a running rebalance operation.

The rebalancing operation can be sped up by increasing the number of background slave processes responsible for the operation. The background process ARBx is responsible for disk rebalancing during storage reconfiguration. To increase the number of slave processes dynamically, you use the init.ora parameter ASM_POWER_LIMIT. It is recommended that you perform rebalancing using only one node when running in RAC. This can be done by shutting down any unused ASM instances. Figure 6-5 shows the rebalancing functionality.

If the POWER clause is not specified in an ALTER DISKGROUP command, or when a rebalance is implicitly invoked by adding or dropping a disk, the rebalance power defaults to the value of the ASM_POWER_LIMIT initialization parameter. You can adjust this parameter dynamically. The higher the limit, the faster a rebalance operation may complete. Lower values cause rebalancing to take longer but consume fewer processing and I/O resources. This leaves these resources available for other applications, such as the database. The default value of 1 minimizes disruption to other applications. The appropriate value is dependent upon your hardware configuration as well as performance and availability requirements.

If a rebalance is in progress because a disk is manually or automatically dropped, increasing the power of the rebalance shortens the window during which redundant copies of that data on the dropped disk are reconstructed on other disks.

The V$ASM_OPERATION view provides information that can be used for adjusting the ASM_POWER_LIMIT and the resulting power of rebalance operations. The V$ASM_OPERATION view also gives an estimate in the EST_MINUTES column of the amount of time remaining for the rebalance operation to complete. You can see the effect of changing the rebalance power by observing the change in the time estimate.

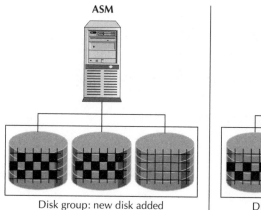
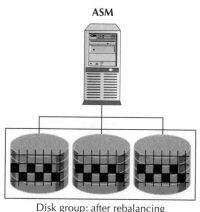

ASM   ASM

Disk group: new disk added   Disk group: after rebalancing

FIGURE 6-5. *ASM rebalancing*

Manually Rebalancing a Disk Group

You can manually rebalance the files in a disk group using the REBALANCE clause of the ALTER DISKGROUP statement. This would normally not be required, because ASM automatically rebalances disk groups when their composition changes. You might want to perform a manual rebalance operation, however, if you want to control the speed of what would otherwise be an automatic rebalance operation.

The POWER clause of the ALTER DISKGROUP...REBALANCE statement specifies the degree of parallelization, and thus the speed of the rebalance operation. It can be set to a value from 0 to 11. A value of 0 halts a rebalancing operation until the statement is either implicitly or explicitly reinvoked. The default rebalance power is set by the ASM_POWER_LIMIT initialization parameter.

The power level of an ongoing rebalance operation can be changed by entering the rebalance statement with a new level.

The ALTER DISKGROUP...REBALANCE command by default returns immediately so that you can issue other commands while the rebalance operation takes place asynchronously in the background. You can query the V$ASM_OPERATION view for the status of the rebalance operation.

If you want the ALTER DISKGROUP...REBALANCE command to wait until the rebalance operation is complete before returning, you can add the WAIT keyword to the REBALANCE clause. This is especially useful in scripts. The command also accepts a NOWAIT keyword, which invokes the default behavior of conducting the rebalance operation asynchronously. You can interrupt a rebalance running in wait mode by typing CTRL-C on most platforms. This causes the command to return immediately with the message "ORA-01013: user requested cancel of current operation," and to continue the rebalance operation asynchronously.

Additional rules for the rebalance operation include the following:

■ The ALTER DISKGROUP...REBALANCE statement uses the resources of the single node upon which it is started.

■ ASM can perform one rebalance at a time on a given instance.

■ Rebalancing continues across a failure of the ASM instance performing the rebalance.

■ The REBALANCE clause (with its associated POWER and WAIT/NOWAIT keywords) can also be used in ALTER DISKGROUP commands that add, drop, or resize disks.

The following example manually rebalances the disk group dgroup2. The command does not return until the rebalance operation is complete.

```
ALTER DISKGROUP dgroup2 REBALANCE POWER 5 WAIT;
```

V$ASM_DISK_STAT and V$ASM_DISKGROUP_STAT can be used to query performance statistics. The following query can be used to get the performance statistics at the disk group level. These views along with V$filestat can provide greater information about the performance of the disk groups and data files.

```
SELECT PATH, READS, WRITES, READ_TIME, WRITE_TIME,
READ_TIME/DECODE(READS,0,1,READS) "AVGRDTIME",
WRITE_TIME/DECODE(WRITES,0,1,WRITES) "AVGWRTIME"
FROM V$ASM_DISK_STAT;
```

PATH	READS	WRITES	READ_TIME	WRITE_TIME	AVGRDTIME	AVGWRTIME
/dev/raw/raw2						
ORCL:DISK1	50477	67683	20.86	724.856718	.000413258	.010709583
ORCL:DISK2	418640	174842	100.259	802.975526	.000239487	.004592578

Backup and Recovery in ASM

An ASM instance is *not* backed up because an ASM instance itself does not contain any files but manages the metadata of the ASM disks. ASM metadata is *triple mirrored*, which should protect the metadata from typical failures. If sufficient failures occur to cause the loss of metadata, the diskgroup must be recreated. Data on the ASM disks is backed up using RMAN. In case of failure, once the disk groups are created, the data (such as database files) can be restored using RMAN.

Each disk group is self-describing, containing its own file directory, disk directory, and other data such as metadata logging information. ASM automatically protects its metadata by using mirroring techniques, even with external redundancy disk groups. An ASM instance caches the information in its SGA. ASM metadata describes the disk group and files, and it is self-describing as it resides inside the disk group. Metadata is maintained in the blocks, and each metadata block is 4K and triple mirrored.

With multiple ASM instances mounting the same disk groups, if one ASM instance fails, another ASM instance automatically recovers transient ASM metadata changes caused by the failed instance. This situation is called *ASM instance recovery* and is automatically and immediately detected by the global cache services.

With multiple ASM instances mounting different disk groups, or in the case of a single ASM instance configuration, if an ASM instance fails while ASM metadata is open for update, the disk groups that are not currently mounted by any other ASM instance are not recovered until they are mounted again. When an ASM instance mounts a failed disk group, it reads the disk group log and recovers all transient changes. This situation is called *ASM crash recovery*.

Therefore, when using ASM clustered instances, it is recommended that you have all ASM instances always mounting the same set of disk groups. However, it is possible to have a disk group on locally attached disks that are visible only to one node in a cluster, and have that disk group mounted only on the node where the disks are attached.

ASM Tools

ASM includes a few tools to provide the API for the file system. The ASM command-line interface and ASM file transfer utilities emulate the UNIX environment within the ASM file system.

ASMCMD ASM Command-Line Utility

In version 10g R2, Oracle introduced a new option to access the ASM files and related information via a command-line interface, which makes ASM management easier and handy for DBAs. This new option can be used on both 10g R1 and 10g R2 but is available by default only in 10g R2. To use this option on 10g R1, you must copy the ASMCMD and ASMCMDCORE files from the 10g R2 installation into the 10g R1 *ORACLE_HOME*/bin directory, where *ORACLE_HOME* is the location where ASM is installed.

Change the ownership of these files to the *oracle* user with *dba* group assigned. Using ASMCMD provides the DBA with a similar look, feel, and privileges as most UNIX-flavor systems, with commands like cd, ls, mkdir, pwd, and so on. Most common commands are shown in the following table:

Command	Purpose
cd	Change current directory to specified directory.
du	Display the total disk space occupied by ASM files in the specified ASM directory and all its subdirectories, recursively.
exit	Exit from ASMCMD.
help	Display syntax and description of ASMCMD commands.
ls	List the contents of an ASM directory, the attributes of the specified file, or the names and attributes of all disk groups.
find	List the paths of all occurrences of the specified name (with wildcards) under the specified directory.
mkalias	Create an alias for a system-generated filename.
lsct	List information about current ASM clients.
lsdg	List all disk groups and their attributes.
mkdir	Create ASM directories.
rm	Delete the specified ASM files or directories.
rmalias	Delete the specified alias, retaining the file to which the alias points.

ASM FTP Utility

Oracle 10g R2 provides a new feature called ASM FTP, by which operations on ASM files and directories can be performed similarly to conventional operations on normal files using conventional File Transfer Protocol (FTP). A typical use of such access to an ASM file can be to copy ASM files from one database to another.

Oracle Database 10g R2 leverages the virtual folder feature of XML DB that provides a way to access the ASM files and directories through XML DB protocols such as FTP, Hypertext Transfer Protocol (HTTP), and programmatic APIs. ASM virtual folder is mounted as /sys/asm within the XML DB hierarchy. The folder is called *virtual* because nothing is physically stored in XML DB. All operations are handled by underlying ASM components.

The virtual folder is created by default during installation of XML DB. If the database is not configured to use automatic storage, this virtual folder will be empty and no operation will be permitted. The /sys/asm virtual folder contains folders and subfolders in line with the hierarchy of the ASM fully qualified naming structure. Figure 6-6 shows the hierarchy of an ASM virtual folder.

As shown in Figure 6-6, the virtual folder contains a subfolder for each mounted disk group in an ASM instance. Each disk group folder contains a subfolder for each database using that disk group subfolder, the database folder contains a file type subfolder, and the file type subfolder

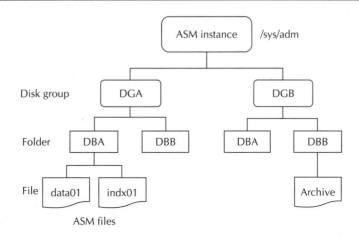

FIGURE 6-6. *ASM virtual folder hierarchy*

contains ASM files, which are binary in nature. Though we can access the ASM files as we can access normal files in a conventional FTP application, some usage/access restrictions are in place. DBA privilege is a must to view the contents of the /sys/asm virtual folder.

The next example demonstrates accessing ASM files via the virtual folder. In this example, we assume that we are in the home directory of user *oracle*, which is /home/oracle, and we are connecting to server using FTP, where the ASM instance is hosted. The ASM instance is hosted on the i3dl045e server. The disk group name is DGA and the database name is *dba* using the DGA disk group.

First we open the FTP connection to i3dl045e and pass on the login information. Only users with DBA privilege can access the /sys/asm folder. After connecting, we change our directory to the /sys/asm virtual folder and list the contents of the /sys/asm folder. A subfolder named DGA is used for the DGA disk group. Then we change to the DGA directory and see another subfolder with a database name, which is *dba* in our case. Then we list the contents of the dba directory that contains the ASM binary files related to the dba database. Finally we download the file data01.dbf to our local directory, which is /home/oracle.

```
ftp> open i3dl045e 7777
ftp> use system
ftp> passwd manager
ftp> cd /sys/asm
ftp> ls
DGA
ftp> cd DGA
ftp> ls
dba
ftp> ls
data01.dbf
indx01.dbf
ftp> bin
ftp> get data01.dbf
```

ASMLib

ASMLib is the storage management interface thet helps simplify the operating system–to–database interface. The ASMLib API was developed and supported by Oracle to provide an alternative interface for the ASM-enabled kernel to identify and access block devices. The ASMLib interface serves as an alternative to the standard operating system interface. It provides storage and operating system vendors the opportunity to supply extended storage-related features that provide benefits such as improved performance and greater integrity than are currently available on other database platforms.

Installing ASMLib

Oracle provides an ASM library driver for the Linux OS. With the advent of this library, steps such as raw device binding become unnecessary. The ASM library driver must be installed prior to installing any Oracle Database software. In addition, it is recommended that any ASM disk devices required by the database be prepared and created before the OUI database installation.

The ASMLib software is available on the Oracle Technology Network (OTN) for free download. Go to http://otn.oracle.com/tech/linux/asmlib/ and chose the link for your version of the Linux platform.

Three packages are available for each Linux platform. The two essential rpm packages are the oracleasmlib package that provides the actual ASM library, and the oracleasm-support package that provides the utilities to configure and enable the ASM driver. Both these packages need to be installed. The third package provides the kernel driver for the ASM library. Each package provides the driver for a different kernel. You must install the appropriate package for the kernel you are running.

Configuring ASMLib

After the packages are installed, the ASMLib can be loaded and configured using the `configure` option in the /etc/init.d/oracleasm utility. For RAC clusters, the oracleasm installation and configuration must be completed on all nodes of the cluster. Configuring ASMLib is as simple as executing the following command:

```
[root@mynode/]# /etc/init.d/oracleasm configure
   Configuring the Oracle ASM library driver.

   This will configure the on-boot properties of the Oracle ASM library
   driver.  The following questions will determine whether the driver is
   loaded on boot and what permissions it will have.  The current values
   will be shown in brackets ('[]').  Hitting  without typing an
   answer will keep that current value.  Ctrl-C will abort.

   Default user to own the driver interface []: oracle
   Default group to own the driver interface []: dba
   Start Oracle ASM library driver on boot (y/n) [n]: y
   Fix permissions of Oracle ASM disks on boot (y/n) [y]: y
   Writing Oracle ASM library driver configuration          [  OK  ]
   Creating /dev/oracleasm mount point                      [  OK  ]
   Loading module "oracleasm"                               [  OK  ]
   Mounting ASMlib driver filesystem                        [  OK  ]
   Scanning system for ASM disks                            [  OK  ]
```

Note that the ASMLib mount point is not a standard file system that can be accessed by operating system commands. It is used only by the ASM library to communicate with the ASM driver. The ASM library dynamically links with the Oracle kernel, and multiple ASMLib implementations could be simultaneously linked to the same Oracle kernel. Each library would provide access to a different set of disks and different ASMLib capabilities.

The objective of ASMLib is to provide a more streamlined and efficient mechanism for managing disks and I/O processing of ASM storage. The ASM API provides a set of interdependent functions that need to be implemented in a layered fashion. These functions are dependent on the backend storage implementing the associated functions. From an implementation perspective, these functions are grouped into three collections of functions.

Each function group is dependent on the existence of the lower-level group. *Device discovery functions* are the lowest-layer functions and must be implemented in any ASMLib library. *I/O processing functions* provide an optimized asynchronous interface for scheduling I/O operations and managing I/O operation completion events. These functions, in effect, extend the operating system interface. Consequently, the I/O processing functions must be implemented as a device driver within the operating system kernel.

The *performance and reliability functions* are the highest-layer functions and depend on the existence of the I/O processing functions. These functions use the I/O processing control structures for passing metadata between the Oracle database and the backend storage devices. The performance and reliability functions enable additional intelligence on the part of backend storage. This is achieved when metadata transfer is passed through the ASMLib API.

Discovery

Device discovery provides the identification and naming of storage devices that are operated on by higher-level functions. Device discovery does not require any operating system code and can be implemented as a standalone library invoked and dynamically linked by the Oracle database. The discovery function makes the characteristics of the disk available to ASM. Disks discovered through ASMLib do not need to be available through normal operating system interfaces. For example, a storage vendor may provide a more efficient method of discovering and locating disks that its own interface driver manages.

I/O Processing

The current standard I/O model imposes a lot of OS overhead, due in part to mode and context switches. The deployment of ASMLib reduces the number of state transitions from kernel-to-user mode by employing a more efficient I/O schedule and call processing mechanism. One call to ASMLib can submit and reap multiple I/Os. This dramatically reduces the number of calls to the OS when performing I/O. Additionally, one I/O handle can be used by all the processes in an instance for accessing the same disk. This eliminates multiple open calls and multiple file descriptors.

One of the critical aspects of the ASMLib I/O interface is that it provides an asynchronous I/O interface enhancing performance and enables database-related intelligence on the backend storage devices. As for additional intelligence in the backend storage, the I/O interface enables passing metadata from the database to the storage devices. Future developments in the storage array firmware may allow the transport of database-related metadata to the backend storage devices and will enable new database-related intelligence in the storage devices.

Automatic Storage Management	Oracle Cluster File System
Oracle Database file system and Volume Manager	Special-purpose cluster file system, no volume manger functionality
Available only from Oracle 10g	Supports Oracle 9i and Oracle 10g
Available in all platforms as part of the RDBMS shipment	Available in Linux and Windows only
Integrated with RDBMS kernel	Not integrated with RDBMS, but works closely with Operating System Services
Supported by Enterprise Manager with GUI interface	No Enterprise Manager support, no management GUIs
Performance equivalent to raw	Performance equivalent to raw
Supports striping and mirroring for high availability	Does not support striping or mirroring; relies on storage hardware or host-based RAID
Oracle data files, redologs, and flash recovery files; not suitable for binaries	Supports all Oracle files and can also be used for binaries
Free with Enterprise Edition and Standard Edition, but source code is proprietary to Oracle	Free source code under GPL on Linux (open source)

TABLE 6-1. *ASM and OCFS Features Compared*

OCFS and ASM Comparison

Oracle Cluster File System (OCFS) is a special-purpose shared file system designed specifically for Oracle RAC. It allows you to have a clustered database using a file system in Windows and Linux environments. In Windows environments, OCFS eliminates the requirement for Oracle database files to be linked to logical drives and enables all nodes to share a single Oracle_Home instead of requiring each node to have its own local copy.

OCFS can be used virtually for all Oracle files including datafiles, control files, log files, and trace files. The Oracle Cluster Registry and voting disk can also be placed in OCFS. OCFS provides the basic cluster file system in Windows and Linux environments and cannot be treated as a replacement or comparable product to ASM. See Table 6-1 for a comparison of the features of ASM and OCFS.

In a Nutshell

Automatic Storage Management is one of the best frameworks for managing data storage, with lots of self-management and self-tuning capabilities. It also provides GUI tools for management and a command-line interface for the command-line lovers. ASM tools like ASMCMD and ASMFTP provide a file system, such as interface to ASM instance, and ASMLib makes the raw devices management easier. With ASM, managing a huge amount of storage is no longer a complex task that involves lots of planning and day-to-day administration issues.

PART
III

RAC Administration and Management

CHAPTER
7

RAC Basic Administration

racle Real Application Clusters database administration is similar to single instance database administration. Accomplishing tasks such as managing users, datafiles, tablespaces, control files, and undos are similar to managing those aspects in a single instance environment. The information in this chapter assumes that you are familiar with single instance database administration and focuses on aspects of RAC that are different from those of a single instance. This chapter covers the tasks of administering an RAC database in an Oracle RAC instance and administering an Oracle RAC database and database objects.

Initialization Parameters

Oracle is a highly flexible, function-rich RDBMS that can be used on a laptop by a single user or used on the world's most powerful computer systems and accessed by thousands of users. How does Oracle offer such flexibility? How does an end user choose which functions to use and optimize the database for the intended use? The answers lie in Oracle's parameter file that contains a set of parameters that allow an end user to customize and optimize an Oracle database instance. When an Oracle instance starts, it reads these parameters, which in turn define the features the database uses, the amount of memory an instance uses, how users interact with the database, and other important information.

Prior to Oracle version 9i, parameters used by an instance could be stored only in a text file (frequently referred to as init.ora). Its name was somewhat operating-system dependent, however—for example, on a UNIX-based system, the parameter file's default name was *init<sid>.ora*. A DBA could use a non-default parameter file by specifying the `pfile` clause of the startup command. The text file used during startup was never referred to by the Oracle instance again, and the only means of updating it was by editing it through a text editor.

Starting with Oracle 9i, Oracle introduced the *server parameter file (SPFILE)*. This binary file can be updated only by Oracle. SPFILE offers the following advantages over the traditional init. ora text file:

■ Any changes made to an instances parameter can be persistent through shutdown and startup. A DBA can control whether the change is intended for the current life of the instance (by specifying `SCOPE=MEMORY`), should be permanent (by specifying `SCOPE=SPFILE`), or should be immediate and permanent (by specifying `SCOPE=BOTH`).

■ When used, an Oracle instance remembers which SPFILE was used to start the instance. The SQL command `show parameter spfile` can be used to display the SPFILE used to start the instance. Oracle does not remember the name of the traditional parameter (init.ora) file used to start the instance.

■ An instance will update the SPFILE whenever the DBA uses the `alter system` command with `SCOPE=SPFILE` or `SCOPE=BOTH`. The DBA does not need to remember the file used to start the instance, and there is no need to edit the file manually.

In an RAC environment a DBA can use a parameter file shared by all the instances, or each instance can have its own dedicated parameter file. Using a shared SPFILE for managing instances in an RAC environment is highly recommended.

NOTE
In an RAC environment, SPFILE must be shared and should be placed on a shareable disk subsystem—that is, either on a raw device, a clustered file system, or Automatic Storage Management (ASM). The typical size of an SPFILE needs not be more than few kilobytes, so if you are using a raw device, allocating a raw device of 5MB is more than adequate.

Oracle instance parameters for the RAC environment can be grouped into three major categories:

- **Unique parameters** These parameters are unique to each instance. Parameters in this category identify resources to be used by an instance exclusively. Some examples of this type of parameter are `instance_name`, `thread`, and `undo_tablespace`.

- **Identical parameters** Parameters in this category need to be the same on all the instances in an RAC environment. Parameters defining the database characteristics, interinstance communication characteristics, and so on, fall in this category. The parameters `max_commit_propagation_delay`, `db_name`, and `control_file` belong to this category. Beginning with Oracle 10g, you can use the ISINSTANCE_MODIFIABLE column of v$parameter view to see a list of such parameters:

```
select name, ISINSTANCE_MODIFIABLE
from v$parameter
where ISINSTANCE_MODIFIABLE='FALSE'
order by name;
```

- **Neither unique nor identical parameters** Those that do not fall in either of the above two categories are included. Parameters that define performance characteristics of an instance generally fall in this section. Some examples of this type of parameter are `db_cache_size`, `large_pool_size`, `local_listener`, and `gcs_server_processes`.

Unique Parameters

The following parameters are unique to each instance.

instance_name   This parameter defines the name of the Oracle instance. Although not required, this parameter is generally chosen to be the same as the `oracle_sid` environment variable defined at the operating system level. The default value for this parameter is also the value of the environment variable `oracle_sid`. In a single instance environment, the instance name is usually the same as the database name. In an RAC environment, the instance name is constructed by appending a suffix to each instance of the database (for example, for a database named *prod*, instance names could be *prod1*, *prod2*, *prod3*, and so on).

Generally the value of this parameter is not set in the parameter file, thus leaving it to its default value of SID. We strongly recommend not specifying this parameter and leaving it to its default setting.

Note that data dictionary views dynamic performance (more than 30 of them) that contain the column *instance_name* or *inst_name* derive the value of this column from the environment variable `ORACLE_SID` and *not* from this parameter.

The following SQL session demonstrates the parameter behavior:

```
$echo $ORACLE_SID
PROD1
$grep instanace_name initPROD1.ora
instance_name=xyz
. . .
SQL>
SQL> select instance_name from v$instance ;
INSTANCE_NAME
----------------
PROD1
SQL> show parameter instance_name
NAME                                 TYPE        VALUE
------------------------------------ ----------- ----------------
instance_name                        string      xyz
```

instance_number   This is a unique number greater than 0 (zero) and smaller than the `max_instance` parameter specified when the database was created. Oracle uses it internally to identify the instance. The INST_ID column in the GV$ corresponds to the value of this parameter for that instance. Generally, the value of this parameter is kept equal to the value of the parameter `thread` to make administrative tasks simple.

If manual segment space management is used (as opposed to automatic segment space management), Oracle uses the instance number to map instance to the freelist group.

The following example line set `instance_number` to 1 for instance prod1:

```
prod1.instance_number=1
```

thread   This parameter specifies the set of redolog files to be used by the instance. All thread values default to 1 if the `thread` parameter is not specified. Therefore, only the first instance will start.

To simplify administrative tasks, it is highly recommended that you use the same thread number for an instance. Also, as mentioned, the value of the parameter `instance_number` should be the same as the value of `thread`. The following example assigns a thread value of 2 to instance prod2:

```
prod2.thread = 2
```

undo_tablespace   This parameter specifies the name of the undo tablespace to be used by an instance. An instance uses its own undo tablespace to write the undo data for its transaction; however, it can read other instances' undo tablespaces. The following line specifies undo tablespace UNDOTBS1 to the instance prod1:

```
prod1.undo_tablespace='UNDOTBS1'
```

For more information on managing the undo tablespace, refer to the "Administering Undo" section of this chapter.

rollback_segments   It is highly recommended that you use Automatic Undo Management. If, due to any reason, an older method of rollback segments is being used, this parameter is used to specify a list of rollback segments. For the best practices on using rollback segments and further details, refer to the Oracle 8i documentation.

The following line assigns rollback segment rbs1, rbs2 to instance prod1:

```
prod1.rollback_segments = (rbs1, rbs2)
```

cluster_interconnects   This optional parameter is used only when the Oracle instance is not able to pick the correct interconnect for interinstance communication automatically. This parameter can also be used to specify multiple networks interconnect to be used for RAC traffic. Use this parameter to specify the IP address of the network to be used for Cache Fusion traffic. In the following example, 10.0.0.1 is the IP address of the private interconnect to be used for the cluster traffic:

```
prod1.cluster_interconnects = "10.0.0.1"
```

The following example line specifies two IP addresses for RAC network traffic:

```
prod1.cluster_interconnects = "10.0.0.1:10.0.0.2"
```

When multiple networks cards/interconnects are to be used for RAC traffic, it is advisable that you use OS-level techniques to configure for the desired failover and traffic sharing features.

NOTE
Specifying multiple interconnects by using the `cluster_`
`interconnets` *parameter enables Cache Fusion traffic to be distributed on all the interconnects. However, if any one of the interconnects is down, Oracle will assume the network is down; thus, it does not provide redundancy and high availability.*

In Oracle Database Release 10g, you can specify a private interconnect during installation and therefore do not need to use this parameter. Oracle 9i should also automatically detect the network to be used for the private interconnect, and generally you do not need to use this parameter. Use this parameter as a last resort to specify network interconnects.

Identical Parameters

Using the query

```
select name, ISINSTANCE_MODIFIABLE
from v$parameter
where ISINSTANCE_MODIFIABLE='FALSE'
order by name;
```

you can determine that more than 100 parameters fall in identical parameters category. However, we will restrict our discussion to parameters that are commonly used. For information on other parameters, refer to the Oracle Database Reference Manual.

In this book, parameters are divided into the following groups:

- RAC-specific parameters
- Database characteristic parameters (parameters that are alike across instances). Here's an example:

  ```
  *.cluster_database = TRUE
  ```

RAC-Specific Parameters
Following are the RAC-specific parameters.

cluster_database   The possible values of this Boolean parameter are TRUE and FALSE. The value of this parameter should be set to TRUE for all the instances. The TRUE value directs the instance during startup to mount the control file in shared mode. If an instance starting first has this parameter set to FALSE, it will be able to mount the control file in exclusive mode. However, this will prevent all subsequent instances from starting up.

During the following maintenance activities, you must start up an instance using `cluster_database = FALSE`:

- Converting from no archive log mode to archive log mode and vice versa
- Enabling the flashback database feature
- Migrating from 9i to 10g
- Performing a media recovery on a system tablespace

The default value for this parameter is FALSE. To start up instances in an RAC environment, this parameter must be set to TRUE.

active_instance_count   This parameter is intended for a primary/secondary RAC environment in which one instance services the workload while another instance acts as a standby for the first instance. In an active/active (true RAC) environment or in an environment consisting of more than two instances, this parameter has no relevance. If this parameter is set, the instance that comes up first becomes the active instance and services the workload. Any instance starting up after the first one acts as a standby instance.

There is no default value for this parameter. This parameter should not be set in an RAC environment where all instances are to be used.

cluster_database_instances   This parameter specifies the number of instances that will be accessing the database. The default value for this parameter is 1. Oracle uses the value of this parameter to compute default values of some other parameters such as `large_pool_size`.

The value of this parameter should be set equal to the maximum number of instances to join the cluster.

dml_locks   This parameter specifies the number of Data Manipulation Language (DML) locks for that instance. (A DML lock is obtained on a table that is undergoing a DML operation, such as insert, update, or delete.) If set to 0 on the instance starting first, it must be set to 0 on all other instances. However, if the value of this parameter is set to any positive number, it can be set to different values for different instances. The default value for this parameter is derived from the transaction parameters.

Leave this parameter at its default value unless the application requires a different setting. Errors such as ORA-00055 require this parameter to be set higher.

In an RAC environment, you might get marginal performance improvement by setting `dml_locks` to 0. However, note that setting `dml_locks` to 0 will prevent users from executing some of the data definition language (DDL) commands. For example, a user can create a table and never be able to drop the table. So it is better to disable the table locks using `ALTER TABLE DISABLE TABLE LOCK` command than setting `dml_locks` to 0.

gc_files_to_locks   This parameter allows you to specify the number of global locks to a data file. Oracle recommends you not set this parameter. Setting this parameter disables the Cache Fusion mechanism for the specified data file and uses the disk ping mechanism to transfer contentious blocks. The following example allocates 100 locks to file number 5:

```
gc_files_to_locks = "5:100"
```

max_commit_propagation_delay   This is an RAC-specific parameter, and its value influences the mechanism Oracle uses to synchronize the System Commit Numbers (SCN) among all instances accessing a database. Its default value is 700 and should not be changed unless necessary. For a default value of this parameter, Oracle uses the Lamport scheme for SCN propagation.

NOTE
This parameter has been deprecated in Oracle Database 10g Release 2, and by default the Broadcast on Commit method is used for SCN propagation.

In situations when application sessions connected to one instance need to read the data recently modified/inserted by another instance and do not find the most recent data, it might be necessary to set `max_commit_propagation_delay` to 0. Setting this parameter to 0 will direct Oracle to use the Broadcast on Commit scheme to generate SCNs. An Oracle instance decides the SCN generation scheme at startup and logs it in the alert.log as follows:

```
This instance was first to open
Picked Lamport scheme to generate SCNs
```

Several packaged applications such as SAP or the Oracle Collaboration Suite recommend that the value of this parameter be set to 0. Review Chapter 10 for information on the performance impact of setting this parameter to a non-default value.

instance_groups   This parameter allows you to specify multiple parallel query execution groups and assigns the current instance to those groups.

parallel_instance_group   This parameter specifies the group of instances to be used for parallel query execution. Oracle will spawn parallel query slaves only on the instances specified by this parameter. It is specifically useful when a parallel query workload should not take away resources intended for other purposes—for example, online transaction processing (OLTP) work. By default, Oracle spawns parallel query slaves on all active instances.

Consider a three-node RAC environment consisting of instances prod1, prod2, and prod3. The following scheme can be used to restrict execution of a parallel query on instances prod2 and prod3, thereby leaving resources on instance prod1 for other purposes:

```
prod2.instances_groups = group23
prod3.instance_groups = group23
prod2.parallel_instance_group = group23
```

When a parallel query is initiated on instance prod2, it will spawn query slaves only on instances prod2 and prod3.

Parameters Specifying Database Characteristics (Alike Across Instances)

The following parameters specify database characteristics that need to be alike across all instances. These parameters behave exactly the same as in a single instance environment; refer to the Oracle Database 10*g* R2 manual for more information about these parameters.

```
archive_lag_target
compatible
control_files
db_block_size
db_domain
db_files
db_name
license_max_users
parallel_execution_message_size
remote_login_passwordfile
spfile
trace_enabled
undo_management
undo_retention
```

Instance-Specific Parameters

Following are the initialization parameters whose influence is generally limited to the local instance's performance characteristics. These parameters can have any value depending on the workload the instance is serving or the capacity of the machine on which they are running. For example, one instance could be serving an OLTP workload, and another instance might be serving a data warehouse (DW) workload; in these situations a DBA is free to choose different values for the parameters, such as db_cache_size to optimize the instance performance with respect to the workload it is executing.

These parameters behave in exactly the same way that they do in a single instance environment; refer to the appropriate Oracle documentation for more information about these parameters.

GCS_SERVER_PROCESSES   This parameter specifies the number of Lock Manager Server (LMS) background processes used by the instance for the Cache Fusion traffic. Its default value is 2 and can be set between 1 and 20 as appropriate for different instances.

remote_listener   This instance-specific parameter is used to register the instance with listeners on remote nodes, generally in a clustered environment. Incoming connection requests received by the Transparent Network Substrate (TNS) listener on a node are directed to the instance running on the least loaded node, thereby distributing the workload among all available nodes. Here is an example of how to specify the parameter in a three-node environment:

```
prod1.remote_listener = listener_prod2, listener_prod3
```

`listener_prod2` and `listener_prod3` are valid tnsnames.ora entries, specifying the listeners on node2 and node3.

Managing the Parameter File

In the RAC environment, a DBA can use a parameter file shared by all instances, or each instance can have its own dedicated parameter file. Following is the syntax for a shared parameter file containing parameters for multiple instances:

```
<instance_name>.<parameter_name>=<parameter_value>
```

An asterisk (*) or no value in place of an *instance_name* implies that the parameter value is valid for all the instances. Here's an example:

```
inst1.db_cache_size = 1000000
     *.undo_management=auto
```

If a parameter appears more than once in a parameter file, the last specified value is the effective value, unless the values are on consecutive lines—in that case values from consecutive lines are concatenated.

The `alter system set` command is available to change initialization parameters for an Oracle instance using SPFILE. Following is the complete syntax of the command:

```
alter system set <parameter>=<value>
                  scope=<memory/spfile/both>
                  comment=<'comments'>
                  deferred
                  sid=<sid, *>
```

- ■ `scope=memory`   Indicates that the parameter should be changed only for the current instance; these changes are lost upon instance restart. If a parameter can be modified only for the local instance, the following error is signaled: "ORA-32018: Parameter cannot be modified in memory on another instance."

- ■ `scope=spfile`   Indicates that the changes are to be made only in the file, and new values of the changed parameter will be effective upon instance restart. The current incarnation of the instance is not affected by this change. If an instance was started using an SPFILE and you try to use this option, the following error is signaled: "ORA-32001: Write to SPFILE requested but no SPFILE specified at startup."

- ■ `scope=both`   Means that the intended parameter change will be effective for the current incarnation of the instance and is persistent through instance restarts.

- ■ `comment`   Allows you to specify comments to be associated with the parameter change.

■ `deferred` Indicates that the changes are effective only for the sessions that are spawned after the command is issued. The sessions that are already active are not affected.

■ `sid` Allows specifying the name of the instance the parameter change is intended for. An asterisk (*) implies that the change is to be made across all the instances. This is the default value as well. Generally in an RAC environment, you can change parameter values for remote instances, with some restrictions depending on the status of the remote instance and the static/dynamic nature of the parameter.

Here are few examples:

```
alter system set db_2k_cache_size=10m scope=spfile sid='prod2';
```

Whenever a parameter is changed using the `alter system` command Oracle logs the command in the alert.log file.

When the Database Configuration Assistant (DBCA) is used to create an RAC database, by default it creates an SPFILE on the shared disk subsystem used for the database. If due to any reason SPFILE is not being used, the `create spfile...` command can be used to create an SPFILE from a parameter file.

Starting and Stopping Instance(s)

An Oracle instance can be started automatically at system boot time. In an RAC environment, you need to ensure that the cluster software is started before database instances can be started. Starting with Oracle Database 10*g* R1, DBCA configures database instances to be started automatically by Cluster Ready Services (CRS) at system boot time.

Using srvctl to Start/Stop Instance(s)

The `srvctl` command is a convenient and highly recommended way to start/stop multiple instances in an RAC environment. Use the following command to start all instances associated with a database:

```
srvctl start database -d prod
```

where the database name is prod. This command can be executed from any of the nodes. The command also starts listeners on each node if not already running.

To shut down all instances associated with the prod database you can use the following command:

```
srvctl stop database  -d prod
```

The command shuts down only instances; the listeners are not stopped, as they might be serving other database instances running on the same machines. You can use the –o option to specify startup/shutdown options. Srvctl uses the Global Services daemon to communicate with other nodes in the cluster, and it invokes SQL *Plus silently to perform start/stop operations. Options specified by –o are directly passed on to SQL *Plus as command-line options for start/stop commands. For example, to stop all the instances with the `immediate` option use the following command:

```
srvctl stop database -d prod -o immediate
```

Similarly, to initiate startup force for all the instances, use the following command:

```
srvctl start database -d prod -o force
```

To perform a normal shutdown of instance prod3 use the following command:

```
srvctl stop database -d prod -i instance prod3
```

Using SQL *Plus to Start/Stop Instance(s)

Similar to a single instance environment, you can use SQL *Plus to start/stop instances individually:

```
$sqlplus '/ as sysdba'
>shutdown immediate;
...
$ sqlplus '/ as sysdba'
...
>startup
```

Note that connecting as `/  as  sysdba` requires OS authentication and needs the logged in user to be a member of the OSDBA group. Refer to the appropriate Oracle Database 10g administrator's guide for more information about the OSDBA group.

Administering Undo

Oracle stores original values of the data called before image in undo segments. The data stored in an undo segment is used to provide read consistency and to roll back uncommitted transactions. Starting with Oracle10g, the flashback feature also makes use of undo data.

Oracle provides two methods of undo management: automatic undo management and manual undo management.

Automatic Undo Management

Automatic undo management was introduced in Oracle Database 9i R1 and is highly recommended. In this method an Oracle instance uses a tablespace of type *undo* to store undo/rollback data. The instance creates the required number of undo segments in the dedicated tablespace and allocates them to transactions to store the undo data; these operations are totally transparent to the DBA and the end user.

Starting with Oracle 9i, DBCA automatically configures the database to use automatic undo management. The following initialization parameters enable automatic undo management:

```
undo_management = "auto"
undo_tablespace = undo_tbs1
```

`undo_retention_time` is another parameter related to automatic undo management. Its default value is 900, which mean that an Oracle instance will make the best effort not to overwrite (reuse) an undo block for 900 seconds after the transaction has been committed. This ensures that transactions/queries that are running for 15 minutes are not likely to get ORA-1555 (the snapshot too old error). If the instance is executing longer running transactions/queries, the DBA needs to size the undo tablespace accordingly. You can use the average undo generation rate to calculate the required size of the undo tablespace.

In the Oracle RAC environment, each instance stores transaction undo data in its dedicated undo tablespace. The DBA can set the undo tablespace for each instance by setting the `undo_tablespace` parameter. The following lines will set `undo_tablespace` for instance prod1 to `undo_tbs1` and for instance prod2 to `undo_tbs2`.

```
prod1.undo_tablespace= undo_tbs1
prod2.undo_tablespace=undo_tbs2
```

All the instances in an RAC environment are required to use either automatic undo management or manual undo management, requiring the parameter `undo_management` to be the same across all the instances. Note that the undo tablespace can't be shared among the instances, requiring that the parameter `undo_tablespace` be unique for each instance.

Any of the following methods can be used to increase the size of an undo tablespace:

- Add another database to undo tablespace.

- Increase the size of the existing datafile(s) belonging to the undo tablespace.

You can change the undo tablespace for an instance. Create the new undo tablespace as follows:

```
create undo tablespace undotbs_big
datafile '/ocfs2/prod/undotbsbig.dbf' size 2000MB;
```

Instruct the instance to use the newly created undo tablespace:

```
alter system set undo_tablespace=undotbs_big scope=both;
```

The instance will start using the new undo tablespace for newer transactions; however, transactions that were active before the new undo tablespace was assigned will continue to use the older undo tablespace until completed. An original undo tablespace can be dropped or taken offline when all the active transactions using it are committed and undo retention time has expired.

Manual Undo Management

The manual method of undo management requires the DBA to create rollback segments. The initialization parameter `rollback_segments` is used to indicate rollback segments to be used by an instance. The DBA can create rollback segments in any desired tablespace; however, the following are recommended:

- Use manual undo management only if you have very good reason for not using automatic undo management.

- Do not create other objects such as tables, indexes, and so on in the tablespace used for rollback segments.

- Create one rollback segment for every four concurrent transactions.

Administering a Temporary Tablespace

Oracle uses a temporary tablespace as a "scratch pad" area to perform sort operation that cannot be done in the memory. Oracle also uses the temporary tablespace to create TEMP tables. Any user who is not assigned a temporary tablespace explicitly will use the default temporary tablespace. Starting with Oracle Database 10g R1, DBCA automatically creates a default temporary tablespace. When you're creating a database with a locally managed system tablespace, a default temporary tablespace must be specified.

Starting with Oracle Release 10g, you can define a temporary tablespace group that can be used wherever a temporary tablespace is used. The use of a temporary tablespace group in an RAC environment is similar to that of a single instance environment. We recommend the use of temporary tablespace group in an RAC environment, as different temporary tablespaces are assigned to the sessions when more than one user connects to the database using the same username. This allows different sessions to use different tablespaces for sort activities—a useful feature when managing packaged applications such as Oracle applications.

In an RAC environment, a user will always use the same assigned temporary tablespace irrespective of the instance being used. Each instance creates a temporary segment in the temporary tablespace it is using. If an instance is running a big sort operation requiring a large temporary tablespace, it can reclaim the space used by other instances' temporary segments in that tablespace. The default temporary tablespace cannot be dropped or taken offline; however, you can change the default temporary tablespace. Use the following commands to do this:

1. Create a new temporary tablespace:

```
create temporary tablespace temp2
tempfile '/ocfs2/prod/temp2.dbf' size 2000MB
autoextend on next 1M maxsize unlimited
extent management local uniform size 1M;
```

2. Make a new temporary tablespace as the default temporary tablespace:

```
alter database default temporary tablespace temp2;
```

3. Drop or offline the original default temporary tablespace.

The following v$ views contain information about temporary tablespaces:

- `gv$sort_segment` Use this view to explore current and maximum sort segment usage statistics.

- `gv$tempseg_usage` Use this view to explore temporary segment usage details such as user name, SQL, and so on.

- `v$tempfile` Use this view to identify temporary datafiles being used for a temporary tablespace.

NOTE
You can use gv$sort_segment and gv$tempseg_usage views to determine the temporary tablespace used by each instance. Use the column INST_ID to separate the data per instance.

In an RAC environment, all instance share the same temporary tablespace. The size of the tablespace should be at least equal to the concurrent maximum requirement of all the instances. If an instance needs a larger sort space, it will ask other instance(s) to release space. In turn, when other instance(s) need more sort space, they will ask this instance to release the sort space. Frequent requests to release temporary space by other instance(s) may impact performance. Pay attention to the columns FREED_EXTENTS and FREE_REQUESTS of V$SORT_SEGMENT; if they grow on a regular basis, consider increasing the size of the temporary tablespace.

Administering Online Redologs

Oracle uses online redolog files to log any changes to data blocks. Each instance has its own set of online redolog files. A set of redologs used in a circular manner by an instance is known as a *thread*. A thread contains at least two online redologs. The size of an online redolog is independent of other instances' redolog sizes and is determined by the local instance's workload and backup and recovery considerations.

Each instance has exclusive write access to its own online redolog files. An instance can read another instance's current online redolog file to perform instance recovery if that instance has terminated abnormally. Thus, an online redolog needs to be located on a shared storage device and cannot be on a local disk.

Operations such as add, delete, and mirror performed on redolog files are similar to those operations performed on a single instance environment.

Use dynamic views V$LOG and V$LOGFILE to explore which log files are allocated to each thread, their sizes, names, and other characteristics.

Enabling Archive Logs in the RAC Environment

As mentioned, online redolog files are reused by Oracle in a circular manner. To facilitate media recovery, Oracle allows you to make a copy of the online redolog files before they are reused. This process called *archiving*.

DBCA allows you to enable archiving at the time of database creation. If the database has been created in no archive log mode, use the following process to change to archive log mode:

1. Set `cluster_database=false` for the instance:

   ```
   alter system set cluster_database=false scope=spfile sid= 'prod1';
   ```

2. Shut down all the instances accessing the database:

   ```
   srvctl stop database -d prod
   ```

3. Mount the database using the local instance:

   ```
   SQL> startup mount
   ```

4. Enable archiving:

   ```
   SQL> alter database archivelog;
   ```

5. Change the parameter `cluster_database=true` for the instance prod1:

   ```
   alter system set cluster_database=true scope=spfile sid='prod1'
   ```

6. Shut down the local instance:

   ```
   SQL> shutdown ;
   ```

7. Bring up all the instances:

   ```
   srvctl start database -d prod
   ```

Once in archive log mode, each instance can archive redologs automatically.

Enabling the Flashback Area

Oracle Database 10g Release 1 introduced the flashback area to roll back the database to a time in the recent past. A flashback log is different from an archive log and is kept in a separate location specified by flashback log location.

The procedure for enabling the flashback is similar to the procedure for enabling the archiving log mode—it requires the database to be mounted in the exclusive mode. If you attempt to enable flashback while mounted/open in shared mode, Oracle will signal an error.

The following steps enable the database's flashback mode. This can be done from any node.

1. Verify that the database is running in archive log mode (if not already enabled, use the preceding procedure to enable archive log mode):

   ```
   SQL> archive log list
   Database log mode              Archive Mode
   Automatic archival             Enabled
   Archive destination            /u01/app/oracle/10g/dbs/arch
   Oldest online log sequence     59
   Next log sequence to archive   60
   Current log sequence           60
   ```

2. Set `cluster_database=false` for the instance to perform this operation.

   ```
   alter system set cluster_database=false scope=spfile sid= 'prod1';
   ```

3. If not already done, set the parameters `DB_RECOVERY_FILE_DEST_SIZE` and `DB_RECOVERY_FILE_DEST`. The `DB_RECOVERY_FILE_DEST` parameter should point to a shareable disk subsystem as it needs to be accessible to all the instances. The value of the `DB_RECOVERY_FILE_DEST_SIZE` parameter should be same for all the instances.

   ```
   alter system set DB_RECOVERY_FILE_DEST_SIZE=200M scope=SPFILE;
   alter system set DB_RECOVERY_FILE_DEST='/ocfs2/flashback' scope=SPFILE;
   ```

4. Shut down all instances accessing the database:

   ```
   srvctl stop database -d prod
   ```

5. Mount the database using the local instance:

   ```
   SQL> startup mount
   ```

6. Enable the flashback by issuing the following command:

   ```
   SQL> alter database flashback on;
   ```

7. Change back the parameter to `cluster_database=true` for the instance prod1:

   ```
   alter system set cluster_database=true scope=spfile sid='prod1'
   ```

8. Shut down the instance:

   ```
   SQL> shutdown;
   ```

9. Start all the instances:

   ```
   $srvctl start database -d prod
   ```

Managing Database Configuration with SRVCTL

SRVCTL, or the server control utility, is a command-line utility. The functions performed by SRVCTL can be divided into two major groups:

- Database configuration tasks
- Database instance control tasks

Oracle stores database configuration information in a repository. In Oracle 9i, the repository is located in a file stored as srvConfig.loc. The file itself should be located on a shared storage device so that it can be accessed from all the nodes. In Oracle 10g, the repository information is stored in the Oracle Cluster Registry (OCR) that is created while installing CRS and must be located on shared storage.

Type **srvctl** without any command-line options to display usage options:

```
$ srvctl
Usage: srvctl <command> <object> [<options>]
command: enable|disable|start|stop|relocate|status|add|remove|modify|getenv|setenv|
unsetenv|config
objects: database|instance|service|nodeapps|vip_range
For detailed help on each command and object and its options use:
srvctl <command> <object> -h
```

As indicated in this output, use the −h option of the `srvctl` command to display detailed help. The following sample output is from a 10.1.0.3.0 database:

```
srvctl -h
Usage: srvctl [-V]
Usage: srvctl add database -d <name> -o <oracle_home> [-m <domain_name>] [-p <spfile>]
[-A <name|ip>/netmask] [-r {PRIMARY | PHYSICAL_STANDBY | LOGICAL_STANDBY}] [-s <start_
options>] [-n <db_name>]
Usage: srvctl add instance -d <name> -i <inst_name> -n <node_name>
Usage: srvctl add service -d <name> -s <service_name> -r "<preferred_list>"
[-a "<available_list>"] [-P <TAF_policy>]
Usage: srvctl add service -d <name> -s <service_name> -u {-r "<new_pref_inst>" | -a
"<new_avail_inst>"}
```

```
Usage: srvctl add nodeapps -n <node_name> -o <oracle_home> -A <name|ip>/netmask
[/if1[|if2|...]]
Usage: srvctl add asm -n <node_name> -i <asm_inst_name> -o <oracle_home> [-p <spfile>]
….. <<<<Part of the out put deleted here>>>>>>>>>>>]
Usage: srvctl status instance -d <name> -i "<inst_name_list>" [-f] [-v] [-S <level>]
Usage: srvctl status service -d <name> -s "<service_name_list>" [-f] [-v] [-S <level>]
Usage: srvctl status nodeapps -n <node_name>
Usage: srvctl status asm -n <node_name>
Usage: srvctl stop database -d <name> [-o <stop_options>] [-c <connect_str> | -q]
Usage: srvctl stop instance -d <name> -i "<inst_name_list>" [-o <stop_options>]
[-c <connect_str> | -q]
Usage: srvctl stop service -d <name> [-s "<service_name_list>" [-i <inst_name>]]
[-c <connect_str> | -q] [-f]
Usage: srvctl stop nodeapps -n <node_name>
Usage: srvctl stop asm -n <node_name> [-i <asm_inst_name>] [-o <start_options>]
Usage: srvctl unsetenv database -d <name> -t "<name_list>"
Usage: srvctl unsetenv instance -d <name> [-i <inst_name>] -t "<name_list>"
Usage: srvctl unsetenv service -d <name> [-s <service_name>] -t "<name_list>"
Usage: srvctl unsetenv nodeapps -n <node_name> -t "<name_list>"
```

Let's have a look at some of the sample commands. To display the databases registered in the repository:

```
$srvctl config database
prod
test
```

To display the status of database prod:

```
$ srvctl status database -d prod
Instance prod1 is running on node node_a
Instance prod2 is running on node node_b
Instance prod3 is running on node node_c
```

To check nodeapps running on a node:

```
$srvctl status nodeapps -n node_a
VIP is running on node: node_a
GSD is running on node: node_a
PRKO-2016 : Error in checking condition of listener on node: node_a
ONS daemon is not running on node: node_a
```

Although mostly transparent to the end user and the DBA, CRS, introduced in Oracle 10g, has changed the mechanism SRVCTL uses to interface with the database. In Oracle 10g, OCR is used to store all the information, including the database configuration information used by SRVCTL utility. SRVCTL uses CRS to communicate and perform startup and shutdown functions on other nodes. On Oracle 9i, SRVCTL uses Global Services Daemon (GSD) to perform instance startup and shutdown operations. GSD should be started before SRVCTL can be used. SRVCTL stores database information in a repository known as the Server Control Repository that must reside on shared storage as it is accessed from all the nodes.

Managing Database Objects

Managing database objects in an RAC environment is similar to managing them in a single instance environment. In this section, we point out particular items to which you should pay special attention in the RAC environment.

Managing Tablespaces

To alleviate any concern for contention in an RAC environment, you should use all tablespaces with Automatic Segment Space Management (ASSM). ASSM was introduced in Oracle 9i and eliminates the need to define freelists, freelist groups, and so on in an RAC environment.

Use the following SQL command to verify whether all your tablespaces are using ASSM.

```
SQL> select tablespace_name, SEGMENT_SPACE_MANAGEMENT
  2  from dba_tablespaces ;
TABLESPACE_NAME                  SEGMENT
------------------------------   -------
SYSTEM                           MANUAL
UNDOTBS1                         MANUAL
SYSAUX                           AUTO
TEMP                             MANUAL
USERS                            AUTO
UNDOTBS2                         MANUAL
EXAMPLE                          AUTO
UNDOTBS3                         MANUAL;
```

By default, the `create tablespace` command creates a tablespace with ASSM. All you need to do is *not* use the `MANUAL` clause.

ASSM characteristics cannot be specified at the object level. For an object to use ASSM, create the object in an ASSM tablespace.

Managing Sequences

It is good practice to increase the cache values for the sequences that are used by multiple concurrent sessions in multiple instances. This will eliminate the possibility of contention on sequences. The default value for cache sequence is 20. However, depending on the frequency of use, cache values as high as 2,000 could be acceptable. The disadvantage of using a very high cache value is that the unused sequence numbers are lost in the event of an instance's crash or when a shared pool is flushed.

Managing Tables

The Oracle RAC environment does not require specific treatment for tables. Best practices, such as partitioning very large tables and avoiding "hot" I/O spots by putting active tables on different spindles that are followed in a single instance environment, are sufficient for RAC as well.

Managing Indexes

Avoiding contention on B-tree index blocks is a huge challenge in designing highly scalable systems. A good application design, whether it is for a single instance environment or for RAC, should use all available techniques for avoiding index block contention. Partitioned indexes and reverse key indexes are the two most commonly used techniques available to avoid index block contention.

In a Nutshell

Administering the RAC database is similar to managing the single instance Oracle database. As more than one instance is accessing the same set of database objects, a little caution is required while managing the RAC database. However, each RAC instance has the dependency of the Oracle Cluster Ready Services, and we will discuss the administration of the Oracle clusterware in the next chapter.

CHAPTER
8

RAC Advanced
Administration

anaging various types of workloads is a challenging task in the RAC environment. Oracle 10g made this process simpler by introducing services where the workload is split and distributed among the available instances. Also, RAC can relocate services among instances in response to planned and unplanned outages, which greatly extends the availability and scalability of RAC environments.

Understanding Services

Services are used to manage the workload in an RAC environment. They provide a logical way to group a workload so that users employing the same set of data and functionalities can be grouped together to use the same services. For example, an online transaction processing (OLTP) service can be defined for the users who execute small, short-lived transactions; a BATCH service can be defined for users executing long-running batch transactions; a data warehousing (DW) service can be defined for users using data warehousing features; and so on. Another useful way to group users could be according to type of functionalities used, such as Sales, Human Resources, Order Entry, and so on.

Following are some of the important features of services:

- Services are used to distribute the workload. The RAC Load Balancing Advisory provides workload execution efficiency and system resource availability information to listeners and mid-tier servers to route the incoming workload in an optimal manner.

- Services can be configured to provide high availability. You can configure multiple instances to provide the same services. If an instance or a node failure occurs, the workload can be relocated to another existing instance.

- Services provide a transparent way to direct workload. In many cases, users may not even notice the instance, node, or the machine from where the services are being provided.

Service Characteristics

The v$services view contains information about services that have been started on that instance—that is, services being currently served by that instance. Here is sample output from v$services:

```
SQL> select name,network_name, creation_date, goal, dtp, AQ_HA_NOTIFICATION,
clb_goal from v$services
SQL> /
NAME              NETWORK_NAME      CREATION_ GOAL         D AQ_ CLB_G
---------------   ---------------   --------- ------------ - --- -----
prodXDB           prodXDB           10-AUG-05 NONE         N NO  LONG
prod              prod              10-AUG-05 NONE         N NO  LONG
SYS$BACKGROUND                      30-JUN-05 NONE         N NO  SHORT
SYS$USERS                           30-JUN-05 NONE         N NO  SHORT
```

Note that services, which have not been started on the instance, are not shown in the view. The characteristics of services are briefly described here, and many of these concepts are explained in detail in Chapter 13.

NOTE
Many of the characteristics of services are applicable only in Oracle Database 10g R2.

Goal   Oracle Database 10g R2 allows you to define a service goal using SERVICE TIME, THROUGHPUT, or NONE.

Connect Time Load Balancing Goal   Listeners and mid-tier servers contain current information about service performance at the available instances. A new connection intending to use the service can be directed to available instances considering the short- or long-term load balancing characteristics of the service.

Distributed Transaction Processing   If an external transaction manager is being used and is required to ensure that all SQL statements of a transaction are processed on the same instance, you must define this characteristic as YES. Distributed transactions must use this service while connecting to the database. For details on how distributed transactions work and how to implement distributed transactions in an application, refer to the Oracle Database Application Developer's Guide.

AQ_HA_Notifications   When set to TRUE, information about an instance being up or down, or about similar events, will be sent to the mid-tier servers via the advance queuing mechanism.

Preferred and Available Instances   *Preferred* instances for a service are instances in which the service will be started, and these instances will serve the users. *Available* instances are the backup instances; the service will be started on these instances in the event of failure of preferred instances.

To view a service's high availability (HA) characteristics, you can use the srvctl command:

```
$srvctl config service -d prod -s hr.us.oracle.com
hr.us.oracle.com PREF: prod1 AVAIL: prod2
```

Administering Services

The following tools are available for administering services:

- **DBCA**   An easy and intuitive GUI tool to create and modify services.
- **EM**   An easy and intuitive GUI tool to manage services.
- **DBMS_SERVICES**   Provides a programmatic interface to manage services.
- **Server control**   A comprehensive command-line RAC administration tool. DBCA and EM in turn call this tool.

Oracle highly recommends the use of DBCA and EM for managing services.

Creating Services

When DBCA is used to create a database, by default it creates a service for the database. The default service is derived from the database name. In addition to the default database service, Oracle also employs the following two services:

- **SYS$BACKGROUND**   This service is used by an instance's background processes only.
- **SYS$USERS**   When users connect to the database without specifying a service they use this service.

These two services are available on all the instances all the time as long as the instance is up. You cannot relocate or disable these two services.

Creating a Service Using DBCA

This is the most preferred and the easiest way to create a service. Using DBCA not only creates the service, it also starts it and creates the required TNS entries in the tnsnames.ora and registers it with the required listeners.

To create a service using DBCA, invoke DBCA and proceed as follows:

1. In the DBCA Welcome Page, choose Oracle Real Application Clusters Database. Click Next.

2. In the Operations screen, choose Services Management. Click Next.

3. In the List of Cluster database page, choose <Select the desired database>and click Next.

4. The Database Services page will appear. Click Add, and then enter the desired service name in the pop-up window. Click Next.

5. Enter the preferred available instance and Transparent Application Failover (TAF) policy by clicking the corresponding radio buttons, and then click Finish.

This will create the service and start it on the preferred instances.

Creating a Service Using Enterprise Manager

Oracle Enterprise Manager (OEM) provides another GUI for managing services. The Create Service page provides all the parameters used to create a service. This page can be located by navigating to the Manage Cluster Database Service page from the Cluster Database Maintenance Home page.

Creating a Service Using the Server Control Utility

Following is the syntax for creating a service using the server control utility:

```
$srvctl add service -d database_name -s service_name -r
preferred_instance(s)-a available_instance(s) [-P TAF_policy]
```

For example, the following command creates a service named *test* defining instances prod1 and prod2 as the preferred instances and instances prod3 and prod4 as available instances and basic TAF policy.

```
$srvctl add service -d prod -s test - r prod1, prod2 -a prod3,
prod4 -P  basic
```

For the service to be available for client connections, the service needs to be started as follows:

```
$srvctl start service -d prod -s test
```

Creating a Service Using the dbms_service Package

The dbms_service package provides a programmatic interface for creating services. Although Database Configuration Assistant (DBCA) and OEM provide easy and intuitive means of creating services, the programmatic interface is useful for packaged applications. Use this package if you need to perform the same operation repetitively.

Table 8-1 describes the parameters for the `create_service` procedure.

Here is an example of creating a service using this procedure:

```
execute dbms_service.create_service ( service_name => 'test.us.oracle.com' -
, network_name => 'test.us.oracle.com' -
, aq_ha_notifications => true -
, failover_method => dbms_service.failover_method_basic -
, failover_type => dbms_service.failover_type_select -
, failover_retries => 180 -
, failover_delay => 5 -
, clb_goal => dbms_service.clb_goal_long);
```

Once created, you can use the `start_service` procedure of the package to start the service:

```
execute dbms_service.start_service('test.us.oracle.com');
```

Parameter	Description
`service_name`	The name of the service to be created.
`network_name`	The name used by clients connecting via SQL*Net. Typically used in tnsnames.ora entry.
`goal`	Defines the workload management goal for the service. The possible values are `goal_service_time`, `goal_thoughtput`, `goal_none`.
`dtp`	A True value for this boolean parameter enables the service for distributed transaction processing. The possible values are TRUE and FALSE.
`aq_ha_notification`	Determines whether HA event notifications are sent via Advanced Qeueing mechanism. This is a boolean parameter with possible values TRUE and FALSE.
`failover_method`	Defines TAF method for the application. Possible values are `basic` and `preconnect`.
`failover_type`	Defines TAF type for the sessions using this service. Possible values are `session`, `select`, and `none`.
`failover_retries`	Specifies the number of tries to attempt in case of failure to connect.
`failover_delays`	Specifies the delay in seconds between the retries.
`clb_goal`	Specifies the connection load balancing goal. Possible values are `clb_goal_short` and `clb_goal_long`.

TABLE 8-1. *Parameters and Descriptions for* `create_service`

For detailed syntax and description of the dbms_service package and procedures, refer to *Oracle Database PL/SQL Packages and Types Reference.*

Other operations such as stopping, removing, modifying service, and so on are similar to the add service operation described here. You can execute them by using the appropriate keywords in the command-line tools or choosing the corresponding options in the GUI tools.

Administering Cluster Ready Services

As you know, CRS is Oracle's cluster software included since Oracle 9i. Oracle CRS can coexist with vendor-supplied clusterware, though third-party clusterware is not required for RAC (except for the HP True64 platform, for which vendor-supplied clustering software is required, even with CRS).

NOTE
The Oracle MetaLink (http://metalink.oracle.com) "Certification and Availability" section on the Web contains information on operating system, clusterware, and RDBMS version certification and compatibility.

Starting and Stopping CRS—Oracle 10g R1

Oracle CRS is started automatically at system boot time. Manually starting and stopping CRS is generally not required, except in the following rare situations:

- Applying a patch set to $ORA CRS HOME
- OS/System maintenance
- Debugging CRS problems

Manual startup of CRS is not supported in Oracle Database 10g R1. Oracle recommends the following procedure to stop CRS in 10g R1 manually:

1. Shut down the end user application accessing the database, including the processes on the middle tier as well as processes running from any of the ORACLE_HOMEs on the server—for example, OEM database control, iSQL*Plus, and so on.

2. Shut down all database instances. Issue commands similar to the following for each database on the system:

   ```
   $ORACLE_HOME/bin/srvctl stop -d database prod
   ```

3. If ASM is used, stop ASM instances on each node by issuing the following command for each node:

   ```
   $ORACLE_HOME/bin/srvctl stop asm -n node1
   ```

4. Stop all nodeapps on all the nodes using the following command for each node:

   ```
   $ORACLE_HOME/bin/srvctl stop nodeapps -n node1
   ```

5. Shut down CRS using the following command. Note that all the commands preceding this were performed as the Oracle *owner* user. However, the following command needs to be executed as *root*:

```
#/etc/init.d/init.crs stop
```

The location of the init.crs is platform dependent; refer to the platform documentation to determine the exact location of init.crs.

Starting and Stopping CRS—Oracle 10g R2

In Oracle Database 10g R2, CRS can be started and stopped using the following command examples.

■ Starting CRS:

```
#ORA_CRS_HOME/bin/crsctl stop crs
Stopping resources.
Successfully stopped CRS resources
Stopping CSSD.
Shutting down CSS daemon.
Shutdown request successfully issued.
```

■ Stopping CRS:

```
#$ORA_CRS_HOME/bin/crsctl start crs
Attempting to start CRS stack
The CRS stack will be started shortly
#
```

It can take few minutes to start CRS. Once started, use the `crsctl check crs` command to verify the CRS and its subcomponents' status:

```
#$ORA_CRS_HOME/bin/crsctl check crs
CSS appears healthy
CRS appears healthy
EVM appears healthy
#$ORA_CRS_HOME/bin /crsctl check evmd
EVM appears healthy
#$ORA_CRS_HOME/bin/crsctl check cssd
CSS appears healthy
#$ORA_CRS_HOME/bin/crsctl check crsd
CRS appears healthy
#
```

Disabling and Enabling CRS

By default, CRS will restart on system reboot. If system maintenance is being done, and CRS needs to be prevented from starting on system reboot, you can disable it. Note that different procedures are used for 10g R1 and 10g R2. Also, the `enable` and `disable` CRS commands are effective only for the future reboots of the node and do not impact the availability of the currently running CRS and its components.

Disabling and Enabling CRS—Oracle 10g R2

In Oracle10g R2 you can use the following commands to enable/disable CRS and it daemons.

- Disable all CRS daemons:

  ```
  #$ORA_CRS_HOME/bin/crsctl disable crs
  ```

- Enable all CRS daemons:

  ```
  #$ORA_CRS_HOME/bin/crsctl enable crs
  ```

Disabling and Enabling CRS—Oracle 10g R1

Follow these steps to disable or enable CRS:

1. Stop all the applications, database instances, ASM instances, and nodeapps as described in the preceding section.

2. Disable CRS using the following command:

   ```
   #/etc/init.d/init.crs disable
   ```

3. Use the enable option of init.crs once the desired system maintenance activity is complete. This will allow CRS to be started on system reboot.

   ```
   #/etc/init.d/init.crs enable
   ```

Rebooting the system in single user node also allows performing system maintenance without disabling/enabling CRS.

CRS Utilities

All CRS utilities are present in the $ORA_CRS_HOME/bin directory. Some of the CRS utilities are also available in ORACLE_HOME; however, you should always use CRS utilities from the $ORA_CRS_HOME/bin directory only. Do not put $ORA_CRS_HOME/bin in your path, but execute these utilities by specifying the full path name.

Table 8-2 briefly describes CRS utilities.

crs_stat

This utility lets you look at the status of various resources controlled by CRS. The command syntax for crs_stat can be obtained by invoking it with the –h option.

```
# ./crs_stat -h
crs_stat [resource_name [...]] [-v] [-l] [-q] [-c cluster_member]
 crs_stat [resource_name [...]] -t [-v] [-q] [-c cluster_member]
 crs_stat -p [resource_name [...]] [-q]
 crs_stat [-a] application -g
 crs_stat [-a] application -r [-c cluster_member]
 crs_stat -f [resource_name [...]] [-q] [-c cluster_member]
 crs_stat -ls [resource_name [...]] [-q]
```

Utility	Description
crs_stat	Queries or displays status of various resources controlled by CRS.
crsctl	CRS control utility used to check, start, stop, get status, enable, and disable CRS components and resources controlled by CRS. Also used for managing OCR and voting disks and debugging various CRS components.
crs_profile	Creates an application resource profile.
crs_register	Registers an application in OCR.
crs_unregister	Unregisters an application from OCR.
crs_start	Starts an application resource controlled by CRS.
crs_stop	Stops an application resources controlled by CRS.
crs_getparam	Finds the permissions associated with a resource.
crs_setparam	Sets permissions for a resource.
crs_relocate	Relocates application resources controlled by CRS.

TABLE 8-2. *CRS Utilities*

Here is a sample output from this command without any command-line argument:

```
#ORA_CRS_HOME/bin/crs_stat
NAME=ora.node_a.gsd
TYPE=application
TARGET=ONLINE
STATE=ONLINE
 . . .
 . . .
```

The output will show GSD, OEM, ONS, and VIP resource status for each node. All the resources are supposed to be online and are available and will be displayed for each TARGET and ONLINE.

crsctl

This diagnostic and debugging utility can also be used to display the status of various CRS components such as css, evm, and so on, and some CSS parameters such as miscount. Following is a sample usage of this utility:

```
$ORA_CRS_HOME/bin/crsctl check install -wait 600
CSS is active on these nodes.
 Node_a
 Node_b
 Node_c
```

```
CSS is active on all nodes.
$ORA_CRS_HOME/bin/crsctl get css misscount
Configuration parameter misscount has value of 60.
$ ORA_CRS_HOME/bin/crsctl check css
CSS daemon appears healthy.
```

This utility can also be used to set the `misscount` parameter, which might be needed if you are using CRS along with third-party clusterware. It is strongly advised to do this with utmost caution and only if directed to do so by Oracle Support Services (OSS). Setting a low value for this parameter can cause sporadic node reboots and make your environment unstable.

olsnodes

Use this utility to check that all the nodes have joined the cluster. The `olsnodes` command syntax is

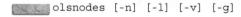 `olsnodes [-n] [-l] [-v] [-g]`

- `-n` displays the member number with the member name
- `-l` displays the local node name
- `-v` activates verbose mode
- `-g` activates logging

You can check the status of Oracle CRS by executing this command without any command-line options. The output should be a listing of the nodes, confirming that CRS is up and running and that all the nodes can communicate to each other via the CRS.

Oracle Interface Configuration—oifcfg

The Oracle Interface Configuration tool helps you to define network interface cards usage in an RAC environment.

NOTE
Network interface configuration that occurs during the installation has changed in 10g R2, as the configuration is done during the CRS install itself. In 10g R1, oifcfg was called by dbca during database creation.

Here are some usage examples for this tool:

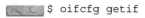 `$ oifcfg getif`

This command should return values for global `public` and global `cluster_interconnect`; for example:

```
en0 144.25.68.0 global public
en5 192.168.100.0 global cluster_interconnect
```

If the command does not return a value for global `cluster_interconnect`, enter the following commands to delete and set the desired interface:

```
# oifcfg delif -global
 # oifcfg setif -global <interface name>/<subnet>:public
 # oifcfg setif -global <interface name>/<subnet>:cluster_interconnect
```

Virtual IP Configuration Assistant—vipca

Starting Oracle 10g RAC requires a virtual IP address in addition to the hardware IP address for the node that is used by the operating system. For a detailed description of VIP, revisit Chapter 3.

This tool helps you configure the VIP address. During CRS installation, vipca is called automatically when root.sh is run. Starting with Oracle 10g R2 you can use Oracle CRS for implementing HA for third-party applications as well. This might require a VIP for each application. Each VIP should be defined in the hosts file and should be in the DNS. When invoked, vipca will ask the network interface to be used for the VIP. Always use a public network interface card (NIC) for VIPs. Once the interface card is chosen, vipca proceeds to ask the VIP address and provide an address in the public domain, as this will be used by client or mid-tier server to connect to the database instance. Once the abovementioned information is collected, vipca proceeds to configure the VIPs and starts the dependent applications such as gsd, ONS, and so on.

Global Services Daemon Control utility—gsdctl

The Global Services daemon can be started using this utility:

```
$gsdctl start
 Successfully started GSD on local node
$gsdctl stat
 GSD is running on the local node
```

Please note that the Global Services daemon is used only for Oracle 9i instances to execute remote control commands via srvctl or OEM.

Cluster Configuration Utility—clscfg

This utility is used during CRS installation and should not be used unless instructed to do so and under guidance from OSS. The command `clscfg -concepts` provides a good description of some CRS concepts, including private interconnect, host names, node names, voting disk, ocssd, evmd, crsd, and ocr.

The following options are available with the Cluster Configuration utility.

```
#$ORA_CRS_HOME/bin/clscfg
clscfg: EXISTING configuration version 3 detected.
clscfg: version 3 is 10G Release 2.
clscfg -- Oracle cluster configuration tool

  This tool is typically invoked as part of the Oracle Cluster Ready
  Services install process. It configures cluster topology and other
  settings. Use -help for information on any of these modes.
```

```
Use one of the following modes of operation.
-install    - creates a new configuration
-upgrade    - upgrades an existing configuration
-downgrade  - downgrades an existing configuration
-add        - adds a node to the configuration
-delete     - deletes a node from the configuration
-local      - creates a special single-node configuration for ASM
-concepts   - brief listing of terminology used in the other modes

-trace      - may be used in conjunction with any mode above for tracing
WARNING: Using this tool may corrupt your cluster configuration. Do not
         use unless you positively know what you are doing.
```

Cluster Name Check Utility—cemutlo

This utility prints the cluster name information. Following is the usage syntax for this utility:

```
#$ORA_CRS_HOME/bin/cemutlo [-n] [-w]
        where:
        -n prints the cluster name
        -w prints the clusterware version in the following format:
                <major_version>:<minor_version>:<vendor_info>
#$ORA_CRS_HOME/bin/cemutlo -n
crs
#$ORA_CRS_HOME/bin/cemutlo -w
2:1:
```

This utility can be used only in Oracle 10g; for Oracle 9i you need to use cemutls.

Add Node Script—addnode.sh

This script must be run when adding a new node to an existing cluster. More details on adding a node to an existing cluster are discussed in Appendix B.

Delete Node Script—deletenode.sh

This script needs to be run when deleting an existing node from a cluster. More details on deleting a node to an existing cluster are discussed in Appendix B.

Administering OCR

OCR is the RAC configuration information repository that manages information about the cluster node list and instance-to-node mapping information. Processes that make up the CRS and other cluster-aware applications use this repository to share information among them. Its contents include but are not limited to the following:

- Node membership information
- Database instance, node, and other mapping information
- Service characteristics
- Characteristics of any third-party applications controlled by CRS (10g R2 and later)

OCR's location is specified during CRS installation. The file pointer indicating the OCR device location is in the file ocr.loc, whose location is somewhat platform dependent. For example, on Linux systems it is located in /etc/oracle, and on Solaris it is located at /var/opt/oracle. The contents of ocr.loc follow:

```
#Device/file  getting replaced by device /ocfs01/ocr2.dbf
ocrconfig_loc=/ocfs01/ocr.dbf
ocrmirrorconfig_loc=/ocfs02/ocr2.dbf
local_only=false
```

The first line offers information about the last operation performed on OCR impacting the contents of the ocr.loc file. The third line is valid for Oracle Database 10g R2 only, which supports mirroring for the OCR device, making it more fault resilient. Version 10g R2 provides a choice of mirroring OCR at the Oracle level or at the OS level to provide high availability.

Little day-to-day maintenance is required for OCR. However, OCR is a critical component of a HA framework, so if anything happens to the OCR you should be prepared to take corrective actions immediately. The following Oracle utilities are used to administer OCR. Practice these commands on a test system to be ready for any eventuality with the OCR:

- ocrcheck   Performs a quick health check on OCR and prints space usage statistics.

- ocrdump   Dumps contents of OCR to an OS file.

- ocrconfig   Performs export, import, add, replace, remove, restore, and show backup operations on OCR.

Checking OCR Integrity

You can use the ocrcheck utility to perform a quick health check on OCR. The command returns the OCR version, total space allocated, space used, free space, location of each device, and the result of integrity check.

```
Status of Oracle Cluster Registry is as follows :
         Version                  :         2
         Total space (kbytes)     :      262144
         Used space (kbytes)      :        3252
         Available space (kbytes) :      258892
         ID                       :    137714859
         Device/File Name         : /ocfs1/ocr.dbf
                              Device/File integrity check succeeded
         Device/File Name         : /ocfs2/ocr2.dbf
                              Device/File integrity check succeeded

         Cluster registry integrity check succeeded
```

The command also creates a log file in the directory $ORACLE_HOME/log/<hostname>/client; the contents of this log file reflect what is displayed in the output.

Dumping OCR Information

The Oracle-supplied utility ocrdump writes the contents of OCR to an OS file. By default it dumps the contents into a file named OCRDUMP in the current directory. Alternatively, you can specify a destination file and can also dump information in XML format. The command-line options available for this command can be viewed by using the command with the -help option.

The contents of the dump file are generally used by OSS to check configuration information in the OCR. The dump file is an ASCII file that you can open using any text editor. The file contains a set of key name, value type, and key value information. The information contained in this file is fairly easy to understand; however, only in very rare situations would you need to consult it.

Managing OCR Backup

Oracle regularly backs up OCR to a default location. The command ocrconfig -showbackup displays the backup destination directory, available backups, and the timestamp for backups:

```
#ocrconfig -showbackup
node2      2005/08/18 19:17:49    /u01/app/oracle/product/10.2.0/crs/cdata/crs
node2      2005/08/18 15:17:48    /u01/app/oracle/product/10.2.0/crs/cdata/crs
node2      2005/08/18 11:17:47    /u01/app/oracle/product/10.2.0/crs/cdata/crs
node2      2005/08/17 03:17:42    /u01/app/oracle/product/10.2.0/crs/cdata/crs
node2      2005/08/10 15:17:20    /u01/app/oracle/product/10.2.0/crs/cdata/crs
```

You can take an offline backup of OCR by making the backup copies from this location at regular intervals. The command ocrconfig - backuploc <dirname> can be used to change the backup directory for OCR.

NOTE
A backup of OCR by copying the OCR file directly at the OS level is not valid and will result in errors after the restore.

Exporting OCR

Export OCR using the ocrconfig -export <filename> command. Export is highly recommended after making significant configuration changes. The command creates a binary file specified in the command line. The binary file can be further backed up using any of the OS commands. Note that you cannot restore OCR from an export file. An OCR import can be used only to import the configuration from an export file.

Restoring OCR

In case all the copies of OCR are lost or the current copy of the OCR becomes unusable, you might need to restore OCR. The command ocrconfig -restore <filename> is the only mechanism available to restore OCR. The command needs to be executed when CRS has been stopped on all the nodes.

Maintaining a Mirror OCR

Version 10g R2 allows you to create mirror OCR, thereby removing OCR as a single point of failure. It also eliminates the need for mirroring OCR using methods external to Oracle.

The following command adds/relocates the ocrmirror file to the specified location:

```
ocrconfig -replace ocrmirror '/ocfs2/ocr2.dbf'
```

NOTE
`ocrconfig -replace` is the only way to add/relocate OCR files. Copying the existing OCR file to new location and manually adding/ changing the file pointer in the ocr.loc file is not supported and will not work.

You can use the following command to relocate an existing OCR file:

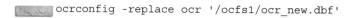

```
ocrconfig -replace ocr '/ocfs1/ocr_new.dbf'
```

You can relocate OCR only when OCR is mirrored. To relocate OCR or mirror to a new location, another copy of OCR should be fully functional.

NOTE
OCR mirror add/relocate operations can be performed while CRS is running and hence does not require any system downtime.

The command `ocrconfig -replace ocr` or `ocrconfig -replace ocrmirror` can be used to remove the OCR or the ocrmirror. There is no need to specify the file location as an option on the command line. It will retrieve the file location and remove the intended file.

Administering the Voting Disk

Oracle CRS uses a voting disk to resolve cluster membership issues in the event of partitioned clusters. Consider an eight-node cluster experiencing a breakdown in communication between the nodes—four nodes cannot communicate with the other four nodes. Situations like this can cause serious data integrity issues. A voting disk or a quorum disk provides a mechanism to resolve such issues. In case of a break in communication and a partitioned cluster, a voting disk helps in deciding which set of nodes should survive if another set of nodes should go down.

All voting disks must be placed on shared storage to be accessible by all the nodes. A voting disk is a small file if you are using a raw device for it; a 20MB raw device should be used for each voting disk. Oracle 10g R1 supports only one disk, but version 10g R2 supports up to 32 voting disks. Having multiple voting disks removes the voting disk as a single point of failure and eliminates the need to mirror them outside Oracle. Oracle Universal Installer (OUI) allows you to specify up to three voting disks during CRS installation. Having three voting disks allows CRS operation to continue uninterrupted when any of the three voting disks fails. For the cluster to survive failure of x number of voting disks, you needs to configure $(2x+1)$ voting disks.

NOTE
Adding and removing voting disks is documented to work with CRS and should not require any cluster-wide downtime. However, this functionality doesn't currently work in Oracle Database 10g R2 and is expected to be fixed in future patch sets.

When functional, as documented, you should be able to use the following commands:

- `crsctl add css votedisk <filename>`   Adds a voting disk.
- `crsctl delete css votedisk <filename>`   Deletes an existing voting disk. This does not remove the physical file at the OS level.
- `crsctl query css votedisk`   Lists the voting disks being used.

In a Nutshell

In this chapter we explored how using RAC services helps in workload management. Managing and administering services become easier with this Oracle-supplied package. We also discussed various utilities for managing Oracle cluster-ready services, including the Oracle cluster registry and voting disk. These utilities make managing Oracle clusterware relatively simple.

CHAPTER
9

RAC Backup
and Recovery

n this chapter we discuss the key concepts in backup and recovery operations of Real Application Clusters (RAC) databases. Basic backup and recovery methods for the RAC database are similar to those for single instance databases. No special considerations for media recovery or any other advanced recovery mechanisms are required, so this chapter does *not* cover generic backup (and recovery) mechanisms. Here we discuss the recovery issues that are specific to RAC, starting from the basics and then delving deeper into RAC-based backup and recovery and other information that is not easily available or accessible.

Introduction to Backups

One of the key features of the Oracle RDBMS engine is its ability to back up and recover from various kinds of faults, disasters, and human errors. The Oracle backup and recovery mechanism has evolved since its early days of Oracle 6 into a near "fault-tolerant" database engine that can guarantee data protection as well as recoverability more than any other database vendor's product. Transaction recovery is possible mainly due to the redolog. The structure of the redolog and its associated buffer has undergone changes since the days of Oracle 6 when it was first introduced, but it largely remains the same and its prime purpose and importance inside Oracle remains.

Oracle has developed its own tools/utilities (Recovery Manager, or RMAN) to perform backups and restore/recover a database in the simplest or easiest ways possible. Oracle also provides the user with the flexibility to choose between RMAN and other tools to make backups and restore data. Recovery of restored data can be done only through an Oracle Interface such as SQL *Plus or RMAN.

Oracle Backup Options

Generally, Oracle's backup options can be classified based on the tools or technologies used to implement them. The following serves as a rough guide to understanding the various tools used for Oracle backups in the industry today.

Small, Noncritical Databases

These include operating system (OS) built-in utilities such as tar, cpio, and so on, that are available to Windows users. The backup media can be a tape or disk. Usually, Windows systems do not have a separate backup tool or framework. This type of backup is almost exclusively a closed database backup, where the business operation has the luxury of performing a *cold backup*—stopping and shutting down the databases for a backup.

Medium to Large Databases

These databases may also use common utilities such as tar and cpio. DBAs generally write or borrow automated scripts to perform these backups. Servers have a fast tape drive or two connected to the database host. Automated tape libraries are used in large organizations. It is common to find backup tools such as Veritas NetBackup, HP OmniBack or Storage Data Protector, IBM Tivoli, and so on, implemented at the database level. RMAN is also widely used but with a lesser degree of integration with the third-party backup tools.

Oracle Data Guard is increasingly becoming a standard choice for disaster recovery in many types of organizations. Since Oracle 8i, Data Guard has presented a "near real-time switchover capability" that was not possible before with an Oracle database. Additional server hardware and disk storage (equivalent to your primary system) is required to implement Data Guard.

Enterprise Databases

These are big-spending mega-corporations that use sophisticated technologies such as disk mirroring and splitting and remote geographical mirroring, which could be in conjunction with cluster technologies such as Oracle RAC. These companies may also deploy large, automated tape libraries or robotic libraries with scores of tape drives and redundancies. It has become increasing difficult for tape libraries to keep up with the rapid pace of Oracle data growth. Backup as well recovery time is critical here. To overcome this time constraint, large enterprises employ disk mirroring as a method of quick data backup and also use the copy for reporting purposes or as a standby database. This comes at an extra cost, which can be millions of dollars.

Oracle Backup Basics

Oracle backups can be taken at the physical level (hot or cold) or at the logical level. A physical backup comprises the following:

- Datafiles
- Control files
- Archived redolog files (if the database is in ARCHIVELOG mode)
- Parameter files (init.ora and SPFILE)

A physical backup is performed by taking an OS copy of these files. Alternatively, RMAN can be used to accomplish the backup of the database files with an exception of the init.ora file. It is a well-known fact that online redologs need not be backed up, irrespective of the fact that a database is in ARCHIVELOG mode or NOARCHIVELOG mode. For detailed information on this topic and other basics mentioned in this chapter, refer to the *Oracle 9i/10g Backup and Recovery Concepts User's Guide*.

Performing Backups in Oracle

Oracle databases exist in every size and shape. With terabyte-sized databases becoming as common as PlayStations and Nintendos, large organizations and corporations no longer depend on tape libraries for backups; sophisticated disk mirroring mechanisms haven taken their place. Oracle as a database company has come up with excellent solutions such as RMAN and Oracle Data Guard, which allow even the largest databases to be backed up. The backup scheme needs to be chosen carefully. Some like to back up to disk and then push data to tape while others like to back up directly to tape.

In Oracle, full and incremental backups can be performed using RMAN by itself or in combination with other third-party backup tools such as IBM Tivoli, Veritas NetBackup, and HP Storage Data Protector. If a third-party tool is to be used without RMAN integration, the traditional method of putting a database in backup mode and pulling it out is to be followed. Oracle 10g allows you to put the whole database in backup mode with a single command, whereas prior to version 10g, each tablespace had to be put in backup mode and pulled out at the end of a backup.

RMAN Backup for RAC Databases

RMAN is capable of handling RAC databases, and it can be configured to perform RAC database backups. Beginning with Oracle 9i, many of the configuration items are now persistent and need to be performed only once during the setup phase. As mentioned, RMAN should be actively considered as the backup solution even for RAC. The only consideration would be the time taken to perform the backup for large databases (larger than 500GB) when tape drives or tape libraries are used, as this would be the same whether RAC is used or not. In such cases, disk mirroring technology can be used if backup and restore time is of prime importance and/or database size exceeds a terabyte.

Choosing the Archive Log Destination in an RAC Database   Configuring the ARCHIVELOG mode in an RAC database is a crucial decision for a DBA. Since archive logs can be placed on a CFS drive (shared) or a local drive (non-shared), it has serious implications on your backup and recovery strategies. The primary consideration is to ensure that all archived redologs can be read from every node during recovery and if possible even during backups, irrespective of whether or not RMAN is used.

The key point to understand is that when a node generates an archived redolog, Oracle always records the file name of the archived log in the control file of the database. If you are using RMAN with a recovery catalog, RMAN also records the archived redolog file names in the recovery catalog when a resynchronization occurs. However, archived log file path names do not include the node name, so RMAN expects to find the files it needs on the nodes where the channels are allocated.

The archived redolog naming scheme that you use is important because when a node writes to a log with a specific file name on its file system (or CFS), the file must be readable by any node that needs to access this archived redolog for backup and/or recovery purposes.

The backup and recovery strategy that you choose depends on how you configure the archiving destinations for each node. It doesn't matter if only one or all nodes perform archived redolog backups; you need to ensure that all archived redologs are backed up.

If a cluster file system is used, all instances can write to a single archive log destination. Backup and recovery of the archive logs are easy because all logs are centrally located. If a cluster file system is not available, Oracle generally recommends that local archive log destinations be used for each instance with Network File System (NFS) read mount points to all other instances. This is known as the *local archive with NFS scheme*. During backup, you can either back up the archive logs from each host or select one host to perform the backup for all archive logs. During recovery, one instance may access the logs from any host without having to copy them first to the local destination. It is still crucial to provide a second archive destination to avoid single points of failure, irrespective of the scheme being used.

If RMAN parallelism is used during recovery, the node that performs recovery must have access to all the archived redologs in your cluster. Multiple nodes can restore archived logs in parallel. However, during recovery, only one node applies the archived logs. Therefore, the node that is performing the recovery must be able to access all of the archived logs that are needed for recovery.

Data Guard and RAC
Data Guard was first introduced in Oracle 8i as Standby Database and has since undergone many enhancements. Oracle 9i introduced Data Guard with support for Real Application Clusters (RAC). By this we mean that the primary database can be RAC and/or the standby database can be RAC. This provides for and extends the maximum availability demands that 24×7 shops place on database and other systems today. Data Guard also works seamlessly with RMAN, and this integration is helpful for creating standby databases using the DUPLICATE DATABASE command. Refer to the *Oracle Recovery Manager Reference* for more details.

Instance Recovery in RAC

Instance recovery in Oracle RAC (9i and 10g) is not radically different from the way it is performed on a single instance. Some additional steps are required since redo entries for a data block can now exist in any redo threads. Hence, global (clusterwide) coordination and synchronization is required to ensure that the consistency and reliability of data blocks are maintained, just like the Oracle recovery mechanism would in the case of a single instance recovery.

At this juncture, it is important that you understand the subtle differences in the terms *instance recovery* and *crash recovery*. Though they generally mean the same thing in terms of operations, some minor contextual differences exist.

In a single instance environment, crash and instance recovery are one and the same. In RAC, *crash recovery* means that all instances in the RAC database have failed and hence all instances have to be recovered or all instances may need recovery, depending on the operations they were performing. The point is, in RAC crash recovery, all instances need to participate and are qualified candidates for recovery operations.

Instance recovery means that one or more instances in the cluster database have failed and need to be recovered by the other surviving instance. Thread recovery is applicable in both situations since a single instance is being recovered, and the term generally describes the recovery of a single thread (or instance) in a cluster database and has more relevance in an RAC database than in a single instance scenario.

The following section looks at the key concepts of recovery operations in the RAC database. Instance recovery and media recovery involve additional steps in the RAC environment as multiple redo streams record database changes, and they should be seamlessly applied to the database during recovery in a chronological order. The following structures ensure the recovery operations in RAC databases.

Redo Threads and Streams

Redo information generated by an instance is called a *thread of redo*. All log files for that instance belong to this thread. An online redolog file belongs to a group and the group belongs to a thread. If the database is running in ARCHIVELOG mode, the thread is nothing but all the archived redolog files. If the server is running in NOARCHIVELOG, then the thread is effectively the size of the online redolog files. A record in the control file describes each and every online redolog file. Details about the log file group and thread association details are stored in the control file.

A *redo stream* consists of all the threads of redo information ever recorded. The stream forms a timeline of changes performed to the database. In a single instance, the terms *thread* and *stream* refer to the same thing since a single instance has only one thread. RAC databases have multiple threads of redo—that is, each active instance has one active thread. In RAC, the threads are parallel timelines and together form the stream.

Redo Records and Change Vectors

When users make changes to the database, Oracle records them in the redolog file as *change vectors*. Each change vector is a description of a single change, usually to a single block. A set of change vector structures makes up the content of each redo record. A redo record contains one or more change vectors and is located by its *Redo Byte Address* (RBA) and points to a specific location in a redolog file (or a thread). It consists of three components: a log sequence number, block number within log, and byte number within block.

Checkpoints

Checkpoints are important database events that synchronize the database buffer cache and the datafiles. Without the various checkpoint mechanisms, recovery of data would be impossible. Checkpoints are used to determine the location or point from where recovery should start. This is the most important use of checkpoints and is indispensable in instance recovery (single and RAC).

In simple but crude terms, a checkpoint is a framework that enables the writing of dirty blocks to disk based on an System Commit Number (SCN) and RBA validation algorithm and, more importantly, limits the number of blocks required for recovery.

Checkpoints ensure that data blocks that have redos generated up to a point in the redolog are written to disk. Checkpoint information is stored in a data structure called the *checkpoint structure*, which defines (points to) a specific location in a given redolog file. Checkpoint structures are stored in datafile headers and in the control file and are usually made up of the checkpoint SCN, checkpoint RBA, thread ID, timestamp, and some other control information. Like an RBA, these structures are used to find the starting point for reading the redolog for redo application.

Checkpoints are triggered by a number of events (such as log switches, hot backups, shutdowns) that in turn produce different types of checkpoints. The most important ones are briefly explained next.

Thread Checkpoint or Local Checkpoint

A thread checkpoint collects all dirty buffers in an instance that contain changes to any online datafile before a designated SCN—the thread checkpoint SCN—and writes them to disk. The SCN is associated with a specific RBA in the log, which is used to determine when all the buffers have been written. A thread checkpoint can occur at a log switch or if any of the thread checkpoint conditions are satisfied.

All blocks dirtied prior to this thread checkpoint SCN in that thread for all online data files are written to disk. In an RAC database, a thread checkpoint occurs independently and separately for each instance, since each has its own thread or redo. This information is recorded in a structure called the *thread checkpoint structure* and in multiple control file records and all online datafile headers.

Database Checkpoint or Global Checkpoint

When a database checkpoint needs to be triggered, Oracle looks for the thread checkpoint that has the lowest checkpoint SCN for all open and enabled threads (highest checkpoint SCN for all closed threads), and that itself becomes the database checkpoint. All blocks in memory that contain changes made prior to this SCN across all instances must be written out to disk. For a single instance database, a database checkpoint is the same as a thread checkpoint. The information is recorded in several control file records and all online datafile headers.

Incremental Checkpoint

When data blocks are modified in the buffer cache, they are placed in a queue called the Checkpoint Queue (CKPTQ) for background writing by the DBWR process. The CKPTQ was introduced in Oracle 8. This queue is ordered by the RBA of the first log record to modify the block, which is nothing but the earliest modification record for that block. The oldest dirty blocks are the first in the queue and are waiting to be written out. Since Oracle 8i, when the touch count mechanism was introduced, some blocks may still remain in the buffer cache if it is an active buffer or a hot buffer.

Log History Considerations

The control file always maintains a record of the archived log files generated for each thread. This enables an instance that is performing media recovery to identify the archived log files that it needs regardless of which instance generated them. The number of entries that are maintained in the control file is determined by the value assigned with the MAXLOGHISTORY setting in the CREATE DATABASE command.

Usually, DBAs overlook or sometimes do not pay much attention to the log history until the following occurs:

- Oracle complains that you cannot create more online redolog files during an attempt to create them.

- Standby redolog files cannot be created in a physical Data Guard setup.

- The DBA is asked to generate metrics about the rate at which redo is generated.

Generally, it is recommended that MAXLOGHISTORY should not be less than the total number of archived log files that are generated across all your instances between each complete database backup. This enables a recovering instance to identify the archived log files that it requires after you restore the most recent backup.

If there are insufficient archived log entries in your control file, you are prompted for the required file names when you initiate the recovery process. This can be hard to do when hundreds or maybe thousands of archived logs needs to be applied. To increase the size of the MAXLOGHISTORY setting, the control file must be recreated.

The idea behind incremental checkpoints is to reduce the amount of redo that has to be read during instance recovery. This allows instance recovery time to be bounded by a DBA. To accomplish this, an "in memory" checkpoint record is updated approximately every 3 seconds and action is also taken to ensure that the number and age of dirty data blocks in the cache are limited.

A CKPTQ enables the incremental checkpoint to avoid having a cache filled with many dirty blocks, which all must be written at once when a checkpoint occurs. By keeping the dirty block count low, the number of blocks that need to be recovered in case of a crash is fewer, resulting in faster database recovery. The length of this list is an indicator of the amount of blocks that need recovery if the block is lost in a crash. Information on this is visible in the V$INSTANCE_RECOVERY view.

Crash Recovery

The internal mechanics of recovery are well beyond the discussion context of this chapter, yet it is important to remind you of some important characteristics of recovering a single instance (non-OPS or RAC). As mentioned earlier, the terms *instance* and *crash recovery* refer to the same recovery aspect. The only notable difference is that in RAC, crash recovery involves *all* the instances. For a single instance, crash recovery and instance recovery are the same. Some of these points are also applicable to RAC databases since the mechanisms are basically the same.

Steps in Crash Recovery (Single Instance)

When an instance failure (which leads to a database crash in a single instance database) occurs, the following is the recovery process.

1. The on-disk version of a block is the starting point for recovery. Oracle will need to consider only the block on disk and the recovery is straightforward. Crash recovery is automatic, using the online redologs that are current or active.

2. The starting point of a thread recovery is at most at the last full checkpoint. The starting point is provided in the control file and compared against the same information in all data file headers. Only the changes from a single redo thread need to be applied.

3. The block specified in the redolog is read into the cache. If the block has the same timestamp as the redo record (SCN match is satisfied), the redo is applied. The block is then written out by a recovery checkpoint at a log switch or when aged out of the cache.

Crash Recovery in RAC

Oracle performs instance recovery automatically upon detecting that an instance has died. Instance/crash recovery is performed automatically when the database is opened for the first time after a crash or when one of the instances of an RAC database fails. In the case of RAC, a surviving instance detects the need to perform instance recovery for one or more failed instances by the following methods:

1. A foreground process in a surviving instance detects an "invalid block lock" condition when an attempt is made to read a block into the buffer cache. This is an indication that another instance died while a block covered by that lock was in a potentially dirty state in its buffer cache.

2. The foreground process sends a notification to its instance's System Monitor (SMON) process, which begins a search for dead instances.

3. The death of another instance is detected if the current instance is able to acquire that instance's redo thread locks, which is usually held by an open and active instance.

NOTE
In RAC, the SMON process in the surviving instance obtains a reliable list of dead instances together with a list of "invalid" block locks. These locks are invalid because the instance that had locked these blocks has crashed and their status remains "fuzzy" and/or unknown. The SMON also performs the recovery (Oracle 8.1.7 onward). The instance performing the recovery would then clean up these locks and make them available for normal use as soon as recovery and cleanup are complete.

Instance Recovery

The procedure used to recover from single instance crash failures as well as RAC instances failures is called *instance recovery*. In case of RAC, a surviving instance recovers all the failed instances. Instance recovery aims to restore the data block changes that were in the cache of the failed instance and to close the thread that was left open. Instance recovery uses only online redolog files and current online datafiles (not restored backups).

Instance Recovery in OPS

In Oracle Parallel Server (OPS), instance recovery processes one thread at a time and recovers one instance at a time. It applies all redo (from the thread checkpoint through the end-of-thread) from each thread before starting on the next thread.

This scheme depends on the fact that only one instance at a time can have a given block modified in its cache (both single instance and OPS). In OPS, if a change is to be made to the block by other instances, the block is written to disk by the holding instance before the requesting instance can make a change. This was the ping protocol mechanism used in pre-RAC days and in some current block copy situations. You may recall that a holding instance must write the block to disk if another instance requests the same block for modification.

The recovery process uses the checkpoint structure to know where to start reading the thread in a database. When a surviving instance is recovering a failed OPS instance, a redo from only one thread (crashed instance) needs to be applied to a given block (as read from disk during instance recovery). This is because only this thread contains the most recent modification for that block. This is also the case for single instance or crash recovery. This kind of recovery is also called *one-thread-at-a-time* recovery since one thread is recovered at a time.

Instance recovery is always done using the online redologs. Recovery starts with the thread with the highest checkpoint SCN. It continues to recover the threads in the order of decreasing thread checkpoint SCNs. This avoids advancing the database checkpoint by each thread recovered. Once the one-thread-at-a-time procedure completes recovering all the threads, the database checkpoint is advanced at the end of recovery.

Note that for OPS, other complex recovery operations such as distributed lock manager (DLM) freeze and reconfiguration, lock invalidation and cleaning, cluster communications, and so on, are not presented here. Some of these will be discussed in the recovery steps later in this chapter.

With Oracle 9i and Cache Fusion Phase II, disk ping is avoided in many situations because the holding instance downgrades its lock (EXL->SHR), keeps a "past image" of the block (which cannot be modified from this point onward by this instance or any other instance), and sends the block across the interconnect to the requesting instance, which can then make the required changes to the block after being granted the required and compatible locks. This topic is discussed in "Internals of Cache Fusion Recovery" later in this chapter.

Instance Recovery in RAC

Oracle 9i introduced a few good optimization techniques in recovery, and one of them is the *thread merge* mechanism. Using this formula, redos from multiple threads are merged when crash recovery or instance recovery is performed in RAC. This is because changes from multiple instances may not have made it to the datafiles. This is termed *thread merge recovery*. Media recovery also uses the thread merge mechanism where redos from all the threads are merged and applied simultaneously. The redo records are merged in increasing SCN order. More on thread merge mechanism is presented in "Two-Pass Recovery" later this chapter.

Crash Recovery and Media Recovery

Some of the basic differences between crash and media recovery are presented here for completeness in understanding recovery structures:

Number	Crash Recovery	Media Recovery
1	Automatic and uses the online redologs that are CURRENT or ACTIVE.	Manual process. Can be performed even without ARCHIVELOG mode, if enough information in the online redologs.
2	No concept of incomplete recovery unless block corruption (data or redo) is identified. This is a complicated situation and is not discussed here.	Can be complete or incomplete. Incomplete recovery requires RESETLOGS to open the database.

Bounded Recovery

Two-pass recovery was introduced in Oracle 8i. Its history is tightly connected to the introduction of bounded recovery. *Bounded time recovery* is a feature that enables the control of the amount of time taken for crash recovery with some predetermined limits by specifying a suitable value for DB_BLOCK_MAX_DIRTY_TARGET. This feature allows the user to specify an upper bound on the time (or number of block) required for instance and crash recovery. The fewer the number of dirty buffers in the buffer cache at the time of the failure, the faster the recovery time. Remember that DB_BLOCK_MAX_DIRTY_TARGET is a hidden parameter since Oracle 9i.

Starting with Oracle 8i, the FAST_START_IO_TARGET parameter controls the target number of I/Os needed for crash recovery. DBWR writes data blocks continuously to meet this target and also writes the oldest dirty buffers first, assuring that the checkpoint will progress. This is where direct control over roll forward I/O was introduced, a feature lacking in Oracle 7. Hence, since Oracle 8i, the definitions of LOG_CHECKPOINT_INTERVAL and LOG_CHECKPOINT_TIMEOUT have been redone and are widely documented: the incremental checkpoint should not lag the tail of the redolog by more than LOG_CHECKPOINT_INTERVAL number of redo blocks (X$KCCLE. LEBSZ). LOG_CHECKPOINT_TIMEOUT is reinterpreted to mean that the incremental checkpoint should lag the tail of the redolog by no more than that many seconds' worth of redo records.

Block Written Record (BWR)

One of the optimization recovery mechanisms used by Oracle 9i and later is the writing of additional (yet critical) information into the redolog about checkpoints. Normally, the cache aging and incremental checkpoint system would write a number of blocks to disk. When DBWR completes a data block write operation, it also adds a redo record (in the redolog file) that states that the block has been written. It basically writes the data block address along with the SCN information. DBWn can write block written records (BWRs) in batches, though in a "lazy" fashion.

In RAC, a BWR is written when an instance writes a block covered by a global resource or when it is told that the past image (PI) buffer it is holding is no longer necessary. Recovery processes that indicate redo information for the block is not needed prior to this point use this record.

The basic use of BWR is to make recovery more efficient, hence the instance does not force a flush of the log buffer after creating it because it is not essential for ensuring the accuracy of recovery.

Past Image (PI)

PI is what makes RAC Cache Fusion version II click. It makes RAC "unbreakable" in terms of recovery and in the context of Cache Fusion. It eliminates the write/write contention problem that existed (or still does in some sites!) in many OPS databases. Because block transfers from one node's buffer cache to another's required an intermediate disk write (a ping), with associated slower I/O and network congestion, OPS's scalability in large environments was limited, particularly for online transaction processing (OLTP). In OPS, time to recover depended upon the number of nodes that touched the buffer, which is a drawback in making OPS an HA solution.

In the simplest of terms, a PI is a copy of a globally dirty block and is maintained in the database buffer cache. It can be created and saved when a dirty block is shipped across to another instance after setting the resource role to global (if it was not already set). A PI must be maintained by an instance until it or a later version of the block is written to disk. The Global Cache Service (GCS) is responsible for informing an instance that its PI is no longer needed after another instance writes a newer (a current) version of the same block. PIs are discarded when GCS posts all the holding instances that a new and consistent version of that particular block is now on disk.

Checkpoints and PI

In Cache Fusion, when an instance needs to write a block to satisfy a checkpoint request, the instance needs to check the role of the resource covering the block. If the role is global, the instance must inform GCS that it needs to write that block to disk. GCS is responsible for finding the most current block image and informing the instance holding that image to perform the block write. GCS then informs all holders of the global resource that they can release their PI copies of the block, hence allowing the global resources to be released.

Two-Pass Recovery

Oracle 9i introduced the concept of two-pass recovery, where the recovery process (SMON or the foreground) performs a two-step "read" process. Basically, this limits the number of I/O reads required for recovery by recording more information in the logs (BWR). The first read builds a list of blocks that are mentioned in the redolog (all data blocks that have redo information). Some of these redo records could be BWR entries, denoting that the block mentioned is up to date until that point in the redo. Therefore the recovery process need not "recover" this block, and it is removed from the list being built. The resultant list of this first pass is a list of blocks that have redo information but were not written to disk (since there was an instance failure). This list is called the *recovery set*.

The second read now processes only blocks from this list or set, which is smaller than the blocks touched in the redo stream in the first pass. Redo is applied in this phase and fewer data blocks are read and written in the second pass, thus offsetting the cost of reading the online redolog files twice. If the system is unable to perform two-pass recovery, it will fall back to the single pass. The alert file states the result from two-pass recovery. Two-pass crash recovery can be suppressed with _two_pass=false.

Two-Pass Recovery in RAC

Two-pass recovery in RAC has some additional steps to be performed since multiple instances (threads) may have failed or crashed. This involves reading and merging all the redo information for a particular block from all the threads. This is called a *log merge* or a *thread merge* operation.

One of the bigger challenges in RAC recovery is that a block could have been modified in any of the instances (dead or alive). This was not the case in OPS. Hence, in RAC, getting hold of the latest version of a dirty block needs an intelligent and efficient mechanism that completes the identification of the latest version of that block and processing it for recovery. The introduction of PI images and BWRs makes it possible to significantly reduce recovery time and efficiently recover from an instance failure or crash.

First Pass   This pass does not perform the actual recovery but merges and reads redo threads to create a hash table of blocks that need recovery and that are not known to have been written back to the datafiles. This is where incremental checkpoint SCN is crucial since the Redo Byte Address (RBA) denotes a starting point for recovery. All modified blocks are added to the recovery set. As BWRs are encountered, the file, DBA, and SCN of each change vector are processed to limit the number of blocks to recover in the next pass. A block need not be recovered if its BWR version is greater than the latest PI present in any of the buffer caches.

Redo threads from all failed instances are read and merged by SCN, beginning at the RBA of the last incremental checkpoint for each thread. When the first change to a data block is encountered in the merged redo stream, a block entry is added in the recovery set data structure. Entries in the recovery set are organized in a hash table.

Second Pass   In this stage, SMON rereads the merges redo stream (by SCN) from all threads needing recovery. The redolog entries are again compared against the recovery set built in the first pass, and any matches are applied to the in-memory buffers as in single pass recovery. The buffer cache is flushed and the checkpoint SCN for each thread is updated upon successful completion. This is also the single pass thread recovery if only one pass is to be done.

Cache Fusion Recovery

Cache Fusion recovery is applicable only in RAC. Since additional steps, such as GRD (re)configuration, internode communication, and so on, are required on top of the existing recovery steps, it is known as Cache Fusion recovery. The SMON from a surviving instance recovers the failed instance. If a foreground process detects instance recovery, it posts SMON. As of Oracle 9i and beyond, foreground processes no longer perform instance recovery.

Crash recovery is a unique case of instance recovery whereby all instances have failed. Yet, in either case, the threads from failed instances need to be merged. The only distinction being, in instance recovery, SMON performs the recovery. In crash recovery, a foreground process performs the recovery.

Let's now examine the main steps involved in Cache Fusion recovery or instance recovery. The main advantages or features of Cache Fusion recovery are that

- Recovery cost is proportional to the number of failures, not the total number of nodes.
- It eliminates disk reads of blocks that are present in a surviving instance's cache.
- It prunes recovery sets based on the global resource lock state.
- The cluster is available after an initial log scan, even before recovery reads are complete.

In Cache Fusion recovery, the starting point for recovery of a block is its most recent PI version. A PI could be located in any of the surviving instances, and multiple PI blocks of a particular buffer can exist. An on-disk version is used for recovery only if no PI is available. It is called Cache Fusion recovery because, from Oracle 9i onward, the on-disk version of a block might not be the latest copy since Cache Fusion allows the shipping of copies of CURRENT blocks across the interconnect by using the PI concept.

Dynamic Reconfiguration and Affinity Remastering

Remastering is the term used to describe the operation whereby the node attempting the recovery tries to own or master the resource(s) that was once mastered by another instance prior to a failure. Hence, the term *remaster* is used for the operation performed during instance recovery or when a node joins or leaves a cluster.

When one instance departs the cluster, the GRD component of that instance needs to be redistributed to the surviving nodes. Similarly, when a new instance enters the cluster, the GRD portions of the existing instances need to be redistributed to create the GRD portion of the new instance.

As an optimization feature during instance recovery, remastering of all resources does not happen across all nodes. From Oracle 9i onward, RAC uses an algorithm called *lazy remastering* to remaster only a minimal number of resources during a reconfiguration. A minimum subset of resources is remastered to maintain consistency of the lock database. This occurs in parallel during the first pass log read where the recovery set is built. The entire Parallel Cache Management (PCM) lock space remains invalid while the DLM and SMON complete the following two crucial steps:

1. Integrated Distributed Lock Manager (IDLM) master node discards locks that are held by dead instances; the space reclaimed by this operation is used to remaster locks that are held by the surviving instance for which a dead instance was mastered.

2. SMON issues a message saying that it has acquired the necessary buffer locks to perform recovery.

While the lock domain is invalid, most PCM lock operations are frozen, making the database unavailable for users requesting a new or incompatible lock. Operations that do not require interaction with the DLM can proceed without affecting the remastering operations. If a second instance fails, its resources are remastered on the other surviving instances evenly. As resources are remastered, they are cleared of any reference to the failed instance.

In addition, the database can automatically adapt and migrate resources in the GRD, based on the affinity of a resource to a particular instance. If a single instance is identified as the sole user of a tablespace, the block resource masters for files of that tablespace are lazily and dynamically moved to that instance.

In both cases, the use of dynamic resource remastering provides the key benefit of greatly increasing the likelihood of local cache access without additional interconnect traffic. Another great advantage of the lazy remastering scheme is that instances keep many of their locks/resources during a reconfiguration, whereas in OPS 8i, all resources and locks were deleted from all instances. Because of this concept, many processes can resume active work during a reconfiguration because their locks/resources do not have to be moved away or deleted.

A good discussion on this topic is available in Metalink Note 139435.1.

Fast Reconfiguration in RAC

Fast reconfiguration is an enhancement feature introduced in Oracle 9i and designed to increase the availability time for RAC instances during instance reconfiguration. Reconfiguration of open DLM locks/resources takes place under the following conditions:

- An instance joins the cluster
- An instance fails or leaves the cluster
- A node is halted

In previous versions (Oracle 7, 8, and 8i OPS), this operation could be relatively instantaneous or could be delayed for several minutes while *lock remastering* takes place. Consider a situation in which an instance leaves a cluster. The lock remastering process is triggered and all open global locks/resources are deleted from the departing instance and all locks/resources on all instances are *distributed evenly* across surviving instances. During this time no lock operations can occur on the database.

The amount of time that reconfiguration took primarily depended on the number of open DLM locks/resources (usually higher with fixed locking) and hardware resources such as memory, interconnect speed, and CPUs. Reconfiguration in Oracle 8i and earlier was prone to performance bottlenecks, as the instance would experience a hang situation until the completion of this task, and the lock database was frozen completely.

Oracle 9i (and 10g RAC) overcomes these issues with optimization techniques whereby the thrust is on decreasing the amount of time it takes to complete reconfiguration and allowing some processes to continue work (in parallel) during reconfiguration.

One of the most significant changes in Oracle 9i RAC is that fixed locks are no longer used. Remember that fixed locks are allocated during instance startup as well as during reconfiguration in Oracle 8i and earlier versions. Fixed PCM locks are initially acquired in null mode. All specified fixed locks are allocated at instance startup and deallocated at instance shutdown. Fixed locks are preallocated and statically hashed to blocks at startup time. The init.ora parameter, `gc_files_to_lock`, determines the fixed PCM locks along with `gc_rollback_locks`.

So in Oracle 9i, fixed locks are no longer used during instance startup or reconfiguration; this speeds up startup time. Second, instead of remastering all locks/resources across all nodes, Oracle uses the lazy remastering algorithm (introduced in the preceding section) to remaster only a minimal number of locks/resources during a reconfiguration. For a departing instance (expected or unexpected), Oracle 9i tries to determine how best to distribute only the locks/resources from the departing instance and a minimal number from the surviving instances.

Let's consider a simple example of this phenomenon in Figure 9-1, though the actual resource mastering process is quite different from this simplified one.

- Instance A masters resources 1, 3, 5, and 7
- Instance B masters resources 2, 4, 6, and 8
- Instance C masters resources 9, 10, 11, and 12

Now, assume that Instance B crashes (Figure 9-2). Now the resources 2, 4, 6, and 8 will be affected by the instance failure. The resources mastered in Instance A and Instance C are not affected by this failure.

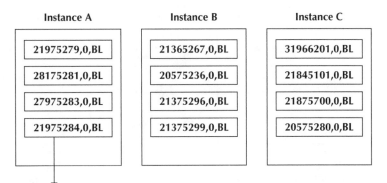

21975284: Decimal representation of the Lock Element Name as found in column
LOCK_ELEMENT_NAME in V$BH. X$KJBL.KJBLNAME2 has the full LE.
0: Class of the block as found in column CLASS# in V$BH
BL: Keyword for PCM Locks meaning **BL**ock

FIGURE 9-1. *Resource mastering example*

Now instances A and C remaster their resources. After remastering, the DLM database (GRD) could look like this (Figure 9-3):

- Instance A masters resources 1, 3, 5, 7, 4, and 8
- Instance C masters resources 9, 10, 11, 12, 2, and 6

So, instead of removing all resources and remastering them evenly across instances, Oracle 9i and 10g RAC will remaster only the resources necessary (in this case those owned by the departing instance), thus using a more efficient means of reconfiguration. With an instance joining the cluster, RAC will remaster a limited number of resources from the other instances to the new instance.

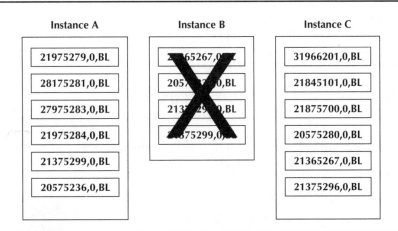

FIGURE 9-2. *Instance crash*

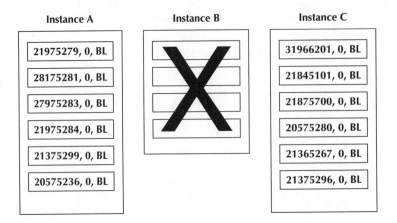

FIGURE 9-3. *Resource remastering*

Assume that Instance B now rejoins the cluster; a minimal number of resources are remastered to Instance B from the other instances. This is much faster than the 8i behavior of redistributing all resources. Here is the configuration after Instance B rejoins the GRD:

- Instance A masters resources 1, 3, 5, and 7
- Instance B masters resources 2, 4, 6, and 8
- Instance C masters resources 9, 10, 11, and 12

Fast reconfiguration is controlled by the parameter _gcs_fast_reconfig. Another parameter, _lm_master_weight, controls which instance will hold or (re)master more resources than others. Similarly, _gcs_resources is also used to control the number of resources an instance will master at a time. Each instance can have a different value.

With the concept of lazy remastering, instances retain many of their locks/resources during a reconfiguration process, whereas in previous versions, all locks were deleted from all instances. Because of this concept, many processes can resume active work during a reconfiguration because their locks/resources do not have to be moved or remastered.

Internals of Cache Fusion Recovery

As mentioned, when you recover an RAC database, additional steps are involved due to the presence of a cluster and multiple instances. When an instance fails, for example, in a two-node RAC database, the failure is detected by the surviving instance, which then performs the following recovery steps, as explained in Figure 9-4. Note that GRD reconfiguration (remastering) and I Pass recovery can be done in parallel.

The steps for GRD reconfiguration are as follows:

- Instance death is detected by the cluster manager.
- Requests for PCM locks are frozen.

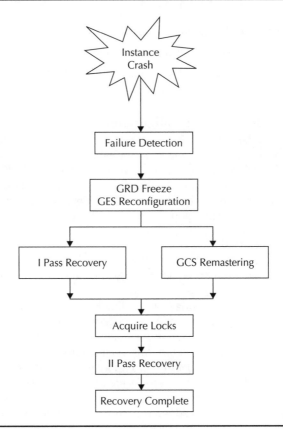

FIGURE 9-4. *Two-pass recovery in RAC*

- Enqueues are reconfigured and made available.
- DLM recovery.
- GCS (PCM lock) is remastered.
- Pending writes and notifications are processed.

The steps for I Pass recovery are as follows:

- The instance recovery (IR) lock is acquired by SMON.
- The recovery set is prepared and built. Memory space is allocated in the SMON Program Global Area (PGA).
- SMON acquires locks on buffers that need recovery.

II Pass recovery steps are as follows:

- II Pass is initiated. The database is partially available.

- Blocks are made available as they are recovered.

- The IR lock is released by SMON. Recovery is complete.

- The system is available.

Global Resource Directory Reconfiguration

An instance failure is detected by the cluster manager (Cluster Group Services). The DLM reconfiguration process is started and all locks owned by the failed instance are remastered. This is when the PCM lock database is frozen and no instance can acquire a PCM lock. The reconfiguration phase (in lazy mode) can continue in parallel along with the first pass read process. During this phase, existing PIs in any of instance buffer caches are identified as potential candidates for recovery. DLM reconfiguration or recovery is performed by LMON.

First Pass Redo Log Read

SMON acquires the IR enqueue. By doing that, Oracle keeps multiple surviving instances from trying to recover a failed instance simultaneously and causing severe inconsistencies and more failures.

The SMON process of a surviving instance that has acquired the IR enqueue starts the first pass log read of the failed instance's redo thread. SMON then merges the redo thread ordered by SCN to ensure that changes are written in a sequential order. The recovery set is built during this phase and contains the first dirty and last dirty version information (SCN, Seq#) of each block. SMON trims the recovery set (removes blocks no longer needed for recovery) based on the DBAs found in the redo stream because these blocks are nothing but PIs already written to disk. The BWR helps in this trimming.

The result of the first pass log read is a recovery set (built into the PGA of SMON) that contains only blocks modified by the failed instance with no subsequent BWR to indicate that the blocks were later written. Each entry in the recovery list is ordered by the first-dirty SCN to specify the order to acquire instance recovery locks.

The recovering SMON process will then inform each lock element's master node for each block in the recovery list that it will be taking ownership of the block and lock for recovery. Logically speaking, only the part of the database requiring recovery is locked and the rest is still available for normal operations. Note that the actual locking is done during the second pass read.

Acquiring block buffers (and their locks) for recovery is a complex process and needs DLM (GES) messaging and coordination. Depending on the lock status of each buffer during the time of recovery, the recovery process has to perform a series of steps before an exclusive lock on the buffer can be held. A detailed description of the various lock states and eventual outcome is discussed in Metalink Note 144152.1.

Recovery Lock Claim   It is in this phase that SMON indicates to DLM (GES) that it needs IR locks on all the buffers identified in the recovery set. SMON continues to acquire locks on all buffers until it runs through the recovery set. If the master node for a resource has failed and the DLM remastering has not completed, SMON waits until the resource is made available. This also implies that DLM recovery is occurring in parallel. Now, SMON sends a cluster-wide message to indicate that all required locks on buffers have been acquired. The DLM lock database is unfrozen and is available for normal operations.

Validate Global Resource Directory   After the DLM completes reconfiguration, only the resources that are locked for recovery are unavailable to foreground lock requests. Once the PCM lock database is released, other foreground processes can continue to acquire buffer locks as long as they are not requesting an "in-recovery" buffer. The GRD is globally resynchronized and flagged off as available.

Second Pass Log Read and Redo Application

It is in this phase that redo threads of failed instances are again read and merged by SCN. Buffer space for recovery is allocated in the database buffer cache and the resources that were identified in the previous reading of the redologs are claimed as recovery resources. This is done to prevent other instances from accessing those resources. Then, assuming that there are PIs or current images of blocks to be recovered in other caches in the cluster, the most recent PI is the starting point of recovery.

If neither the PI buffers nor the current buffer for a data block are in any of the surviving instances' caches, SMON performs a log merge of the failed instances. Then redo is applied to each buffer identified in the first pass until its SCN matches the last dirty SCN that was identified in the first pass. SMON recovers and posts DBWR to write the recovery buffer and clear the "in-recovery" state of the buffer. Soon after the write, SMON releases the recovery resources so that more blocks become available as recovery proceeds. Recovery time is determined by this phase.

After all blocks have been recovered and the recovery resources have been released, the system is again fully available. In summary, the recovered database or recovered portions of the database become available earlier and before the completion of the entire recovery sequence. This makes the system available sooner and it makes recovery more scalable.

NOTE
The performance overhead of a log merge is proportional to the number of failed instances and to the size of the redologs for each instance.

Online Block Recovery for Cache Fusion   When a data buffer becomes corrupt in an instance's cache, the instance will initiate online block recovery. Block recovery will also occur if either a foreground process dies while applying changes or an error is generated during redo application. In the first case, SMON initiates block recovery and in the second case the foreground process initiates block recovery. Online block recovery consists of finding the block's predecessor and applying redo changes from the online logs of the thread in which corruption occurred. The predecessor of a fusion block is its most recent past image. If there is no past image, the block on disk is the predecessor. For non-fusion blocks, the disk copy is always the predecessor.

If the lock element of the block needing recovery is held in XL0 (Exclusive, Local, no past images) status, the predecessor will be located on disk. If the Lock Element (LE) of the block needing recovery is held in XG# (Global Exclusive) status, the predecessor will exist in another instance's buffer cache. The instance with the highest SCN PI image of the block will send a consistent read copy of the block to the recovering instance.

Backup and Recovery of the Voting Disk and OCR

The voting disk and OCR are the two critical components in Oracle Clusterware. Here we discuss the backup and recovery of the voting disk and OCR.

Oracle Clusterware backups should include the voting disk and OCR components. The voting disk is a disk partition that stores information about the status of the nodes and membership details. The OCR is a file that manages the configuration and the details about the services. We recommended mirroring the voting disk and the OCR using Oracle-provided mirroring techniques. Mirroring the voting disk and OCR can be configured during installation or at later stages dynamically.

Backup and Recovery of Voting Disks

Voting disks can be backed up by the standard operating system commands: the UNIX dd command or Windows ocopy command. Adding voting disks can be done using the crsctl commands. The following commands back up the voting disk in UNIX and Windows.

For UNIX:

```
dd if=voting_disk_name of=backup_file_name
```

For Windows:

```
ocopy voting_disk_name backup_file_name
```

Recovering Voting Disks

Voting disks can be recovered by the simple restore of the backup file. The following commands recover the voting disks from the backup.

For UNIX:

```
dd if=backup_file_name of=voting_disk_name
```

For Windows:

```
copy backupfile_name voting_disk_name
```

Backup and Recovery of OCR

The Oracle Clusterware automatically creates OCR backups every four hours. At any one time, Oracle always retains the last three backup copies of the OCR in the master node. By default, the second node is selected as master node and OCR is backed up and stored in the master node. The CRS daemon (CRSd) process that creates the backups also creates and retains an OCR backup for each full day and at the end of each week.

The default location for generating backups on UNIX-based systems is CRS_HOME/cdata/ <cluster_name>, where <cluster_name> is the name of your cluster. The Windows-based default location for generating backups uses the same path structure. To recover the OCR from automated backup, the ocrconfig command can be used. The following command lists the successful backups of the OCR:

```
ocrconfig -showbackup
```

To recover the OCR, Oracle Clusterware should be stopped from all the nodes. This can be done by executing `init.crs stop` in the all the nodes. Once the CRS demons are stopped in all the nodes, the following command restores the OCR:

`ocrconfig -restore <file_name>`

Restart the Oracle Clusterware on all of the nodes in your cluster by restarting each node or by running the `init.crs start` command.

OCR can also be exported and imported. This can be used as an alternative recovery mechanism for OCR recovery. The following command can be used to export the contents of OCR:

`ocrconfig -export <file_name>`

This will create the binary copy of the OCR. This file cannot be edited by text editors. Human-readable information about OCR can be obtained by using the `ocrdump` command. This command dumps the contents of the OCR to a text file in the current directory.

To import the OCR, stop Oracle CRS by executing `init.crs stop`. Once the CRS daemon is stopped in all the nodes, you can use the following command to import the OCR:

`ocrconfig -import <file_name>`

NOTE
It is recommended that you manually backup the OCR from other nodes as the clusterware-initiated automatic OCR backup process backs up the OCR only for master node. If master node is down and cannot be rebooted, OCR backups are lost. Hence it is important to integrate the OCR backup process to the regular backup schedules.

In a Nutshell

We have discussed the concepts and inner workings of RAC recovery. For the exact commands and syntaxes, refer to *Oracle 10g Recovery Manager Reference*. Oracle RAC backup and recovery processes are the same as single instance backup and recovery except for the thread merging and two-pass recovery concepts. We have also discussed the backup and recovery for the voting disk and OCR. In the next chapter we discuss performance tuning in the RAC environment.

CHAPTER
10

RAC Performance
Management

n this chapter we look at considerations and procedures for optimizing the performance in the Oracle RAC environment, which consists of a database opened by multiple instances. Interinstance coordination and communication are necessary to preserve data integrity and other database characteristics. This requires CPU, network bandwidth, and memory resources. However, this need for additional system resources should not impact the end user's transaction processing time. Techniques mentioned in this chapter should help you to identify and address user response time problems and optimize performance in an RAC environment.

Traditionally, the capacity of a database tier could be increased by adding hardware to the existing system or by replacing the system with a higher capacity system. Oracle RAC offers an alternative to this approach by allowing the database tier to scale horizontally by adding one or more database servers to the existing machine(s). This also lets you make use of low cost servers, including those running Linux operating systems, thereby reducing the overall cost of ownership.

Overall, the RAC database instance tuning process is similar to that of single instance database tuning. The same principles of SQL tuning—identifying hot spots and tuning contentions—are applicable to the RAC environment. Tools used for monitoring Oracle instance and system usage are also the same.

Cluster interconnect tuning and cache synchronization delays are some of the additional components that need to be considered while tuning RAC. Automatic Workload Repository (AWR) and STATSPACK reports contain additional information required for tuning the RAC instance and database.

RAC Design Considerations

The best application, database designs, and coding practices that are applicable to a single instance Oracle database are also applicable to RAC. A well-tuned application in a single instance environment on a symmetric multiprocessing (SMP) machine should run well in an RAC environment.

An application that has known performance problems will not run better in an RAC environment. If an application has capacity issues, moving to the RAC environment will not solve them; it will provide only temporary relief. So is there anything you can do to make an application run better in an RAC environment? The following sections address this question.

Oracle Design Best Practices

Let's quickly recall the Oracle design best practices for application and database layout:

- Optimize connection management. Ensure that the middle tier and programs that connect to the database are efficient in connection management and do not log on or off repeatedly.

- Ensure that the SQL execution is well tuned. Optimize execution plans and data access paths. Text books have been devoted to this subject, and many tools are available to tune SQL automatically. A majority of database performance problems are due to inefficient SQL execution plans. Tools such as ADDM and SQL Tuning Advisor go a long way in pointing out SQL statements that can be optimized and how to optimize them. Consider optimizing SQL statements if this has not already been done.

- Ensure that the application is using bind variables to minimize parsing. Introduction of the initialization parameter `cursor_sharing` has addressed this problem to some extent, but it still remains an important consideration for online transaction processing (OLTP) applications. For data warehouse applications, using bind variables may not be desirable.

- Use packages and procedures in place of anonymous PL/SQL blocks and big SQL statements. Packages and procedures are compiled and stored in the database and can be reused without runtime compilation overhead.

- Use the latest database space management features. Features such as locally managed tablespace and automatic segment space management help performance and simplify database administration. These features are used by default if you are creating a database using the Database Configuration Assistant (DBCA). Upon migrating a pre–Oracle 8 database, consider using these features as soon as possible.

- The use of features such as automatic undo management and temporary tablespace simplify administration and optimize performance. Ensure that you are using automatic undo management. Using a permanent tablespace for sorting is a thing of the past. Be sure that the database is configured with default temporary tablespace.

- If a sequence is being used frequently and by multiple concurrent sessions, ensure that a large cache is used. The default value for cache sequence is 20.

- Avoid use of data definition languages (DDLs) in a production environment that operates during normal business hours. Use of DDLs increases invalidations of the already parsed SQL statements, and they need to be recompiled before reuse.

- Index leaf block contention is the single largest cause of buffer busy waits in a single instance environment and can cause buffer cache contention (buffer busy global cr) in an RAC environment. Indexes are a necessary evil as they help to retrieve data access. However, they become a drag on Data Manipulation Language (DML) statements, as indexes need to be updated during insert, update, and delete operations. Consider using reverse key index and index only tables. Partitioning tables and indexes is another effective way to minimize contention.

- Optimize contention on data blocks by avoiding small tables with too many rows in a block. You can use the `minimize records per block` clause of the `alter table` command to restrict the number of rows per block.

RAC-Specific Design Best Practices

Following are some application design considerations that can help you optimize performance specifically in an RAC environment:

- Do not re-read the recently modified/inserted data just to validate it. There is no need to read and compare the data to confirm what has been inserted or committed. Built-in checks and balances help ensure data integrity and avoid corruptions.

- If business requirements do not dictate otherwise, consider using application partitioning. This is discussed in detail in the following section.

- Consider restricting DML-intensive users to one instance. If few users are performing DMLs on certain sets of data, allow these users to access the same instance; although not necessary, this strategy helps in reducing cache contention.

- Group read-only data together and put it in a read-only tablespace(s). Read-only tablespaces require little resource and lock coordination. Keeping read-only and read-intensive data separate from DML-intensive data will help optimize RAC Cache Fusion performance.

- Avoid auditing in an RAC environment. It has lots of negative side effects as it creates more shared library cache locks.

- Use full table scans sparingly as they cause the global cache service to service lots of block requests. Tuning the inefficient SQLs and collecting system statistics for the optimizer to use CPU costing will also help. The statistics "table scans (long tables)" in V$SYSSTAT provides the number of full table scans done by the instance.

- If the application makes a large number of new session "logon storms," increase the cache value of the sys.audsess$ sequence:

```
alter sequence sys.audses$ cache 10000;
```

Partitioning the Workload

In workload partitioning, a certain type of workload is executed on an instance—that is, partitioning allows users who access the same set of data to log on from the same instance. This limits the amount of data shared among the instances and therefore saves resources used for messaging and Cache Fusion data block transfer.

Whether to partition or not to partition? The decision is a fine balance between business needs and system resources conservation. You can save system resources by implementing workload partitioning in an RAC environment. If the system's processing resources are being used to their full capacity, partitioning might help. However, if the system has enough spare resources, partitioning probably isn't necessary.

Consider the following before implementing workload partitioning:

- RAC can handle buffer cache contention, and if the system CPU resources and private interconnect bandwidth is sufficient, you do not need to partition.

- At times, it might be much easier and more economical to add extra CPU power or interconnect bandwidth rather than implementing a workload partitioning scheme.

- You don't need to consider partitioning the user workload unless evidence indicates that contention is impacting performance and partitioning the workload will improve performance.

- Establish baseline statistics with and without workload partitioning. If the comparison shows significant performance improvements with partitioning, consider implementing workload partitioning.

Scalability and Performance

Scalability and high availability are the two most significant advantages offered by RAC. If you were to look up the word *scalability* on http://www.dictionary.com, you'd see the following definition: "How well a solution to some problem will work when the size of the problem increases."

A system is said to be *fully scalable* if its response time remains unchanged whether it serves 1,100, 1,000, or any other number of users. Consider a real-life example: If the freeways are 100 percent scalable, travel time from point A to point B will always remain the same, whether one car is on the highway or millions of cars. Are highways fully scalable? Probably not! A four lane freeway with properly designed exit and entrance ramps might support hundreds or even thousands of cars, but if the number of cars increases beyond a limit, the drivers will have to slow down to avoid accidents and to yield. A freeway that is scalable for thousands of cars and allows them to travel at a speed of 65 mph may not be able to support the same number of trucks at that speed. So the scalability of a system not only depends on the number of users but also on the type of workload. It is reasonable to expect that the same freeway cannot support 10,000 mixed vehicles (cars, trucks, bikes, and so on).

The points to be noted are as follows:

- No real-life system is fully scalable all the time.

- Each and every system has a limit beyond which it may not be able to support additional users without compromising the response time.

- A system that is scalable for a certain number of users of some type may not be able to support the same number of different type users.

However, for all practical purposes, a system is assumed to be fully scalable as long as its response time does not degrade (or remains within service level agreements) for an intended maximum number of users. With reference to Oracle RAC, scalability is generally discussed in terms of ability to support additional user workload when a node, identical to the existing node, is added. For example, consider the following data:

3,000 = Number of user transactions per second processed with 3 nodes

4,000 = Number of user transactions processed per second with 4 nodes

Scalability = (4,000 − 3,000) / 3,000 / 3) × 100 = 100%

These are the assumptions for this example:

- All nodes have the same hardware configuration.

- Response time and the user workload characteristics remain unchanged. Only numbers of user transactions are increased.

A real-life system consists of multiple components. For a system to be scalable, each of its components need to support the increased user workload—that is, all its components need to be scalable. For an RAC system to be fully scalable, all the following components need to be scalable:

- Application
- Network

- Database
- Operating system
- Hardware

If any of the components cannot perform for the intended number of users, the system will not be scalable.

A specific application's scalability may vary depending on several factors. In general, scalability of an application is built during the design process by avoiding any point of serialization. An application's scalability in the RAC environment might be limited if the same data blocks are frequently needed by all the instances, thereby increasing the Cache Fusion activity. For example, if each transaction is updating a running total maintained in a row, the block containing the row needs to be updated by each transaction, thereby causing the block to travel among the instances very rapidly. This behavior would limit the application's scalability.

Choosing the Block Size for an RAC Database

Most operating systems have a buffer cache that keeps frequently used data in memory to minimize disk access. To optimize I/O efficiency, the first choice is to make Oracle block size equal to the file system buffer size. If that is not acceptable, the Oracle block size should be set to a multiple of the OS file system cache block size. For example, if the file system buffer is 4K, then the preferred Oracle block sizes will be 4K, 8K, 16K, and so on. If the OS buffer cache is not being used or the OS being used does not have a buffer cache (as in Windows), you can choose any block size without compromising the I/O efficiency. Oracle RAC data is accessed from multiple systems simultaneously; the OS buffer cache cannot be used. This is achieved either by using raw devices, a shared file system, or Automatic Storage Management (ASM). Therefore, you do not need to consider file system buffer size while choosing a block size for RAC.

Note that Oracle 9i and later versions support multiple block sizes, so different tablespaces can have different block sizes. The parameter db_block_size represents the standard block size for the database and is used by the system tablespace, temporary tablespace, auxiliary tablespace, and any other tablespace for which a different block size is not specified while creating it.

Most of the applications use the 8K block size for the database. While designing a decision support system (DSS)/data warehouse system, consider larger block sizes. For data that is mostly read-only or retrieved using full table scans, a large block size is helpful. A large block size is also helpful when row size is larger—for example, while using large objects (LOBs) to store documents, images, and so on. Using a small block size for an index is sometimes helpful as it reduces contention on index branch blocks. Similarly for tables with smaller row sizes, using smaller block sizes will reduce contention. Wait events such as buffer busy waits, global cache busy, buffer busy global cr, and so on, are indications of block level contention, and moving the index/table with high contention to a tablespace with a smaller block size will help reduce contention.

Using Automatic Segment Space Management

Automatic Segment Space Management (ASSM) was introduced in Oracle 9i and is the preferred way to manage space within a segment. Oracle uses bitmaps stored within the segment to manage free space for the segment. This is a more efficient and simpler way to manage space within a segment compared to the traditional linked-list–based space management algorithm. The traditional method uses the PCTUSED, FREELISTS, and FREELIST GROUPS parameters for managing space usage for tables, indexes, and so on. Using ASSM also provides dynamic affinity of space to instance, because there is no association of extents to instance as present while using FREELIST GROUPS. Therefore, there is no performance degradation or wasted space when instances are added or removed form an RAC environment.

To ensure that an object uses ASSM, create that object in a tablespace that has been created with a segment space management clause auto. The following lines of code provide the basic syntax for creating a tablespace with ASSM:

```
SQL> create tablespace data_assm
  2   datafile '$ORADATA/data_assm01.dbf' size 1000M
  3   extent management local
  4   segment space management auto ;
```

Column SEGMENT_SPACE_MANAGMENT of the DBA_TABLESPACES data dictionary view can be queried to view this characteristic of existing tablespaces. Performance of a frequently, concurrently executed insert statement can be improved by migrating the inserted object from a tablespace with manual segment space management to ASSM. Once these objects are identified, the following methods are available to move them from one tablespace to another:

- Export/import
- Alter table...move
- Alter index...rebuild
- Online table redefinition

Select one of these methods to move the object to the desired tablespace, keeping availability requirements for the application in mind while the move operation is being performed. If the system has enough resources, consider using parallel query/DML to optimize the elapsed time for the operation.

Limitations of ASSM

Following are the limitation of the ASSM feature:

- ASSM cannot be used for a system tablespace.
- It can be used only for a locally managed tablespace. If, due to any reason, a dictionary managed tablespace is created, the ASSM clause cannot be used.
- ASSM cannot be used with temporary tablespaces.
- ASSM does not offer any control over space management, as the parameters freelists and freelist groups are not available.

Introduction to V$ and GV$ Views

The dynamic performance (V$) view contains database statistics and is commonly used for performance analysis and tuning. In the Oracle RAC environment, a global (GV$) view corresponds to each V$ view. V$ views contain statistics for one instance, whereas GV$ views contain information from all the active instances. Each GV$ view contains an `INST_ID` column of type `NUMBER`, which can be used to identify the instance associated with the row data.

When a query is issued against a GV$ view, the instance gets statistics from remote instances using the parallel query mechanism. In Oracle 10g, special parallel query slaves are dedicated to this task. They are named pz98, pz99, and so on, to distinguish them from general parallel query slaves. Here's an example:

```
$ ps -ef | grep PROD
oracle     6810     1   0 Jun07 ?        00:00:59 ora_pmon_PROD2
oracle     6812     1   0 Jun07 ?        00:00:00 ora_diag_PROD2
oracle     6824     1   0 Jun07 ?        00:01:17 ora_dbw0_PROD2
<<<unwanted lines deleted from here>>>
oracle     7168     1   0 Jun07 ?        00:01:41 ora_pz99_PROD2
oracle    25130     1   0 Jun29 ?        00:00:07 ora_pz98_PROD2
```

Most of the performance tuning tools (Oracle Enterprise Manager, AWR, STATSPACK) and scripts make use of these views, and there should be little need for you to query these views directly.

V$ Views Containing Cache Fusion Statistics

Generally, an AWR report should suffice to analyze the performance in an RAC environment. Seven or eight RAC-specific segments (described later in this chapter) are included in the AWR report and provide statistical information about Cache Fusion performance. Refer to Appendix A for a discussion on some of the important V$ views that can be used to manage performance in an RAC environment.

RAC Wait Events

An *event* can be defined as an operation or a particular function that the Oracle kernel performs on behalf of the user session or its own background process. Tasks such as reading and writing data blocks to and from data files, receiving data from other instances' memory, or waiting for the permission to read and acquire the block from the resource master are known as *database events*, and they have specific names. But why are these events called *wait events*?

All sessions accessing Oracle database instances need resources to perform their tasks concurrently and independently. A resource may be a data buffer, a latch, an enqueue (lock), or a piece of code to be executed exclusively. Some of these resources are serialized by access, and at any point of time only one process can have an exclusive access; the others wanting the resource must wait in the queue. Whenever a session has to wait for something, the wait time is tracked and charged to the event that is associated with that wait. For example, a session that needs a block that is not in the current instance's cache makes a read call to the operating system to be delivered from another instance's cache and waits for the block. The wait time is charged to the waiting session's account. If the block is read from the disk, the wait time is charged to the requesting instance's *db file sequential read* wait event. If the block is coming from the other instance's cache, the wait time is charged against *global cache* wait events. Another session may have completed the last instruction and is now waiting for user input. This is generally termed an *idle wait*, and the wait time is charged to the *SQL*Net message from client* event. In short, when a session is not using the CPU, it may be waiting for a resource, for an action to complete, or simply for more work. Events that are associated with all such waits are known as *wait events*.

Wait Class	Number of Wait Events in the Class
Commit	1
Scheduler	2
Application	12
Configuration	23
User I/O	17
System I/O	24
Concurrency	24
Network	26
Administrative	46
Cluster	47
Idle	62
Other	590

TABLE 10-1.   *Wait Classes in Oracle Database 10g R2*

Wait events are further classified by their type—Cluster, I/O, or Network, for example. Table 10-1 lists different wait classes and the number of wait events in each class. Note that even though more than 874 wait events are available in Oracle Database 10g R2 and they are divided into 12 different categories, you would normally deal with less than 50 events while analyzing RAC performance.

The remainder of this section describes wait events specific to the RAC environment. Starting with version 10g, Oracle has enhanced RAC-related wait events. We begin with a description of these enhancements.

Place Holder Event

When a session requests access to a data block in CR/CUR (Consistent Read/Current) mode, it sends a request to the lock master for proper authorization. However, whether it will receive the block via the Cache Fusion mechanism or a permission to read from the disk is not known until the request is satisfied. Two placeholder events, `global cache cr request` and `global cache cur request`, keep track of the time a session spends in this state. For example, when a session sends a request for a CR block, its wait time is counted against `global cache cr request`. Let's assume that the lock master grants the lock to the requestor, thereby authorizing it to read the block from the disk so all the wait time is now logged against the wait event `gc cr grant 2-way`. Similarly, the wait time would be logged against `gc cr block 2-way` if the requesting instance receives the CR copy of the block from the master. In the end, there should not be any wait time logged against these two placeholder wait events.

Two-Way and Three-Way Wait Events

Oracle 10g and later versions track whether a lock request was satisfied with just two-way communication between requestor and master/holder. In two-way events, the master instance is also the current holder of that block and is able to send the needed CR/current copy of the block via Cache Fusion to the requestor. In case of three-way events, the master forwards the request to the holder. The holder in turn sends the CR/current copy of the block as desired by the requestor.

We will describe important RAC wait events and the possible action plan when the wait event appears in the "Top 5 timed wait events" section of the AWR report. We will also look at messages and data flow during some of the important global cache wait events.

gc current block 2-way As indicated in Figure 10-1, an instance requests authorization for a block to be accessed in current mode to modify the block. The instance mastering the corresponding resource receives the request. The master has the current version of the block and sends the current copy of the block to the requestor via the Cache Fusion mechanism. This event indicates write/write contention.

NOTE
The appearance of gc current block 2-way and the following three events in the "Top 5" event section doesn't necessarily indicate performance issues. It merely indicates that the instances are accessing copies of data present in each other's cache and that Cache Fusion mechanism is being used to transfer copies of the data among the instances. However, if the average wait time for each event is very high, it might be impacting performance and needs further analysis.

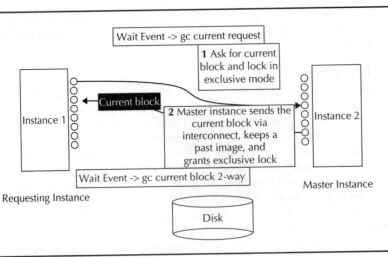

FIGURE 10-1. *Wait event: gc current block 2-way*

If this wait event appears in the "Top 5" timed events, do the following:

- Analyze the contention. Segments in the "Current Blocks Received" section of the AWR report should help you identify top contentious objects.

- Ensure that good database object design practices, database object layout, and space management practices are being followed for top contentious objects.

- Optimize the application contention by using an appropriate application partitioning scheme.

- Look at "Tips for Avoiding RAC Wait Events" at the end of this section.

gc current block 3-way   Figure 10-2 shows this wait event. An instance requests authorization for a block to be accessed in current mode. The instance mastering the corresponding resource receives the request and forwards the message to the current holder, telling it to relinquish ownership. The holding instance sends a copy of the current version of the block to the requestor via the Cache Fusion mechanism and transfers the exclusive lock to the requesting instance. This event indicates write/write contention.

If this wait event appears in the "Top 5" timed events list, your plan of action should be similar to that for a gc current block 2-way event.

gc current block 2-way   Figure 10-3 shows a pictorial representation of the event. An instance requests authorization for a block to be accessed in current mode. The instance mastering the corresponding resource receives the request. The master has the current version of the block. It makes a current copy using the current block and undo data it has and sends the current copy of the block to the requestor via the interconnect. This event indicates write/read contention.

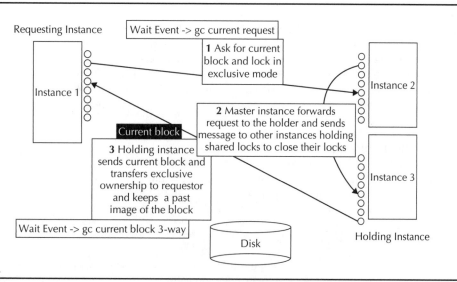

FIGURE 10-2.   *Wait event: gc current block 3-way*

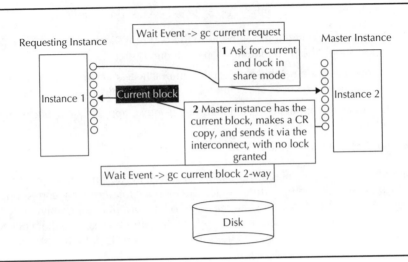

FIGURE 10-3. *Wait event: gc current block 2-way*

If this wait event appears in the Top 5 timed events, then do the following:

■ Analyze the contention. The "Segments by Current Blocks Received" section of the AWR report should help you to identify top contentious objects.

■ Optimize the application contention by using an appropriate application partitioning scheme.

■ Look at "Tips for Avoiding RAC Wait Events" at the end of this section.

gc current block 3-way Figure 10-4 shows a pictorial representation of this event. An instance requests authorization for a block to be accessed in current mode. The instance mastering the corresponding resource receives the request. The master forwards the request to the current holder of the block. The holding instance sends a current copy of the block to the requestor via the Cache Fusion mechanism. This event indicates write/read contention.

If this wait event appears in the "Top 5 timed events" list, the plan of action should be similar to that for the gc current block 2-way event.

gc current grant 2-way Figure 10-5 shows a pictorial representation of this event. When an instance needs a block in current mode, it sends the request to the master instance. The master instance finds that currently no instances, including itself, has any lock on the requested block. It sends a message back to the requesting instance granting it the shared lock on the block. The requesting instance then reads the block from the disk. This event doesn't indicate any contention.

The presence of this event in the "Top 5" list indicates that the instance is spending a significant amount of time in obtaining the locks.

■ Tune the SQL to optimize the number of blocks accessed by the application, thereby reducing the number of blocks it is requesting.

■ Look at "Tips for Avoiding RAC Wait Events" at the end of this section.

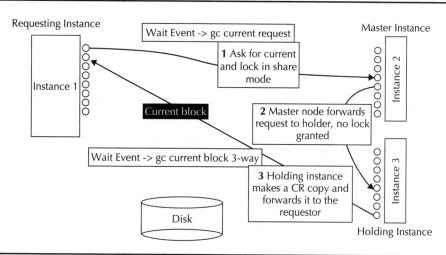

FIGURE 10-4. *Wait event: gc current block 3-way*

gc current grant 2-way Figure 10-6 represents this wait event. When an instance needs a block in current mode, it sends the request to the master instance. The master instance finds that currently no other instance, including itself, has any locks on the requested block. It sends a message back to the requesting instance granting it the exclusive lock on the block. The requesting instance then reads the block from the disk. This event doesn't indicate any contention.

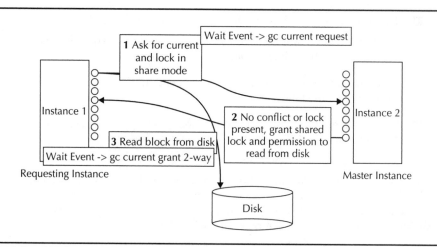

FIGURE 10-5. *Wait event: gc current grant 2-way*

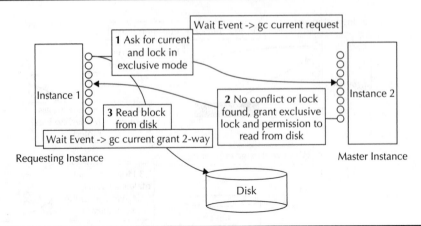

FIGURE 10-6. *Wait event: gc current grant 2-way*

The presence of this event the "Top 5" list indicates that the instance is spending significant amount of time in obtaining the locks.

■ Tune the SQL to optimize the number of blocks accessed by the application, thereby reducing the number of block it is requesting.

■ Look at "Tips for Avoiding RAC Wait Events" at the end of this section.

gc current block busy   When a request needs a block in current mode, it sends a request to the master instance. The requestor eventually gets the block via Cache Fusion transfer; however, the block transfer is delayed due to either of the following reasons:

■ The block was being used by a session on another instance.

■ The block transfer was delayed as the holding instance could not write the corresponding redo record to the online redolog file immediately.

This event indicates significant write/write contention. If the event appears in the "Top 5" list of the AWR report, do the following:

■ Ensure that the Log Writer (LGWR) is tuned. Refer to the *Oracle Performance Tuning Guide* for information about tuning the LGWR performance.

■ Use an appropriate application partitioning to avoid contention.

■ Look at "Tips for Avoiding RAC Wait Events" at the end of this section.

gc current block busy   This event is the same as a gc current block busy event except in this case the requesting instance has requested the block in current mode.

gc current buffer busy   This event is also the similar to the gc current block busy event. In this case the session does not wait because the transfer from another instance was delayed, but because another session on the same instance has already initiated the lock request and is waiting for the response from the master instance. Thus, multiple sessions on the local instance are accessing the same block simultaneously. This event indicates local contention for the block.

If this wait event appears in the "Top 5" list in the AWR report, tune the SQLs to optimize the number of blocks accessed by the application, thereby reducing the number of blocks it is requesting.

gc current block congested   When an instance needs a block in current mode, it sends the request to the master instance. The requestor gets the block via Cache Fusion; however, the block transfer process is delayed due to heavy workload on Cluster Group Services (GCS).

This event doesn't indicate any contention. However, it does indicate that GCS is heavily loaded and the background processes involved with the GCS's work need more CPU time. Lack of CPU resources on the holding instance might cause this to happen.

If this wait event appears in the "Top 5" list of the AWR report, consult the "Tips for Avoiding RAC Wait Events" section.

gc current block congested   This event is same as the gc current block congested event except that in this case the requesting instance has requested the block in current mode.

Tips for Avoiding RAC Wait Events
Following are some generic quick checks for avoiding excessive waits on the global cache:

- Ensure that the system has enough CPU resources. Check the average run queue length, which should be set to less than 1.

- Interconnect network transfer speed and bandwidth should not impact the Cache Fusion data transfer. Have a look at the AWR report, including how much network traffic is generated by each instance. Ensure that the overall network traffic is well below the bandwidth of the private interconnect. If multiple RAC database instances are running on each node, evaluate the network bandwidth against the sum total of traffic generated by all instances. Refer to the "Tuning the Cluster Interconnect" section near the end of this chapter.

- Ensure that the socket send and receive buffers are configured appropriately. Refer to the platform/protocol information available from Oracle.

Enqueue Tuning in RAC
Oracle RDBMS preserves the integrity of user data during simultaneous use of the same data block by using GCS. In addition to data blocks, many other shared resources can be concurrently accessed by end users. Oracle uses a queuing mechanism to ensure proper use of these shared resources. In an RAC environment Global Enqueue Services (GES) protects and regulates access to these shared resources.

Enqueue wait is the time spent by a session waiting for shared resources. A user's response time and hence the database performance might be negatively impacted if a user session spends a long time waiting for a shared resource (or an enqueue). Waiting for the updating of the control file (CF enqueue), of individual row (TX enqueue), or of an exclusive lock on a table (TM enqueue) are examples of enqueue waits.

In an RAC environment, some enqueues are similar to single instance counterparts and need to be coordinated only at the instance level. However, many of the enqueues need to be coordinated globally. GES is responsible for coordinating the global enqueues. Due to global coordination, some enqueues might have higher performance impacts in the RAC environment.

The number of enqueue resources allocated during the instance startup is calculated as follows:

$$\text{GES Resources} = \text{DB\_FILES} + \text{DML\_LOCKS} + \text{ENQUEUE\_RESOURCES}$$
$$+ \text{PROCESSES} + \text{TRANSACTIONS} + 200) \times (1 + (N - 1) / N)$$

where N = Number of RAC instances

Dynamic performance view V$RESOURCE_LIMIT contains the initial allocation, `current_utilization`, `max_utilization`, and `limit_value` statistics for enqueues. The following SQL session output shows enqueue-related statistics from V$RESOURCE_LIMIT:

```
SQL> column current_utilization heading CURRENT
SQL> column MAX_UTILIZATION heading MAX_USAGE
SQL> column  INITIAL_ALLOCATION heading INITIAL
SQL> column resource_limit format a23
SQL>select * from v$resource_limit;
RESOURCE_NAME              CURRENT  MAX_USAGE INITIAL    LIMIT_VALU
------------------------   -------- --------- ---------  ----------
processes                      35       44       150        150
sessions                       40       49       170        170
enqueue_locks                  16       35      2261       2261
enqueue_resources              16       52       968   UNLIMITED
ges_procs                      33       41       320        320
ges_ress                        0        0      4161   UNLIMITED
ges_locks                       0        0      6044   UNLIMITED
ges_cache_ress                346     1326         0   UNLIMITED
ges_reg_msgs                   46      225      1050   UNLIMITED
ges_big_msgs                   22      162       964   UNLIMITED
ges_rsv_msgs                    0        0       301        301
gcs_resources                7941    10703     13822      13822
 <<<output lines not relevant are deleted >>>>
```

AWR and STATSPACK

AWR is Oracle's mechanism for gathering and preserving statistics useful for performance analysis. Oracle 10g introduced a new background process, MMON (Manageability Monitor), to do this work. Every 60 minutes, it takes a snapshot of statistics needed for performance tuning and diagnostics. Snapshots older than one week are automatically purged. Snapshot data is stored in a set of tables in the SYSAUX tablespace; these tables are owned by SYS. AWR is fully RAC aware and is active by default on all the instances. One of the MMON processes acts as the master and coordinates snapshots on all the active instances. AWR takes concurrent snapshots on all the instances and statistics from all the instances stored in the AWR repository with the same `snap_id`. The column `inst_id` is used to differentiate statistics for different instances from the same snapshot.

The package DBMS_WORKLOAD_REPOSITORY is available for managing snapshots manually. You can use this package to create, drop, and modify snapshots. This package can also be used to establish baseline snapshots. Following are some sample commands using this package.

The following command takes an immediate snapshot and archives the data in the repository:

```
sql> execute DBMS_WORKLOAD_REPOSITORY.CREATE_SNAPSHOT ();
```

To modify the snapshot retention interval to 30 days (43,200 minutes) from its default setting of 7 days, you can use the following command:

```
sql> execute DBMS_WORKLOAD_REPOSITORY.MODIFY_SNAPSHOT_SETTINGS
( retention => 43200);
```

You can also change the default snapshot interval of 60 minutes to any other desired value. The following command changes the snapshot interval to 4 hours (240 minutes):

```
sql> execute DBMS_WORKLOAD_REPOSITORY.MODIFY_SNAPSHOT_SETTINGS
( interval => 240);
```

A baseline snapshot is a snapshot that is taken when the database instances and the application are running at optimal performance level. Baseline snapshots are used for comparative analysis. To mark a range of snapshots as baseline snapshots use the following command:

```
sql> execute DBMS_WORKLOAD_REPOSITORY.CREATE_BASELINE
(start_snap_id => 20, end_snap_id => 25, baseline_name => 'normal  baseline');
```

Baseline snapshots are not removed during normal purge operations and need to be removed manually using the DROP_BASELINE procedure as follows:

```
sql> execute DBMS_WORKLOAD_REPOSITORY.DROP_BASELINE
(baseline_name => 'optimal baseline', cascade => FALSE);
```

Even though AWR is RAC aware and snapshots are taken simultaneously on all the active instances, reporting and analysis need to be done at the individual instance level. The script $ORACLE_HOME/rdbms/admin/awrrpt.sql is used to create an AWR report. Here is a sample session to generate an AWR report:

```
SQL> @awrrpt.sql
Current Instance
~~~~~~~~~~~~~~~~

   DB Id           DB Name        Inst Num  Instance
----------      ------------   --------  ------------
 3553717806      PROD               2    PROD2
Specify the Report Type
~~~~~~~~~~~~~~~~~~~~~~~~~
Would you like an HTML report, or a plain text report?
Enter 'html' for an HTML report, or 'text' for plain text
Defaults to 'html'
Enter value for report_type:text

<<<lines for other snapshots deleted from here>>>
                          1384 30 Jul 2005 10:00       1
                          1385 30 Jul 2005 11:00       1
Specify the Begin and End Snapshot Ids
~~~~~~~~~~~~~~~~~~~~~~~~~~~~~~~~~~~~~~~~
Enter value for begin_snap: 1384
Begin Snapshot Id specified: 1385
```

```
Specify the Report Name
~~~~~~~~~~~~~~~~~~~~~~~~~
The default report file name is awrrpt_2_1384_1385.txt. To use this
name, press <return> to continue, otherwise enter an alternative.

Enter value for report_name:PROD2_SAT_JULY3005_10to11.txt
```

> **TIP**
> *Instead of accepting the default name for the report file, give it a name that includes the instance name, day and date, and interval for which the report is generated. This will make the report comparison and tracking easy.*

Interpreting the AWR Report

Oracle performance tuning is a complex and evolved subject—books have been written about it. It is not possible to explain the contents of an AWR report in a few paragraphs here. However, we will attempt to familiarize you with the structure of the report and point out some important RAC-specific statistics to which you should pay attention.

An AWR report generated in an RAC environment contains the following RAC-specific sections, which are not present in an AWR report generated in a single instance database environment:

- Number of instances
- Instance global cache load profile
- Global cache efficiency percentage
- GCS and GES—workload characteristics
- Messaging statistics
- Service statistics
- Service wait class statistics
- Top 5 CR and current blocks segments

Number of Instances Section

This section lists the number of instances at the beginning and end of the AWR report interval.

```
RAC Statistics  DB/Inst: PROD/PROD1  Snaps: 2239-2240
                          Begin    End
                          -----  -----
        Number of Instances:    3      3
```

Global Cache Load Profile Section

This section contains information about the interinstance cache fusion data block and messaging traffic.

```
Global Cache Load Profile
~~~~~~~~~~~~~~~~~~~~~~~~~~~        Per Second    Per Transaction
                                  ----------    ---------------
    Global Cache blocks received:   312.73           12.61
    Global Cache blocks served:     230.60            9.30
```

```
GCS/GES messages received:          514.48              20.74
GCS/GES messages sent:              763.46              30.78
DBWR Fusion writes:                  22.67               0.91
```

The first two statistics indicate the number of blocks transferred to or from this instance. If the database does not contain tablespaces with multiple block sizes, you can use these statistics to calculate the amount of network traffic generated by the instance. Assuming the database block size is 8K, you can calculate the amount of data sent by this instance:

$230 \times 8{,}192 = 1{,}884{,}160$ bytes/sec $= 1.9$ MB/sec

You can also calculate the amount of data received by this instance:

$313 \times 8{,}192 = 2{,}564{,}096$ bytes/sec $= 2.5$ MB/sec

To determine the amount of network traffic generated due to messaging, you first need to find the average message size. Use the following message SQL query to find the average message size:

```
select sum(kjxmsize*
(kjxmrcv+kjxmsnt+kjxmqsnt))/sum((kjxmrcv+kjxmsnt+kjxmqsnt))
from x$kjxm
where kjxmrcv > 0 or kjxmsnt > 0 or kjxmqsnt >0 ;
```

For the system from which the sample report was taken, the average message size was about 300 bytes.

Calculate the amount of messaging traffic on the network like this:

$300 (763 + 514) = 383{,}100 = 0.4$ MB

In case the system for which the report is being analyzed is not available to determine the average message size, you can add 10 to 12 percent of the data traffic to estimate the messaging traffic. Assuming the report is from a two-node RAC environment, then calculate the total network traffic generated by cache fusion activity like this:

$= 1.9 + 2.5 + 0.4 = 4.8$ MBytes/sec

$= 4.8 \times 8 = 38.4$ Mbits/sec

To estimate the network traffic generated in an RAC environment consisting of two or more nodes, first generate an AWR report from all the instances for the same interval. Then calculate the total network traffic generated due to cache fusion activity:

$= \Sigma \text{ block received} + \Sigma \text{ Msg Recd} \times \text{Avg Msg size}$

Please note that Σ block received $= \Sigma$ block served, and Σ Msg Sent $= \Sigma$ Msg Recd. These calculations would require an AWR report from all the instances for the same interval.

NOTE
The AWR report from Oracle Database 10g Release 2 contains an extra line that indicates the interconnect traffic generated by the instance Estd Interconnect traffic (KB). *A quick sum of this statistic from all the instances will provide the overall interconnect traffic, avoiding the trouble of the abovementioned calculations.*

The DBWR Fusion writes statistic in this section indicates the number of times the local DBWR was forced to write a block to disk due to remote instance(s). This number should be low; it is better to analyze this as a fraction of overall DBWR writes, which is available as Physical writes statistics in the Load Profile section of the report:

```
Load Profile
~~~~~~~~~~~~                          Per Second            Per Transaction
                                    ---------------         ---------------
                 Redo size:          700,266.45               28,230.88
              Logical reads:          17,171.74                  692.27
             Block changes:            2,394.61                   96.54
             Physical reads:             208.42                    8.40
            Physical writes:             215.54                    8.69
                User calls:             275.03                   11.09
                   Parses:              22.06                    0.89
```

In this case, DBWR Fusion writes is approximately 10.5 percent of the overall Physical writes. Establish a baseline percentage when the performance is good. You can fine-tune this number by ensuring that instances do not step on each other's data or partitioning the application.

Global Cache Efficiency Percentages Section

This section of the report shows how the instance is getting all the data blocks it needs.

```
Global Cache Efficiency Percentages (Target local+remote 100%)
~~~~~~~~~~~~~~~~~~~~~~~~~~~~~~~~~~~~~~~~~~~~~~~~~~~~~~~~~~~~~~~~~
Buffer access -  local cache %:    97.19
Buffer access - remote cache %:     1.82
Buffer access -         disk %:     0.99
```

The most preferred method is to get data in the local buffer cache, followed by the remote instances' cache, and lastly from the disk. The sum of the first two rows gives the *cache hit ratio* for the instance. The value for remote cache hit should be typically less than 10 percent. Consider implementing an application partitioning scheme if this value is higher than 10 percent.

GCS and GES Workload Characteristics Section

This section contains timing statistics for global enqueue and global cache. The statistics are further subdivided into the following four subsections:

- Average time to obtain an enqueue.
- Time the instance has to wait before receiving a block in consistent read (CR) or in current mode.

- Amount of time/delay an instance is seeing while processing a CR request.

- Amount of time/delay an instance is seeing while processing a current block request.

```
Global Cache and Enqueue Services - Workload Characteristics
~~~~~~~~~~~~~~~~~~~~~~~~~~~~~~~~~~~~~~~~~~~~~~~~~~~~~~~~~~~~~~~~~~
                    Avg global enqueue get time (ms):    951.5

         Avg global cache cr block receive time (ms):      3.9
    Avg global cache current block receive time (ms):      3.0

           Avg global cache cr block build time (ms):      0.7
            Avg global cache cr block send time (ms):      0.3
     Global cache log flushes for cr blocks served %:     50.5
           Avg global cache cr block flush time (ms):     10.1

      Avg global cache current block pin time (ms):        1.4
      Avg global cache current block send time (ms):       0.3
 Global cache log flushes for current blocks served %:     1.4
      Avg global cache current block flush time (ms):      4.4
```

As a rule of thumb, all timings related to a CR block should be less than 10 msec, and all timing related to current block processing should be less than 20 msec.

GCS and GES Messaging Statistics Section

The first section contains statistics related to sending a message, and generally all these statistics should be less than 1 millisecond. The second section details the breakup of direct and indirect messages.

```
Global Cache and Enqueue Services - Messaging Statistics
~~~~~~~~~~~~~~~~~~~~~~~~~~~~~~~~~~~~~~~~~~~~~~~~~~~~~~~~~~~~~~
                  Avg message sent queue time (ms):     0.5
         Avg message sent queue time on ksxp (ms):     1.7
              Avg message received queue time (ms):     0.2
                Avg GCS message process time (ms):     0.5
                Avg GES message process time (ms):     0.2

                      % of direct sent messages:    52.22
                    % of indirect sent messages:    46.95
                   % of flow controlled messages:     0.83
```

Direct messages are the messages sent by an instance foreground or the user processes to remote instances, whereas indirect messages are the messages that are not urgent and are pooled and sent. Indirect messages are low priority messages. These statistics generally depend on the nature of the workload among the instances, and not much can be done to fine-tune them. Establish a baseline for these during normal user workloads. Also observe these statistics after any significant change in the user workload and establish a new baseline after any changes.

Service Statistics Section

Statistics in this section show the resources used by all the service instance supports.

```
Service Statistics  DB/Inst: PROD/PROD1  Snaps: 2239-2240
-> ordered by DB Time
-> us - microsecond - 1000000th of a second
                                                    Physical    Logical
                                                    Reads       Reads
Service Name                DB Time (s)   DB CPU (s)  Reads       Reads
--------------------------  -----------   ----------  ----------  ----------
PROD                        1,198,708.4    17,960.0    491,498    9,998,798,201
SYS$USERS                       3,903.3       539.7    245,724      2,931,729
SYS$BACKGROUND                     29.3         4.8      7,625      4,801,655
```

The instance PROD1 is serving the workload connected using the service PROD. If multiple services are configured, the breakup will appear here. There are two internal services in addition to the application services that are defined by the DBA. SYS$BACKGROUND is used by all background processes. SYS$USERS is the default service for user sessions that are not associated with applications services—for example, connecting as `sqlplus / as sysdba`.

Service Wait Class Statistics Section

This section summarizes waits in different categories for each service. If a service response is not acceptable, these statistics can show where the service is waiting.

```
Service Wait Class Stats  DB/Inst: PROD/PROD1  Snaps: 2239-2240
-> Wait Class info for services in the Service Statistics section.
-> Total Waits and Time Waited displayed for the following wait
   classes:  User I/O, Concurrency, Administrative, Network
-> Time Waited (Wt Time) in centisecond (100th of a second)
```

Service Name							
User I/O Total Wts	User I/O Wt Time	Concurcy Total Wts	Concurcy Wt Time	Admin Total Wts	Admin Wt Time	Network Total Wts	Network Wt Time
PROD							
2227431	4136718	3338963	95200428	0	0	1660799	15403
SYS$USERS							
259502	188515	274	486	0	0	1676	3
SYS$BACKGROUND							
10412	1404	4135	12508	0	0	0	0

Top 5 CR and Current Blocks Segments Section

These sections contain the names of the top 5 contentious segments (index or tables). If a table or an index is being subject to a very high percentage of CR and current block transfers, you need to analyze its usage pattern, database layout characteristics, and other parameters that might cause contention.

Segments by CR Blocks Received DB/Inst: PROD/PROD1 Snaps: 2239-2240

Owner	Tablespace Name	Object Name	Subobject Name	Obj. Type	CR Blocks Received	%Total
ES_MAIL	ESINFREQID	ES_INSTANCE		TABLE	136,997	58.65
ES_MAIL	ESINFREQID	ES_INSTANCE_IX_TYPE		INDEX	21,037	9.01
ES_MAIL	ESFREQTBL	ES_FOLDER		TABLE	14,616	6.26
ES_MAIL	ESFREQTBL	ES_USER		TABLE	6,251	2.68
ES_MAIL	ESSMLTBL	ES_EXT_HEADER		TABLE	2,467	1.06

Segments by Current Blocks Received DB/Inst: PROD/PROD1 Snaps: 2239-2240

Owner	Tablespace Name	Object Name	Subobject Name	Obj. Type	Current Blocks Received	%Total
ES_MAIL	ESINFREQID	ES_INSTANCE		TABLE	602,833	80.88
ES_MAIL	ESSMLTBL	ES_EXT_HEADER		TABLE	18,527	2.49
ES_MAIL	ESINFREQID	ES_INSTANCE_IX_TYPE		INDEX	13,640	1.83
ES_MAIL	ESFREQTBL	ES_FOLDER		TABLE	11,242	1.51
ES_MAIL	ESINFREQID	ES_INSTANCE_IX_FOLDE		INDEX	5,026	.67

Oracle Database 10g R2 contains the following additional information in these sections:

```
-> Total Current Blocks Received:        2,328
-> Captured Segments account for         93.1% of Total
```

The additional information allows you to compare the top segment's activity with respect to the overall system activity in that category.

STATSPACK

AWR is intended to supersede STATSPACK. AWR is automated and works out of the box without needing customizations. STATSPACK is available in the form of a package, but it is not installed automatically.

Although AWR and STATSPACK serve similar objectives and their reports look alike, there are differences, especially starting with Oracle Database 10g R2. STATSPACK is extensively used by Oracle developers and DBAs. When STATSPACK snapshots are taken at a level higher than the default level of 5, it provides much more statistical information. Generally it should not be necessary to run STATSPACK at a level greater than 5. Due to the scope of this book, we will limit our discussions to the AWR report only, with a quick introduction to STATSPACK.

Refer to the $ORACLE_HOME/rdbms/admin/spdoc.txt to install, configure, and use STATSPACK. Complete the following steps to install and begin using the package:

1. Execute the script spcreate.sql; this script creates the required schema and the corresponding schema objects.

2. Execute the script spauto.sql; this script configures an automatic snapshot for every hour on the hour. Execute this script on each instance.

3. Use the script spreport.sql to generate the STATSPACK report.

All these scripts are located in the $ORACLE_HOME/rdbms/admin directory.

ADDM

Automatic Database Diagnostic and Monitor (ADDM) is Oracle's major step toward making the database self-tuning. The following infrastructure components are introduced in Oracle 10g:

- **MMON** Manageability Monitor is a new background process that does all the work required for ADDM.

- **AWR** Automatic Workload Repository is a set of database objects that is used to gather and store database performance statistics.

- **Packages** The package DBMS_ADVISOR is available to manage ADDM.

- **Parameters** The STATISTICS_LEVEL initialization parameter should be set either to TYPICAL or ALL for ADDM to function. The DBIO_EXPECTED parameter needs to be set to represent the average read time for a database block. Its default value is 10000 (10 milliseconds). Use the following command to set this parameter:

  ```
  Sql> execute DBMS_ADVISOR.SET_DEFAULT_TASK_PARAMETER
  ('ADDM','DBIO_EXPECTED'. 30000)
  ```

- **Auxiliary Tablespace** Oracle uses auxiliary tablespace (SYSAUX) as the storage space for the tools and other components such as AWR, ADDM, and so on. This tablespace is created by default during database creation.

The goal of ADDM is to optimize the time spent by the database for servicing the user workload. Its sole objective is to reduce DB Time, which consists of the following two components:

- **Wait Time** Time spent by user sessions while waiting for any resources.
- **CPU Time** Time spent by user sessions while processing user work.

MMON analyzes the data stored in the AWR repository and uses predefined, built-in rules to suggest how DB Time can be reduced. It generates a report with recommendations but does not implement them automatically. Its findings include the following:

- **System Capacity Issues** CPU, I/O subsystem usage.

- **Instance management** Analyzes instance memory management parameters such as SGA, redolog buffers, buffer cache, and so on. Also analyzes other initialization parameters for optimal setting.

- **Java, SQL, and PL/SQL Tuning** Analyzes high resource-consuming Java, SQL, and PL/SQL statements and whether the optimal data access path is being used.

- **Contention** In a single instance environment, analyzes contention in single instances as well as in the RAC environment. Takes into account buffer_busy_waits and all global cache related wait events.

- **Database Structure** Analyzes things like online redolog file size.

- **Miscellaneous** Analyzes application connection patterns.

Tuning the Cluster Interconnect

Oracle uses cluster interconnect for sending messages to coordinate data block access and for sending copies of data blocks from one instance's cache to another instance's cache to optimize disk I/O. Therefore, cluster interconnect performance is crucial to RAC performance. Its configuration and proper functioning is one of the most important parts of RAC performance tuning.

Verify That Private Interconnect Is Used

In Oracle Database 10g, you can specify the private interconnect while configuring the CRS. Ensure that the private interconnect is used for Cache Fusion traffic. Also ensure that the private interconnect is not used by other network-intensive functions such as FTP and rcp commands between the cluster nodes as it might impact the RAC performance.

In Oracle 9i and in Oracle 10g, you can use the following commands to verify that the intended private interconnect is being used for the Cache Fusion traffic:

```
SQL> oradebug setmypid
SQL> oradebug ipc
```

This will dump a trace file to the user_dump_dest. The output will look something like this:

```
SSKGXPT 0x5382dc4 flags SSKGXPT_READPENDING    info for network 0
socket no 8     IP 138.2.205.104         UDP 31691
sflags SSKGXPT_UP
info for network 1
socket no 0     IP 0.0.0.0      UDP 0
```

This indicates that IP 138.2.205.104 with a UDP protocol is being used for cache fusion traffic.

Starting with Oracle Database 10g R2, cluster interconnect information is printed in the alert.log:

```
Interface type 1 eth1 192.168.2.0 configured from OCR for
use as a cluster interconnect

Interface type 1 eth0 138.2.151.0 configured from OCR for
use as  a public interface
```

Verify That Network Interconnect Is Not Saturated

As mentioned in the preceding sections, you can use the AWR report to analyze the following:

- Network traffic generated by Oracle instances; ensure that at no point in time the traffic generated is saturating the private interconnect.
- Whether the network delays and latency as indicated in the AWR report are excessive. In Oracle Database 10g R2, you can use the OEM to monitor the interconnect traffic.

In a Nutshell

Performance tuning in the RAC environment is similar to tuning in a single instance environment, with a few additional considerations for RAC. New wait events and enhanced statistics collection tools are available with Oracle Database 10g. AWR is a powerful tool; the AWR report provides an excellent place to start analyzing performance in an RAC environment. In the next chapter, we will look at resource management in an RAC environment.

PART
IV

Advanced Concepts
in RAC

CHAPTER
11

Global Resource Directory

elcome to the world of resource management and administration in a parallel computing environment. This chapter provides a detailed discussion about resource management and locking issues and the interinstance coordination activities that take place in the cluster. Understanding the internal workings of locking will help you in architecting RAC solutions and administering the RAC. Be warned that the concepts discussed here are specific to the current versions of Oracle and may not be applicable to past or future versions.

The RAC environment includes numerous resources, such as multiple versions of data block buffers in buffer caches in different modes. Oracle uses different types of locking and queuing mechanisms within a cluster to coordinate lock resources, data, and interinstance data requests. We will examine how Oracle coordinates these resources to maintain the integrity of shared data and resources.

Coordination of concurrent tasks within a cluster is called *synchronization.* Resources such as data blocks and locks must be synchronized between the nodes as nodes within a cluster acquire and release ownership of them frequently. The synchronization provided by the Global Resource Directory (GRD) maintains clusterwide concurrency of the resources and in turn ensures the integrity of shared data. The amount of synchronization depends on the amount of resources and the number of users and tasks working on them. Little synchronization may be needed to coordinate a small number of concurrent tasks, but with many concurrent tasks, significant synchronization is required.

Synchronization is also required for buffer cache management, as it is divided into multiple caches, and each instance is responsible for managing its own local version of the buffer cache. Copies of data blocks may be exchanged between the nodes in the cluster. This concept is sometimes referred to as the *global cache*, although in reality each node's buffer cache is separate and copies of blocks are exchanged through traditional distributed locking mechanisms. Global Cache Services (GCS) maintain the cache coherency across the buffer cache resources. Global Enqueue Services (GES) controls the resource management across the clusters' non-buffer cache resources.

Cache Coherency

In *cache coherency*, the contents of the caches in different nodes are in a well-defined state with respect to each other. Cache coherency identifies the most up-to-date copy of a resource, also called the *master copy*. In case of node failure, no vital information is lost (such as a committed transaction state) and atomicity is maintained. This requires additional logging or copying of data but is not part of the locking system.

Cache coherency is the mechanism by which multiple copies of an object are kept consistent between Oracle instances. Parallel Cache Management (PCM) ensures that a master copy of a data block is stored in one buffer cache and consistent copies of the block are stored in other buffer caches. The background process LCKx is responsible for this important task. This process dialogues with LMD0 to synchronize access to resources.

The lock and resource structures for instance locks reside in the GRD (also called the Distributed Lock Manager, or DLM), a dedicated area within the shared pool. The GRD maintains information about the shared resources such as data blocks. Details about the data block resources and cached versions are maintained by GCS. Additional details—such as the location of the most current version, state of the buffer, role of the data blocks (local or global), and ownership details such as most current versions—are maintained by GES. Global cache, together with GES, forms the GRD.

Each instance maintains a part of the GRD in its System Global Area (SGA). The GCS and GES nominate one instance, called the *resource master*, to manage all information about a particular resource. Each instance knows which instance masters which resource. GCS maintains cache coherency by using the Cache Fusion algorithm.

GES manages all non-Cache Fusion interinstance resource operations and tracks the status of all Oracle enqueue mechanisms. The primary resources of the GES controls are dictionary cache locks, library cache locks, and standard enqueues. GES also performs deadlock detection of all deadlock-sensitive enqueues and resources.

Resources and Enqueues

A *resource* is an identifiable entity—that is, it has a name or reference. The referenced entity is usually a memory region, a disk file, a data block, or an abstract entity; the name of the resource *is* the resource. A resource can be owned or locked in various states, such as *exclusive* or *shared*. By definition, any shared resource is lockable. If it is not shared, no access conflict can occur. If it is shared, access conflicts must be resolved, typically with a lock. Although the terms *lock* and *resource* refer to separate objects, they are often used interchangeably. A global resource is visible and used throughout the cluster. A local resource is used by only one instance. It may still have locks to control access by the multiple processes of the instance, but no access to it is available from outside the instance.

Each resource can have a list of locks, called the *grant queue,* that are currently granted to users. A *convert queue* is a queue of locks that are waiting to be converted to particular modes. Conversion is the process of changing a lock from the mode it currently holds to a different mode. Even if the mode is NULL, it is regarded as holding a lock without any conflicts of interest on that resource.

Acquiring a lock (known as a *grant* on that resource) is the process of acquiring a lock on a resource that currently does not have a lock (mode = no-lock). In addition, a resource has a lock value block (LVB) that can contain a small amount of data.

Figure 11-1 shows the grant and convert queue representation for a block and the structure. The data block resource (also known as *PCM resource*) is identified using the following format:

```
[LE] [Class] [BL]
```

- **LE** Lock element that denotes the data block address (DBA—not to be confused with the other DBA, database administrator). It is visible in V$BH.LOCK_ELEMENT_ADDR.

- **Class** Class of the block. Visible in V$BH.CLASS# (data, undo, temp, and so on).

- **BL** Buffer cache management locks (or buffer locks).

```
[0x10000c5] [0x1], [BL]
Grant Queue
Convert Queue
Lock Value Block
```

FIGURE 11-1. *Grant and convert queues*

Data buffer cache blocks are the most obvious and most heavily used global resource. Other data item resources are also global in the cluster, such as transaction enqueues and database data structures. The data buffer cache blocks are handled by the GCS (Parallel Cache Management, or PCM). The non-data block resources are handled by GES (non-Parallel Cache Management, or non-PCM). The Global Resource Manager (GRM, the old DLM) keeps the lock information valid and correct across the cluster. The evaluation of a vendor-supplied DLM to Oracle Clusterware was discussed in Chapter 2.

Grants and Conversions

Locks are placed on a resource grant or convert queue. If the lock mode changes, it is moved between the queues. If several locks exist on the grant queue, they must be compatible. Locks of the same mode are not necessarily compatible with each other.

NOTE
Lock conversation and the compatibility matrix of DLM locks were discussed in Chapter 2. We discuss management of GES locks later in this chapter.

A lock leaves the convert queue under any of the following conditions:

- The process requests the lock termination (that is, removes the lock).
- The process cancels the conversion; the lock is moved back to the grant queue in the previous mode.
- The requested mode is compatible with the most restrictive lock in the grant queue and with all the previous modes of the convert queue, and the lock is at the head of the convert queue.

Figure 11-2 shows the lock conversion mechanisms. Convert requests are processed First In, First Out (FIFO).

The grant queue and convert queue are associated with each and every resource that is managed by the GES. The sequence of operations is discussed in detail in the following example with respect

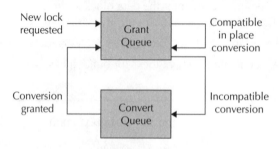

FIGURE 11-2. *Lock conversion*

to the compatibility of lock modes. This is an example of a resource getting locks placed on its grant or resource queues:

1. A shareable read lock is granted.

2. Another shareable read lock is granted. They are compatible and can reside on the grant queue.

3. Another shareable read lock is placed on the grant queue.

4. One lock converts to shareable NULL. This conversion can be done in place because it is a simple downgrade.

5. Another lock attempts to convert to exclusive write. It has to be placed on the convert queue.

Figure 11-3 shows the interested resource's grant and convert queue structure in all five stages.

Locks and Enqueues
Enqueues are basically locks that support queuing mechanisms and that can be acquired in different modes. An enqueue can be held in exclusive mode by one process, and others can hold in non-exclusive mode depending on the type. Enqueues in RAC are the same as the enqueues used in a single instance of the Oracle RDBMS except for the scope. Few enqueues are local to the instance and few are global. A transaction is protected by a TX (transaction) enqueue irrespective of whether it is for a single instance or a clustered environment. But the temporary tablespace enqueue is local to the instance where it is held.

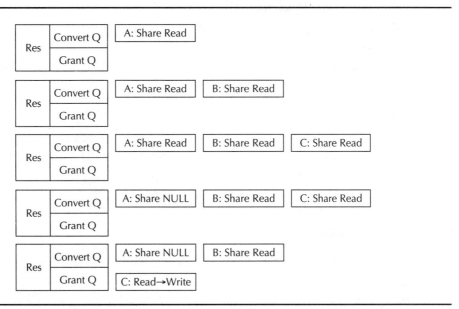

FIGURE 11-3. *Grant and convert queue operations*

Global Enqueue Services

GES coordinates the requests of all global enqueues (any non-buffer cache resources). This is the single point of contact for lock management in the RAC. It is also involved in deadlock detection and request timeouts. During normal operation, it manages caching and performs the cleanup operation during cluster reconfiguration.

Latches and Enqueues

There are two types of local locks, latches and enqueues. Latches are instance specific and do not affect database-wide operations. Latches do not affect the global operations of clustered environments. Enqueues, however, can be both local to an instance and global to a cluster.

Latches are lightweight, low-level serialization mechanisms that protect in-memory data structures in the SGA. They do not support queuing and do not protect database objects such as tables or data files. They are atomic and are held for a very short time. They do not support multiple levels and are always acquired in exclusive mode. Since latches are synchronized within a node, they do not facilitate internode synchronization.

Enqueues are shared structures that serialize access to database resources. Enqueues support multiple modes and are held longer than latches. They have a database-wide scope, as they protect persistent objects such as tables or library cache objects. For example, if you update a row in a block, no one from any other instance should be able to update the same row. A transaction (TX) enqueue protects the update for your operation; this enqueue is a global lock in RAC.

Enqueues are associated with a session or transaction, and Oracle can use them in any of the following modes:

- Shared or protected read
- Exclusive
- Protected write
- Concurrent read
- Concurrent write
- NULL

Depending on the operation on the resource, an enqueue lock is obtained on that resource. The following listing provides the most common locking modes for the associated operations:

```
Operation                    Lock Mode LMODE Lock Description
---------------------------- --------- ----- ----------------
Select                       NULL      1     null
Lock For Update              SS        2     sub share
Select for update            SS        2     sub share
Insert/Delete/Update         SX        3     sub exclusive
Lock Row Exclusive           SX        3     sub exclusive
Create Index                 S         4     share
Lock Share                   S         4     share
Lock Share Row Exclusive     SSX       5     share/sub exclusive
Alter/Drop/Truncate table    X         6     exclusive
Drop Index                   X         6     exclusive
Lock Exclusive               X         6     exclusive
Truncate table               X         6     exclusive
```

The following matrix explains the compatibility matrix of the enqueue modes:

Compatible	NULL	SS	SX	S	SSX	X
NULL	Yes	Yes	Yes	Yes	Yes	Yes
SS	Yes	Yes	Yes	Yes	Yes	No
SX	Yes	Yes	Yes	No	No	No
S	Yes	Yes	No	Yes	No	No
SSX	Yes	Yes	No	No	No	No
X	Yes	No	No	No	No	No

Lock Modes   Enqueues are acquired in various lock modes. Table 11-1 summarizes each lock mode and provides a detailed description; this information is common to both single instance and multi-instance databases.

Mode	Summary	Description
NULL	Null mode. No lock is on the resource.	Conveys no access rights. Typically, a lock is held at this level to indicate that a process is interested in a resource, or it is used as a placeholder. Once created, NULL locks ensure the requestor always has a lock on the resource; there is no need for the DLM to create and destroy locks constantly when ongoing access is needed.
SS	Subshared mode (concurrent read). Read—there may be writers and other readers.	The associated resource can be read in an unprotected fashion; other processes can read and write the associated resource. This lock is also known as an RS (row share) table lock.
SX	Shared exclusive mode (concurrent write). Write—there may be other readers and writers.	The associated resource can be read or written to in an unprotected fashion: other processes can both read and write to the resource. This lock is also known as an RX (row exclusive) table lock.
S	Shared mode (protected read). Read—no writers are allowed.	A process cannot write to the associated resource, but multiple processes can read it. This is the traditional shared lock. Any number of users can have simultaneous read access to the resource. Shared access is appropriate for read operations.
SSX	Subshared exclusive mode (protected write). One writer only—there may be readers.	Only one process can hold a lock at this level. This allows a process to modify a resource without allowing other processes to modify the resource at the same time. Other processes can perform unprotected reads. This traditional update lock is also known as an SRX (shared row exclusive) table lock.
X	Exclusive mode. Write—no other access is allowed.	When a lock is held at this level, it grants the holding process exclusive access to the resource. Other processes cannot read or write to the resource. This is the traditional exclusive lock.

TABLE 11-1.   *Lock Mode Summary*

NOTE
*For a complete and detailed discussion on the fundamentals of locking,
refer to the Oracle document* Oracle Database Concepts, 10g Release
2 (Part No. B14220-01), *Chapter 13, "How Oracle Locks Data."*

Global Locks Database and Structure

Each node holds directory information for a set of resources. To locate a resource, the directory service uses a hashing function on the resource name to determine which nodes hold the directory tree information for the resource. The lock request is sent directly to the holding node. The GRD also stores information on resource locks and the converter and granter queues. When a process requests a lock that is owned by the same node, the structure is created local to the node. In this case, the directory node is the same as the master node.

The GES layer in RAC synchronizes global locks among all active instances in a cluster. Global locks are mainly of two types:

- Locks used by the GCS for buffer cache management. Those locks are called Parallel Cache Management (PCM) locks.

- Global locks, such as global enqueues, that Oracle synchronizes within a cluster to coordinate non-PCM resources. These locks are used to protect the enqueue structures (and are managed by GES). They are called non-PCM locks.

GES tracks the status of all Oracle locks and their corresponding resources. Global locks are allotted and created during instance startup, and each instance owns or masters some set of resources or locks.

Global locks are held by background processes within instances rather than by transactions. An instance *owns* a global lock that *protects* a resource, such as a data block or data dictionary entry, when the resource enters the instance's SGA. The GES manages locking only for resources accessed by more than one instance. In the following sections we discuss non-PCM coordination (non-PCM locks) only.

GES Locks

Many non-PCM locks control access to data files and control files and also serialize interinstance communication. They also control library caches and dictionary caches. These locks protect data files, not the data file blocks inside the file. Examples of these are data manipulation language (DML) enqueues (table locks), transaction enqueues, and data definition language (DDL) locks or dictionary locks. The System Change Number (SCN) and the mount lock are global locks, not enqueues.

Transaction Locks or Row-level Locks   Oracle's row-level locking is one of the most sophisticated features in the RDBMS; it is also one of the least understood topics. Row-level locks protect selected rows in a data block during a transaction. A transaction acquires a global enqueue and an exclusive lock for each individual row modified by one of the following statements: INSERT, UPDATE, DELETE, and SELECT with the FOR UPDATE clause.

These locks are stored in the block, and each lock refers to the global transaction enqueue. Since they are stored in the block level, their scope is wider at the database level. A transaction lock is acquired in exclusive mode when a transaction initiates its first change. It is held until the transaction does a COMMIT or ROLLBACK. SMON also acquires it in exclusive mode when recovering (undoing) a transaction. Transaction locks are used as a queuing mechanism for processes awaiting the release of an object locked by a transaction in progress.

Internal Implementation of Row-level Locks   Every data block in the data file with the exception of the temp and rollback segments will be created with a predefined number of transaction slots. (Undo segments have different types of transaction slots, called transaction tables.) These transaction slots are called *interested transaction lists* (ITLs) and are controlled by the INITRANS parameter. The default value for INITRANS is 2 for tables and 3 for index segments.

Every transaction slot occupies 24 bytes of free space in the variable part of the data block header. The maximum number of transaction slots is controlled by the MAXTRANS parameter. However, the size of the variable part of the database block header cannot exceed 50 percent of the data block size. This limits the total number of transaction slots in the data block.

ITL slots are acquired for every DML lock that affects that data block. An ITL contains the transaction ID (XID), which is the pointer to an entry in the transaction table of a rollback segment. Another transaction can always read the data from the rollback segment. If new transactions want to update the data, they must to wait until the current transaction commits or rolls back.

Any transaction that is interested in performing a DML lock on the rows belonging to that block *must* get an ITL slot before proceeding. An ITL entry consists of the XID, undo byte address (UBA), flags indicating the transaction status (Flag), and lock count (Lck) showing the number of rows locked by this transaction within the block and the SCN at which the transaction is updated. The XID uniquely identifies the transaction and provides the information about the undo for that transaction. Figure 11-4 shows the relational links between the block and ITL and the transaction tables.

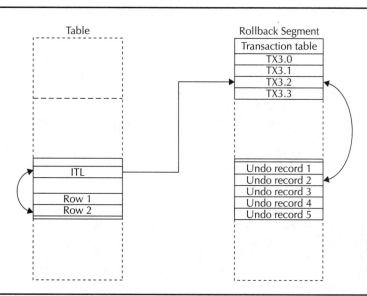

FIGURE 11-4.   *Internal implementation of row-level locks*

Transaction Table

The transaction table is the data structure within the rollback segment that holds the transaction identifiers of the transactions using that rollback segment. The number of rows in the transaction table is equal to the number of transaction slots in that rollback segment and is visible via the internal view X$KTUXE (available only when logged in as SYS).

A transaction ID (XID) is the three-part information that consists of the undo segment number, undo segment slot number, and the wrap number in the undo segment. (USN.SLOT#.WRAP#). The dynamic performance view V$TRANSACTION can be queried to get more details on that particular transaction.

While the transaction commits, Oracle completes the bare minimum requirements for the transaction commit operation as the system is optimized for higher throughput. This involves updating the flag in the transaction table in the rollback segment, and the block is not revisited. This process is known as *fast commit*. During this time, the ITL in the data block (called *open ITL*) is still pointing to the transaction table of the corresponding rollback segments. If the instance crashes before the transaction is committed (or rolled back), transaction recovery is performed while opening the database next time by the data from the rollback segments.

If at the same time or a later time another transaction visits the data block, which has an open ITL, to get a consistent-read copy (CR), the transaction looks up the transaction table to find the status of the transaction. If the transaction is uncommitted, the second transaction creates a copy of the data or index block in memory, gets the UBA from the ITL, reads the data from the undo, and uses it to roll back the change defined by the undo. If the undo does not populate the ITL with an SCN, or the SCN is old enough, another copy of the data block is made and the undo is read from the undo block once again to undo the next change. The UBA in the transaction table is used to roll back the entire transaction as a result of a rollback command, process failure, or shutdown immediate command.

If the status of the transaction in the table is committed, the transaction is deemed committed. Now the rows are no longer locked by the transaction, but the lock byte in the row header is not cleared until the next time DML is performed on the block. The lock byte cleanout is piggy-backed with the DML operation. The block cleanout is delayed by some discrete time interval because of the fast commit—this is called *delayed block cleanout*. This cleanout operation closes the open ITLs for the committed transactions and generates the redo information, as a block cleanout may involve updating the block with a new SCN. This is why you see the redo generation for some select statements.

Table Locks

Table locks (TM) are DML locks that protect entire tables. A transaction acquires a table lock when a table is modified by one of the following statements: INSERT, UPDATE, DELETE, SELECT with the FOR UPDATE clause, and LOCK TABLE. A table lock can be held in any of several modes: null (N), row share (RS), row exclusive (RX), share lock (S), share row exclusive (SRX), and exclusive (X).

Messaging in RAC

The synchronization effort to achieve parallel processing among nodes ideally uses a high-speed interconnect linking the parallel processors. For parallel processing within a single node, messaging is not necessary; shared memory is used instead. The DLM handles messaging and locking between nodes. Interrupts are used when more than one process wants to use the processor in a uniprocessor architecture. Shared memory and semaphores are used when more than one process wants to communicate in a symmetric multiprocessing (SMP) system.

In RAC, GES uses messaging for interinstance communication. The implementation of interprocess/internode communication is done by messages and asynchronous traps (ASTs). Messaging is used for both intra-instance communication (between the processes of the same instance on the same node) and interinstance communication (between processes on other nodes).

The LMON process of an instance communicates with the other LMON processes on other servers and uses the same messaging framework. Similarly, the LMD process from one instance communicates with other LMD processes using messages. Any process's lock client performs direct sends. Though the GRD has been a part of the RDBMS kernel, processes requiring the lock handle on the resource do not directly access the resource directory. This is done by a background message from the requesting instance's LMD to the master instance. Once the message is received, the lock handle in the GRD is updated with the new information. The returning message confirms the acknowledgment of the grant for a set of operations on that resource and management of those resources. This helps in deadlock detection and avoidance. The messaging traffic information can be obtained from the fixed view V$GES_MISC.

Three-Way Lock Messages

Messaging is used by GES for interinstance and interprocess communication. Interinstance messaging is used between the LMON process from one instance to the LMON process of another instance. Intra-instance or interprocess communication is used when LMON wants to communicate to the LMD process.

In interinstance messaging, a maximum of three parties is involved. Let's look a typical three-way communication. The three-way lock message involves up to a maximum of three nodes, namely the master (M) instance, holding (H) instance, and requesting (R) instance. The sequence of messages is shown in Figure 11-5, where requesting instance R is interested in block B1 from holding instance H. The resource is mastered in master instance M.

1. Instance R gets the ownership information about a resource from the GRD, which maintains details such as lock ownership and current state. Instance R then sends the message to master instance M, requesting access to the resource. This message is sent by a direct send, as it is critical.

2. Instance M receives the message and forwards that request to holding instance H. This message is also sent by a direct send message. This message to the holder is known as a *blocking asynchronous trap* (BAST), which is discussed in the next section.

3. Instance H sends the resource to instance R. It uses high-speed interconnect to transfer the resource. The resource is copied to the requesting instance's memory.

4. Upon receipt of the resource and lock handle on that resource, instance R sends an acknowledgment to instance M. This message is queued for propagation; it is not a critical message. This is called *acquisition asynchronous trap* (AAST) and is discussed in the next section.

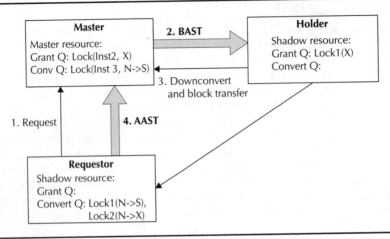

FIGURE 11-5. *Three-way lock messages*

Asynchronous Traps

When a process requests a lock on a resource, the GES sends a blocking AST (BAST) to notify the holder, another process that currently owns locks on that resource in incompatible modes. When the holder receives the BAST from the requestor, owners of locks can relinquish them to permit access by the requester. When a lock is obtained, an acquisition AST (AAST) is sent to tell the requester that it now owns the lock. ASTs are delivered by LMD or LMS to the process that has submitted a lock request. This is done by sending all messages to the LMD on the remote node, which then forwards the messages to the actual waiting process in earlier versions.

Messaging Deadlocks

Deadlocks can occur if one process (A) is waiting to send a BAST to another process to acquire a lock, and another process (B) is waiting on the lock that the waiting process hold. In this condition, the first process (A) will not be checking on BASTs, so it will not see that it is blocking another process. As too many writers are trying to send messages (known as BAST-only messages) and no one is reading messages to free up buffer space, a deadlock occurs.

Message Traffic Controller (TRFC)

GES totally depends on messages for resource management. These messages are typically small in size (128 bytes) and interconnect plays a great role if the number of messages is high, depending on the number of resources. The interconnect is also expected to be lightweight or low latency so that it can reduce deadlocks. To streamline the messaging traffic and to avoid deadlocks, the message traffic controller introduces the ticketing mechanism for a smooth flow of messages.

Normally, messages are sent with the message sequence number along with tickets that control the message flow. This way, the receiver ensures that all the messages are received from the sender. The TRFC is used to control the DLM traffic between all the nodes in the cluster by buffering sender sends (in case of network congestion) and making the sender wait until the network window is large enough to accommodate the traffic.

The traffic controller will keep a predefined number of tickets in the reserve pool. The size of the ticket pool is dependent on the function of network send buffer size. Any process that sends messages should acquire a ticket before sending and return the ticket to the pool once the message is sent. Used tickets are released back to the pool by the receivers (LMS or LMD), according to the remote receiver report of how many messages the remote receiver has received. This is similar to the transaction slot entry in the data blocks, where any DML lock should get the ITL slot before modifying the block. If no tickets are available, the messages are buffered at the sender side and sent when a ticket is available. The number of tickets can be manually controlled by the hidden parameter_lm_tickets, for which no tweaking is required unless a big send queue is affecting system performance.

The ticket availability and send queue details can be obtained from V$GES_TRAFFIC_ CONTROLLER. A node relies on messages to return from the remote node to release tickets for reuse. This ticketing mechanism allows smooth flow of messages.

The following query provides a snapshot of ticket usage details:

```
SQL> SELECT LOCAL_NID LOCAL ,REMOTE_NID REMOTE,TCKT_AVAIL AVAILABILITY,
  2  TCKT_LIMIT LIMIT,SND_Q_LEN SEND_QUEUE,TCKT_WAIT WAITING
  3  FROM V$GES_TRAFFIC_CONTROLLER;

     LOCAL     REMOTE AVAILABILITY      LIMIT SEND_QUEUE WAITING
---------- ---------- ------------ ---------- ---------- ----------
         0          1          750       1000          0 NO
         0          1          750       1000          0 NO
         0          1          750       1000          0 NO
```

Another mechanism is implemented to help avoid running out of tickets. If the number of available tickets goes beyond 50, the active send backing is enabled for aggressive messaging. This helps the traffic controller maintain speed. The number of tickets which triggers active send back is configurable via the _lm_ticket_active_sendback parameter. This query can be run to monitor ticket usage and availability. Pay particular attention to the TCKT_WAIT column, which shows *YES* when messages are waiting for tickets. If it is waiting for tickets, you need to check the TCKT_LIMIT and TCKT_AVAIL columns, which show the ticket limit and ticket availability at that time.

In extreme situations, the preceding query may hang, because to get information about ticket availability, tickets are required. Under those conditions, the sessions will be waiting for the "*KJCTS: client waiting for tickets*" wait event. Alternatively, using the lkdebug -t option to oradebug can also dump the ticket information to the trace files:

```
oradebug setmypid
oradebug unlimt
oradebug lkdebug -t
```

Global Cache Services

GCS also uses locks to coordinate shared data access by multiple instances. These are different from the enqueue locks used by GES. These GCS locks protect only data blocks in the global cache (previously known as parallel cache, and the locks were known as *PCM locks*).

A GCS lock can be acquired in shared mode or in exclusive mode. Each lock element can have the lock role set to either local or global. If the lock role is local, the block can be handled as it is usually handled in a single instance. Local mode reads the block from the disk if it is not seen in the buffer cache and can write the block to disk when it holds the lock mode X.

In a global role, three lock modes are possible—shared, exclusive, and null. The instance can modify the block only with the exclusive (X) mode. When the lock role is global, the instance cannot read the block from the disk as it does in the single instance mode. It has to go through the master and can write to or read from the disk only when directed by the master. Otherwise, it has to wait for the buffer from the other instance.

GCS maintains the lock and state information in the SGA. It is stored in an internal data structure called *lock elements*. It also holds a chain of cache buffer chains that are covered by the corresponding lock element. The lock elements are exposed as fixed table view V$LOCK_ELEMENT, which shows the lock element and the buffer class and state of the buffer. The hidden parameter _db_block_hash_buckets controls the number of hash buffer chain buckets. The number of hash chain buckets defaults to the nearest prime number lower than the _db_block_buffers parameter.

Lock Modes and Lock Roles

A lock mode describes the access rights to a resource. The compatibility matrix is clusterwide. For example, if a resource has an S lock on one instance, an X lock for that resource cannot exist anywhere else in the cluster. A lock role describes how the resource is to be handled. The treatment differs if the block resides in only one cache.

Cache Fusion changes the use of PCM locks in the Oracle server and relates the locks to the shipping of blocks through the system via IPC. The objectives are to separate the modes of locks from the roles that are assigned to the lock holders, and to maintain knowledge about the versions of past images of blocks throughout the system.

Global Lock Modes

GCS locks use the following modes: exclusive (X), shared (S), and null (N). An instance can acquire the global lock that covers a set of data blocks in either shared or exclusive mode, depending on the access type required.

Exclusive (X) lock mode is used during UPDATE or any of the DML operations. DML operations require that the blocks be in *exclusive* mode. If one instance needs to update a data block that is owned by another instance in an incompatible mode, the first instance asks GES to request that the second instance disown the global lock.

Shared (S) lock mode allows the instance to read (SELECT) blocks. Multiple instances can own a global lock in shared mode as long as they are reading the data. All instances can read the block without any change in lock state of the other instance. This means instances do not have to disown global locks to allow another instance to read the data block. In other words, reading does not require any explicit locking or lock conversion whether it is single instance or cluster implementation of Oracle.

Null (N) lock mode allows instances to keep a lock without any permission on the block(s). This mode is used so that locks need not be continually created and destroyed. Locks are simply converted from one mode to another.

Lock Roles

Lock roles are introduced to handle the Cache Fusion functionality. A lock role can be either local or global. The lock role for a resource is local if the block is dirty only in the local cache. The role becomes global if the block is dirty in a remote cache or in several caches.

Initially, a block is acquired in a local lock role with no past images. If the block is modified locally and other instances express interest in the block, the instance holding the block keeps a past image (PI) and ships a copy of the block, and then the role becomes global.

A PI represents the state of a dirty buffer. Initially, a block is acquired in Local role, with no PIs present. The node that modifies the block keeps PIs, as the lock role becomes Global, only after another instance expresses interest in this block. A PI block is used for efficient recovery across the cluster and can be used to satisfy a CR request, remote or local.

The node must keep a PI until it receives notification from the master that a write to disk has completed covering that version. The node then logs a block written record (BWR). The BWR is not necessary for the correctness of recovery, so it need not be flushed.

When a new current block arrives on a node, a previous PI is kept untouched because some other node might need it. When a block is pinged out of a node carrying a PI and the current version, it might or might not be combined into a single PI. At the time of the ping, the master tells the holder whether a write is in progress that will cover the older PI. If a write is not in progress, the existing current block replaces the older PI. If a write is in progress, this merge is not completed and the existing current block becomes another PI. An indeterminate number of PIs can exist.

Local and Global Roles   In the local role, only S and X modes are permitted. All changes are on the disk version, except for any local changes (mode X). When requested by the master instance, the holding instance serves a copy of the block to others. If the block is globally clean, this instance's lock role remains local. If the block is modified by this instance and passed on dirty, a PI is retained and the lock role becomes global. The lock mode reads from disk if the block is not in the cache and may write to the block if lock mode is X.

The local role states that the block can be handled similarly to the way it is handled in single instance mode. In the local role, the lock mode reads from disks and writes the dirty block back to disk when it ages out without any further DLM activity.

In the global lock role, possible lock modes are N, S, or X. When the lock role for a block is global, that block may be dirty in any of the instances and the on-disk version may be obsolete. So interested processes can modify the block only with mode X. The instance cannot read from disk, as it is not known whether the disk copy is current. The holding instance may send a copy to others when instructed by the master. The instance may write a block in X mode or PI and the write requests must be sent to the master.

Lock Elements   A lock element (LE) holds lock state information (converting, granted, and so on). LEs are managed by the lock processes to determine the mode of the locks. LEs also hold a chain of cache buffers that are covered by the LE and allow the Oracle database to keep track of cache buffers that must be written to disk in case a LE (mode) needs to be downgraded (X -> N)

Figure 11-6 shows the LEs and hash chains.

LEs protect all the data blocks in the buffer cache. The following table describes the classes of the Oracle data blocks, which are managed by the LEs using GCS locks. The class of the lock elements directly maps to X$BH.CLASS.

Column state of X$BH can contain following value:
0 or FREE
1 or EXLCUR
2 or SHRCUR
3 or CR
4 or READING
5 or MRECOVERY
6 or IRECOVERY
7 or WRITING
8 or PI

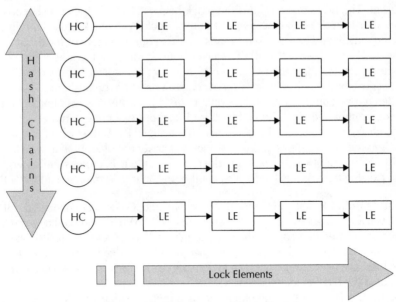

FIGURE 11-6. *Hash chains and lock elements*

GCS manages PCM locks in the GRD. PCM locks manage the data blocks in the global cache. Since the buffer cache is global, if a buffer is not found in the local cache, a block may be cached in the other instance's buffer cache. If the block is not found in any of the instances, the GCS instructs the requesting instance for a disk read. The GCS monitors and maintains the list and mode of the blocks in all the instances. Based on the request and availability, the GCS asks the holding instance to ship the block to the requesting instance, or instructs the requesting instance to read the block from the disk. All types of blocks are copied between instances in a coherent manner, and requests can be for write or read.

The database blocks from the shared database can be cached in the buffer cache of any instance that is used by the application. A local cache miss will consult the GCS to determine whether a requested block is cached by another instance. If the block is in cache, the GCS will inform the instance which node holds a lock on the block (the potential holder) of the request. If that node still has the block in its cache, it will send a copy of the block to the requestor. If the block is not in the node's cache, the GCS will grant an access right to the requestor and the block will be read from disk into the requestor's cache. The frequency and distribution of these events depends on the application.

Each database block has a master instance, where the complete lock state of the block is known. Each instance will be a master for some data blocks. Resource instances and master instances have a one-to-one relation. One resource cannot be mastered in more than one instance, but one instance can master more than one resource.

Though more than one instance may use the same set of resources in the RAC, only one instance is allowed to modify a block. GCS ensures cache coherency by requiring that instances acquire a lock before modifying or reading a database block. GCS locks are *not* to be confused with the row-level locks in single instance environments. Row-level locks are still used in conjunction with PCM locks.

Row-level locks are independent of GCS locks. GCS locks ensure the block is used by only one instance, and row-level locks manage blocks at row-level. GCS ensures that current mode buffer is exclusive for one instance and pre-images are allowed for other instances as shared mode.

If another instance needs to read a block, the current version of the block may reside in many buffer caches under shared locks. Thus, the most recent copy of the block in all SGAs contains all changes made to that block by all instances, regardless of whether any transactions on those instances have been committed.

At the same time, if a data block is updated in one buffer cache, the cached copies in other buffer caches are no longer current. New copies can be obtained after the modification operation completes. This is called *CR block fabrication*. Normally CR building occurs when a request is made for a block in that mode for a query. In simple terms, if a query wants a copy of a modified block, a CR copy is built. The process is quite simple and straightforward in a single instance environment as the process can find all the required information in the local cache. In RAC, additional processing and messaging occurs to have the buffer cache synchronization occur across all the nodes.

In CR building, the master of a block may be the local instance where the request is made, the instance where the block is cached, or any other instance. In clusters with only two nodes, blocks cached in another instance can be accessed after two hops, because the master is on the requesting mode or the caching node. In clusters with more than two nodes, a block access may require at most three hops but may complete in two hops if the master is the local node or the caching node. If the block is not cached anywhere, the request will complete after two hops.

NOTE
Block access between instances is done on a per-block level. When an instance locks a block in exclusive mode, other instances cannot access the block in the same mode. Every time Oracle tries to read a block from the database it must obtain a global lock. Ownership of the lock is thus assigned to the instance. Block lock is also known as BL type enqueues.

Consistent Read Processing

Readers do not block writers and SELECT does not require any lock in the Oracle RDBMS. This means readers never block writers. The consistent read (CR) mechanism in the RDBMS kernel enables read consistency across the instances. Read consistency ensures that the behavior of data returned by a query or transaction is consistent with respect to the start of the query to the end of the query or transaction. At the same time, the transaction sees its own committed and uncommitted changes. Read consistency is guaranteed with the help of undo segments. The consistent read version of blocks is called CR blocks, and its processing is called CR processing.

During the start of the query or transaction, the Snap SCN (SCN of the block during that particular point in time) along with the UBA is obtained. During the transaction, any time the other interested session is looking for the CR buffer, the block version at a particular point in time is obtained from the undo segments. The interested process clones the buffer and scans the undo chain to construct the CR copy of the buffer at a particular point in time. Sometimes the process has to loop to take the buffer back to the required point in time. The information to go back to a previous point in time is available from the undo segments. The CR building process is the same for single instance and RAC.

During CR processing, one ITL is scanned during every pass and the undo records are applied to the cloned buffer. Sometimes applying undo information may involve block cleanout. Once the block is cleaned or no open ITLs are listed, or when the SNAP SCN is less than or equal to the query SCN, the block is deemed valid and that buffer is returned as a CR buffer. But a few regulations are implemented to make the CR building efficient in both single instance and RAC. A buffer cannot be cloned an infinite number of times, as a built-in mechanism limits the number of CR copies per DBA. This controls the CR versions of a hot object filling the buffer cache. The hidden parameter _db_ block_max_cr_dba limits the number of CR copies per DBA on the buffer cache.

In a multi-instance environment, when a buffer is transferred to another instance during Cache Fusion transfer, the past image buffer is kept in the home instance. Undo records can also be applied on top of this PI buffer during CR processing. CR processing does not generate any redo information.

This process becomes a little complex when the block is held in the other instance's cache. When the requestor wants a CR copy, it sends a message to the holder of the block. On receipt of the CR request, the holder walks through the undo block(s), constructs the CR copy, and ships the block to the requesting instance. Figure 11-7 shows the steps in the CR fabrication process.

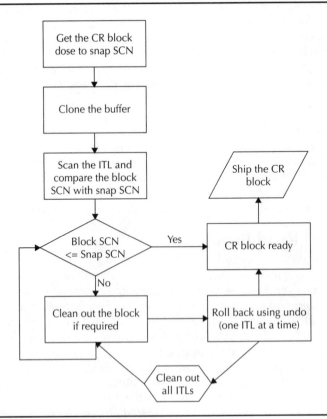

FIGURE 11-7. *CR block fabrication process*

Sometimes creating a CR block to the Snap SCN may involve too much work for the holder, going back too far in time or reading the blocks from disk; in that case, the holder may not construct the CR block as it will be too expensive. After all, the holder does a "favor" to the requestor by constructing the CR block and sending it. In this case, the holder just ships the block to the requesting instance and CR fabrication is done at requestor's instance.

Holder construction of CR copies to the requesting instances sometimes impacts the equilibrium of the instances, if one instance is always used for queries. In this case, the reading instance always has the privilege of getting all the required blocks to its cache, as CR fabrication is done by another instance. Because CR fabrication can be expensive when the fabricator has to scan through the chain of undo blocks and read the blocks from disks, a couple of optimization techniques are used to avoid CR request thrashing. One such technique is the "lightwork rule," which is implemented using the "fairness threshold" and discussed in the following section.

Lightwork Rule and Fairness Threshold

When too many CR requests arrive for a particular buffer, the holder can disown the lock on the buffer and write the block to the disk. Then the requestor can read the block from the disk after acquiring the required lock on the object. The process of disowning the block is technically known as *fairness downconvert*. The number of consecutive requests after the holder converts the lock elements is configurable via the `_fairness_threshold` parameter. This parameter defaults to 4, which is usually enough for most instances. However, it requires a special setting when one instance in the cluster is always used for queries.

The lightwork rule is invoked when CR construction involves too much work and no current block or PI block is available in the cache for block cleanouts. The number of times the instance performs a fairness downconversion and the lightwork rule is invoked is shown in the V$CR_BLOCK_SERVER view. The V$CR_BLOCK_SERVER view also lists details about the CR request processing and the distribution of block requests:

V$CR_BLOCK_SERVER

Name	Type	Notes
CR_REQUESTS	NUMBER	CR+CUR =Total Requests
CURRENT_REQUESTS	NUMBER	
DATA_REQUESTS	NUMBER	
UNDO_REQUESTS	NUMBER	
TX_REQUESTS	NUMBER	DATA+UNDO+TX= CR+CUR
CURRENT_RESULTS	NUMBER	
PRIVATE_RESULTS	NUMBER	
ZERO_RESULTS	NUMBER	
DISK_READ_RESULTS	NUMBER	
FAIL_RESULTS	NUMBER	
FAIRNESS_DOWN_CONVERTS	NUMBER	# of downconverts from X
FAIRNESS_CLEARS	NUMBER	# of time Fairness counter cleared
FREE_GC_ELEMENTS	NUMBER	
FLUSHES	NUMBER	Log Flushes
FLUSHES_QUEUED	NUMBER	
FLUSH_QUEUE_FULL	NUMBER	
FLUSH_MAX_TIME	NUMBER	
LIGHT_WORKS	NUMBER	# of times light work rule evoked
ERRORS	NUMBER	

The number of times a downconvert occurs and the lightwork rule is invoked from the instance startup can be obtained using the following query:

```
SQL> SELECT CR_REQUESTS, LIGHT_WORKS ,DATA_REQUESTS, FAIRNESS_DOWN_CONVERTS
  2 FROM
  3 V$CR_BLOCK_SERVER;

CR_REQUESTS LIGHT_WORKS DATA_REQUESTS FAIRNESS_DOWN_CONVERTS
----------- ----------- ------------- ----------------------
      80919        5978         80918                  17029
```

When the data request to downconvert ratio is more than 40 percent, lowering the `_fairness_threshold` value may improve the performance and greatly reduce the interconnect traffic for the CR messages. This parameter can be set to 0 when the systems are used for query purposes only. Setting `_fairness_threshold` to 0 disables the fairness downconverts. This parameter can be altered only with the consent of Oracle Support.

Lock Mastering and Remastering

GRD is like a central repository for locks and resources. It is distributed in all the nodes and no single node has information about all the resources. Only one node maintains complete information about one resource and that node is called the *master node* for that resource. Other nodes need to maintain information only about locally held locks on that resource. The process of maintaining information about the resources is called *lock mastering* or *resource mastering*.

Resource Affinity and Dynamic Resource Remastering

Starting with Oracle 9i, the GRD includes a feature called *resource affinity*. Resource affinity allows the resource mastering of the frequently used resources on its local node. It uses dynamic resource remastering to move the location of the resource masters. This technique optimizes the system for situations in which certain transactions are always being executed on one instance. This happens in an application-partitioning environment or an activity-based, load-balancing environment. When activity shifts to another instance, the resource affinity will correspondingly move to the new instance. If activity is not localized, the resource ownership is distributed to the instances equitably.

Dynamic resource remastering is the ability to move the ownership of a resource between instances of RAC during runtime without affecting availability. When one resource or set of resources is frequently accessed by one node more than the other nodes, it would be better to have that resource mastered by the frequently requesting instance. In normal conditions, a resource can be mastered only during instance reconfiguration. This happens when an instance joins or leaves the cluster. Other than a node joining or leaving the cluster, the ownership is remastered from one node to another node (outside the reconfiguration jurisdiction) based on the frequency of the usage. This kind of online resource mastership change is called *dynamic remastering*.

Few applications do the applications partitioning, and a set of requests is always directed to one particular node. This happens when application partitioning is implemented or where some third-party load balancers are employed to route the connections based on the user or application type.

In these situations, one node may always be requesting a particular subset of resources. During these situations it will be beneficial to have those resources mastered at the same instance. This greatly reduces interconnect messaging traffic as the resources are mastered by the requesting instance.

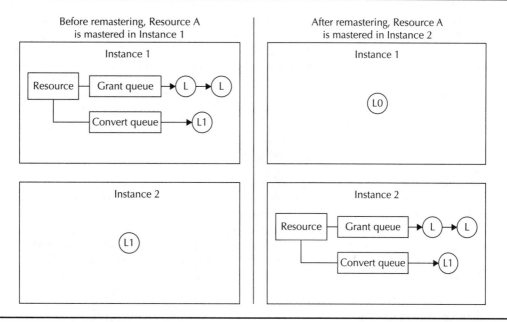

FIGURE 11-8. *Dynamic remastering*

The resource can be of an object or file based on the version of Oracle being used. Starting from 10g R2, remastering occurs at the object level, which helps fine-grained object remastering. For example, table partitions will have a different object ID and can be remastered to different instances based on their affinity. Figure 11-8 shows dynamic remastering.

Note that remastering is done only on very stringent conditions. The resources and their access patterns are evaluated in a predefined time interval. Moreover, only resources that are heavily accessed are considered candidates for resource mastering. Once the resources are identified as hot resources or frequently used resources, they are eligible for remastering evaluation.

NOTE
To have one resource remastered from one instance to another instance, the resource should have been accessed by one node 50 times more than the other node within that interval. The interval at which the resource access pattern evaluation occurs is controlled by the hidden parameter $\_gc\_affinity\_time$. This parameter specifies interval minutes as the resource usage statistics are evaluated for remastering. The parameter $\_gc\_affinity\_limit$ defines the number of times one node must access a resource before affinity can be defined as that resource and remastered. The candidate selection is based on the settings of the $\_gc\_affinity\_minimum$ parameter. Setting the parameter $\_lm\_dynamic\_remastering$ to FALSE disables dynamic remastering. Note that none of these parameters should be changed without prior approval from Oracle Support.

Dynamic resource remastering requires the acquisition of the RM (remastering) enqueue at exclusive level. The RM enqueue is a single-threaded enqueue, and only one enqueue exists per database. So at any point in time, only one node can be performing the remastering operation, and the other node has to wait for the current node to complete the operation. Once the node acquires the RM enqueue, it broadcasts the message to all other nodes and starts the remastering of resources selected based on the candidate selection algorithm. If too many resources are queued for remastering, the remastering occurs in batches. Up to 100 resources are selected for remastering after acquisition of the RM enqueue. LMD processes from the entire instances request the corresponding LMON process on respective instances to remaster the resource, and the GRD is updated to reflect the current resource ownership.

Figure 11-9 explains the remastering process.

Disabling Dynamic Remastering   Resources are initially mastered to instances based on the simple hashing algorithm. But resource remastering is quite expensive in terms of the messages and resource ownership transfers to the other instances in a busy environment. For benchmarks or an application-partitioned environment that does not require dynamic remastering, you can disable it using the hidden parameter _lm_dynamic_remastering. Setting the hidden parameter _lm_file_affinity disables dynamic remastering for the objects belonging to those files. Setting the _gc_affinity_time to 0 also disables dynamic remastering.

In a Nutshell

Congratulations. You have just completed learning about the foundations of the GRD. You have also learned about the internal workings of GES messaging and ticketing. Next you will take a closer look at Cache Fusion, which is a foundation for high performance in RAC systems.

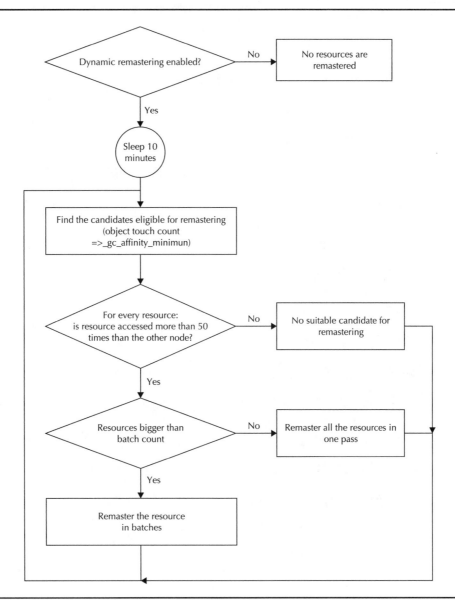

FIGURE 11-9. *Flowchart of dynamic remastering*

CHAPTER
12

A Closer Look
at Cache Fusion

scalable high performance system should spend the least amount of time in message transits and should use the most efficient communication methods for I/O processing. Cache Fusion makes this possible. In this chapter we look under the hood of Cache Fusion to understand the various kinds of block transfers that occur between instances. Understanding the internal operations of the block transfers will help you appreciate the intelligence built in to this component of Real Application Clusters.

We also take a look at how and why Oracle moves data blocks from one instance to another instance in an RAC environment. We also explain concepts closely associated with the Cache Fusion technology and wherever possible provide relevant database instance statistics.

RAC appears to merge the database buffer cache of multiple instances so that the end user sees only a single large buffer cache. In reality, the buffer caches of each node remain separate; copies of data blocks are shared through distributed locking and messaging operations. A data block present in an instance's buffer cache can be copied to another instance's buffer cache over the high-speed interconnect, thereby eliminating a re-read from disk by other instance(s). Figure 12-1 depicts the notion of a single large buffer cache spread across all the database instances among the nodes of a cluster.

Starting with version 8.1.5, Oracle introduced the framework of sharing data using private interconnects between the nodes, which was used only for messaging purposes in previous versions. This protocol is Cache Fusion. Data blocks are shipped throughout the network similar to messages, reducing the most expensive component of data transfer, disk I/O, to data sharing. Using the private interconnect greatly increases performance and scalability while preserving availability benefits of the classic implementation of a shared disk architecture in which the disk is the medium of data sharing. Simply put, while the basic data sharing and coherency mechanisms remain largely the same (distributed locks and messaging), copies of data blocks can now be passed from one node to another with one high-speed network hop instead of the two relatively slow hops required for a disk ping.

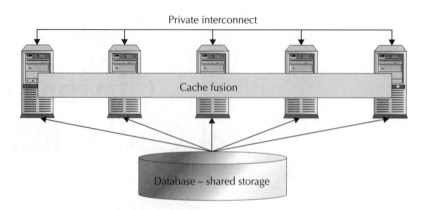

FIGURE 12-1. *Cache Fusion creates merged buffer caches of participating instances*

Oracle Release	Feature	Description
Prior to 8.1.5	OPS	OPS used disk-based pings
8.1.5	Cache Fusion I or Consistent Read Server	Consistent read version of the block is transferred over the interconnect
9i	Cache Fusion II (write/write cache fusion)	Current version of the block is transferred over the interconnect
10g R1	Oracle Cluster Ready Services (CRS)	CRS eliminates the need for third-party clusterware, though it can be used
10g R2	Oracle CRS for High Availability	CRS provides high availability for non-Oracle applications

TABLE 12-1. *History of Cache Fusion*

The Cache Fusion technology has evolved and has been refined to run applications efficiently without any specific changes to those applications. As one would expect, with every release of Oracle RDBMS, Oracle has introduced newer concepts and improved efficiency. Table 12-1 shows the history of Cache Fusion and Oracle RAC.

Key Components in Cache Fusion
The following sections cover a few terms and concepts used in the discussion of Cache Fusion.

Ping
The transfer of a data block from one instance's buffer cache to another instance's buffer cache is known as a *ping*. Whenever an instance needs a block, it sends a request to the lock master to obtain a lock in the desired mode. If another lock resides on the same block, the master will ask the current holder to downgrade/release the current lock. As you learned in an earlier chapter, this process is known as a *blocking asynchronous trap* (BAST). When an instance receives a BAST it downgrades the lock as soon as possible. However, before downgrading the lock, it might have to write the corresponding block to disk. This operation sequence is known as *disk ping* or a *hard ping*.

NOTE
The definitions of AST and BAST used in this book are based on Oracle context. Various implementations (such as VMS) use different definitions for AST and BAST.

Starting with Oracle 9i, disk pings have been reduced, as blocks are transferred from one instance's buffer cache to another instance's buffer cache via the private interconnect in many cases. This type of transfer is known as Cache Fusion block transfer. Some amount of block transfers in the RAC environment is healthy, as it indicates sharing of data among the instances and minimizes disk I/O. However, excessive block transfers can impact performance, consuming CPU and network resources.

As discussed in Chapter 10, the amount of data sent and received by an instance via Cache Fusion can be viewed in the Automatic Workload Repository (AWR) report in the Global Cache Load Profile section.

Deferred Ping

Oracle uses various mechanisms to mitigate pinging. When BAST is received by an instance, it might defer sending the block or downgrading the lock by tens of milliseconds. This extra time might allow the holding instance to complete an active transaction and mark the block header appropriately. This will eliminate any need for the receiving instance to check status of the transaction immediately after receiving/reading a block. Checking status of an active transaction is an expensive operation that might require access (and pinging) to the related undo segment header and undo data blocks as well. Prior to Oracle 9i, you could use the parameter gc_defer_time to define the duration by which an instance deferred downgrading a lock. In Oracle versions 9i and later, this parameter has been replaced by the hidden parameter _gc_defer_time.

Past Image (PI) Blocks

PI blocks are copies of blocks in the local buffer cache. Whenever an instance has to send a block it has recently modified to another instance, it preserves a copy of that block, marking it as PI. An instance is *obliged* to keep PIs until that block is written to the disk by the current owner of the block. PIs are discarded after the latest version of the block is written to disk. When a block is written to disk and is known to have global role, indicating the presence of PIs in other instances' buffer caches, Global Cache Services (GCS) informs the instance holding the PIs to discard the PIs. With Cache Fusion, a block is written to disk to satisfy checkpoint requests and so on, not to transfer the block from one instance to another via disk.

When an instance needs to write to a block—to satisfy a checkpoint request, for example—the instance checks the role of the resource covering the block. If the role is global, the instance must inform the GCS of the write requirement. The GCS is responsible for finding the most current block image and informing the instance holding that image to perform the block write. The GCS then informs all holders of the global resource that they can release the buffers holding the PI copies of the block, allowing the global resources to be released.

A block written record (BWR) is placed in its redolog buffer when an instance writes a block covered by a global resource or when it is told it can free up a PI buffer. This record is used by recovery processes to indicate that redo information for the block is not needed for recovery prior to this point. Although the BWR makes recovery more efficient, the instance does not force a flush of the log buffer after creating it because it is not essential for accurate recovery.

The fixed table X$BH can be used to find the number of past image blocks present in the buffer cache:

```
SQL> select state, count(state) from X$BH group by state;
     STATE  COUNT(STATE)
---------- ------------
         1  403
         2  7043
         8  15
         3  659
```

There are 15 past image blocks indicated in the STATE column of the X$BH table.

Lock Mastering

The memory structure where GCS keeps information about a data block (and other sharable resources) usage is known as the *lock resource*. The responsibility of tracking locks is distributed among all the instances and the required memory also comes from the participating instances' System Global Area (SGA). Due to this distributed ownership of the resources, a master node exists for each lock resource. The master node maintains complete information about current users and requestors for the lock resource. The master node also contains information about the PIs of the block.

Whenever an instance needs a data block, it must contact the master of lock resources corresponding to that data block. The master instance for the required lock resource could be local or remote. If local, fewer messages or no messages need to be sent over the interconnect to obtain the required lock for that block. (For more information, see Chapter 11.)

Types of Contention

Contention of a resource occurs when two or more instances want the same resource. If a resource such as a data block is being used by an instance and is needed by another instance at the same time, a contention occurs. There are three types of contention for data blocks:

- **Read/Read contention**   Read/read contention is never a problem because of the shared disk system. A block read by one instance can be read by other instances without the intervention of GCS.

- **Write/Read contention**   Write/read contention was addressed in Oracle 8i by the consistent read server. The holding instance constructs the CR block and ships the requesting instance using interconnects.

- **Write/Write contention**   Write/write contention is addressed by the Cache Fusion technology. Since Oracle 9i, cluster interconnect is used in some cases to ship data blocks among the instances that need to modify the same data block simultaneously.

In the following sections, we look at how these components work seamlessly in a real-world situation. We explore how these contentions were addressed before Cache Fusion was introduced and how they work with Cache Fusion.

Cache Fusion I or Consistent Read Server

Cache Fusion I (also known as consistent read server) was introduced in version 8.1.5. Oracle keeps a list of recent transactions that have changed a block. The original data contained in the block is preserved in the undo segment, which can be used to provide consistent read versions of the block to other readers or to recover an uncommitted transaction after an instance or a process crash.

Generally, when a transaction is committed, the server process places a flag in the undo segment header indicating the transaction status as "committed." To save time, it does not stamp each and every block it has modified with a commit flag. Thus, in the future, whenever another process reads that block and finds an active transaction in the block, the reader refers to the corresponding undo segment header to determine whether the transaction has been committed. If the undo segment header indicates that the transaction has been committed, the reader updates the block with the System Commit Number (SCN) in the transaction layer of the block to signify the commit and moves on to read the block. However, if the transaction has not yet been committed, the reader locates the undo block where original data is stored and makes a consistent read image of the block for its use.

This discussion leads us to infer the following:

■ When a reader reads a recently modified block, it might find an active transaction in the block.

■ The reader will need to read the undo segment header to decide whether the transaction has been committed or not.

■ If the transaction is not committed, the process creates a consistent read (CR) version of the block in the buffer cache using the data in the block and the data stored in the undo segment.

■ If the undo segment shows the transaction is committed, the process has to revisit the block and clean out the block and generate the redo for the changes.

In an RAC environment, if the process of reading the block is on an instance other than the one that has modified the block, the reader will have to read the following blocks from the disk:

■ **Data block**   To get the data and/or transaction ID and Undo Byte Address (UBA)

■ **Undo segment header block**   To find the last undo block used for the entire transaction

■ **Undo data block**   To get the actual undo record to construct a CR image

Before these blocks can be read, the instance modifying the block will have to write those blocks to disk. This will result in at least six disk I/O operations. The number of I/O operations can be optimized if the modifying instance, knowing that an instance needs a CR copy of the block it recently modified, can construct a CR copy of the block and send it to the requesting instance. It is highly probable that the data block, undo segment header block, and undo block will still be in this instance's buffer cache. Thus, by making a CR copy and sending it over the private interconnect, potentially six disk I/Os have been replaced by a single data block transfer over the interconnect.

Prior to Cache Fusion, whenever an instance needed to modify a data block that had been recently modified by another instance, the sequence of operation shown next and in Figure 12-2 occurred.

1. An instance sends a message to the lock manager requesting a shared lock on the block.

2. Following are the possibilities in the global cache:

■ If there is no current user for the block, the lock manager grants the shared lock to the requesting instance.

■ If another instance has an exclusive lock on that block, the lock manager asks the owning instance to downgrade the lock.

3. Based on the result, either of the following can happen:

■ If the lock is granted, the requesting instance reads the block from the disk.

■ The owning instance writes the block to disk and disowns the lock on that resource.

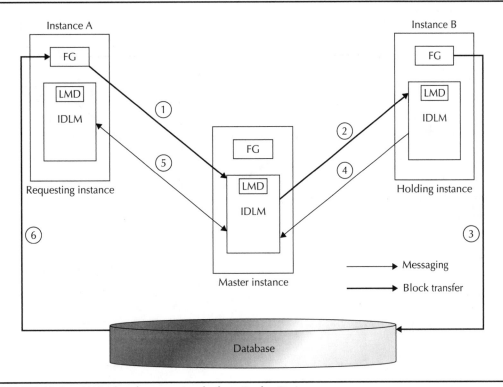

FIGURE 12-2. *Write/read contention before Cache Fusion*

4. The owning instance also informs the lock manager and the requesting instance that it has released the lock.

5. The requesting instance now has the lock granted. The lock manager updates the IDLM with the new holders of that resource.

6. The requesting instance reads the block from disk. If it is looking for the previous version of the block, it can proceed with the regular CR block fabrication in its own buffer cache.

CR fabrication can be an expensive operation, especially when the undo information is cached in the remote node. The requesting instance has to make a few additional disk I/Os to get the blocks to its own cache. Since the disk is used as a data transfer medium, latency issues will crop up and application scalability and performance will degrade when the data is not partitioned across the instances.

If the CR block fabrication occurs at the holding instance, part of the disk I/O can be avoided as the data blocks and undo blocks are local to that instance. Upon undo block fabrication, the holder can ship the *processed* block to the requestor. Read/write contention is avoided by building CR in the holding instance, and this is the first phase in Cache Fusion.

Following is the sequence of operations with the implementation of CR server engine in Oracle 8i. The newly introduced background process, the Block Server Process (BSP), makes the CR fabrication

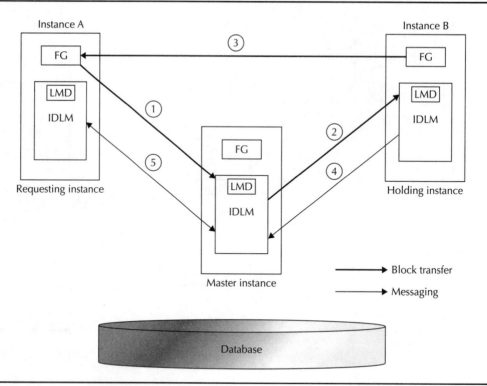

FIGURE 12-3. *CR block transfer in Cache Fusion*

at the holder's cache and ships the CR version of the block across the interconnect. The sequence of operations is shown in Figure 12-3.

1. An instance sends a message to the lock manager requesting a shared lock on the block.

2. Following are the possibilities in the global cache:

   ■ If there is no current user for the block, the lock manager grants the shared lock to the requesting instance.

   ■ If another instance has an exclusive lock on that block, the lock manager asks the owning instance to build a CR copy and ship it to the requesting instance.

3. Based on the result, either of the following can happen:

   ■ If the lock is granted, the requesting instance reads the block from disk.

   ■ The owning instance creates a CR version of the buffer in its own buffer cache and ships it to the requesting instance over the interconnect.

4. The owning instance also informs the lock manager and the requesting instance that it has shipped the block.

5. The requesting instance now has the lock granted. The lock manager updates the IDLM with the new holders of that resource.

While making a CR copy needed by another instance, the holding instance may refuse to do so if

- It doesn't find any of the needed blocks in its buffer cache. It will not perform a disk read to make a CR copy for another instance.

- It is repeatedly asked to send a CR copy of the same block. After sending CR copies of the same block four times, it will voluntarily relinquish the lock, write the block to disk, and let other instances get the block from disk. The number of copies it will serve before it does so is governed by the hidden parameter `_fairness_threshold`.

While downgrading the lock and writing the block to disk, the holding instance will send a copy of the block it has constructed so far, and the requesting instance will continue the construction of the CR copy needed by it. This is known as the lightwork rule. Refer to Chapter 11 for a detailed discussion on the lightwork rule and fairness threshold.

Cache Fusion II or Write/Write Cache Fusion

Read/write contention was addressed by the CR server in the first phase of Cache Fusion. The second phase of Cache Fusion, introduced in Oracle 9i, implements the framework for current block transfers for write/write contention. Prior to Oracle 9i, whenever an instance needed to modify a data block that had been recently modified by another instance, the following sequence of operations would take place, as illustrated in Figure 12-4.

1. An instance sends a message to the lock manager requesting an exclusive lock on the block.

2. Following are the possibilities in the global cache:

   - If there is no current user for the block, the lock manager grants the exclusive lock to the requesting instance.

   - If another instance has an exclusive lock on that block, the lock manager asks the owning instance to release the lock.

3. Based on the result, either of the following can happen:

   - If the lock is granted, the requesting instance reads the block from the disk.

   - The owning instance writes the block to disk and disowns the lock on that resource.

4. The owning instance also informs the lock manager and the requesting instance that it has released the lock.

5. The requesting instance now has the exclusive lock. It can read the block from disk and proceed with the intended changes to the block.

6. The lock manager updates the resource directory with the new information about the holder.

Often, the requesting instance will find an active transaction in the active transaction list of the block, and it might need the corresponding undo block header and undo data block to clean out the block. Thus, multiple disk I/Os might be needed before the requesting instance can

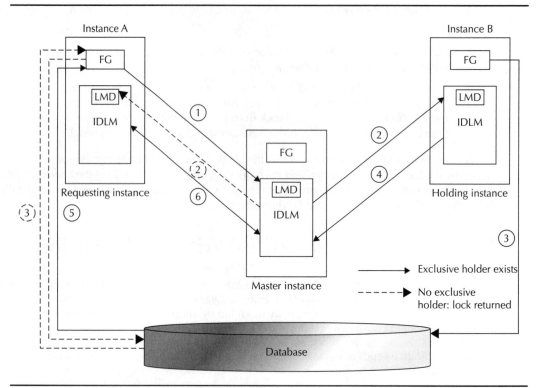

FIGURE 12-4. *Write/write contention in pre-Cache Fusion*

modify the block. Cache Fusion makes this operation relatively efficient and fast, as shown in Figure 12-5.

1. The instance sends a message to the lock manager to request an exclusive lock on the block.

2. Following are the possibilities in the global cache based on whether any other user is holding the lock:

   ■ If there is no current user for the block, the lock manager grants the exclusive lock to the requesting instance.

   ■ If another instance has an exclusive lock on that block, the lock manager asks the owning instance to release the lock.

3. Based on the result, either of the following can happen:

   ■ If the lock is granted, the requesting instance reads the block from the disk.

   ■ The owning instance sends the current block to the requesting instance via the interconnect. To guarantee recovery in the event of instance death, the owning

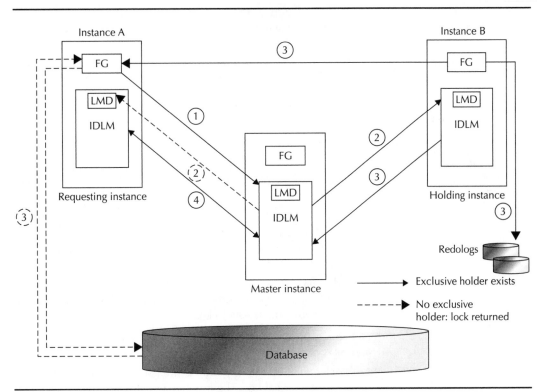

FIGURE 12-5. *Cache Fusion current block transfer*

instance writes all the redo records generated for the block to the online redolog file. It will keep a past image of the block and inform the master instance that it has sent the current block to the requesting instance.

4. The lock manager updates the resource directory with the current holder of the block.

Cache Fusion in Operation

Before we get into Cache Fusion operation, here's a quick recap of GCS resource roles and modes. A GCS resource can be *local* or *global*. It is local if it can be acted upon without consulting other instances. It is global if it cannot be acted upon without consulting or informing remote instances. GCS is used as a messaging agent to coordinate manipulation of a global resource.

Depending on the type of operation an instance intends to do on a block (resource), an instance will acquire the block in shared or exclusive mode. When an instance needs a block to satisfy a query request, it requires the block to be in consistent read mode or in shared mode. When an instance needs a block to satisfy a DML (update, insert, delete) request, it needs the block in exclusive mode. The Null (N) mode indicates that the instance does not currently hold the resource in any mode. This is the default status for each instance.

An instance having a resource with a local role can have the resources in X, S, or N mode. The following table denotes the different states of a resource:

Mode/Role	Local	Global
Null: N	NL	NG
Shared: S	SL	SG
Exclusive: X	XL	XG

- **SL** When an instance has a resource in SL form, it can serve a copy of the block to other instances and it can read the block from disk. Since the block is not modified, there is no need to write to disk.

- **XL** When an instance has a resource in XL form, it has sole ownership and interest in that resource. It also has the exclusive right to modify the block. All changes to the blocks are in its local buffer cache, and it can write the block to disk. If another instance wants the block, it will contact the instance via GCS.

- **NL** A NL form is used to protect consistent read blocks. If a block is held in SL mode and another instance wants it in X mode, the current instance will send the block to the requesting instance and downgrade its role to NL.

- **SG** In SG form, a block is present in one or more instances. An instance can read the block from disk and serve it to other instances.

- **XG** In XG form, a block can have one or more PIs, indicating multiple copies of the block in several instances' buffer caches. The instance with the XG role has the latest copy of the block and is the most likely candidate to write the block to disk. GCS can ask the instance with the XG role to write the block to disk or to serve it to another instance.

- **NG** After discarding PIs when instructed by GCS, the block is kept in the buffer cache with NG role. This serves only as the CR copy of the block.

Consider the following: a four-instance RAC environment, with instances A, B, C, and D. Instance D is the master of the lock resources for the data block BL. In this example, we'll work with only one block BL to begin with, and it will reside on disk at SCN 987654.

We will choose a three-letter code for the lock state: The first letter will indicate the lock mode: N = Null, S = Shared, and X = Exclusive. The second letter will indicate the lock role: L = Local, and G = Global. The third letter will be a digit indicating the past image: 0 = block does not have any past image, and 1 = a PI of the block.

The following examples will undergo a sequence of operations to help you understand the current block and CR block transfers from the instances. These scenarios include reading from disk, reading from cache, getting the block from cache for update, performing an update on a block, performing an update on the same block, reading a block that was globally dirty, performing a rollback on a previously updated block, and reading the block after commit. Although these examples do not cover all the functionalities of Cache Fusion, they are the most common operations in a real-world environment.

Example 1: Reading a Block from Disk

In this example, instance C wants to read the block. It will request a lock in shared mode from the master instance.

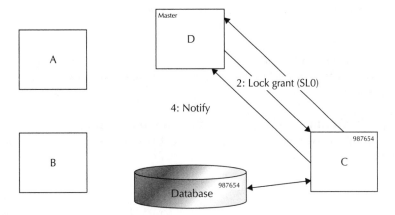

1. Instance C requests the block by sending a shared lock request (S, C) to master instance D. (S represents the type of the lock requested and C represents the requesting instance.)

2. The block has never been read into the buffer cache of any instance and it is not locked. Master instance D grants the lock to instance C. The lock granted is SL0, indicating that it is a shared lock with local interests, and no past images of this block exist.

3. Instance C reads the block from the shared disk in to its buffer cache.

4. Instance C has the block in shared mode. The lock manager updates the resource directory.

Example 2: Reading a Block from the Cache

We begin at the end of example 1. Instance B wants to read the same block that is cached in instance C.

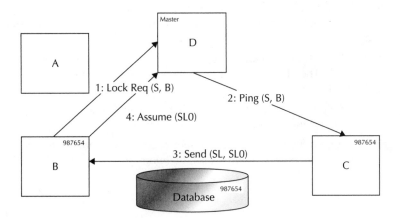

1. Instance B sends a shared lock request, Lock Req (S, B), to master instance D.

2. The lock master at instance D knows that the block may be available at instance C and hence sends a ping message to instance C.

3. Instance C sends the block to instance B over interconnect. Along with the block, instance C also indicates that instance B should take the current lock mode and role from instance C.

4. Instance B sends a message to instance D that it has assumed the SL lock for the block. This message is not critical (yet it is important) for the lock manager; hence, this message is sent asynchronously.

Example 3: Getting a (Cached) Clean Block for Update

We begin at the end of the example 2. Instance A wants to modify the same block that is already cached in instances B and C.

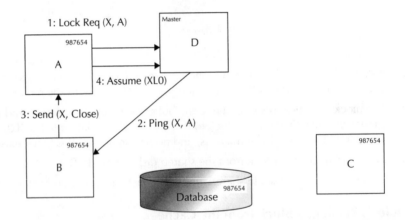

1. Instance A sends an exclusive lock request, Lock Req (X, A), to master instance D.

2. The lock master at D knows that the block may be available at instance B in SCUR mode and C in CR mode. It also sends a ping message to the shared lock holders. The most recent access was at instance B, and instance D sends a BAST message to instance B.

3. Instance B sends the block to instance A over the interconnect and closes its shared (SCUR) lock. The block may still be in its buffer to be used as CR; however, it releases any lock on it.

4. Instance A now has the block in exclusive mode and sends an assume message to instance D. Instance A holds the lock in XL0 mode.

5. Instance A modifies the block in its buffer cache. The changes are not committed and the block has not yet been written to disk; therefore, the SCN on disk remains at 987654.

Example 4: Getting a (Cached) Modified Block for Update and Commit

This example begins at the end of example 3. Instance C now wants to update the block BL. Note that instance A has already updated the block and the block has an open transaction on it. If instance C tries to update the same row, it will wait for the previous update to commit or roll back. However, in this case, instance C updates a different row and after the update, it issues a commit.

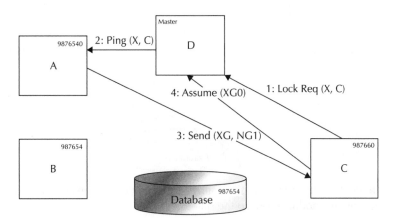

1.   Instance C sends an exclusive lock request, Lock Req (X, C), to master instance D.

2.   The lock master at D knows that instance A holds an exclusive lock on the block and hence sends a ping message to instance A.

3.   Instance A sends the dirty block to instance C over the interconnect. It downgrades the lock on the buffer from XCUR to NULL. It keeps a PI version of the block and disowns any lock on that buffer. Before shipping the block, instance A has to create a PI image and flush any pending redo for the block changed. The block mode on instance A is now NG1.

4.   Instance C sends a message to instance D indicating it now has the block in exclusive mode. The block role G indicates that the block is in global mode and if it needs to write the block to disk it must coordinate it with the other instances that have past images of that block. Instance C modifies the block and issues a commit. This takes the SCN to 987660.

NOTE
Row level locks and block locks operate independently in the RAC environment. In this example, we update the same block in two different instances, but not the same row. Refer to Chapter 11 for a detailed discussion of Oracle's implementation of row level locking. Row locks (known as enqueue type TX) and GCS buffer locks (known as enqueue type BL) can run in parallel for a transaction.

Example 5: Commit the Previously Modified Block and Select the Data

Now instance A issues a commit to release the row level locks held by the transaction and flush the redo information to the redolog files. Global locks on the resources remain the same.

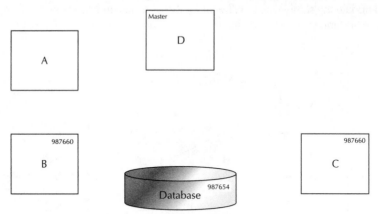

1. Instance A wants to commit the changes. Commit operations do not require any synchronous modifications to the data block.

2. The lock status remains the same as the previous state and change vectors for the commits are written to the redologs.

Example 6: Write the Dirty Buffers to Disk Due to Checkpoint

Continuing at the end of example 5, instance B writes the dirty blocks from the buffer cache due to a checkpoint.

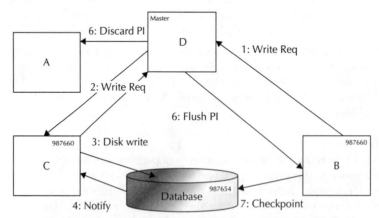

1. Instance B sends a write request to master D with the necessary SCN.

2. The lock master at D knows that the most recent copy of the block may be available at instance C and hence sends a message to instance C asking to write.

3. Instance C initiates a disk write and writes a BWR into the redolog file.

4. Instance C gets the write notification that the write is completed.

5. Instance C notifies the master that the write is completed.

6. On receipt of the notification from C, master instance D tells all PI holders to discard their PIs, and the lock at instance C writes the modified block to the disk.

7. All instances that have previously modified this block will also have to write a BWR. The write request by instance C has now been satisfied, and instance C can now proceed with its checkpoint as usual.

Example 7: Master Instance Crash

This example continues from example 6.

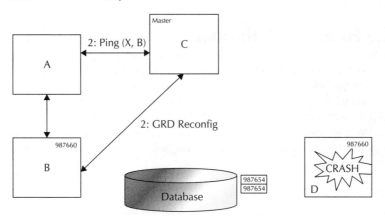

1. The master instance D crashes.

2. The Global Resource Directory (GRD) is frozen momentarily and the resources held by master instance D will be equally distributed in the surviving nodes.

NOTE
Mode details on the GRD are discussed in Chapter 11, and GRD and fast reconfiguration after node failure are discussed in Chapter 9.

Example 8: Select the Rows from Instance A

Now instance A queries the rows from that table to get the most recent data.

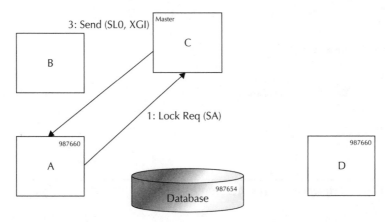

1. Instance A sends a shared lock request, Lock Req (S, D), to master instance C.

2. Master instance C knows that the most recent copy of that block may be in instance C (which is the current master) and asks the holder to ship the CR block to instance A.

3. Instance C ships the CR block to instance A over the interconnect.

Sequence of Operations

Table 12-2 lists the sequence of operations on the nodes and corresponding modes of the buffers in various caches.

Cache Fusion Walkthrough

In the following Cache Fusion example, we will use the V$SEGMENT_STATISTICS, X$BH, XLE, XKJBL, V$DLM_RESS, and V$GES_ENQUEUE views to trace blocks and lock status in a four-node environment. We will use the EMP table contained in the SCOTT schema. The EMP table can be created using the script demobld.sql contained in the $ORACLE_HOME/sqlplus/demo directory. For this example, a primary key on column EMPNO was added to make it more selective for the retrieval. We also manually master the EMP table to instance D for demonstration purposes. The command `oradebug lkdebug -m pkey <objected>` can be used to remaster an object to one instance manually.

Example	Operation on Node A	Operation on Node B	Operation on Node C	Operation on Node D	A	Buffer Status B	C	D
1			Read the block from disk				SCUR	
2		Read the block from cache				CR	SCUR	
3	Update the block				XCUR	CR	CR	
4			Update the same block		PI	CR	XCUR	
5	Commit the changes				PI	CR	XCUR	
6		Trigger checkpoint				CR	XCUR	
7				Instance crash				
8	Select the rows				CR		XCUR	

TABLE 12-2. *Sequence of Operations on Nodes and Buffer Status in Examples 1 through 8*

Run the following SQL script as any DBA user to get the data_object_id for the EMP table owned by the user *SCOTT*:

GET_OBJECT_ID

The data dictionary view dba_objects contains details about all the objects in the database. We query this view to get details about the data_object_id for the EMP table.

```
REM We get the object id of the EMP table
column owner format a10
column data_object_id format 999999
column object_name format a15
select owner, data_object_id, object_name
from dba_objects
where owner='SCOTT'
and object_name='EMP';

SQL> @GET_OBJECT_ID

OWNER      DATA_OBJECT_ID OBJECT_NAME

---------- -------------- ---------------

SCOTT               51151 EMP
```

The dictionary view dba_extents keeps storage detail information for all segments in the database. We can get the details about the file_id and block_id of the EMP table by querying this view:

SEG_DETAILS.SQL

You can query the dba_extents view or use the dbms_rowid package to get the details:

```
REM We get the File ID, Starting Block ID for EMP Table
col owner format a8
col segment_name format a12
select owner,segment_name,file_id,block_id,blocks
from dba_extents
where owner='SCOTT'
and segment_name='EMP'

SQL> @GET_SEGMENT_DETAILS
OWNER    SEGMENT_NAME   FILE_ID   BLOCK_ID    BLOCKS

-------- ------------ ---------- ---------- ----------

SCOTT    EMP                 4          25          8
```

Alternatively, we can get the details about the file number and block number of the rows from the EMP table using the following method. The `rowid` is the physical address of the row inside the database and uniquely identifies a row in database.

```
SQL> select rowid,empno,ename from scott.emp where empno in(7788,7876);
ROWID                    EMPNO ENAME
------------------ ---------- ----------

AAAMfPAAEAAAAAgAAH        7788 SCOTT

AAAMfPAAEAAAAAgAAK        7876 ADAMS

SQL> select
  2  dbms_rowid.rowid_block_number('AAAMfPAAEAAAAAgAAH') Block_No
  3  from dual;
  BLOCK_NO

----------

        32
SQL> select
  2  dbms_rowid. rowid_relative_fno('AAAMfPAAEAAAAAgAAH') File_no
  3  from dual;
  FILE_NO
----------

         4
```

Queries Used to Get Lock and Buffer Status

Following is a quick explanation of the queries used to get the lock and buffer status information. The following four queries were used and need to be run in a session logged in with SYS as *sysdba*, as few of them reference the internal views and they are visible only to SYS users.

GET_SEGMENT_STATS.SQL The dynamic performance view v$segment_statistics contains statistics for each segment such as number of reads, writes, row lock waits, and ITL waits. This view is used to get information about how data blocks belonging to the EMP table are received by the instances.

```
column stat format a35
column value format 99999
select STATISTIC_NAME stat, value val
from v$segment_statistics
where value > 0
and OWNER='SCOTT' and OBJECT_NAME='EMP';
```

GET_BUFFER_STAT.SQL The internal view X$BH contains the status of the block in the buffer cache. We can get the status of any cached buffer in the buffer cache from this view. A predicate `obj = 51151` is used to restrict our interest on the EMP table. To get the status of the block that contains the rows of EMPNO 7788 and 7369, `dbablk = 32` is used. The last condition in the predicate, `class = 1`, is used to get the details about the data blocks of the EMP table.

```
SELECT
state, mode_held, le_addr, dbarfil, dbablk, cr_scn_bas, cr_scn_wrp
FROM x$bh
WHERE obj=51151
AND dbablk=32
AND class = 1;
```

Column STATE of X$BH contains information about the mode of the block in the buffer cache. You can also query V$BH to get the same information. However, querying V$BH may be an expensive operation in production as it accesses all buffers (joining with X$LE) and may consume a large amount of CPU cycles. Hence it is always better to query the X$BH whenever you access the buffer cache information.

The following table contains information about the various block statuses in the buffer cache:

State	Explanation
0	Buffer is free, unused
1	Buffer current, locked in X mode
2	Buffer current, locked in S mode
3	Consistent read buffer
4	Buffer being read
5	Buffer under media recovery
6	Buffer under instance recovery
7	Write clone buffer
8	Past Image buffer

State values 1, 2, 3, and 8 are the most commonly seen buffers modes in the buffer cache; we will use these values in our demo example.

GET_RESOURCE_NAME.SQL The GCS resource name to be used in the query GET_RESOURCE_STAT was retrieved using the following query:

```
column hexname format a25
column resource_name format a15
select
b.kjblname hexname,b.kjblname2 resource_name,
b.kjblgrant,b.kjblrole,b.kjblrequest
from
X$LE a, X$KJBL b
where a.le_kjbl=b.kjbllockp
and a.le_addr=(select le_addr from
x$bh where dbablk=32 and obj=51151
and class=1 and state! =3);

SQL> @GET_RESOURCE_NAME
```

HEXNAME	RESOURCE_NAME	KJBLGRANT	KJBLROLE KJBLREQUE
[0x20] [0x40000], [BL]	32,262144,BL	KJUSEREX	0 KJUSERNL

The kjblname column in the internal view X$KJBL provides the resource name in hexadecimal format and kjblname2 provides the resource name in decimal format. We will be using the hex format *([id1],[id2],[type])* to query the resource in the V$GC_ELEMENT and V$DLM_RESS views.

GET_RESOURCE_STAT.SQL The following query was used to monitor the resource allocated to the data block from the EMP table:

```
column resource_name format a22
column state format a8
column mast format 9999
column grnt format 9999
column cnvt format 9999
select
a.resource_name,b.state,a.master_node mast,a.on_convert_q cnvt ,
a.on_grant_q grnt,b.request_level,b.grant_level
from v$dlm_ress a,
V$ges_enqueue b
where upper(a.resource_name)=upper(b.resource_name1)
and a.resource_name like '%[0x20] [0x40000], [BL]%';

SQL> @GET_RESOURCE_STAT
```

RESOURCE_NAME	STATE	MAST	CNVT	GRNT	REQUEST_L	GRANT_LEV
[0x20][0x40000], [BL]	GRANTED	3	0	1	KJUSERNL	KJUSERPR
[0x20][0x40000], [BL]	GRANTED	3	0	1	KJUSERNL	KJUSERPR

Example Operation Details

We will perform an example operation. At the end of each SQL operation, we'll take a snapshot using the aforementioned four queries to monitor the status change in blocks and locks in the participating instances. User statements should be run as *SCOTT* and monitoring queries should be run as user *SYS* as they refer to internal views.

The sequence of operations is as follows:

1. Select instance C to get the row with EMPNO = 7788 from the EMP table:

   ```
   SELECT EMPNO, ENAME, SAL from EMP where EMPNO=7788;
   ```

2. Select the same row on instance B:

   ```
   SELECT EMPNO, ENAME, SAL from EMP where EMPNO=7788;
   ```

3. Update the row on instance A:

   ```
   UPDATE EMP SET SAL=SAL+1000 where EMPNO=7788;
   ```

4. Update a new row (EMPNO=7369) in instance C:

   ```
   UPDATE EMP SET SAL=SAL*2 where EMPNO=7369;
   ```

5. Commit the changes in instance A:

```
COMMIT;
```

6. Write the changes to the disk because of a checkpoint in instance B:

```
ALTER SYSTEM CHECKPOINT; ALTER SYSTEM SWITCH LOGFILE;
```

7. Master node crash occurs.

8. Select the data from instance A and verify the status of the current master:

```
SELECT EMPNO,ENAME,SAL FROM EMP WHERE EMPNO IN (7788,7369)
```

At the beginning of the example, the buffer cache does not contain any block belonging to the EMP table:

```
Lock status queries run on instance A at the beginning
$ sqlplus '/ as sysdba'
SQL*Plus: Release 10.2.0.1.0 - Production on Sun May 14 19:39:26 2006
Copyright (c) 1982, 2005, Oracle.  All rights reserved.
Connected to:
Oracle Database 10g Enterprise Edition Release 10.2.0.1.0 - 64bit Production
With the Partitioning, RAC, OLAP and Data Mining options
SQL> @GET_SEGMENT_STATS
no rows selected
SQL>@GET_BUFFER_STAT
no rows selected
SQL> @GET_RESOURCE_NAME
no rows selected
SQL>@GET_RESOURCE_STAT
no rows selected

Lock status queries run on instance B at the beginning
$ sqlplus '/ as sysdba'
SQL*Plus: Release 10.2.0.1.0 - Production on Sun May 14 19:41:10 2006
Copyright (c) 1982, 2005, Oracle.  All rights reserved.
Connected to:
Oracle Database 10g Enterprise Edition Release 10.2.0.1.0 - 64bit Production
With the Partitioning, RAC, OLAP and Data Mining options
SQL> @GET_SEGMENT_STATS
no rows selected
SQL>@GET_BUFFER_STAT
no rows selected
SQL> @GET_RESOURCE_NAME
no rows selected
SQL>@GET_RESOURCE_STAT
no rows selected

Lock status queries run on instance C at the beginning
$ sqlplus '/ as sysdba'
SQL*Plus: Release 10.2.0.1.0 - Production on Sun May 14 19:42:01 2006
Copyright (c) 1982, 2005, Oracle.  All rights reserved.
```

```
Connected to:
Oracle Database 10g Enterprise Edition Release 10.2.0.1.0 - 64bit Production
With the Partitioning, RAC, OLAP and Data Mining options
SQL> @GET_SEGMENT_STATS
no rows selected
SQL>@GET_BUFFER_STAT
no rows selected
SQL> @GET_RESOURCE_NAME
no rows selected
SQL>@GET_RESOURCE_STAT
no rows selected

Lock status queries run on instance D at the beginning
$ sqlplus '/ as sysdba'
SQL*Plus: Release 10.2.0.1.0 - Production on Sun May 14 19:44:12 2006
Copyright (c) 1982, 2005, Oracle.  All rights reserved.
Connected to:
Oracle Database 10g Enterprise Edition Release 10.2.0.1.0 - 64bit Production
With the Partitioning, RAC, OLAP and Data Mining options
SQL> @GET_SEGMENT_STATS
no rows selected
SQL>@GET_BUFFER_STAT
no rows selected
SQL> @GET_RESOURCE_NAME
no rows selected
SQL>@GET_RESOURCE_STAT
no rows selected
```

As you can see, the buffer cache does not contain any block belonging to the table EMP. Since no blocks are in the buffer cache, no resources are needed to keep track of them. Thus no rows are returned by the queries. The table EMP is mastered by instance D and every request on the table will be routed through instance D.

Example 1: Retrieve the Data from Disk

The first example retrieves the data from disk and monitors the resource movements between master and holder instances. To start, we'll query the data from the EMP table on instance C. Connect as *SCOTT* and run the following query to load a buffer from disk to the buffer cache of instance C. Instance D is the master of the resource. You can query the X$KJBR.KJBRMASTER view to find the master node for a particular resource.

```
REM Let us query the EMP data from instance C
REM This query is run as user SCOTT

SQL> select empno,ename,sal from emp
  2   where empno=7788;
     EMPNO ENAME              SAL

---------- ---------- ----------

      7788 SCOTT             3000
```

Now we run the lock status queries on instance C. We run the monitoring queries as user *SYS,* since we query the internal tables. These queries yield the following results:

```
REM #### Result of lock queries on instance C,
REM after a select from emp table on instance C
REM This query is run as user SYS
SQL> @get_segment_stats
OBJECT_NAM STAT                                          VALUE
---------- ---------------------------------- -------

EMP        physical reads                                 1

SQL> @get_resource_name
HEXNAME                          RESOURCE_NAME    KJBLGRANT    KJBLROLE KJBLREQUE
------------------------------   --------------   ---------    --------- ---------
[0x20][0x40000],[BL]             32,262144,BL     KJUSERPR             0 KJUSERNL
SQL> @get_resource_stat
no rows selected
SQL> @get_buffer_stat
STATE  MODE_HELD      FILE#       BLOCK#    SCN_BASE   SCN_WRAP
-----  ----------   ----------  ----------  ---------- ----------
  2          0          4           32          0           0
```

Observe the following:

- The block was retrieved from disk, indicated by physical reads for the segment in the v$segment_statisics view.

- The block is held in the current shared mode, as indicated by 2 in the STATE column of the x$bh table. X$BH STATE is 2 (SCUR).

- The master node is node 3 (where instance D is running; the node numbering starts with 0).

- A protected read lock (shared read) as indicated by KJUSERPR has been granted on this resource.

- The row data resides in the File# 4 and Block# 32 in the database. The following excerpt from the block dump shows that all the 14 rows of the EMP table reside in the same block. The block dump output has been edited for brevity.

```
Start dump data blocks tsn: 4 file#: 4 minblk 32 maxblk 32
buffer tsn: 4 rdba: 0x01000020 (4/32)
scn: 0x0000.000adca3 seq: 0x01 flg: 0x04 tail: 0xdca30601

Block header dump:  0x01000020
 Object id on Block? Y
 seg/obj: 0xc7cf  csc: 0x00.adca2  itc: 2  flg: E  typ: 1 - DATA
     brn: 0  bdba: 0x1000019 ver: 0x01 opc: 0
     inc: 0  exflg: 0

Itl         Xid                  Uba       Flag  Lck       Scn/Fsc
0x01    0x0014.017.00000102  0x01400239.0023.06  C---     0  scn 0x0000.000a9cb9
0x02    0x000a.012.000001ea  0x0080118f.00d1.11  C-U-     0  scn 0x0000.000ad663
```

```
data_block_dump,data header at 0x64c6664
===============
tsiz: 0x1f98
hsiz: 0x2e
pbl: 0x064c6664
bdba: 0x01000020
      76543210
flag=--------
ntab=1
nrow=14
```

In this block dump, `nrow=14` shows that all 14 rows are stored in the same block. The data block address (bdba) is `0x01000020`; this will be used later to verify the block written records in the redologs.

The block dump belongs to the EMP table and the object ID of the block is shown as `seg/obj`: `0xc7cf`, where the object ID 51151 is represented as `0xc7cf`.

Here's the result of lock queries on master instance D after a select from EMP table on instance A:

```
REM Lock status on the Master Node D
SQL> @get_segment_stats
no rows selected
SQL> @get_buffer_stat
no rows selected
SQL> @get_resource_name
no rows selected
SQL> @get_resource_stat
RESOURCE_NAME          STATE      MAST  CNVT  GRNT  REQUEST_L  GRANT_LEV
---------------------  --------   ----- ----- ----- ---------  ---------
[0x20] [0x40000], [BL] GRANTED       3     0     1  KJUSERNL   KJUSERPR
```

Observe the following:

- There is no physical read or logical read on the EMP table in the master node. The query `GET_SEGMENT_STATS` on V$segment_statistics confirms this.

- Since there is no read on the EMP table, no blocks from the EMP table are cached in the master node.

- Since no blocks are cached, no resource is allocated to protect that block in instance D.

- The query `GET_RESOURCE_STAT` tells us that the resource is granted on a protected read level.

Example 2: Read the Block from Cache

Continuing from example 1, we run the same query from instance B. The data is already cached in instance C and we should get the block from instance C. The block was read to instance C from disk by the disk read and the block is not changed yet. The on-disk version and the cache version are same as no modifications were made from instance C.

```
REM Execute the following query on instance B: (User SCOTT's session)
SQL> select empno,ename,sal from emp
```

```
    2   where empno=7788;
        EMPNO ENAME                SAL


    ---------- ---------- ----------


        7788 SCOTT               3000
#### Result of lock queries on instance B,
after a select from emp table on instance B
SQL> @get_segment_stats
OBJECT_NAM STAT                                        VALUE
---------- ----------------------------------- -------


EMP         gc cr blocks received                       1

SQL> @get_buffer_stat
     STATE   MODE_HELD      FILE#      BLOCK#    SCN_BASE   SCN_WRAP
---------- ---------- ---------- ---------- ---------- ----------
        3           0          4          32     665905          0
SQL> @get_resource_name
no rows selected
SQL> @get_resource_stat
no rows selected
```

Observe the following:

- The block was retrieved from the cache and not from the disk, as indicated by gc cr blocks received for the segment in the v$segment_statisics view.
- The block is held in the current shared mode as indicated by 3 in the STATE column of the x$bh table. X$BH.STATE is 3 (CR).
- As the buffer is CR state, it does not require any locks to protect it, and no resources are allocated for that buffer in the master node.
- Master node is node 3 (where instance D is running, the node numbering starts with 0).

Now we will look at activity in the master instance D and the instance served the block, which is instance C.

Here are lock statistics in the master instance:

```
SQL> @get_resource_stat
RESOURCE_NAME            STATE    MAST  CNVT  GRNT REQUEST_L GRANT_LEV
-------------------- -------- ----- ----- ----- --------- ---------
[0x20][0x40000],[BL]  GRANTED     3     0     1 KJUSERNL  KJUSERPR

#### Result of lock queries on instance C
after a select from emp table on instance B


SQL> @get_buffer_stat
STATE  MODE_HELD      FILE#      BLOCK#    SCN_BASE   SCN_WRAP
----- ---------- ---------- ---------- ---------- ----------
    2          0          4          32          0          0
```

```
SQL> @get_resource_name
HEXNAME                         RESOURCE_NAME    KJBLGRANT    KJBLROLE KJBLREQUE
------------------------------- ---------------- --------- ---------- ---------
[0x20][0x40000],[BL]            32,262144,BL     KJUSERPR             0 KJUSERNL
```

Observe the following:

■ The master instance granted the shared access to instance C.

■ The SCUR lock mode is compatible with another CR mode without any conflicts.

■ Instance C shipped the block to instance B over the interconnect as instructed by master instance D.

■ The column KJBLGRANT shows KJUSERPR for the lock in SCUR mode in instance C.

■ No additional locks are required to protect the CR buffer in instance A, so no lock status changes are in the master instance.

■ A block present in the buffer cache in CR mode can be used locally by the instance for the query. However, it cannot be used for update and cannot be served to other instances; hence the block does not require a lock.

At the end of example 2, the global cache has two copies of the buffer in two of its caches. Instance C has the buffer in SCUR mode and instance B has the buffer in CR mode. The buffer is still in the local role; no one has yet updated the block; and there is no past image in any of the caches.

Example 3: Update the Row in Instance A

The block that holds the data about user *SCOTT* (EMPNO = 7788) is now cached in instances B and C. Instance C reads the block from disk and serves it to instance B via the interconnect. Then instance A updates the data and makes the buffer incompatible. Instance A does not commit the changes.

Now let's update the block on instance A:

```
REM Let us update DML on instance A:

UPDATE EMP SET SAL=SAL+1000 WHERE EMP=7788;

#### Result of lock queries on instance A

SQL> @get_segment_stats
OBJECT_NAM STAT                                         VALUE
---------- ------------------------------------- -------

EMP        gc current blocks received                       1


SQL> @get_buffer_stat
STATE   MODE_HELD       FILE#       BLOCK#   SCN_BASE    SCN_WRAP
-----   ----------      ----------  -------- ----------  ----------
    1           0            4           32         0           0
```

```
SQL> @get_resource_name
HEXNAME                         RESOURCE_NAME      KJBLGRANT    KJBLROLE  KJBLREQUE
----------------------------    ---------------    ---------    --------  ---------
[0x20][0x40000],[BL]            32,262144,BL       KJUSEREX            0  KJUSERNL
SQL> @get_resource_stat
no rows selected
```

Observe the following:

- State 1 in x$bh shows that the block is held by the instance A in exclusive mode in the current state.

- Statistics gc current blocks received indicates that the block is obtained from the global cache through Cache Fusion and not from the disk.

- Column KJBLGRANT has a value of KJUSEREX, indicating that an instance has an exclusive lock on this resource.

- Instance A has upgraded its lock from Null to X mode.

```
REM Lock and Block statistics from node B and C


REM Buffer Status in Node B (After Instance A updated the Block)
SQL> @get_buffer_stat
STATE  MODE_HELD     FILE#      BLOCK#     SCN_BASE    SCN_WRAP
-----  ----------    ----------  ----------  ----------  ----------
    3           0         4          32      669341            0
SQL> @get_resource_name
no rows selected

SQL> @get_resource_stat
no rows selected

REM  Buffer Status from Node C
SQL> @get_buffer_stat
STATE  MODE_HELD     FILE#      BLOCK#     SCN_BASE    SCN_WRAP
-----  ----------    ----------  ----------  ----------  ----------
    3           0         4          32      669340            0
SQL> @get_resource_name
no rows selected

SQL> @get_resource_stat
no rows selected

REM Resource Statistics from Master Node
SQL> @get_resource_stat
RESOURCE_NAME           STATE     MAST  CNVT  GRNT  REQUEST_L  GRANT_LEV
----------------------  --------  ----  ----  ----  ---------  ---------
[0x20][0x40000],[BL]    GRANTED      3     0     1  KJUSERNL   KJUSEREX
```

Observe the following:

- Instance C downgraded its lock from SCUR to Null mode and has the buffer in CR mode only.

- The buffer status in instance C is changed from 2 (SCUR) to 3 (CR).

- Instances B and C no longer have any lock on the resource. A block present in the buffer cache in CR mode can be used locally by the instance for query. However, the block cannot be used for update and cannot be served to other instances, so it does not require any lock.

- The master instance shows the lock covering the resource is granted in exclusive mode.

- Instance A has the most recent block in the buffer cache. Now any instance requesting the block will be served by instance A.

Example 4: Update a New Row (in the Same Block) in Instance C

Continuing from example 3, we update the same block from another instance, but here we update a different row. Updating the same row will cause waits for TX enqueue, as we are working with a single instance. The buffer holding block 32 is held exclusively by instance A and protected by a BL enqueue. Row level locks in an RAC instance operate similarly to those in a single instance. In this example, we update the same block but a different row.

Let's update the same block on instance C. The block already has an open transaction operating on empno 7788.

```
REM On instance C's scott session:
UPDATE EMP SET SAL = SAL*2 WHERE EMPNO=7369;
COMMIT;


Result of lock queries on instance C, after an update to emp table on instance C
SQL> @get_segment_stats
OBJECT_NAM STAT                                              VALUE
---------- ---------------------------------------- -------
EMP        physical reads                                       1
EMP        gc current blocks received                           1


SQL> @get_buffer_stat
STATE  MODE_HELD      FILE#      BLOCK#    SCN_BASE   SCN_WRAP
-----  ----------  ----------  ---------- ---------- ----------
    1           0       4          32           0          0
SQL> @get_resource_name
HEXNAME                      RESOURCE_NAME   KJBLGRANT   KJBLROLE KJBLREQUE
-------------------------- --------------- --------- ---------- ---------
[0x20][0x40000],[BL]        32,262144,BL    KJUSEREX           0 KJUSERNL

SQL> @get_resource_stat
no rows selected
```

Observe the following:

- The statistic `gc current blocks received . . .1` indicates that the instance received one block belonging to this segment (table) from a remote instance via GCS.

- A value of 1 in the STATE column of the X$BH view on instance C indicates that the block is current and is locked exclusively by this instance.

- The resource is held in exclusive mode as shown as `KJUSEREX` in the third query.

Now let's query the master node to see lock statistics:

REM Statistics from Master Node (Instance D)

```
SQL> @get_resource_stat
RESOURCE_NAME           STATE     MAST  CNVT  GRNT  REQUEST_L  GRANT_LEV
----------------------  --------  ----- ----- ----- ---------  ---------
[0x20][0x40000],[BL]    GRANTED     3     0     1   KJUSERNL   KJUSEREX
[0x20][0x40000],[BL]    GRANTED     3     0     1   KJUSERNL   KJUSERNL
```

Now we will go back to the instance that served the block to this instance. Instance A served the current block to instance C:

REM Resource statistics in node A
```
SQL> @get_buffer_stat
     STATE  MODE_HELD     FILE#     BLOCK#  SCN_BASE  SCN_WRAP
---------- ---------- ---------- ---------- --------- ----------
       8          0          4         32         0          0

SQL> @get_resource_name
HEXNAME                    RESOURCE_NAME    KJBLGRANT    KJBLROLE KJBLREQUE
-------------------------  ---------------  ---------    -------- ---------
[0x20][0x40000],[BL]       32,262144,BL     KJUSERNL            0 KJUSERNL
```

Note the following:

- Instance A downconverts the block from XCUR to PI (STATE equals 8).

- The PI is protected by a Null mode lock as indicated by `KJUSERNL`.

- Master node D shows the locks covering instance C as exclusive (`KJUSEREX`) and the lock covering instance A (`KJUSERNL`) for the PI image.

- The master keeps track of the PI images across the buffer cache. All these instances will be asked to discard the PI copies once the current block is written to disk.

If you look at examples 3 and 4 closely, you can understand that the buffer locks are independent of row level locks. When the block is updated in instance C, a row level lock is placed in the block. When the block is updated again, another row level lock is placed in the block.

The block level storage parameter `INITRANS` controls the initial number of row level locks that can be taken on that block. As demand grows, the number of row level locks in the block grows as long as the block has enough space to record the transaction information. Refer to Chapter 11 for a better understanding of Oracle's internal implementation of row level locks.

Example 5: Commit the Block in Instance A and Select the Rows

Now the process operating on instance A decides to commit the changes. Commit operations in the RAC environment work the same as operations in a single instance environment as far as transactional locks are concerned. In the global cache, level commits do not make any lock status changes in the lock management layer. Now we will explore the query results after issuing a commit in instance A.

```
REM Let us commit our update done in example 3
REM In SCOTT's session, we will issue a commit.
COMMIT;
```

The following are the results in instance A after issuing a commit:

```
Resource statistics in node A
SQL> @get_buffer_stat
     STATE  MODE_HELD     FILE#     BLOCK#    SCN_BASE   SCN_WRAP
---------- ---------- ---------- ---------- ---------- ----------
         8          0          4         32          0          0
SQL> @get_resource_name
HEXNAME                    RESOURCE_NAME   KJBLGRANT   KJBLROLE KJBLREQUE
------------------------   -------------   ---------- ---------- ---------
[0x20][0x40000],[BL]       32,262144,BL    KJUSERNL            0 KJUSERNL


SQL> @get_segment_stats
OBJECT_NAM STAT                                       VALUE
---------- ---------------------------------- -------


EMP        gc current blocks received                     1



REM Resource Statistics in  Instance C
SQL> @get_segment_stats


OBJECT_NAM STAT                                       VALUE
---------- ---------------------------------- -------


EMP        physical reads                                 1
EMP        gc current blocks received                     1



SQL> @get_buffer_stat
STATE  MODE_HELD     FILE#     BLOCK#    SCN_BASE   SCN_WRAP
----- ---------- ---------- ---------- ---------- ----------
    1          0          4         32          0          0
SQL> @get_resource_name
HEXNAME                    RESOURCE_NAME   KJBLGRANT   KJBLROLE KJBLREQUE
------------------------   -------------   ---------- ---------- ---------
[0x20][0x40000],[BL]       32,262144,BL    KJUSEREX            0 KJUSERNL

REM Statistics from Master Node (Instance D)
```

```
SQL> @get_resource_stat
RESOURCE_NAME              STATE      MAST  CNVT  GRNT  REQUEST_L  GRANT_LEV
-------------------        --------   ----- ----- ----- ---------  ---------
[0x20][0x40000],[BL]       GRANTED      3     0     1   KJUSERNL   KJUSEREX
[0x20][0x40000],[BL]       GRANTED      3     0     1   KJUSERNL   KJUSERNL
```

Observe the following:

■ Commits do not make any major changes in the global cache locks.

Example 6: Disk Writes Due to a Checkpoint

Continuing from example 5, the modified buffer from instance C is written to disk due to a checkpoint. We will explore the resource statistics after the checkpoint.

```
REM Let us trigger a checkpoint in Instance C
SQL> alter system checkpoint global;
System altered.

REM Resource Statistics in Instance A
SQL> @get_buffer_stat
STATE   MODE_HELD      FILE#       BLOCK#     SCN_BASE    SCN_WRAP
-----   ----------   ----------   ----------  ----------  ----------
  3          0           4           32        669387         0
SQL> @get_resource_name
no rows selected
SQL> @get_resource_stat
no rows selected

REM Resource Statistics in  Instance C
SQL> @get_segment_stats
OBJECT_NAM STAT                                      VALUE
---------- ----------------------------------- -------

EMP        physical reads                          1
EMP        gc current blocks received              1

SQL> @get_buffer_stat
STATE   MODE_HELD      FILE#       BLOCK#     SCN_BASE    SCN_WRAP
-----   ----------   ----------   ----------  ----------  ----------
  1          0           4           32          0            0
SQL> @get_resource_name
HEXNAME                   RESOURCE_NAME    KJBLGRANT    KJBLROLE KJBLREQUE
----------------------    --------------- ---------- ---------- ---------
[0x20][0x40000],[BL]      32,262144,BL     KJUSEREX          0 KJUSERNL

Statistics from Master Node (Instance D)

SQL> @get_resource_stat
RESOURCE_NAME              STATE      MAST  CNVT  GRNT  REQUEST_L  GRANT_LEV
-------------------        --------   ----- ----- ----- ---------  ---------
[0x20][0x40000],[BL]       GRANTED      3     0     1   KJUSERNL   KJUSEREX
```

Here are observations:

- The checkpoint request from instance C to the master does not change any lock status in the current node.

- The PI from node A is discarded and the buffer is changed to CR mode. Hence the status of the buffer is changed from 8 to 3.

- Since the PI buffer is changed to CR, there is no need for the master to protect that resource. So the KJUSERNL lock is destroyed.

- Instance C also generates a BWR and writes it to redolog files. The BWR dump is shown here:

Block Written Record Dump in Redo Log File of Instance C

```
CHANGE #1 MEDIA RECOVERY MARKER SCN:0x0000.00000000 SEQ:  0 OP:23.1
 Block Written - afn: 4 rdba: 0x01000020 BFT:(1024,16777248) non-BFT:(4,32)
                 scn: 0x0000.001778e1 seq: 0x01 flg:0x00

REDO RECORD - Thread:1 RBA: 0x000006.00004d4a.0010 LEN: 0x0070 VLD: 0x06
SCN: 0x0000.00178185 SUBSCN:  1 06/21/2006 22:36:35
CHANGE #1 MEDIA RECOVERY MARKER SCN:0x0000.00000000 SEQ:  0 OP:23.1
```

Example 7: Instance Crash

At this time, instance D (master instance for our interested resource EMP) crashes. Here is the reconfiguration information from the alert log of instance A:

```
List of nodes:
  0 1 2
  Global Resource Directory frozen
  * dead instance detected - domain 0 invalid = TRUE
  Communication channels reestablished
  * domain 0 valid = 0 according to instance 0
Wed Jun 21 23:22:22 2006
  Master broadcasted resource hash value bitmaps
  Non-local Process blocks cleaned out
Wed Jun 21 23:22:22 2006
  LMS 0: 0 GCS shadows cancelled, 0 closed
Wed Jun 21 23:22:22 2006
  LMS 2: 0 GCS shadows cancelled, 0 closed
Wed Jun 21 23:22:22 2006
  LMS 3: 0 GCS shadows cancelled, 0 closed
Wed Jun 21 23:22:22 2006
  LMS 1: 0 GCS shadows cancelled, 0 closed
  Set master node info
  Submitted all remote-enqueue requests
  Dwn-cvts replayed, VALBLKs dubious
  All grantable enqueues granted
Wed Jun 21 23:22:22 2006
  LMS 0: 2189 GCS shadows traversed, 332 replayed
```

```
Wed Jun 21 23:22:22 2006
 LMS 2: 2027 GCS shadows traversed, 364 replayed
Wed Jun 21 23:22:22 2006
 LMS 3: 2098 GCS shadows traversed, 364 replayed
Wed Jun 21 23:22:22 2006
 LMS 1: 2189 GCS shadows traversed, 343 replayed
Wed Jun 21 23:22:22 2006
 Submitted all GCS remote-cache requests
 Fix write in gcs resources
Reconfiguration complete
```

Example 8: Select the Data from Instance A

After instance reconfiguration, we select the data from instance A. Here are the resource statistics on the master node:

```
SQL> @get_segment_stats
OBJECT_NAM STAT                                      VALUE
---------- ------------------------------------- -------
EMP          gc cr blocks received                     1
EMP          gc current blocks received                1

SQL> @get_buffer_stat


      STATE MODE_HELD       FILE#      BLOCK#   SCN_BASE  SCN_WRAP
---------- ----------  ---------- ----------  ---------- ----------
         3          0           4          32     670125          0
SQL> @get_resource_name
no rows selected
SQL> @get_resource_stat
no rows selected
```

Upon instance recovery, the EMP table is remastered in instance C. We query X$KJBR with the resource name and confirm the resource is remastered in instance C. Alternatively oradebug lkdebug -a <pkey> can be used to determine the details about the master of that resource.

```
REM Resource Statistics from the (new) master node
SQL> @get_master_info
   INST_ID KJBRNAME                 KJBRROLE KJBRMASTER
---------- ----------------------  ---------- ----------

         3 [0x20][0x40000],[BL]            0          2


SQL> @get_resource_stat
RESOURCE_NAME            STATE    MAST  CNVT  GRNT REQUEST_L GRANT_LEV
--------------------    -------- ----- ----- ----- --------- ---------
[0x20][0x40000],[BL]     GRANTED     3     0     1 KJUSERNL  KJUSEREX
```

Observe the following:

- Instance ID 3 is instance C, as instance numbers for the INST_ID start from 1. KJBRMASTER shows 2 because for KJBR the numbering starts from 0.

- Upon the master instance crash, the resources are equally distributed to the surviving nodes and the example object (obj=51151, EMP) is remastered to instance C.

Resource Mastering and Remastering

If you have carefully read the concepts of Cache Fusion so far, the following should be clear:

- Resource usage (including locks on the data blocks) is tracked by GCS. GCS resources and responsibilities are equally distributed among all the instances.

- Every resource has a master and the master instance knows the complete lock state of the resource at any point in time.

- When an instance needs a resource, it requests the desired lock from the master instance by sending a message.

- Based on the current status of the resource, the master grants access to the resource or asks the holder to disown the lock on that resource.

- If one instance accesses a particular resource more often than the others, it would be beneficial to master the resource to that instance to reduce the number of messages on ownership transfers.

- At any point in time a resource can be accessed at the maximum of three hops. This is true irrespective of the number of instances as only three parties are involved in any resource management operation.

- If the application's data access patterns are such that a set of data blocks is generally accessed by only one instance, then the amount of messages sent to remote instances can be optimized by making the local instance the master of those resources. Oracle keeps track of data block access patterns by instances and remasters the resources to optimize the messaging. By default, the Oracle kernel invokes the remastering algorithm every 10 minutes.

Background Process and Cache Fusion

The following sections describe functions performed by each background process as it relates to GCS.

LMON: Lock Monitor Process

LMON maintains GCS memory structures. It handles the abnormal termination of processes and instances. Reconfiguration of locks and resources when an instance joins or leaves the cluster are handled by LMON. Activities that occur during instance reconfigurations are tracked by it in its trace file. In versions 10*g* R2 and later, LMON is responsible for executing dynamic lock remastering every 10 minutes.

LMS: Lock Manager Server

LMS is the most active RAC background process; it can become very active, consuming significant amounts of CPU time. Oracle recommends that this process be allocated the needed CPU time by increasing its priority. In 10g R2, Oracle has implemented a feature to ensure that the LMS process does not encounter CPU starvation.

This process is responsible for receiving remote messages and executing the desired GCS requests, which include the following operations:

- Retrieves requests from the server queue queued by LMD to perform requested lock operations.

- Rolls back any uncommitted transactions for any blocks that are being requested for consistent read by the remote instance.

- Copies blocks from the holding instance's buffer cache and sends a read consistent copy of the block to the requesting foreground process on the requesting instance to be placed into the buffer cache.

LMS also sends messages to remote instances that are not sent by the user processes. Each RAC instance can have two or more LMS processes. Internal view X$KJMSDP contains statistics for the work performed by each LMS process for the instance.

The number of LMS processes can also be set with the `init` parameter `GCS_SERVER_PROCESSES`. Oracle has been optimizing the default number of LMS processes and this varies from version to version. In most of the versions, the default value is `MIN(CPU_COUNT/2, 2)`. However, starting 10g R2, in a single CPU machine, only one LMS process is started. You can consider increasing the value of this parameter if global cache activity is very high.

LMD: Lock Manager Daemon Process (LMDn)

The LMD process performs global lock deadlock detection. It also monitors for lock conversion timeouts. It manages lock manager service requests for GCS resources and sends them to a service queue to be handled by the LMSn process. This process primarily handles lock requests for Global Enqueue resources. Internal view X$KJMDDP contains statistics for the work done by each LMD process for the instance.

LCKn: Lock Process (LCK0)

This process manages instance resource requests and cross instance calls for shared resources. During instance recovery, it builds a list of invalid lock elements and validates lock elements.

DIAG: Diagnostic Daemon (DIAG)

The diagnostic daemon process was introduced in Oracle 10g as a part of the new enhanced diagnosability framework. It regularly monitors the health of the instance. It also checks for instance hangs and deadlocks. Most importantly, it captures the vital diagnostics data for instance and process failures.

In a Nutshell

Cache Fusion contributes to the high performance of the Oracle Database RAC. In this chapter, you saw examples of how it actually works and what happens "under the hood" to enable the transparency of the sessions and connected applications. Understanding the workings of Cache Fusion will help you to appreciate the functionalities and enable designing highly scalable system architecture.

CHAPTER
13

Workload and
Connection Management

he fundamental features of a good, scalable database management system include connection and workload balancing of database connections. Efficient management of these connections, once established, is very important. Fault-tolerant services must be provided by the database engine so that users can take appropriate actions as alternatives to failures and errors.

In a large installation, potentially thousands of users could log on or off from a database within a short span of time. An efficient database engine ensures minimal delays in processing their requests and managing the resources used by these connections. Complex installations are required on external hardware and/or software mechanisms to aid them in integrating messaging and notifications within the cluster when a failure occurs in a cluster service such as an RAC instance, network interfaces, disks, and so on.

Workload Distribution and Load Balancing

Workload distribution can sometimes be called *load balancing*. *Workload distribution* is the management of user connections in such a way that the work they perform is distributed uniformly across RAC nodes. It does not necessarily mean that the *work itself* is evenly spread between nodes due to this mechanism. The distribution of work is an indirect result of the connection distribution.

The workload distribution strategy must be determined during the test implementation phase of application deployment (if not earlier) to make it clear how the application is actually going to connect to the various nodes and database instances. Designers and architects should work out the application behavior with adequate testing to understand how the system performs under a given workload; this information provides a benchmark for the live implementation.

Workload distribution can occur on a per-connection basis, based on server-CPU load or on application/module usage. Certain strategies may be more appropriate than others depending on the implementation and type of usage. The implementation architecture also plays a crucial role in the performance of the system as well as the way the workload is distributed.

Consider, for example, a four-node RAC database running the Oracle E-Business Suite 11i. Multiple application and web servers on the system may or may not be clustered. A total of 8,000 users (connections) access the database via a dedicated server mechanism, and no external, intelligent network devices route the connection request(s) to a particular RAC instance based on some predetermined criteria.

Using Oracle's workload distribution mechanism, you can ensure that about 2,000 clients connect to each RAC node, thereby ensuring that the *connections* are balanced—but not necessarily the *work* these connections perform. In this system, one particular node is more heavily loaded than the others, because the users connected to that node are firing many batch jobs, while the other nodes are running user modules—Inventory, Payables, GL, and the like. Nevertheless, you would like these connections to perform equal units of work, thereby achieving the ever-elusive and mirage-like *load balanced* system. But one of the most difficult tasks to achieve is a complete and perfectly balanced system—unless the application behavior is very well analyzed, the users are well educated, and the application access is restricted to one node, ensuring a uniform usage pattern. This is easier said than done, however, as many of us may have discovered over the years.

If only one database server responds to all the incoming requests, the capacity of the server will not be able to handle high volumes of incoming traffic once the workload increases. Needless to say, application as well as database response time takes a beating—and so do the DBAs. An increase in work and connections to the database server can lead to a point at which upgrading the server hardware will no longer be cost effective.

To achieve server scalability, more servers need to be added to distribute the load among the cluster. The load distribution among these clustered servers is known as *load balancing*.

Such situations are nothing new for someone who has been in the IT industry since the early 1990s, when clustered solutions took off like a rocket. Load balancing and clustering go hand in hand and can be applied to various types of applications such as Internet web servers, telecom applications, and network information servers.

Generic load balancing can become a highly technical and complicated topic and is best treated by network and systems professionals who operate large networks. Load balancing is decided at the system architecture design level though the implementation mechanisms, and methods could differ depending on the application and type of load balancing being done. In this discussion, we look at load balancing particularly from an Oracle perspective.

In Oracle Database applications, load balancing is the attempt to achieve a balanced number of database connections across all the database servers. Load balancing also distributes the services across all the nodes in a cluster implementation. Load balancing can be accomplished using a hardware device or by using Oracle's own software mechanism, as you will learn in the following few sections.

Oracle attempts load balancing by introducing the workload distribution principle. By ensuring a uniform set of connections across all the nodes, we can hope that all the servers are equally loaded to achieve maximum scalability, of course depending on many other factors—too many to discuss here. We can hope that each user will perform equivalent amounts of work, irrespective of the node into which each user is logged.

Application designers and implementers like to restrict usage of an application/module to a particular node only in hopes of achieving balance. For example, if we have deployed General Ledger, Payables, Accounts Receivable, and Inventory in our organization on a four-node cluster for 8,000 users, we might restrict usage of General Ledger and Payables to nodes 1 and 2, respectively. Nodes 3 and 4 can run only Accounts Receivable and Inventory, respectively. This method, commonly known as *application partitioning*, can sometimes cause an imbalanced cluster. In such cases, each node accepts a maximum of 2,000 connections, and a node runs only one application at a time.

Using this method, we could end up in a situation where nodes 1 and 2 are loaded evenly and the other two nodes are heavily loaded. It is also possible that between the last two nodes, node 4 could be running at near 100 percent CPU and memory utilization due to the intense workload generated by the Inventory users. Therefore, it is quite possible that an acceptable approach such as application partitioning can sometimes yield unexpected or undesirable results. Overcoming these challenges is one of the best things about working in clustered environments. See Chapter 16 for more information about this topic.

Problems occur because the work patterns and resource usage of each application can be different. The way they scale and their behavior with increased workload can be vastly different. Hence, it is extremely crucial to test and measure workload profile and performance statistics *before* implementing an application and/or before deploying soft load balancing (application partitioning).

Hardware and Software Load Balancing

The deciding factors for choosing one method of load balancing over another depends on the requirements, available features, complexity of implementation, and cost. We will consider hardware- and software-based load balancing here, as they are more applicable to the Oracle Database application.

Hardware load balancing devices can route TCP/IP packets to various servers in a cluster. These types of load balancers provide a robust topology with high availability but come at a much higher cost. On one hand, this method uses a circuit-level network gateway to route traffic. However, its implementation is more expensive than software implementations.

The most commonly used load balancers are software based and are used mainly as additional/optional features of software applications such as web servers. Oracle provides some form of load balancing as an integrated component of its database software. Software-based load balancers are cheaper than their hardware counterparts. Software is more configurable based on requirements, and it can incorporate intelligent routing based on multiple input parameters. On the other hand, additional hardware can be needed to isolate the load balancing application.

Let's look at some of the features Oracle provides in terms of load balancing connections to the database.

Load Balancing and Oracle Net Services

Many applications like to balance their workloads across all the instances of an Oracle RAC database. Usually, load balancing with Oracle (excluding the parallel feature) meant connection load balancing—that is, the connections to the database are balanced on a "round robin" basis, CPU load, or session count at connect time. With Oracle Net Services, there are two types of connection load balancing, one on the client side and the other on the server side. Starting with Oracle 10g, the Database Configuration Assistant (DBCA) can balance the workload automatically for you when you're creating a database.

NOTE
The discussion about connect time load balancing is for dedicated connections only. Shared server connections can also take advantage of these features but are not discussed here.

Client-Side Load Balancing

Oracle's client-side load balancing feature enables clients to randomize connection requests among all the available listeners. Oracle Net Services progresses through the list of protocol addresses in a random sequence, balancing the load on various listeners. This normally is referred to as *client-side connect-time load balance*. Without client-side load balancing, Oracle Net Services progresses through the list of protocol addresses sequentially until one succeeds. Figure 13-1 illustrates client-side load balancing.

Client-side load balancing is defined in the client connection definition file (tnsnames.ora) by setting the parameter LOAD_BALANCE = ON. Oracle documentation (*Oracle 9i Real Application Clusters Concepts Release 2 (9.2) Part No. A96597-01*) also suggests that you can use LOAD_ BALANCE = YES or LOAD_BALANCE = TRUE, though it is recommended that this approach be tested thoroughly before implementing it. When set to ON, Oracle Net Services progresses through

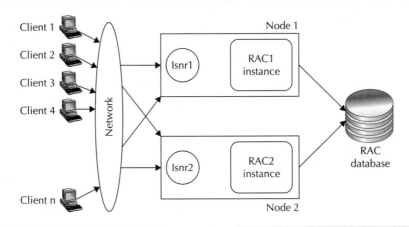

FIGURE 13-1. *Client-side load balancing*

the list of listener addresses in a random sequence, balancing the load on the various listeners. When set to OFF, the addresses are tried sequentially until one succeeds. This parameter must be correctly specified in the Net Services name (connect descriptor). By default, this parameter is set to ON for the DESCRIPTION_LIST.

Load balancing can be specified for an ADDRESS_LIST or associated with a set of addresses or set descriptions. If you use ADDRESS_LIST, LOAD_BALANCE = ON should be within the (ADDRESS_LIST =) portion. If you do not use ADDRESS_LIST, LOAD_BALANCE = ON should be within the (DESCRIPTION =) portion. Here is the example tnsnames.ora (client and server) configuration for a four-node RAC database:

```
RAC =
  (DESCRIPTION =
    (LOAD_BALANCE = ON)
    (ADDRESS = (PROTOCOL = TCP)(HOST = node1)(PORT = 1541))
    (ADDRESS = (PROTOCOL = TCP)(HOST = node2)(PORT = 1551))
    (ADDRESS = (PROTOCOL = TCP)(HOST = node3)(PORT = 1561))
    (ADDRESS = (PROTOCOL = TCP)(HOST = node4)(PORT = 1571))
    (CONNECT_DATA = (SERVICE_NAME = RAC)
  ))
```

Alternatively, you can configure it in another way. Since LOAD_BALANCE is ON by default, the reference is not needed unless you want to turn it off. Most examples show LOAD_BALANCE = ON when the Oracle Connection Manager is being used.

```
RAC =
  (DESCRIPTION =
    (ADDRESS_LIST =
      (LOAD_BALANCE = ON)
      (ADDRESS = (PROTOCOL = TCP)(HOST = node1)(PORT = 1541))
      (ADDRESS = (PROTOCOL = TCP)(HOST = node2)(PORT = 1551))
```

```
      (ADDRESS = (PROTOCOL = TCP)(HOST = node3)(PORT = 1561))
      (ADDRESS = (PROTOCOL = TCP)(HOST = node4)(PORT = 1571))
    )
    (CONNECT_DATA = (SERVICE_NAME = RAC)
  ))
```

The listener.ora file on *each* node will look like this NODE1 file:

```
LISTENER =
  (DESCRIPTION_LIST =
    (DESCRIPTION =
      (ADDRESS_LIST =
        (ADDRESS = (PROTOCOL = IPC)(KEY = EXTPROC))
      )
      (ADDRESS_LIST =
        (ADDRESS = (PROTOCOL = TCP)(HOST = NODE1)(PORT = 1541))
      )
    )
  )
SID_LIST_LISTENER =
  (SID_LIST =
    (SID_DESC =
      (SID_NAME = PLSExtProc)
      (ORACLE_HOME = /app/oracle/product/ora9i)
      (PROGRAM = extproc)
    )
    (SID_DESC =
      (ORACLE_HOME = /app/oracle/product/ora9i)
      (SID_NAME = RAC1)
    )
  )
```

The tnsnames.ora on each node (as well as your client PCs or other hosts) may also contain the individual entries for each of the RAC instances. This is useful when a client program wants to connect to a specific node.

```
RAC1 =
  (DESCRIPTION =
    (ADDRESS_LIST =
      (ADDRESS = (PROTOCOL = TCP)(HOST = NODE1)(PORT = 1541))
    )
    (CONNECT_DATA =
      (SERVICE_NAME = RAC)
      (INSTANCE_NAME = RAC1)
    ))

RAC2 =
  (DESCRIPTION =
    (ADDRESS_LIST =
      (ADDRESS = (PROTOCOL = TCP)(HOST = NODE2)(PORT = 1551))
    )
```

```
      (CONNECT_DATA =
        (SERVICE_NAME = RAC)
        (INSTANCE_NAME = RAC2)
    ))

RAC3 =
  (DESCRIPTION =
    (ADDRESS_LIST =
      (ADDRESS = (PROTOCOL = TCP)(HOST = NODE3)(PORT = 1561))
    )
    (CONNECT_DATA =
      (SERVICE_NAME = RAC)
      (INSTANCE_NAME = RAC3)
    ))

RAC4 =
  (DESCRIPTION =
    (ADDRESS_LIST =
      (ADDRESS = (PROTOCOL = TCP)(HOST = NODE4)(PORT = 1571))
    )
    (CONNECT_DATA =
      (SERVICE_NAME = RAC)
      (INSTANCE_NAME = RAC4)
    ))
```

The tnsnames.ora on each node should be able to resolve the individual listeners also. First, ensure that each instance has the init.ora/SPFILE parameter `local_listener` configured correctly, especially when the listener is running in a non-default port:

```
rac1.local_listener='LISTENER_RAC1'
rac2.local_listener='LISTENER_RAC2'
rac3.local_listener='LISTENER_RAC3'
rac4.local_listener='LISTENER_RAC4'
```

Here's the tnsnames.ora entry on node 1:

```
LISTENER_rac1 =
  (DESCRIPTION =
      (ADDRESS = (PROTOCOL = TCP)(HOST = node1)(PORT = 1541))
  )
```

And here's the tnsnames.ora entry on node 2:

```
LISTENER_rac2 = ....
```

```
..
```

In this way, the tnsnames.ora on each node should be able to resolve its own listener. With this, the configuration is complete; now when clients start to connect using the RAC service name (which matches the init.ora/SPFILE parameter `SERVICE_NAME`) from a PC using SQL

*Plus or any application, the connections are randomly sent to each of the active nodes. This is the round robin feature mentioned earlier. An `lsnrctl services` command can reveal the statistics for each node.

Note that provisioning a "random" method of a database connection mechanism can also be done using a hardware device that is configured appropriately. Cost is a major factor to be considered, and if the *database instance* is down for some reason, the hardware device has no way of knowing it, even though it has the intelligence to recognize that the node is up and running. This lack of *database knowledge* can cause delays or timeouts for connections. Oracle helps you overcome these limitations with its simple client-side load-balancing feature.

One of the disadvantages of the client-side method of load balancing is that client connections won't be able to gauge the load and other resource consumption factors on the instance/node to which they are trying to connect. Hence, timeouts can also occur if the node being attempted for connection is heavily loaded and unable to respond quickly.

Server-Side Load Balancing

Server-side load balancing is also known as *listener-connection load balancing*. This feature improves connection performance by balancing the number of active connections among multiple dispatchers and instances. In a single instance environment (when shared servers are used), the listener selects the least loaded dispatcher to handle the incoming client requests. In an Oracle 9i RAC environment, connection load balancing also has the ability to balance the number of active connections among multiple instances.

Due to dynamic service registration (by Performance Monitor, or PMON), a listener is always aware of all instances and dispatchers regardless of their locations. Depending on the load information, a listener decides to which instance, and, if a shared server is configured, to which dispatcher the incoming client request will be sent. Figure 13-2 illustrates typical server-side load balancing.

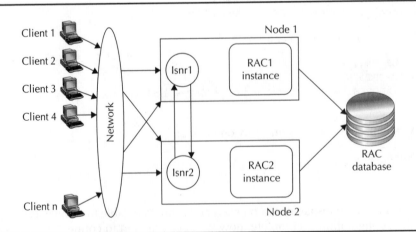

FIGURE 13-2. *Server-side load balancing*

In a shared server configuration, a listener selects a dispatcher in the following order:

1. Least loaded node

2. Least loaded instance

3. Least loaded dispatcher for that instance

In a dedicated server configuration, a listener selects an instance in the following order:

1. Least loaded node

2. Least loaded instance

If a database service has multiple instances on multiple nodes, the listener chooses the least loaded instance on the least loaded node. If a shared server is configured, the least loaded dispatcher of the selected instance is chosen.

As mentioned, the initialization parameter `remote_listener` is used to enable listener connection load balancing. The entry on every node would look like this:

```
*.remote_listener='LISTENERS_RAC'
```

And the tnsnames.ora file for every node would contain this:

```
LISTENERS_RAC =
  (DESCRIPTION =
    (ADDRESS_LIST =
      (ADDRESS = (PROTOCOL = TCP)(HOST = NODE1)(PORT = 1541))
      (ADDRESS = (PROTOCOL = TCP)(HOST = NODE2)(PORT = 1551))
      (ADDRESS = (PROTOCOL = TCP)(HOST = NODE3)(PORT = 1561))
      (ADDRESS = (PROTOCOL = TCP)(HOST = NODE4)(PORT = 1571))
    ))
```

The listener considers the current workload being executed on all the available instances for the requested database service. With server-side load balancing, the listener routes incoming client connections to instances on the least loaded nodes. The listener determines connection distribution based on profile statistics that are dynamically updated by PMON. The higher the node load, the more frequently PMON updates the load profile. Updates occur in as little as 3 seconds on heavily loaded nodes and may take up to 10 minutes on lightly loaded nodes.

The service updates are printed to the listener log as follows:

```
19-DEC-2005 18:07:25 *
(CONNECT_DATA=(SERVICE_NAME=PROD)(INSTANCE_NAME=PROD1)(CID=(PROGRAM=)(HOST=erpa
s2)(USER=applprod))) * (ADDRESS=(PROTOCOL=tcp)(HOST=130.188.1.214)(PORT=48604))
* establish * PROD * 0
19-DEC-2005 18:07:27 * service_update * PROD2 * 0
19-DEC-2005 18:07:29 * service_update * PROD1 * 0
19-DEC-2005 18:10:12 *
(CONNECT_DATA=(SERVICE_NAME=PROD)(INSTANCE_NAME=PROD1)(CID=(PROGRAM=)(HOST=erpd
b1)(USER=applprod))) * (ADDRESS=(PROTOCOL=tcp)(HOST=130.188.1.215)(PORT=47933))
* establish * PROD * 0
19-DEC-2005 18:10:12 *
```

```
(CONNECT_DATA=(SERVICE_NAME=PROD)(INSTANCE_NAME=PROD1)(CID=(PROGRAM=)(HOST=erpd
b1)(USER=applprod))) * (ADDRESS=(PROTOCOL=tcp)(HOST=130.188.1.215)(PORT=47934))
* establish * PROD * 0
19-DEC-2005 18:12:13 * service_update * PROD2 * 0
19-DEC-2005 18:12:15 * service_update * PROD1 * 0
19-DEC-2005 18:12:24 * service_update * PROD1 * 0
19-DEC-2005 18:13:42 * service_update * PROD1 * 0
```

Depending on the load information sent by each PMON process, the listener, by default, redirects the incoming connection request to the listener of the least loaded instance on the least loaded node. By default, Oracle uses the run queue length to distribute the load. To trace the load balancing, you can set the debug event 10237 in the init.ora file, and the PMON trace file in `background_dump_dest` can be examined to confirm the load balancing:

```
event="10257 trace name context forever, level 16"
```

If you want to guarantee that the listener redirects the connection request based on session load, set `PREFER_LEAST_LOADED_NODE_[listener_name]` to `OFF` in the listener.ora file. This is suited for applications that use connection pools.

Note that the init.ora/SPFILE parameters `local_listener` and `remote_listener` need to be set correctly for server-side load balancing to work.

Table 13-1 summarizes the overall details about the different types of load balancing with their advantages and disadvantages.

Type	Hardware Load Balancing (Switch)	Software Load Balancing (Server)	Software Load Balancing (Client)
Implementation	Implemented at network level. Depending on the address the connection is routed to specific node.	Implemented at server level. Based on the CPU usage of the server the connection is accepted or forwarded to other node.	Implemented using client configuration files. Connections distributed to different nodes from the list of nodes
Operation parameters	At network level. Network address of the incoming connection.	Implemented at OS level; CPU usage statistics from OS.	Application level; from the application or module.
Cost	Additional cost involved, as it requires additional hardware.	No additional cost.	No additional cost.
Optimization for logon storms	Well optimized for logon storms—huge number of connection requests during very short time.	Not optimized for logon storm. All connections may land in one node.	Partial optimization for logon storm as requests are distributed to nodes on round robin basis.

TABLE 13-1. *Types of Load Balancing*

Transparent Application Failover

Transparent Application Failover (TAF) enables an application user to reconnect to a database automatically if a connection fails. Active transactions roll back, but the new database connection, achieved using a different node, is identical to the original node. This is true regardless of how the connection fails.

TAF notifications are used by the server to trigger TAF callbacks on the client side. TAF is configured using either a client-side specified Transparent Network Substrate (TNS) connect string or using server-side service attributes. However, if both methods are used to configure TAF, the server-side service attributes will supersede the client-side settings, because the server-side service attributes are the preferred way to set up TAF.

When a failure occurs, callback functions are initiated on the client-side via Oracle Call Interface (OCI) callbacks. This will work with standard OCI connections as well as connection pool and session pool connections.

TAF Considerations

TAF works very well for the reporting and query only applications, without requiring any additional code changes at the application layer. However, it does not fail over or protect the following elements:

- Active insert, update, and delete transactions
- PL/SQL server-side package variables
- Applications not using OCI 8

Even with Oracle 10g R2, TAF supports only failover of SELECT statements and client applications built using OCI. Custom application code may be required to trap errors or exceptions and perform alternative actions. Any application written using OCI 8 or later can take advantage of TAF. Many Oracle tools use OCI transparently; therefore, SQL *Plus, the Pro*C precompiler, the ODBC driver, and thick Java Database Connectivity (JDBC) driver all work with TAF.

For an application to utilize the TAF feature, it must incorporate appropriate OCI 8 (or later) usages and provide certain network configuration information. This requires the manual configuration of the tnsnames.ora and listener.ora files. It is possible to utilize TAF in a configuration where connected clients are performing update transactions; however, additional coding is required to achieve this.

Uncommitted changes at the time of failure are automatically rolled back by the database. To ensure that the application does not think that changes still exist, an error is returned to the application, which can then trigger the application to execute its own rollback statement. The application can then retry the transaction. In most cases, the application will receive another error during the rollback phase, indicating that the connection has been lost. This error must be trapped, but it can be ignored, as the database will have already undone any transactional changes active during the failover.

Alternatively, Oracle Net Services can also preconnect users to a second node. If the primary node dies, the second connection already will be in place, bypassing network bottlenecks at reconnect time.

Configuring TAF

For a client to use TAF, it must connect to the database using a connect descriptor that contains a `FAILOVER_MODE` portion. An example of a tnsnames.ora entry for a four-node RAC database follows:

```
RAC =
  (DESCRIPTION =
    (ADDRESS = (PROTOCOL = TCP)(HOST = NODE1)(PORT = 1531))
    (ADDRESS = (PROTOCOL = TCP)(HOST = NODE2)(PORT = 1541))
    (ADDRESS = (PROTOCOL = TCP)(HOST = NODE3)(PORT = 1551))
    (ADDRESS = (PROTOCOL = TCP)(HOST = NODE4)(PORT = 1561))
    (CONNECT_DATA =
      (SERVICE_NAME = RAC)
      (FAILOVER_MODE=(TYPE=SELECT)(METHOD=BASIC))
  ))
```

It is assumed that the `SERVICE_NAME` parameter in init.ora or SPFILE is accurately configured. Services can also be configured using the Server Control utility (SRVCTL), DBCA, or Enterprise Manager. Most importantly, the service entries have to be updated in the OCR repository. The tnsnames.ora and listener.ora files should be configured as shown earlier in the chapter. Initialization parameters such as `local_listener` and `remote_listener` should also be accurately configured. Using the `GLOBAL_DBNAME` parameter in listener.ora will disable TAF and hence should not be used in this configuration.

Note that we have not used `FAILOVER=ON`. This default parameter is set to `ON` if you use `DESCRIPTION_LIST`, `DESCRIPTION`, or `ADDRESS_LIST` in tnsnames.ora. `FAILOVER=ON`/ `TRUE`/`YES` provides for *connect-time failover,* where Oracle Net Services tries the first address in the list and if that fails, it fails over to the next one in the address list. Without this, Oracle would try only one address (if `LOAD_BALANCE=ON`, a random address is selected or else the first one in the list is used for a connection attempt) from the list and report an error on connection failure.

This type of service configuration for service RAC tells Oracle Net Services to fail over to another instance providing the service RAC only when the instance to which we are currently connected fails.

TAF Configuration Options

The notable part of TAF configuration is shown here:

```
(FAILOVER_MODE=(TYPE=SELECT)(METHOD=BASIC))
```

The `TYPE` parameter can take any of the following three values:

- **SESSION** Set to failover the session. If a user's connection is lost, a new session is automatically created for the user on the backup node using the service name specified in the tnsnames.ora. This type of failover does not attempt to recover selects.

- **SELECT** Set to enable users with open cursors to continue fetching on them after failure. Using this mode can incur overhead on the client side in normal select operations.

- **NONE** This is the default. No failover functionality is used. This can also be explicitly specified to prevent failover from happening.

The `METHOD` parameter can accept either of the following two values and basically determines which method of failover takes place on instance failure from primary node to the secondary:

- **BASIC** Set to establish connections at failover time. This option requires almost no work on the backup server until failover time.

- **PRECONNECT** Set to pre-established connections. This means that a separate database connection to the secondary (backup instance) is maintained all the time while there is a connection to the primary instance. This provides faster failover but requires that the backup instance be able to support all connections from every supported instance. Note that the `BACKUP=` clause is mandatory when using the `PRECONNECT` method of failover.

Here is an example configuration with connect time failover, connection load balancing and TAF for a four-node RAC database:

```
RAC =
(DESCRIPTION=
(LOAD_BALANCE=ON)
(FAILOVER=ON)
(ADDRESS=(PROTOCOL=tcp)(HOST=NODE1)(PORT=1541))
(ADDRESS=(PROTOCOL=tcp)(HOST=NODE2)(PORT=1551))
(ADDRESS=(PROTOCOL=tcp)(HOST=NODE3)(PORT=1561))
(ADDRESS=(PROTOCOL=tcp)(HOST=NODE4)(PORT=1571))
(CONNECT_DATA=
(SERVICE_NAME=RAC)
(FAILOVER_MODE=(TYPE=select)(METHOD=basic)(BACKUP=RAC2)))
```

The `BACKUP=RAC2` clause is crucial here to avoid failover-related issues. Assume that we are connected to an instance and a failure occurs on that instance. When TAF is triggered, Oracle Net Services tries to fail over to another instance as per the TNS configuration. It will try connecting using the service name *RAC* and can attempt to reconnect to the failed node itself since RAC is a service being offered by *n* number of nodes. Though Oracle Net Services would fail over to another address in the list due to the `FAILOVER=ON` parameter (which provided connect time failover), we can avoid unnecessary connect time delays and errors. With the `BACKUP=RAC2` clause, Oracle Net Services will ensure that once TAF is triggered, the connection request is only sent to the `BACKUP=RAC2` node, and this is done immediately without trying any other address.

It is recommended that TAF be configured using the `BACKUP` parameter in the `CONNECT_DATA` of the connect string; this makes it obvious which connect string will be used for failover. Without the `BACKUP` parameter, failover can still occur but you may see some strange effects, such as disconnected sessions returning to the same node from which they were disconnected.

The `BACKUP` TNS alias is not actually verified to be a valid node of an RAC cluster that connects to the same database as the main connection. So, it is possible to set `BACKUP` to a totally different machine and database with different schema objects. This could cause some confusion, such as a failed over select returning ORA-942 "Table or view does not exist" if the table does not exist at the `BACKUP` connection.

Validating the Failover

To check whether your TNS entries are working correctly and if TAF is indeed being triggered, use the following query. (Ensure that this is a test system or that your database is running in ARCHIVELOG mode if data protection is important.)

1. Log into the primary node as *SYS* where a user connection is made using the new TAF-enabled TNS service entry.

```
col sid format 999
col serial# format 9999999
col failover_type format a15
col failover_method format a15
col failed_over format a12

SQL> select instance_name from v$instance ;

INSTANCE_NAME
----------------
RAC1


SQL> select sid, serial#, failover_type, failover_method, failed_over
from v$session where username = 'SCOTT';

       SID    SERIAL# FAILOVER_TYPE FAILOVER_METHOD FAILED_OVER
---------- ---------- ------------- --------------- -----------
        26          8 SELECT        BASIC           NO
```

This shows that the user *SCOTT* has logged into instance RAC1. You could also use the following method:

```
SQL> select inst_id, instance_name from gv$instance ;


INST_ID INSTANCE_NAME
------- -------------
      1 RAC1
      2 RAC2
      3 RAC3
      4 RAC4

SQL> select inst_id, sid, serial#, failover_type, failover_method,
failed_over from gv$session where username = 'SCOTT';

INST_ID       SID    SERIAL# FAILOVER_TYPE FAILOVER_METHOD FAILED_OVER
------- --------- ---------- ------------- --------------- -----------
      1        26          8 SELECT        BASIC           NO
```

2. As user *SCOTT*, run a long query that would last for a period of 45 seconds or more. Here's a commonly used query:

```
SQL> select count(*) from
(select * from dba_source
union
select *  from dba_source
union
```

```
select *    from dba_source
union
select *    from dba_source
union
select *    from dba_source)
```

At this juncture, SHUTDOWN ABORT the instance on which *SCOTT* is running the query—which is instance RAC1 in this case. *SCOTT*'s user screen (SQL *Plus) should hang for a few seconds or more depending on various factors such as cluster communication and node failure detection, network delays, and timeout parameters.

3. After the failover is completed internally by Oracle, the screen should return to normal and the query should continue to process and display results as follows:

```
COUNT(*)
----------
    128201
```

(Note that the resultant value 128201 is an example and the exact value that you get depends on the number of objects in your system.)

4. As user *SYS*, run the query to find out if *SCOTT*'s session was indeed failed over to the other node. The advantage of using GV$ views is that you don't need to log into each instance and query them individually to find out if *SCOTT* has been transferred here.

```
SQL> select inst_id, sid, serial#, failover_type, failover_method,
failed_over from gv$session where username = 'SCOTT';

INST_ID     SID     SERIAL# FAILOVER_TYPE FAILOVER_METHOD FAILED_OVER
------- --------- ---------- ------------- --------------- -----------
      3        16        10 SELECT        BASIC           YES
```

The YES for FAILED_OVER specifies that *SCOTT*'s session did fail over to instance RAC3 when RAC1 failed due to a shutdown abort.

TAF Setup with Services

Let's assume that our service is called ERP instead of RAC and is created in DBCA or using SRVCTL. RAC is the name of the database and RAC1, RAC2, and so on, are the instances. Node1 and Node2 are the RAC cluster nodes. The ERP service is defined so that Node1 is the "preferred" instance for connections, and Node2 is the "available" instance for connections. At startup, Cluster Ready Services (CRS) tries to run the service on Node1. TAF clients connect to the service transparent to where the service executes. If there is a failure with the instance on Node1, the service will be failed over to Node2 by CRS, and all client connections will be routed to Node2. In Oracle 10g, TAF operates with load balancing. If you encounter a scenario with more than two instances, on any failure, the clients load-balance across surviving instances.

Following is the configuration information for the RAC service (the output of $ORA_CRS_ HOME/bin/crs_stat was edited):

```
[node1]/> $ORA_CRS_HOME/bin/./crs_stat

NAME=ora.RAC.ERP.RAC1.sa
TYPE=application
```

```
TARGET=ONLINE
STATE=ONLINE on node1

NAME=ora.RAC.ERP.RAC1.srv
TYPE=application
TARGET=ONLINE
STATE=ONLINE on node1

NAME=ora.RAC.ERP.cs
TYPE=application
TARGET=ONLINE
STATE=ONLINE on node1

NAME=ora.node1.LISTENER_RAC1.lsnr
TYPE=application
TARGET=ONLINE
STATE=ONLINE on node1

NAME=ora.node1.vip
TYPE=application
TARGET=ONLINE
STATE=ONLINE on node1

NAME=ora.node2.LISTENER_RAC2.lsnr
TYPE=application
TARGET=ONLINE
STATE=ONLINE on node2

NAME=ora.node2.vip
TYPE=application
TARGET=ONLINE
STATE=ONLINE on node2

[node1]/> srvctl status service -d RAC -s ERP
  Service ERP is running on instance(s) RAC1


  [node1]/> srvctl status nodeapps -n node1
  VIP is running on node: node1
  GSD is running on node: node1
  Listener is running on node: node1
  ONS daemon is running on node: node1

  [node1]/> srvctl status nodeapps -n node2
  VIP is running on node: node2
  GSD is running on node: node2
  Listener is running on node: node2
  ONS daemon is running on node: node2
```

Troubleshooting TAF Issues

Troubleshooting TAF in 10g RAC differs from that of previous versions because of the additional CRS layer involved. With 10g RAC, one or more services would be created for application and client connections. These services could be started, stopped, or failed over by CRS.

CRS also manages virtual IPs (VIPs) on which the listeners listen. If a node goes down, the service and VIPs that are managed by CRS will fail over to a surviving node. By having the listener listen on the VIPs, we can avoid waiting for a TCP timeout if a node goes down. Connections will be routed to surviving nodes and will be able to resume their work when the failover is completed. When troubleshooting TAF issues in 10g RAC, it is important to look at the CRS layer, the network layer, and the database layer to identify where a problem may reside.

To check whether TAF is working, we can analyze the output of crs_stat once failover has happened. Here is an excerpt from the crs_stat output:

```
[node2]/> $ORA_CRS_HOME/bin/./crs_stat
NAME=ora.RAC.ERP.RAC1.sa
TYPE=application
TARGET=ONLINE
STATE=OFFLINE


NAME=ora.RAC.ERP.RAC1.srv
TYPE=application
TARGET=ONLINE
STATE=ONLINE on node2

NAME=ora.RAC.ERP.cs
TYPE=application
TARGET=ONLINE
STATE=ONLINE on node2


NAME=ora.node1.LISTENER_RAC1.lsnr
TYPE=application
TARGET=ONLINE
STATE=OFFLINE


NAME=ora.node1.vip
TYPE=application
TARGET=ONLINE
STATE=ONLINE on node2


NAME=ora.node2.LISTENER_RAC2.lsnr
TYPE=application
TARGET=ONLINE
STATE=ONLINE on node2


NAME=ora.node2.vip
TYPE=application
TARGET=ONLINE
STATE=ONLINE on node2

[node2]/> srvctl status service -d RAC -s ERP
  Service ERP is running on instance(s) RAC2
```

Looking at the highlighted sections, you can see that node1's virtual IP and the ERP service failed over to node2. Compare this output with the earlier one and you can understand what has happened. The CRS and CSS log whose default location is ORA_CRS_HOME/crs/log and $ORA_CRS_HOME/css/log also provides detailed output about the CRS reconfiguration and node membership details.

Relocation of Failed Service(s)   Once a set of services fails over to another surviving instance and eventually when the failed instance is restarted, all the migrated services do not automatically come back to the restarted instance. For instance, in Oracle 10*g* RAC, once the failed node restarts, it reclaims its own VIP, which was temporarily taken over by node2.

Services have to be manually relocated. An example of the ERP service is provided next, in which the service is relocated from node2 back to node1:

```
[node1]/> srvctl relocate service -d RAC -s ERP -i RAC2 -t RAC1
```

(Oracle Metalink Notes: 97926.1 and 226880.1 provide detailed discussions of TAF and load balancing issues.)

Workload Management

Workload management enables users to manage the distribution of workloads to provide optimal performance for users and applications. Workload management comprises the following:

- **Services**   Oracle Database 10g introduces the powerful automatic workload management facility, called *services*, to enable the enterprise grid vision. You can define services in RAC databases that enable you to group database workloads and route work to the optimal instances that are assigned to offer the service.

- **Load Balancing Advisory**   Provides information to applications about the current service levels being supplied by the database and its instances, and provides recommendations to applications about where to direct application requests to obtain the best service based on the defined policy.

- **High Availability Framework**   Enables the Oracle Database application to maintain components in a running state at all times.

Oracle Services

To manage workloads, you can define and assign services to a particular application or to a subset of an application's operations. You can also group other types of work under services. For example, online users can be a service, batch processing can be another, and reporting can be another service type. It is recommended that all users who share a service have the same service level requirements. You can define specific characteristics for services, and each service is a separate unit of work. A service is the building block that can be used to divide work into logical workloads.

Services allow applications to benefit from the reliability of the redundant parts of the cluster. The services hide the complexity of the cluster from the client by providing a single system image for managing work.

Each service represents a workload with the following:

- Globally unique name
- Common service level policies—performance, HA, and so on
- Common priority
- Common function and footprint

Services supply many benefits. They provide a single system image to manage competing applications, and they allow each workload to be managed in isolation and as a unit. Using standard user interfaces in DBCA, NetCA, SRVCTL, and Enterprise Manager (EM) with services, a workload is configured, administered, enabled and disabled, and measured as a single entity. EM supports viewing and operating services as a whole, with the ability to drill down to the instance level when needed. A service can span one or more instances of an Oracle database or multiple databases in a global cluster, and a single instance can support multiple services. The number of instances offering the service is transparent to the application.

Services enable the automatic recovery of work. This is achieved according to business rules. Following outages, the service is recovered fast and automatically at the surviving instances. When instances are later repaired, services that are not running are restored fast and automatically by CRS. Immediately, the service changes state—up or down, and a notification is available for applications using the service—to trigger immediate recovery and load balancing actions.

Services are dynamic. The resources assigned to a service can be augmented when load increases and they can be reduced when load declines. This dynamic resource allocation provides a cost-effective solution for meeting demands as they occur. For example, services are measured automatically and the performance is compared to service level thresholds. Performance violations are reported to EM, allowing the execution of automatic or scheduled solutions.

A number of RDBMS features act in concert to support services. The Automatic Workload Repository (AWR) collects a service's performance metrics, recording the service performance, including SQL execution times, wait classes, and resource consumed by service. AWR alerts warn when service response time thresholds are exceeded. The dynamic views report current service status with one hour of history as configured by default.

Configuring Services

To configure services in Oracle single instance environments, you use the DBMS_SERVICE package. For backward compatibility, services are also created implicitly when the `service_names` parameter is set for the instance. To configure the service level thresholds and Database Resource Manager for services, use EM or PL/SQL.

Available and Preferred Instances   To configure the high availability features of services in Oracle 10g RAC environments, use the DBCA and/or NETCA or SRVCTL. This definition process creates a number of high availability (HA) resources that are managed by the clusterware to keep the services available. The DBCA and SRVCTL interfaces for service ask the administrator to enter the list of instances that are the preferred location for the service, plus any additional instances that are available to support the service in the event of an outage or planned operation.

The definition of the preferred set of instances are a hint to the HA framework integrated with RAC 10g about how to distribute the service when the system first starts. Some or all instances of the database may be configured to support the service. Once the service is created, Database Resource Manager can be used to create consumer groups that control the priority of the service.

When you define a service, you define which instances will normally support that service. These are known as the *preferred* instances. You can also define other instances to support a service if the service's preferred instance fails. These are known as *available* instances.

When you specify the preferred instances, you are specifying the number of instances on which a service will initially run. For example, on a three node cluster, the preferred configuration may offer the Payroll service from instance 1 and the ERP service from instances 2 and 3.

Afterwards, due either to instance availability or planned service relocations, a service may be running on an available instance. When a service moves to an available instance, Oracle does not move the service back to the preferred instance when the preferred instance comes back online. This is because the service is already running on the desired number of instances. All this provides a higher level of continual service availability and avoids a second service outage due to failback processing.

Oracle Net Services provides connection load balancing that lets you to spread user connections across all of the instances that are supporting a service. RAC uses FAN to notify applications about configuration changes and the current service level that is provided by each instance where the service is enabled.

The easiest way to use FAN is to use the Oracle clients that have Fast Connection Failover (FCF), which means the clients have been integrated with the HA FAN events. These include JDBC, OCI, and ODP.NET. OCI clients can include clients with TAF enabled. For OCI and ODP .NET, you must enable the service to send FAN high availability events—in other words, set AQ_HA_NOTIFICATIONS to TRUE.

By default, when you create a database, Oracle defines one special database service for your RAC database. The default database service is always available on all instances in an RAC environment, unless the instance is in restricted mode. You cannot alter this service or its properties.

Workload Balancing

When it comes to workload balancing, connection placement uses connection load balancing and work request placement uses runtime load balancing. The benefit of managing work across multiple servers as a single unit is that it increases the utilization of the available resources. Work requests can be distributed across instances offering a service according to the current service performance. Balancing work requests occurs at two different times—at *connect time* and at *runtime*.

Connection Pooling and Load Balancing Advisory

Historically, load balancing within a pool of connections was based on the initial load information provided by Oracle to the middle tier. So the load information was outdated in no time as the workload on the system was bound to increase as more users connected. Hence, load balancing involved distributing an even number of connections across all the RAC instances. When an application asked for a connection, it was given a random connection (to an instance) from a set of inactive connections in the pool. There was no way of knowing how loaded the instance was before connecting to it.

Oracle 10g R2 introduced connection pool load balancing—also called the Load Balancing Advisory. With this new feature configured, an RAC database will periodically send load information and the current service level to the connection pool. The information is collated from all active instances and sent as a FAN to the connection pool manager in the middle tier. Since there is a periodic update about the service information and the listener is able to route connections based on intelligence, this is also referred to as *runtime load balancing*.

RAC's Load Balancing Advisory monitors the work for each service in an instance and provides a percentage value of how much of the total workload should be sent to this instance as well as a service quality flag. The feedback is provided as an entry in the AWR and a FAN event is published.

Well-designed and built applications generally tend to make good use of connection pools built into the middle tier of an application. For example, applications using Common Object Request Broker Architecture (CORBA), BEA WebLogic, and other Java-based applications can take advantage of the connection pooling mechanism in the middle layer. This mechanism is not new to Oracle 10g but has existed since the early days of TP monitors and the evolution of large-scale OLTP application deployment.

In simple terms, the connection pool is a named group of identical connections to the database. Applications borrow connections from the connection pool and use the connections to perform database calls. When that work is complete, the connection channel is released back to the connection pool to be reused.

Connection caching or pooling is used to preserve connections and minimize the overhead of creating new connections at the OS level. By maintaining the connection(s) for a long time, the OS does not need to spend time allocating process space, CPU time, and so on, every time a connection is made. Even disconnection from the database requires quite a bit of OS coordination, such as database lock cleanup and other housekeeping activities that can be avoided by using connection pooling.

Standard architectures that can use the Load Balancing Advisory include connection load balancing, TP monitors, application servers, connection concentrators, hardware and software load balancers, job schedulers, batch schedulers, and message queuing systems. All of these applications can allocate work.

The Load Balancing Advisory is deployed with key Oracle clients, such as Listener, JDBC Implicit Connection Cache 10g, and ODP.NET Connection Pool. The Load Balancing Advisory is also open for third-party subscription by way of Oracle Notification Service.

Connection Load Balancing

Good applications connect once to the database server and stay connected. This is best practice for all applications—connection pools, client/server, and server side. Since connections are relatively static, the method for balancing connections across a service should not depend on metrics that vary widely during the lifetime of the connection.

Three metrics are available for the listeners to use when selecting the best instance:

- **Session count by instance**   For symmetric services and the same capacity nodes, the absolute session count evenly distributes the sessions.

- **Run queue length of the node**   For asymmetric services or different capacity nodes, the run queue length places more sessions on the node with the least load at the time of connection.

- **Goodness by service**   For all services and any capacity nodes, the goodness of the service is a ranking of the quality of service experienced at an instance. The ranking compares the service time to the service's threshold value. It also considers states such as whether access to an instance is restricted. Example goodness ratings are excellent, average, violating, and restricted. To avoid a listener routing all connections to the excellent instance between updates to the goodness values, each listener adjusts its local ratings by a delta as connections are distributed. The delta value used is the resource consumed by each connection using a service.

Oracle 10g R2 also introduced changes to connection load balancing on the server side. When services are created using the DBMS_SERVICE.CREATE_SERVICE package, you also need to specify a connection load balancing goal using the parameter CLB_GOAL. It accepts two values, CLB_GOAL_LONG or CLB_GOAL_SHORT. LONG is the default value, which means connections are held for longer periods, based on session count.

To specify a method of load balancing, a database service needs to be created. Here's an example:

```
EXECUTE DBMS_SERVICE.CREATE_SERVICE(service_name=>'rac.acme.com',-
network_name=>'rac.acme.com',-
goal=>dbms_service.goal_service_time,-
clb_goal=>dbms_service.clb_goal_short);
```

With CLB_GOAL_SHORT, connection load balancing uses the Load Balancing Advisory, when it is enabled (either GOAL_SERVICE_TIME or GOAL_THROUGHPUT). When CLB_GOAL_NONE (no Load Balancing Advisory) is used, connection load balancing uses an abridged advice based on CPU utilization.

With CLB_GOAL_LONG, connection load balancing balances the number of connections per instance using session count per service. This setting is recommended for applications with long connections such as SQL *Forms. This setting can be used with Load Balancing Advisory when connection pools are used. As the name suggests, CLB_GOAL_LONG creates long-lived connections and CLB_GOAL_SHORT creates connections of short duration.

The parameter goal=>dbms_service.goal_service_time is concerned with connection pool load balancing or runtime load balancing, which also requires the configuration of database services and configuration Oracle Net Services connection load balancing. This feature is described in the next section.

So, when an application requests a connection, the connection pool is able to provide a connection to the instance that will best service the client request. This load balancing algorithm is able to route work requests based on a defined policy. When database services are created, a goal is specified along with it, which can be GOAL_THROUGHPUT, GOAL_SERVICE_TIME, or GOAL_NONE.

GOAL_THROUGHPUT means that the load balancing will be based on the rate that work is completed in the service plus the available bandwidth. If GOAL_SERVICE_TIME is specified, load balancing is based the elapsed time for work done in the database service plus the available bandwidth to the service.

For a detailed discussion on the basics and configuration steps, refer to the Oracle document *Oracle Clusterware and Oracle Real Application Clusters Administration and Deployment Guide 10g Release 2 (10.2) Part No: B14197-01.*

If the connection pool load balancing feature is used, the GOAL_* parameters are set using the DBMS_SERVICE and CLB_GOAL is ignored. Having PREFER_LEAST_LOADED_NODE_[listener_name] in listener.ora will disable/override new functionality.

Runtime Load Balancing

Runtime load balancing (RLB) is used when selecting connections from connection pools. For connection pools that act on services at one instance only, the first available connection in the pool is adequate. When connection pools act on services that span multiple instances, for runtime load balancing, a metric is needed that is responsive to the current state of each service at each instance.

The AWR measures the response time, CPU consumption, and service adequacy for each service and is integrated with the Load Balancing Advisory. The views V$SERVICE_METRICS and V$SERVICE_METRICS_HISTORY contain the service time for every service and are updated every 60 seconds with 1 hour of history. These views are available to applications to use for their own runtime load balancing. For example, a middle tier application using connection pools can use the service metrics when routing the runtime requests to instances offering a service.

The Database Resource Manager maps services (in place of users) to consumer groups, thereby automatically managing the priority of one service relative to others. The RAC high availability features keep the services available, even when some or all components are unavailable. The Data Guard Broker, in conjunction with RAC, is capable of migrating the primary service across various Data Guard sites for disaster tolerance.

Using Service Time for Load Balancing   Using the service time for load balancing is a major improvement over earlier approaches that use round robin or run queue length. The run queue length metric does not consider sessions that are blocked in wait—for example, interconnect wait, IO wait, and application wait—and unable to execute. Run queue length and session count metrics also do not consider session priority.

Using service time for load balancing recognizes machine power differences, sessions that are blocked in wait, failures that block processing, and competing services of different importance. Using service time prevents sending work to nodes that are overworked, hung, or failed.

The Load Balancing Advisory takes into consideration different sized nodes and in cases where a node is heavily loaded, the connection pool is capable of removing connections for that instance from the pool (as they become inactive or hung). The connection pool is then able to create new connection(s) to another instance, providing better service levels.

The response times DB time and CPU time are available for each service at each instance in V$SERVICE_METRICS_HISTORY. Just as the listener uses this data to deal connections across the service, the connection pool algorithm can use the data when selecting connections from the connection pool. Using this approach distributes the work across instances that are serving the service well and avoids sending work to slow, hung, failed, and restricted instances.

Assuming that an ODP.NET–based application uses connection pooling with the grid runtime load balancing attribute enabled, an ODP.NET connection pool registers for an RLB notification with a particular service in an RAC or grid environment. If the environment is properly configured, the service periodically sends notifications to ODP.NET with information on the responsiveness of each service member.

For optimal performance, ODP.NET dispenses connections to service members based on information received about their responsiveness. This attribute can be used only against Oracle instances within an RAC database. Its value is also ignored if `pooling=False`.

The grid runtime load balancing attribute is enabled by setting the grid runtime load balancing connection string attribute to True. The default is False. The following connection string enables the grid runtime load balancing attribute:

```
"user id=apps;password=apps;data source=erp;grid runtime load" + "balancing=true;"
```

Measuring Workloads by Service
If configured, the AWR maintains performance statistics, including response times, resource consumption, and wait events, for all services and for all the work that is being done in the system. Selected metrics, statistics, wait events, and wait classes, plus SQL level traces are maintained for

the service, optionally augmented by module and action names. The statistics aggregation and tracing by service are new in their global scope for RAC and in their persistence across instance restarts and service relocation for both RAC and single instance Oracle.

By default, statistics are collected for the work attributed to every service. Each service can be further qualified by module and action names to identify the important transactions within the service. This eliminates the hard work associated with measuring the time for all calls for the service. The service, module, and action name provide a user-explicable unit for measuring elapsed time per call and for setting and resource consumption thresholds.

As most programmers know by now, module and action can be set with the following:

```
DBMS_APPLICATION_INFO.SET_MODULE(module_name => 'add_customer',
action_name => 'CUST_ADD');
```

Module and action are visible in V$SESSION. This naming format is a way of tying a portion of the application code to the database work done on its behalf. The module name is set to a user recognizable name for the program that is currently executing (script or form). The action name is set to a specific action that a user is performing within a module (such as reading mail or entering new customer data). Setting these tags using OCI in 10g does not result in additional round trips to the database.

We can use the DBMS_MONITOR package to control the gathering of statistics that quantify the performance of services, modules, and actions. DBMS_MONITOR is also used for tracing services, modules, and actions.

High Availability Features

For HA clients connected to an RAC database, HA event notification can provide a best-effort programmatic signal to the client in the event of a failure. Client applications can register a callback on the environment handle to signal interest in this information. When a significant failure event occurs (which applies to a connection made by this client), the callback is invoked, with information concerning the event (the event payload) and a list of connections (server handles) that were disconnected as a result of the failure.

The HA event notification mechanism improves the response time of the application in the presence of failure. In the past, a failure would result in the connection being broken only after the TCP timeout expired, which could take minutes. With HA event notification, standalone, connection pool, and session pool connections are automatically broken and cleaned up by OCI, and the application callback is invoked within seconds of the failure event. If any of these server handles are TAF-enabled, failover will also automatically be engaged by OCI.

Applications must connect to an RAC instance to enable HA event notification. Furthermore, these applications must initialize the OCI environment in OCI_EVENTS mode. Then these applications can register a callback that is invoked whenever an HA event occurs.

Grid Connection Recovery—ODP.NET

When the grid connection recovery attribute is enabled, the ODP.NET connection pool subscribes to an RAC FAN event. FAN notifies ODP.NET whenever a node or a service is down. This allows ODP.NET to properly clean up resources from connections that have been severed and establish new connections to healthy service members. This provides better availability with minimal application management, and applications can quickly recover from downed nodes or services.

The grid connection recovery attribute is enabled by setting the grid connection recovery connection string attribute to True. The default is False. The `grid connection recovery` attribute can be used only against Oracle instances within an RAC or grid environment. The attribute value is ignored if `pooling=False`. The following connection string enables the grid connection recovery attribute:

```
"user id=apps;password=apps;data source=erp;grid connection recovery=true;"
```

Notifications and FAN

One of the main principles of a highly available application is that it be able to receive fast notification when the status of a critical resource or component changes. This resource or component could be within a cluster or outside, but it is critical to the functioning of the application. The FAN feature provides a framework to achieve higher levels of availability and reliability for a cluster database.

Using notifications, applications are able to perform some form of retaliatory action or handle this event (by executing a program or script) so that application availability is not compromised or a certain set of predetermined actions are taken to minimize the impact of this status change known as an event.

The timely execution of these handler programs minimizes the impact of cluster component failures by avoiding connection timeouts, application timeouts, and reacting to cluster resource reconfiguration in both planned and unplanned scenarios.

Event-based Notification   The concept of event-based notification is not new. Customers who have deployed Oracle Enterprise Manager or monitored enterprise IT resources using third-party management console products that rely on low-overhead protocols such as SNMP are already familiar with the usage and benefits of receiving component up, down, or threshold violation alerts from the database layer. Production sites may also implement their own polling mechanisms by capturing events and delivering proper notifications to higher application layers.

Traditionally, client or mid-tier applications connected to the database have relied on connection timeouts, out-of-band polling mechanisms, or other custom solutions to realize that a system component has failed. This approach has huge implications in application availability, because down times are extended and more noticeable.

The other area where the traditional approach falls short is in the management of complex database cluster environments, because of the exponential growth in the number of server-side components, both horizontally (across all cluster nodes) and vertically (across cluster node components such as listeners, instances, and application services). Furthermore, with the introduction of grid computing to the enterprise, such levels of component complexity must be interconnected, monitored, and managed in a proactive and automated way.

When the state of an Oracle 10g database service changes (up, down, restart failure), the new status is posted or relayed to interested subscribers through FAN events. Applications can use these events to achieve very fast failure detection and recreate, reestablish, and balance a connection pool following a failure as well as failback detection to restore normal services.

A FAN event is issued whenever a service becomes available, whenever it becomes unavailable, and whenever it is no longer being managed by CRS. The notification events occur for status changes in resources under CRS for services, service members, database, and instances. Databases and instances are included to accommodate applications that depend on these resources directly. The notification event is used to eliminate the HA problems of sessions waiting to timeout when blocked in receive and/or wasting time processing in think-time after their service has terminated. This is done by providing a notification in the form of an out-of-band event to the client side. In this way, sessions are notified fast when the application changes state.

Since important HA events are pushed as soon as they are detected, this method results in a more efficient use of existing computing resources and a better integration with enterprise applications, including mid-tier connection managers or IT management consoles such as trouble ticket loggers and email/paging servers.

FAN is a distributed system that is enabled on each participating node. This makes it reliable and fault-tolerant because the failure of one component is detected by another one. Therefore, event notification can be detected and pushed by any of the participating nodes.

FAN events are tightly integrated with Oracle Data Guard Broker, Oracle JDBC implicit connection cache, and Enterprise Manager. Oracle Database 10g JDBC applications managing connection pools do not need custom code development. They are automatically integrated with the Oracle Notification Service (ONS) if implicit connection cache and fast connection failover are enabled. Figure 13-3 shows the FAN architecture.

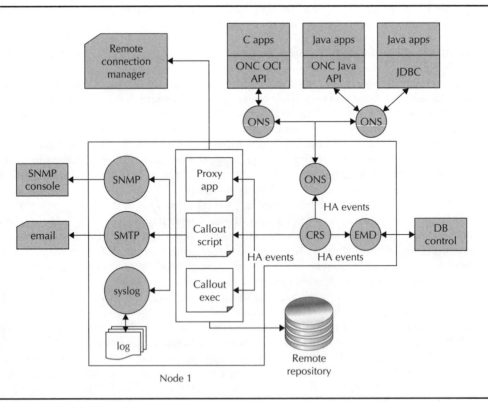

FIGURE 13-3. *FAN architecture*

Application Failure Issues   When a service goes down in a cluster, applications end up wasting time trying one or some of these activities:

■   Waiting for TCP/IP timeout when a node fails without closing sockets and for every subsequent connection while that particular IP is down.

■   Attempting to connect when services are down and not connecting when services resume.

■   Attempting to execute work on slow, hung, or dead nodes.

The existing mechanisms in Oracle do not allow for these types of problems to be reported, so accounting for downtime or performance issues caused by them is not possible or at best an estimation.

When a node fails without closing the network sockets, all sessions that are blocked in an I/O use the transport layer configuration (`tcp_keepalive`) for a predefined period before timing out. The problem could be worse for sessions that are processing something at the client end and are not aware that the server is down. The status is known only after the last result set is to be fetched or processed. This causes severe delays or timeouts.

For cluster configuration changes, the RAC HA framework publishes a FAN event immediately when a state change occurs in the cluster. Instead of waiting for the application to poll the database and detect a problem, applications receive FAN events and can react immediately to them.

On receipt of a FAN event, applications can abort sessions in communication with the failed instance or node, relocate them to another node, notify sessions waiting to resume operations, and reorganize incoming work on the fly as additional resources become available or lost. For example, if a service is down, a DOWN event is published. For DOWN events, the disruption to the application can be minimized because sessions to the failed instance or node can be terminated. Incomplete transactions are terminated and the application user is immediately notified. Application users who request connections are directed to available instances only.

You can also use server-side callouts to do the following:

■   Page DBAs or open support tickets when resources fail to start.

■   Automatically start dependent external applications that need to be co-located with a service.

■   Change resource plans or shut down services when the number of available instances decreases—for example, if nodes fail.

■   Automate the failback of a service to PREFERRED instances if needed.

For UP events, when services and instances are started, new connections can be created so that the application can immediately take advantage of the extra resources.

FAN also publishes load balancing advisory events. Applications can take advantage of the load balancing advisory FAN events to direct work requests to the instance in the cluster that is currently providing the best service quality.

Using FAN   FAN can be used in three ways. First, applications can take advantage of FAN without programmatic changes by utilizing an integrated Oracle client. The integrated clients for FAN events include Oracle Database 10g JDBC (Oracle Database 10g R2 is required for load balancing), Oracle Database 10g R2 Oracle Data Provider for .NET (ODP.NET), and Oracle

Database 10g R2 Oracle Call Interface (OCI). This includes applications that use TAF. Second, applications can use the ONS API to subscribe to FAN events and execute event-handling actions upon receipt. Third, applications can implement FAN server-side callouts on the database tier.

Applications can also enable the Oracle JDBC implicit connection cache and let FAN events be handled by the Oracle JDBC libraries directly. Using this method, you no longer need to write any custom Java or C code to handle FAN events, nor do you need to invoke the ONC API directly. They are automatically integrated with ONS if implicit connection cache and fast connection failover are enabled. Consider this as an out-of-the-box integration with the ONS.

The easiest way to receive all the benefits of FAN with no effort is to use an Oracle connection pool that is integrated with FAN. Oracle Enterprise Manager (Oracle 10g Grid Control) is also tightly integrated with FAN and no extra configuration is required to use it.

Fan Events and Notification   FAN events consist of a header and payload information delivered as a set of name-value pairs accurately describing the name, type, and nature of the cluster event. Based on this payload, the event recipient can take concrete management, notification, or synchronization steps. These could include actions such as shutting down the application connection manager, rerouting existing database connection requests, refreshing stale connection references, logging trouble tickets, or sending a page to the database administrator. The objective is to deliver FAN events so that they precede any other polling intervals or connection timeouts.

Notification is the first step in the processes for application recovery, service recovery, offline diagnosis, and fault repair. Notification occurs in several forms:

- **In-band notification**   Using strong and weak dependencies in CRS and special CRS events for check and fail actions, dependent resources receive an in-band notification to start and stop. These events occur as a result of starting or stopping interdependent resources, and as a result of dependent resources failing and restarting. These notifications are considered in-band because they are posted and processed synchronously as part of CRS managing the system.

- **Out-of-band notification**   FAN provides callouts, events, and paging; email from the enterprise console, status changes, fault notifications, and fault escalation are forwarded to invoke repair and to interrupt applications to respond to the service change. These FAN events are considered out-of-band because they are issued asynchronously through gateway processes out of RAC/HA to listeners, enterprise console, and callouts.

- **Error and event logs**   When a fault occurs in any layer, details of the error are reported to persistent event logs. This is the case for all error conditions, including those that are automatically recovered by the CRS system. For expediency, all event logs should have a consistent format and should be logged to a consistent location. Data collection is essential to ensure that a root cause for the condition can be found early. Once the problem is identified, a resolution can be produced.

Three categories of events are currently supported in FAN:

- Service events, which include both application services and database services

- Node events, which include cluster membership states and native join/leave operations

- Load balancing events sent from the RAC Load Balancing Advisory

In addition to application services, RAC standardizes the generation, presentation, and delivery of events pertaining to managed cluster resources, which include these event types:

Event Type	Description
SERVICE	Primary application service event
SRV_PRECONNECT	Shadow application service event (mid-tiers and TAF using primary and secondary instances)
SERVICEMEMBER	Application service on a specific instance event
DATABASE	Oracle database event
INSTANCE	Oracle instance event
ASM	Oracle ASM instance event
NODE	Oracle cluster node event

This table describes the event status for each of these managed cluster resources:

Event Status	Description
status=up	Managed resource comes up
status=down	Managed resource goes down
status=preconn_up	Shadow application service comes up
status=preconn_down	Shadow application service goes down
status=nodedown	Managed node goes down
status=not_restarting	Managed resource cannot fail over to a remote node
status=restart_failed	Managed resource fails to start locally after discrete number of retries
status=unknown	Unrecognized status

The event status for each managed resource is associated with an event reason. The reason further describes what triggered the event, as shown in the following table:

Event Reason	Activity Type	Event Trigger
reason=user	Planned	User initiated commands, such as srvctl and sqlplus
reason=failure	Unplanned	Managed resource polling checks detected a failure
reason=dependency	Unplanned	Dependency of another managed resource that triggered a failure condition
reason=unknown	Unhandled	Unknown or internal application state when event is triggered
reason=autostart	CRS boot	Initial cluster boot (managed resource has profile attribute AUTO_START=1, and was offline before the last CRS shutdown)
reason=boot	CRS boot	Initial cluster boot (managed resource was running before the last CRS shutdown)

Other event payload fields further describe the unique cluster resource whose status is being monitored and published. They include the following:

Event Resource Identifier	Description
`VERSION=<n.n>`	Event payload version (currently `VERSION=1.0`)
`timestamp=<eventDate> <eventTime>`	Server-side date and time when the event was detected
`service=<serviceName.dbDomainName>`	Name of the (primary or shadow) application service (excluded from NODE events)
`database=<dbName>`	Name of the RAC database (excluded from NODE events)
`instance=<sid>`	Name of the RAC instance (excluded from SERVICE, DATABASE, and NODE events)
`host=<hostName>`	Name of the cluster node as returned by the clusterware (excluded from SERVICE and DATABASE events)
`card=<n>`	Service membership cardinality (excluded from all events except `SERVICE status=up`)

The combination of all these attributes and types result in a FAN event with the following payload structure:

```
<Event_Type> VERSION=<n.n>
service=<serviceName.dbDomainName>
[database=<dbName> [instance=<sid>]] [host=<hostname>]
status=<Event_Status> reason=<Event_Reason> [card=<n>]
timestamp=<eventDate> <eventTime>
```

Here's an example:

```
Service events:

SERVICE VERSION=1.0 service=homer.simpsons.com database=BART status=up
reason=user card=4 timestamp=16-Feb-2006 21:09:15

SERVICEMEMBER VERSION=1.0 service=barney.simpsons.com database=BEER
instance=DRAUGHT host=moesplace status=down reason=user timestamp=16-Mar-2006 19:01:34

DATABASE VERSION=1.0 service=skywalker.starwars.com database=STARS
host=galaxy status=up reason=boot timestamp=08-Mar-2006 15:31:00

INSTANCE VERSION=1.0 service=robinhood.thieves.com database=RANSOM
instance=SCOTLAND host=locksley status=down reason=failure
timestamp=12-Mar-2006 17:25:09
```

```
ASM VERSION=1.0 instance=ASM1 host=apps status=down reason=failure
timestamp=12-Mar-2006 11:54:46

Node events:

NODE VERSION=1.0 host=sales status=nodedown timestamp=16-Mar-2006 13:54:51
```

In a Nutshell

Oracle was one of the first commercial databases to foresee the need for an efficient mechanism to deal with a large user population and workload distribution in a single instance database as well as RAC environments. Oracle started providing load balancing and simple failover with version 7.3 and enhanced them as it progressed to version 10g. With so many features and options in load balancing and connection management, the user has plenty of choices for managing the connections.

CHAPTER
14

RAC Troubleshooting

n this chapter we look into the details of debugging Oracle Real Application Clusters, from simple startup problems to complex system hang or crash problems. As a single piece of software, Oracle RDBMS is the one of the most complex commercial products in the world. But with the help of a solid and extensive diagnostics framework, you can usually diagnose even complex problems simply by viewing and interpreting Oracle's detailed trace files.

Each instance in a cluster has its own alert logs, which will be the first and foremost thing to examine whenever a problem is reported. Alert logs show detailed information about the basic settings of the database, including the non-default parameters used. Alert logs also contain information about startup and shutdown, and details of node(s) joining and leaving with timestamps. The alert log is specific to each instance and the location of the log is specified by the initialization parameter background_dump_dest, which also defines the location of the background process trace files. The trace files of the other background process such as LMON or LMD traces are also written in the location specified by this parameter. If the shared server is configured, trace files of the shared servers are also written in the directory.

Log Directory Structure in Cluster Ready Services

To diagnose any problem, the first thing examined by Oracle Support are the installation log files. Anyone who knows anything about database administration knows the importance of the dump directories (bdump, udump, and cdump). Similarly, each component in the CRS stack has its respective directories created under the CRS home:

- **$ORA_CRS_HOME/crs/log**   Contains trace files for the CRS resources.
- **$ORA_CRS_HOME/crs/init**   Contains trace files of the CRS daemon during startup. Good place to start with any CRS login problems.
- **$ORA_CRS_HOME/css/log**   The Cluster Synchronization (CSS) logs indicate all actions such as reconfigurations, missed check-ins, connects, and disconnects from the client CSS listener. In some cases, the logger logs messages with the category of auth.crit for the reboots done by Oracle. This could be used for checking the exact time when the reboot occurred.
- **$ORA_CRS_HOME/css/init**   Contains core dumps from the Oracle Cluster Synchronization Service daemon (OCSSd) and the process ID (PID) for the CSS daemon whose death is treated as fatal. If abnormal restarts for CSS exist, the core files will have the format of core.<pid>.
- **$ORA_CRS_HOME/evm/log**   Log files for the Event Volume Manager (EVM) and evmlogger daemons. Not used as often for debugging as the CRS and CSS directories.
- **$ORA_CRS_HOME/evm/init**   PID and lock files for EVM. Core files for EVM should also be written here.
- **$ORA_CRS_HOME/srvm/log**   Log files for Oracle Cluster Registry (OCR), which contains the details at the Oracle cluster level.
- **$ORA_CRS_HOME//log**   Log files for Oracle Clusterware (known as the cluster alert log), which contains diagnostic messages at the Oracle cluster level. This is available from Oracle database 10*g* R2.

Log Directory Structure in the Oracle RDBMS

In a 10g RAC installation, a node consists of a CRS home and an Oracle RDBMS home. The RDBMS home is where you install the Oracle software with the RAC option. You create databases from this home. The log files are related to each of the database instances running out of this Oracle home. The most important log file that every database generates is the alert.log file that is created in the directory specified by the init.ora parameter `background_dump_dest`. For most sites, this directory is kept under $ORACLE_BASE/admin.

Suppose, for example, that you have a database named *test*. All its background process trace files, along with the alert.log, would be available in the $ORACLE_BASE/admin/test/bdump directory; that's the norm. Its not a hard and fast rule that you use this directory structure, but it does help to follow conventions.

These directories are also important for the RDBMS home:

- **$ORACLE_BASE/admin/udump** Contains any trace file generated by a user process.

- **$ORACLE_BASE/admin/cdump** Contains core files that are generated due to a core dump in a user process.

Let's take a closer look at the startup of an instance in a two-node RAC cluster running version 10.1.0.4. We use SQL *Plus to issue startup on node1 and then on node2. The sequence of events follows with additional explanations added as and when required:

```
SQL> startup nomount;
Cluster communication is configured to use the following interface(s) for this instance
   192.168.0.1
Mon Aug 29 07:25:09 2005
cluster interconnect IPC version:Oracle UDP/IP
IPC Vendor 1 proto 2 Version 1.0
PMON started with pid=2, OS id=31242
```

The correct interconnect must be used for the Cache Fusion traffic. Some may choose the public network for the interconnect traffic, but doing so will bring the database to its knees. To identify the network used for Cache Fusion or private traffic, you can do any of the following:

```
$ oifcfg getif
```

```
SQL> select INST_ID,PUB_KSXPIA,PICKED_KSXPIA,NAME_KSXPIA,IP_KSXPIA
from x$ksxpia;

   INST_ID P PICK NAME_KSXPIA      IP_KSXPIA
---------- - ---- --------------- ----------------
         1   OCR  prod1           192.168.0.1
```

Depending on the source of the information, the `PICKED_KSXPIA` is populated with the values OSD, OCR, and CI. If the `cluster_interconnects` parameter is set in the SPFILE, the query will return the following output:

```
SQL> select INST_ID,PUB_KSXPIA,PICKED_KSXPIA,NAME_KSXPIA,IP_KSXPIA
from x$ksxpia;
   INST_ID P PICK NAME_KSXPIA      IP_KSXPIA
---------- - ---- --------------- ----------------
         1   CI   prod1           192.168.0.1
```

Another option is the conventional method of finding the interconnect information from an Interprocess Communications (IPC) dump. This was the only method available in Oracle versions prior to 10g, but this method is also possible in Oracle 10g. Starting from 10g R2, X$KSXPIA is exposed as GV$CONFIGURED_INTERCONNECTS.

Log in to the database as user *SYS*:

```
SQL> oradebug setmypid
SQL> oradebug ipc
```

This will dump a trace file to user_dump_dest. The output will look something like this:

```
SSKGXPT 0x1a2932c flags SSKGXPT_READPENDING info for network 0
socket no 10 IP 192.168.0.1 UDP 43749
sflags SSKGXPT_WRITESSKGXPT_UP info for network 1
socket no 0 IP 0.0.0.0 UDP 0...
```

You can see that we are using IP 192.168.0.1 with a User Datagram Protocol (UDP).

To change the network that RAC uses, you can change the order of the network(s) in the operating system–dependent network configurations, such as /etc/hosts or by using the cluster_interconnects parameter.

NOTE
A little caution is required while using the cluster_interconnects parameter. With Oracle 10g, interconnect information is stored in OCR, so you don't need to specify the interconnect using the cluster_interconnects parameter. Although this parameter supports load balancing among the specified interfaces, it does not provide failover capabilities, and in case one of several interfaces goes down, Oracle will treat it as a complete failure and start evicting instances. You can still use cluster_interconnects with one IP address—for example, to work around a bug in the network selection or to use a specific NIC for a particular instance for test purposes.

The moment the first instance is started, its alert log gets populated with important information. The first thing to notice in the preceding example after the list of non-default parameters is the IP address used for the interconnect. On the first instance, mentioning the cluster_interconnects parameter is necessary so that the correct interface is picked up—due to a bug that doesn't pick up the correct interface for the interconnect. Also shown is the protocol used—in our case, UDP. The value shown would depend on your platform-specific usage—RSM could be used on Sun, HyperFabric on HP, and so on. Ensure that you see the correct protocol that you have configured for the interconnect usage. The supported interconnect protocols with respect to various operating systems are listed in Chapter 3.

```
Mon Aug 29 07:25:11 2005
lmon registered with NM - instance id 1 (internal mem no 0)
Mon Aug 29 07:25:11 2005
Reconfiguration started (old inc 0, new inc 1)
```

```
List of nodes:
 0
 Global Resource Directory frozen
 Update rdomain variables
 Communication channels reestablished
 Master broadcasted resource hash value bitmaps
 Non-local Process blocks cleaned out
Mon Aug 29 07:25:11 2005
 LMS 1: 0 GCS shadows cancelled, 0 closed
Mon Aug 29 07:25:11 2005
 LMS 0: 0 GCS shadows cancelled, 0 closed
 Set master node info
 Submitted all remote-enqueue requests
 Dwn-cvts replayed, VALBLKs dubious
 All grantable enqueues granted
 Post SMON to start 1st pass IR
Mon Aug 29 07:25:11 2005
 LMS 0: 0 GCS shadows traversed, 0 replayed
Mon Aug 29 07:25:11 2005
 LMS 1: 0 GCS shadows traversed, 0 replayed
Mon Aug 29 07:25:11 2005
 Submitted all GCS remote-cache requests
 Post SMON to start 1st pass IR
 Fix write in gcs resources
Reconfiguration complete
LCK0 started with pid=17, OS id=31272
```

When an instance starts up, it's the Lock Monitor's (LMON) job to register with the Node Monitor (NM). That's what we see in the alert.log with the instance ID that is getting registered. When any node joins or leaves a cluster, the global resource directory undergoes a reconfiguration event. We see the start of the reconfiguration event along with the old and new incarnation. Next, we see the number of nodes that have joined the cluster. As this was the first node to be started up, in the list of nodes we see only one node listed, and the number starts with 0. A reconfiguration event is a seven-step procedure and upon completion the "reconfiguration complete" message is logged into the alert.log.

The messages logged in the alert.log are summaries of the reconfiguration event. The LMON trace file would have more information about the reconfiguration. Following are the contents of the LMON trace file:

```
*** 2005-08-29 07:25:11.235
kjxgmrcfg: Reconfiguration started, reason 1
kjxgmcs: Setting state to 0 0.
```

Here, you can see the reason for the reconfiguration event. The most common reasons would be 1, 2, or 3. Reason 1 means that the NM initiated the reconfiguration event, as typically seen when a node joins or leaves a cluster. A reconfiguration event is initiated with reason 2 when an instance death is detected. How is an instance death detected? Every instance updates the control file with a heartbeat through its Checkpoint (CKPT) process. If heartbeat information is not present for *x* amount of time, the instance is considered to be dead and the Instance Membership Recovery (IMR) process initiates reconfiguration. This type of reconfiguration is commonly seen when significant time changes occur across nodes, the node is starved for CPU or I/O times, or some problems occur with the shared storage.

A reason 3 reconfiguration event is due to a communication failure. Communication channels are established between the Oracle processes across the nodes. This communication occurs over the interconnect. Every message sender expects an acknowledgment message from the receiver. If a message is not received for a timeout period, then a "communication failure" is assumed. This is more relevant for UDP, as Reliable Shared Memory (RSM), Reliable DataGram protocol (RDG), and Hyper Messaging Protocol (HMP) do not need it, since the acknowledgment mechanisms are built into the cluster communication and protocol itself.

When the block is sent from one instance to another using wire, especially when unreliable protocols such as UDP are used, it is best to get an acknowledgment message from the receiver. The acknowledgment is a simple side channel message that is normally required for most of the UNIX systems where UDP is used as the default IPC protocol. When user-mode IPC protocols such as RDG (on HP Tru64 UNIX TruCluster) or HP HMP are used, the additional messaging can be disabled by setting _reliable_block_sends=TRUE. For Windows-based systems, it is always recommended to leave the default value as is.

```
Database mounted in Shared Mode (CLUSTER_DATABASE=TRUE).
Completed: alter database mount
```

Since this is an RAC database, every instance mounts the database in shared mode. Sometimes you want to mount the database in exclusive mode, as in completing the actions of a patch set application. Checking the alert log is one way to confirm that:

```
Mon Aug 29 15:36:53 2005
alter database open
This instance was first to open
Picked Lamport scheme to generate SCNs
```

You may see the message depending on the version of the RAC and setting of the parameter max_commit_propagation_delay. In version 9i, every commit System Commit Numbers (SCN) is broadcasted to all the nodes, and the log writer is held up until all the interested redos are written to the disk. Starting with 10g, the wait is greatly reduced as the broadcast and commit are asynchronous. This means the system waits until it is sure that all nodes have seen the commit SCN. Any message with an SCN greater than commit SCN is deemed sufficient.

Before doing a broadcast, the process checks whether it has already received a higher SCN from that instance. It used the same SCN to determine whether a foreground or an LMS has to be posted. With 10g, this is decoupled: an SCN to release foregrounds and an SCN needed for shipping buffers. The init.ora parameter _lgwr_async_broadcasts = true can be used to change the broadcast method.

The Lamport Algorithm

The Lamport algorithm is fast and scalable in RAC as it generates the SCNs in parallel and the SCNs are assigned to the transactions on a first come, first serve basis. The Distributed Lock Manager (DLM) controls and monitors the lock management and conflict resolution.

Another algorithm that is simpler than Dr. Lamport's bakery algorithm is based on the broadcasting operation after a commit operation, and this is the default SCN generation algorithm in single instance Oracle implementations. In this method, the SCN is broadcasted to the participating nodes immediately after a commit operation. This ensures that read consistency is at the highest level so that the participating nodes know the current state of the transaction irrespective of the workload. This method puts additional load on the systems, as it has to broadcast the SCN for every commit; however, the other nodes can see the committed SCN immediately.

The initialization parameter `max_commit_propagation_delay` limits the maximum delay allowed for SCN propagation to the participating nodes and controls the SCN scheme used in the OPS/RAC environment. This parameter defaults to 7 seconds (700 centiseconds) in most of the platforms except for the Compaq Tru64 UNIX. When we set the `max_commit_propagation_delay` initialization parameter to any value less than 100, the broadcast on commit algorithm is used. The alert log is updated immediately after startup with the method used for SCN generation.

Let's start the second instance and check the reconfiguration event entries in the alert.log:

```
SQL> startup nomount;
```

In the alert log of the second instance we see this:

```
Mon Aug 29 17:40:35 2005
lmon registered with NM - instance id 2 (internal mem no 1)
Mon Aug 29 17:40:37 2005
Reconfiguration started (old inc 0, new inc 2)
List of nodes:
 0 1
 Global Resource Directory frozen
 Update rdomain variables
```

Now two nodes in the clusters have internal IDs of 0 and 1. The rest of the messages are pretty much the same as in the first instance's alert log file.

RAC ON and OFF

In some cases, you may want to disable the RAC options for testing purposes—perhaps to run a benchmark or convert the RAC binaries to single instance binaries. In such a case, you can use the following procedure to convert the RAC installation to non-RAC. Disabling and enabling RAC options are available only for UNIX platforms. Windows installations do not support relinking binaries with RAC ON and OFF.

Use the following steps to disable RAC (known as RAC OFF):

1. Log in as the Oracle software owner (which is typically the UNIX account *oracle*) in all nodes.

2. Shut down all the instances from all the nodes using a NORMAL or IMMEDIATE option.

3. Change the working directory to $ORACLE_HOME/lib:

   ```
   cd $ORACLE_HOME/lib
   ```

4. Run the following `make` command to relink the Oracle binaries without the RAC option:

   ```
   make -f ins_rdbms.mk rac_off
   ```

   This normally runs for few minutes and should not pose any errors.

5. Now relink the Oracle binaries:

   ```
   make -f ins_rdbms.mk ioracle
   ```

Now the Oracle binaries are relinked with the RAC OFF option. You may have to edit the init.ora or SPFILE parameters accordingly. If errors occur in step 4, you may need to contact Oracle Support and log a service request with the trace and log files.

Use the following steps to enable RAC (known as RAC ON):

1. Log in as the Oracle software owner (typically the UNIX account *oracle*) in all nodes.

2. Shut down all the instances from all the nodes using a NORMAL or IMMEDIATE option.

3. Change the working directory to $ORACLE_HOME/lib:

   ```
   cd $ORACLE_HOME/lib
   ```

4. Run the following make command to relink the Oracle binaries without the RAC option:

   ```
   make -f ins_rdbms.mk rac_on
   ```

   This normally runs for a few minutes and should not pose any errors.

5. Now relink the Oracle binaries:

   ```
   make -f ins_rdbms.mk ioracle
   ```

Now the Oracle binaries are relinked with the RAC ON option. You may need to edit the init.ora or SPFILE parameters accordingly. If any errors occur in step 4, you may need to contact Oracle Support and log a service request with the trace and log files.

Database Performance Issues

RAC databases have more than one instance using the same set of resources, and a resource may be requested by more than one instance. Resource sharing is well managed by Global Cache Services (GCS) and Global Enqueue Services (GES). However, in some cases, the resource management operations could run into a deadlock situation and the entire database may hang because of serialization issues. Sometimes, software bugs also cause database-hang issues, and these situations almost always require the intervention of Oracle Support in the form of a service request.

Database hang issues can be placed in the following categories:

- Hung database
- Hung session(s)
- Overall instance/database performance
- Query performance

We will examine only the hung database, as that is more critical and complex than the others and also related to our point of interest. Detailed texts are available for analyzing the database and query performance.

Hung Database

Oracle Support defines a "true" database hang as "an internal deadlock or a cyclical dependency between two or more processes." When dealing with DML locks (that is, enqueue type TM), Oracle is able to detect this dependency and roll back one of the processes to break the cyclical condition. On the other hand, when this situation occurs with internal kernel-level resources (such as latches or pins), Oracle is usually unable to automatically detect and resolve the deadlock.

If you encounter a database hang situation, you need to take system state dumps so that Oracle Support can begin to diagnose the root cause of the problem. Whenever you take such dumps for a hang, it is important to take at least three of them a few minutes apart, on all instances of your database. That way, evidence shows whether a resource is still being held from one time to the next.

The maxdump file size should be set to unlimited, as this will generate bigger and larger trace files, depending on the size of the System Global Area (SGA), the number of sessions logged in, and the workload on the system. The SYSTEMSTATE dump contains a separate section with information for each process. Normally, you need to take two or three dumps in regular intervals. Whenever you make SYSTEMSTATE dumps repetitively, make sure you reconnect every time so that you get a new process ID and also the new trace files. Expect HUGE trace files!

Starting with Oracle Database 10g, a SYSTEMSTATE dump includes session wait history information. If you are using Oracle 10g or later, you don't need to take multiple system state dumps. The SYSTEMSTATE dump can be taken by any of the following methods.

From SQL *Plus:

```
alter session set max_dump_file_size = unlimited;
alter session set events 'immediate trace name systemstate level 10';
```

Using oradebug:

```
REM The select below is to avoid problems on pre 8.0.6 databases
select * from dual;
oradebug setmypid
oradebug unlimit
oradebug dump systemstate 10
```

When the entire database is hung and you cannot connect to SQL *Plus, you can try invoking SQL *Plus with the `prelim` option if you're using Oracle 10g or later. This attaches the process to the Oracle instance and no SQL commands are run. No login triggers or no pre-processing is done, and no SQL queries are allowed to run. See the change in banner from normal sqlplus and prelim sqlplus.

```
$sqlplus -prelim
SQL*Plus: Release 10.2.0.1.0 - Production on Wed Nov 9 11:42:23 2005
Copyright (c) 1982, 2005, Oracle.  All rights reserved.
Enter user-name: / as sysdba
SQL>
```

Alternatively, oradebug allows you to dump the global system state by connecting to one node. The following shows the global SYSTEMSTATE dump from oradebug:

```
oradebug -g all dump systemstate 10
```

The –g option is used for RAC databases only. This will dump system states for all the instances. The SYSTEMSTATE dump/trace file can be found in the user_dump_dest directory on the instance where the dump was generated.

Hanganalyze Utility

A severe performance problem cam be mistaken for a hang. This usually happens when contention is so bad that it *seems like* the database is completely hung. Usually, a SYSTEMSTATE dump is used to analyze these situations. However, if the instance is large with more than a few gigabytes of SGA and with a heavy workload, a SYSTEMSTATE dump may take an hour or more and often fails to dump the entire SGA and lock structures. Moreover, a SYSTEMSTATE dump has the following limitations when dealing with hang issues:

- Reads the SGA in a "dirty" manner, so it may be inconsistent when the time to dump all the process is long.

- Usually dumps a lot of information (most of which is not needed to determine the source of the hang), which makes it difficult to determine quickly the dependencies between processes.

- Does not identify "interesting" processes on which to perform additional dumps (ERRORSTACK or PROCESS STATE).

- Often very expensive operation in for databases that have large SGAs. A SYSTEMSTATE dump can take hours, and taking few continuous dumps within a few minutes interval is nearly impossible.

To overcome the limitations of the SYSTEMSTATE dump, a new utility called hanganalyze was introduced in Oracle 8i. In Oracle 9i, the `hanganalyze` command was enhanced to provide clusterwide information in RAC environments on a single shot. This uses the DIAG daemon process in the RAC process to communicate between the instances. Clusterwide, hanganalyze will generate information for all the sessions in the cluster regardless of the instance that issued the command.

Hanganalyze can be invoked from SQL *Plus or through oradebug (which is available when you connect as *SYS* in the SQL *Plus utility). The following syntax can be used to get a hanganalyze trace when connected to SQL *Plus:

```
alter session set events 'immediate trace name hanganalyze level <level>';
```

Or when logged in as *SYS*:

```
oradebug hanganalyze <level>
```

Clusterwide, hanganalyze can be obtained like so:

```
oradebug setmypid
oradebug setinst all
oradebug -g def hanganalyze <level>
```

The `<level>` sets the amount of additional information that will be extracted from the processes found by hanganalyze (ERROSTACK dump) based on the STATE of the node. The following table describes the various levels and the trace information emitted when they are set:

Level	Trace Information
1-2	Only hanganalyze output, no process dump at all
3	Level 2 + Dump only processes thought to be in a hang (IN_HANG state)
4	Level 3 + Dump leaf nodes (blockers) in wait chains (LEAF, LEAF_NW, IGN_DMP state)
5	Level 4 + Dump all processes involved in wait chains (NLEAF state)
10	Dump all processes (IGN state)

Hanganalyze uses internal kernel calls to determine whether a session is waiting for a resource and reports the relationships between blockers and waiters. In addition, it determines which processes are "interesting" to be dumped, and it may perform automatic PROCESS STATE dumps and ERRORSTACKs on those processes, based on the level used while executing hanganalyze.

NOTE
Hanganalyze is not intended to replace a SYSTEMSTATE dump, but it may serve as a road map to interpret a system state while diagnosing complex issues. Performance issues related to row cache objects, enqueues, and latches can be analyzed only with hanganalyze and/ or a SYSTEMSTATE dump. The process state information in these dumps provides an accurate snapshot of the locks/latches held by each process or session. It also tells us which event the process was waiting for and if any TM locks were held for a transaction. Problems associated with DDL statement locks and row cache lock issues can be debugged using only these dumps.

Debugging Node Eviction Issues

One of the most common and complex issues in RAC is performing the root cause analysis (RCA) of the node eviction issues. A node is evicted from the cluster after it kills itself because it is not able to service the applications. This generally happens during the communication failure between the instances, when the instance is not able to send heartbeat information to the control file and various other reasons.

During failures, to avoid data corruption, the failing instance evicts itself from the cluster group. The node eviction process is reported as Oracle error ORA-29740 in the alert log and LMON trace files. To determine the root cause, the alert logs and trace files should be carefully analyzed; this process may require assistance from Oracle Support. To get into deeper levels of the node eviction process, you need to understand the basics of node membership and Instance Membership Recovery (IMR), also referred to as Instance Membership Reconfiguration.

Instance Membership Recovery

When a communication failure occurs between the instances, or when an instance is not able to issue the heartbeat information to the control file, the cluster group may be in danger of possible data corruption. In addition, when no mechanism is present to detect the failures, the entire cluster will hang. To address the issue, IMR was introduced in Oracle 9i and improved in Oracle 10g. IMR removes the failed instance from the cluster group. When a subset of a cluster group survives during failures, IMR ensures that the larger partition group survives and kills all other smaller groups.

IMR is a part of the service offered by Cluster Group Services (CGS). LMON is the key process that handles many of the CGS functionalities. As you know, cluster software (known as Cluster Manager, or CM) can be a vendor-provided or Oracle-provided infrastructure tool. CM facilitates communication between all nodes of the cluster and provides information on the health of each node—the node state. It detects failures and manages the basic membership of nodes in the cluster. CM works at the cluster level and not at the database or instance level.

Inside RAC, the Node Monitor (NM) provides information about nodes and their health by registering and communicating with the CM. NM services are provided by LMON. Node membership is represented as a bitmap in the GRD. A value of 0 denotes that a node is down and a value of 1 denotes that the node is up. There is no value to indicate a "transition" period such as during bootup or shutdown. LMON uses the global notification mechanism to let others know of a change in the node membership. Every time a node joins or leaves a cluster, this bitmap in the GRD has to be rebuilt and communicated to all registered members in the cluster.

Node membership registration and deregistration is done in a series of synchronized steps—a topic beyond the scope of this chapter. Basically, cluster members register and deregister from a group. The important thing to remember is that NM always communicates with the other instances in the cluster about their health and status using the CM. In contrast, if LMON needs to send a message to LMON on another instance, it can do so directly without the help or involvement of CM. It is important to differentiate between cluster communication and RAC communication.

A simple extract from the alert log file about member registration is provided here:

```
Thu Jan 1 00:02:17 1970
alter database mount
Thu Jan 1 00:02:17 1970
lmon registered with NM - instance id 1 (internal mem no 0)
Thu Jan 1 00:02:17 1970
Reconfiguration started
List of nodes: 0,
 Global Resource Directory frozen
```

Here you can see that this instance was the first to start up and that LMON registered itself with the NM interface, which is a part of the Oracle kernel.

When an instance joins or leaves the cluster, the LMON trace of another instance shows the reconfiguration of the GRD:

```
kjxgmpoll reconfig bitmap: 0 1 3
*** 1970-01-01 01:20:51.423
kjxgmrcfg: Reconfiguration started, reason 1
```

You may find these lines together with other lines asking SMON to perform instance recovery. This happens when any instance crash occurs or when an instance departs the cluster without deregistering in a normal fashion:

```
Post SMON to start 1st pass IR
*** 1970-01-01 01:20:51.423
kjxgmpoll reconfig bitmap: 0 1 3
*** 1970-01-01 01:20:51.423
kjxgmrcfg: Reconfiguration started, reason 1
kjxgmcs: Setting state to 2 0.
*** 1970-01-01 01:20:51.423
    Name Service frozen
```

The CGS is present primarily to provide a coherent and consistent view of the cluster from an OS perspective. It tells Oracle that *n* number of nodes are in the cluster. It is designed to provide a synchronized view of the cluster instance membership. Its main responsibility involves regular status checks of the members and measures whether they are valid in the group, and very importantly, it detects split-brain scenarios in case of communication failures.

Specific rules bind together members within the cluster group, which keeps the cluster in a consistent state:

- Each member should be able to communicate without any problems with any other registered and valid member in the group.

- Members should see all other registered members in the cluster as valid and have a consistent view.

- All members must be able to read from and write to the control file.

So, when a communication failure occurs between the instances, or when an instance is not able to issue the heartbeat information to the voting disk, IMR is triggered. Without IMR (there is no mechanism to detect the failures), the entire cluster could hang.

Member Voting

The CGS is responsible for checking whether members are valid. To determine periodically whether all members are alive, a voting mechanism is used to check the validity of each member. All members in the database group vote by providing details of what they presume the instance membership bitmap looks like. As mentioned, the bitmap is stored in the GRD. A predetermined master member tallies the vote flags of the status flag and communicates to the respective processes that the voting is done; then it waits for registration by all the members who have received the reconfigured bitmap.

How Voting Happens   The CKPT process updates the control file every 3 seconds in an operation known as the *heartbeat.* CKPT writes into a single block that is unique for each instance, thus intra-instance coordination is not required. This block is called the *checkpoint progress record.*

All members attempt to obtain a lock on a control file record (the *result record*) for updating. The instance that obtains the lock tallies the votes from all members. The group membership must conform to the *decided (voted)* membership before allowing the GCS/GES reconfiguration to proceed. The *control file vote result record* is stored in the same block as the heartbeat in the control file checkpoint progress record.

In this scenario of dead instances and member evictions, a potentially disastrous situation could arise if pending I/O from a dead instance is to be flushed to the I/O subsystem. This could lead to potential data corruption. I/O from an abnormally departing instance cannot be flushed to disk if database integrity is to be maintained. To "shield" the database from data corruption in this situation, a technique called *I/O fencing* is used. I/O fencing implementation is a function of CM and depends on the clusterware vendor.

I/O fencing is designed to guarantee data integrity in the case of faulty cluster communications causing a split-brain condition. A split-brain occurs when cluster nodes hang or node interconnects fail, and as a result, the nodes lose the communication link between them and the cluster. Split-brain is a problem in any clustered environment and is a symptom of clustering solutions and not RAC. Split-brain conditions can cause database corruption when nodes become uncoordinated in their access to the shared data files.

For a two-node cluster, split-brain occurs when nodes in a cluster cannot talk to each other (the internode links fail) and each node assumes it is the only surviving member of the cluster. If the nodes in the cluster have uncoordinated access to the shared storage area, they would end up overwriting each other's data, causing data corruption because each node assumes ownership of shared data. To prevent data corruption, one node must be asked to leave the cluster or should be forced out immediately. This is where IMR comes in, as explained earlier in the chapter.

Many internal (hidden) parameters control IMR and determine when it should start. If a vendor clusterware is used, split-brain resolution is left to it and Oracle would have to wait for the clusterware to provide a consistent view of the cluster and resolve the split-brain issue. This can potentially cause a delay (and a hang in the whole cluster) because each node can potentially think it is the master and try to own all the shared resources. Still, Oracle relies on the clusterware for resolving these challenging issues.

Note that Oracle does not wait indefinitely for the clusterware to resolve a split-brain issue, but a timer is used to trigger an IMR-based node eviction. These internal timers are also controlled using hidden parameters. The default values of these hidden parameters are not to be touched as that can cause severe performance or operational issues with the cluster.

An obvious question that pops up in your mind might be, Why does a split-brain condition take place? Why does Oracle say a link is down, when my communication engineer says its fine? This is easier asked than answered, as the underlying hardware and software layers that support RAC are too complex, and it can be a nightmare trying to figure out why a cluster broke in two when things seem to be normal. Usually, configuration of communication links and bugs in the clusterware can cause these issues.

As mentioned time and again, Oracle completely relies on the cluster software to provide cluster services, and if something is awry, Oracle, in its overzealous quest to protect data integrity, evicts nodes or aborts an instance and assumes that something is wrong with the cluster.

Cluster reconfiguration is initiated when NM indicates a change in the database group, or IMR detects a problem. Reconfiguration is initially managed by the CGS and after this is completed, IDLM (GES/GCS) reconfiguration starts.

Cluster Reconfiguration Steps

The cluster reconfiguration process triggers IMR, and a seven-step process ensures complete reconfiguration.

1. Name service is frozen. The CGS contains an internal database of all the members/ instances in the cluster with all their configuration and servicing details. The name service provides a mechanism to address this configuration data in a structured and synchronized manner.

2. Lock database (IDLM) is frozen. The lock database is frozen to prevent processes from obtaining locks on resources that were mastered by the departing/dead instance.

3. Determination of membership and validation and IMR.

4. Bitmap rebuild takes place, instance name and uniqueness verification. CGS must synchronize the cluster to be sure that all members get the reconfiguration event and that they all see the same bitmap.

5. Delete all dead instance entries and republish all names newly configured.

6. Unfreeze and release name service for use.

7. Hand over reconfiguration to GES/GCS.

Now that you know when IMR starts and node evictions take place, let's look at the corresponding messages in the alert log and LMON trace files to get a better picture. (The logs have been edited for brevity. Note all the lines in boldface define the most important steps in IMR and the handoff to other recovery steps in CGS.)

Problem with a Node   Assume a four-node cluster (instances A, B, C, and D), in which instance C has a problem communicating with other nodes because its private link is down. All other services on this node are assumed to be working normally.

Alter log on instance C:

```
ORA-29740: evicted by member 2, group incarnation 6
Thu Jun 30 09:15:59 2005
LMON: terminating instance due to error 29740
Instance terminated by LMON, pid = 692304
...
...
...
```

Alter log on instance A:

```
Thu Jun 30 09:15:59 2005
Communications reconfiguration: instance 2
Evicting instance 3 from cluster
Thu Jun 30 09:16:29 2005
Trace dumping is performing id=[50630091559]
Thu Jun 30 09:16:31 2005
Waiting for instances to leave:
3
Thu Jun 30 09:16:51 2005
Waiting for instances to leave:
3
Thu Jun 30 09:17:04 2005
Reconfiguration started
List of nodes: 0,1,3,
 Global Resource Directory frozen
 Communication channels reestablished
 Master broadcasted resource hash value bitmaps
Thu Jun 30 09:17:04 2005
Reconfiguration started
```

LMON trace file on instance A:

```
*** 2005-06-30 09:15:58.262
kjxgrgetresults: Detect reconfig from 1, seq 12, reason 3
kjxgfipccb: msg 0x1113dcfa8, mbo 0x1113dcfa0, type 22, ack 0, ref 0,
stat 3
kjxgfipccb: Send timed out, stat 3 inst 2, type 22, tkt (10496,1496)
*** 2005-06-30 09:15:59.070
kjxgrcomerr: Communications reconfig: instance 2 (12,4)
Submitting asynchronized dump request [2]
kjxgfipccb: msg 0x1113d9498, mbo 0x1113d9490, type 22, ack 0, ref 0,
stat 6
kjxgfipccb: Send cancelled, stat 6 inst 2, type 22, tkt (10168,1496)
kjxgfipccb: msg 0x1113e54a8, mbo 0x1113e54a0, type 22, ack 0, ref 0,
stat 6
kjxgfipccb: Send cancelled, stat 6 inst 2, type 22, tkt (9840,1496)
```

Note that Send timed out, stat 3 inst 2 is LMON trying send message(s) to the broken instance.

```
kjxgrrcfgchk: Initiating reconfig, reason 3 /* IMR Initiated */
*** 2005-06-30 09:16:03.305
kjxgmrcfg: Reconfiguration started, reason 3
kjxgmcs: Setting state to 12 0.
*** 2005-06-30 09:16:03.449
    Name Service frozen
kjxgmcs: Setting state to 12 1.
*** 2005-06-30 09:16:11.570
Voting results, upd 1, seq 13, bitmap: 0 1 3
```

Note that instance A has not tallied the vote; hence it has received only the voting results. Here is an extract from the LMON trace file on instance B, which managed to tally the vote:

```
Obtained RR update lock for sequence 13, RR seq 13
*** 2005-06-30 09:16:11.570
Voting results, upd 0, seq 13, bitmap: 0 1 3

...
...
```

Here's the LMON trace file on instance A:

```
Evicting mem 2, stat 0x0007 err 0x0002
kjxgmps: proposing substate 2
kjxgmcs: Setting state to 13 2.
    Performed the unique instance identification check
kjxgmps: proposing substate 3
kjxgmcs: Setting state to 13 3.
    Name Service recovery started
    Deleted all dead-instance name entries
kjxgmps: proposing substate 4
kjxgmcs: Setting state to 13 4.
    Multicasted all local name entries for publish
    Replayed all pending requests
kjxgmps: proposing substate 5
kjxgmcs: Setting state to 13 5.
    Name Service normal
    Name Service recovery done
*** 2005-06-30 09:17:04.369
kjxgmrcfg: Reconfiguration started, reason 1
kjxgmcs: Setting state to 13 0.
*** 2005-06-30 09:17:04.371
    Name Service frozen
kjxgmcs: Setting state to 13 1.
```

GES/GCS recovery starts here:

```
Global Resource Directory frozen
node 0
node 1
```

```
node 3
res_master_weight for node 0 is 632960
res_master_weight for node 1 is 632960
res_master_weight for node 3 is 632960
...
...
...
```

Death of a Member   For the same four-node cluster (A, B, C, and D), instance C has died unexpectedly:

```
kjxgrnbrisalive: (3, 4) not beating, HB: 561027672, 561027672
*** 2005-06-19 00:30:52.018
kjxgrnbrdead: Detected death of 3, initiating reconfig
kjxgrrcfgchk: Initiating reconfig, reason 2
*** 2005-06-19 00:30:57.035
kjxgmrcfg: Reconfiguration started, reason 2
kjxgmcs: Setting state to 6 0.
*** 2005-06-19 00:30:57.037
     Name Service frozen
kjxgmcs: Setting state to 6 1.
*** 2005-06-19 00:30:57.239
Obtained RR update lock for sequence 6, RR seq 6
*** 2005-06-19 00:33:27.261
Voting results, upd 0, seq 7, bitmap: 0 2
Evicting mem 3, stat 0x0007 err 0x0001
kjxgmps: proposing substate 2
kjxgmcs: Setting state to 7 2.
     Performed the unique instance identification check
kjxgmps: proposing substate 3
kjxgmcs: Setting state to 7 3.
     Name Service recovery started
     Deleted all dead-instance name entries
kjxgmps: proposing substate 4
kjxgmps: proposing substate 4
kjxgmcs: Setting state to 7 4.
     Multicasted all local name entries for publish
     Replayed all pending requests
kjxgmps: proposing substate 5
kjxgmcs: Setting state to 7 5.
     Name Service normal
     Name Service recovery done
*** 2005-06-19 00:33:27.266
kjxgmps: proposing substate 6
...
...
...
kjxgmps: proposing substate 2
```

GES/GCS recovery starts here:

```
Global Resource Directory frozen
node 0
node 2
res_master_weight for node 0 is 632960
res_master_weight for node 2 is 632960
 Total master weight = 1265920
 Dead  inst 3
Join  inst
 Exist inst 0 2
...
...
```

Debugging CRS and GSD Using DTRACING

Oracle Server management configuration tools include a diagnostic and trace facility. For verbose output for SRVCTL, GSD, GSDCTL, or SRVCONFIG, tracing can be enabled to provide additional screen output. The following steps explain the process of setting and tracing the other programs:

1. vi the gsd.sh/srvctl/srvconfig file in the $ORACLE_HOME/bin directory. In Windows, right-click the OraHome\bin\gsd.bat file and choose Edit.

2. At the end of the file, look for the following line:

   ```
   exec $JRE -classpath $CLASSPATH oracle.ops.mgmt.daemon.OPSMDaemon $MY_OHOME
   ```

3. Add the following just before the -classpath in the exec $JRE line:

   ```
   -DTRACING.ENABLED=true -DTRACING.LEVEL=2
   ```

4. At the end of the gsd.sh file, the string should now look like this:

   ```
   exec $JRE -DTRACING.ENABLED=true -DTRACING.LEVEL=2 -classpath.....
   ```

NOTE
Beginning with Oracle Database 10gd, setting the environment variable SRVM_TRACE to true traces all the SRVM files such as GSD, SRVCTL, and OCRCONFIG.

In a Nutshell

In this chapter, you have seen the basic to advanced methods of collecting diagnostic information when a hang situation occurs. You also studied the steps in node reconfiguration and IMR internals. Most of the complex problems may require assistance from Oracle Support, and this chapter will help you when dealing with Oracle Support personnel.

PART
V

Deploying RAC

CHAPTER
15

RAC Extensions

s Real Application Clusters is an increasingly common solution for scalability across enterprises, it is time to think beyond the obvious usage of the technology. RAC is designed primarily as a scalability and availability solution that resides in a single data center. However, it is possible, under certain circumstances, to build and deploy an RAC system in which the nodes in the cluster are separated by great distances.

The choice of extending RAC depends on the failure it is designed to address. To protect against multiple points of failure, a cluster must be geographically dispersed: nodes can be put in different rooms, on different floors of a building, or even in separate buildings or separate cities. Your decision as to the distance between the nodes rests on the types of disaster from which you need protection and the technology used to replicate data between the storage systems.

Modern data center clusters are built around high-performance storage area networks (SANs) that provide secure, reliable, and scalable data storage facilities. An effective business continuance and disaster recovery plan mandates the deployment of multiple data centers located at optimal distances to protect against regional power failures or disasters, yet close enough for synchronous data replication without affecting the application performance. Achieving this balance for successful business continuance poses a significant challenge.

The time in which a business needs to recover during a disaster determines the type of data replication that is required. Synchronous data replication provides the least amount of downtime but requires the data centers to be close enough so that the application performance is not affected by the latencies introduced for every I/O operation. Asynchronous or semi-synchronous replication allows for greater distance, but the data centers are in lock step with each other, with the secondary data center lagging behind the primary by a fixed amount of time. This in turn implies that a loss of data occurs for that period of time. An optimal solution is to increase the distance between the data centers without introducing additional latency for I/O operations.

For example, if a business has a corporate campus, the individual RAC nodes could be placed in separate buildings. This configuration provides a degree of disaster tolerance in addition to the normal RAC high availability, since a fire in one building would not bring the database down. Extended RAC, if properly set up, provides continuous data availability even during regional disasters. Figure 15-1 shows the basic architecture of an extended RAC configuration.

Implementing RAC on an extended cluster provides double advantages. Being able to distribute any and all work across all nodes, including running as a single workload across the whole cluster, allows for the greatest flexibility in usage of resources. Should one site fail, for example because of a fire at a site, all work can be routed to the remaining site that can rapidly (in less than a minute) take over the processing.

Design Considerations

Before going to the design and implementation of extended clusters, let's take a look at the key points to consider when designing a solution that involves "geo-clusters." Network infrastructure plays a major role in extending RAC, as performance is greatly impacted by round-trip latency. An optimal solution is to increase the distance between the data centers without introducing additional latency for I/O operations.

Speed of Light

In a vacuum, light travels at 186,282 miles per second. To make the math simpler, we can round that off to 200,000 miles per second, or 200 miles per millisecond. We require confirmation

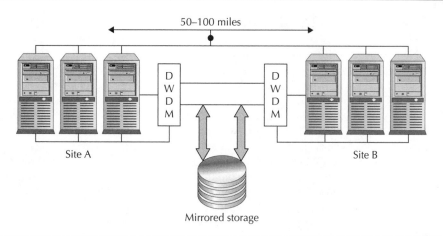

FIGURE 15-1. *Extended RAC architecture*

of any message, so we must use round-trip distances. Light can travel up to 100 miles away and back in 1 millisecond, but the actual transit time is longer, in part because the speed of light is slowed by about 30 percent through an optical fiber and straight lines rarely occur in global communications situations, but also because delays are created when the signal passes through an electronic switch or signal regenerator.

While considering all the factors like the inevitable switch delays, the conservative rule of thumb is that it takes 1 millisecond for every 50 miles of distance round trip. Therefore, 500 miles adds 10 milliseconds to the latency of a disk access. Given the normal disk access latency of 10 to 15 milliseconds, this distance merely doubles the total latency; however, the shadowing software layer can cope with that. But if the latency is more than double, the software might think the disk at the other end has gone offline and will incorrectly break the shadow set. So the speed of light becomes the limiting factor due to the latency caused by distance between the data centers, even with the use of dark fiber.

Network Connectivity

Network interconnect has a great impact on performance in a normal RAC environment. It has even greater impact in an extended RAC environment. Planned redundancy should be introduced at every component level to avoid failures and interconnect. In addition, SAN and IP networking need to be kept on separate dedicated channels.

A scalable and reliable lightweight and protocol-independent network is required for extended RAC. Traditional networks are limited to about 6 miles before repeaters are needed. Repeaters or any other intermediate switches introduce inevitable delays, introducing latency between the switches. Dark fiber networks allow the communication to occur without these repeaters across at much greater distance. Dark fiber networks with dense wavelength-division multiplexing (an optical technology used to increase bandwidth over existing fiber-optic backbones) provide low latency/high bandwidth communication over longer distances.

Dense Wavelength Division Multiplexing

In optical communications, wavelength-division multiplexing (WDM) technology multiplexes multiple optical carrier signals on a single optical fiber by using different wavelengths of laser light to carry different signals. This allows for a multiplication in capacity and makes it possible to perform bidirectional communications over one strand of fiber.

WDM technology is further divided into two market segments—dense and coarse WDM. Systems with more than eight active wavelengths per fiber are generally considered dense WDM (DWDM) systems, while those with fewer than eight active wavelengths are classed as coarse WDM (CWDM).

CWDM and DWDM technologies are based on the same concept of using multiple wavelengths of light on a single fiber, but the two technologies differ in the spacing of the wavelengths, number of channels, and the ability to amplify signals in the optical space.

CWDM is also used in cable television networks, where different wavelengths are used for the downstream and upstream signals. DWDM works by combining and transmitting multiple signals simultaneously at different wavelengths on the same fiber. In effect, one fiber is transformed into multiple virtual fibers that provide the extended bandwidth. With this over-bandwidth extension, single fibers have been able to transmit data at speeds up to 400 gigabits per second (Gbps).

A key advantage to DWDM is that it is protocol and bit-rate independent. DWDM-based networks can transmit data in IP, ATM, SONET/SDH, and Ethernet and can handle bitrates between 100 megabits per second (Mbps) and 2.5 Gbps. Therefore, DWDM-based networks can carry different types of traffic at different speeds over an optical channel.

Data Storage

The next important factor in designing an extended RAC solution is the storage for the data files across the clusters. The storage should be concurrently available with both the instances, yet at the same time should be continuously synchronized in real time. *Synchronous replication* means that an I/O is not complete until both sides acknowledge its completion.

While it is possible to implement RAC on extended distance clusters with storage at only one site, should the site with the storage fail, the storage is no longer available to any surviving nodes and the whole cluster becomes unavailable. This defeats the purpose of having had RAC nodes at different locations. Hence we mirror the storage in both the sites, and nodes use the storage at their respective sites transparently. In addition, to maintain consistency of data, every write to the primary storage is written over to the secondary storage in the same sequence before the application write is considered successful. This method helps ensure that data stored at both sites is always consistent, with the only data that could be lost in the event of a failure is the data that was not committed or was being transmitted at the time of the failure.

Figure 15-2 shows the components involved in the physical implementation of the extended RAC cluster.

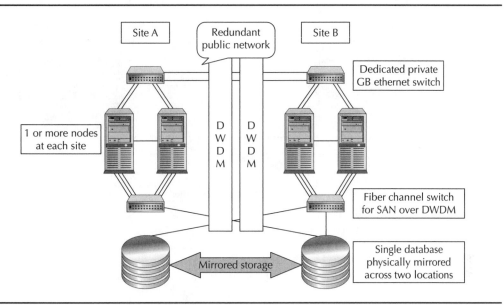

FIGURE 15-2.   *Extended RAC component architecture*

Common Techniques for Data Mirroring

A couple of mirroring techniques are commonly used in the industry. But the choice of storage is totally dependent on the hardware, as some hardware configuration support the array mirroring and few support host-based mirroring. The most common techniques available for clusters are *array-based mirroring* and *host-based mirroring*.

Array-Based Mirroring

In array-based mirroring, all the writes are forwarded to one site and then mirrored to the other node using the disk technologies. Array mirroring means having a primary/secondary site setup. Only one set of disks is always used and all the reads and writes are serviced by that storage. If the node or site fails, all the instances will crash and need to be restarted after bringing the secondary site to life.

Array-based mirroring is quite simple to implement, as the mirroring is done by the storage system and is transparent to the database applications. It is the only option available if you use only Oracle Clusterware and it comes with an obvious limitation. If the primary site fails, all access to the primary disks is lost. An outage may be incurred before the system can switch to the secondary site. Figure 15-3 explains the architecture of array-based mirroring.

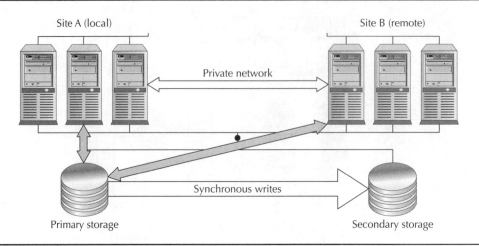

FIGURE 15-3. *Array-based mirroring*

Host-Based Mirroring

Host-based mirroring, as the name suggests, mirrors at the host level. It requires closely integrated clusterware and Logical Volume Manager (LVM), which does not exist with Oracle Clusterware at this time. The underlying Cluster Logical Volume Manager (CLVM) mirrors the writes to both nodes synchronously. But from the database or operating system point of view, only one set of disks exists. The disk mirroring is done transparently to the database.

Oracle Automatic Storage Management (ASM) can also be used to mirror the storage. However, the voting disk and Oracle Cluster Registry (OCR) cannot be mirrored using Oracle Clusterware. Thus, it would be necessary to implement third-party clusterware to use host-based mirroring. Figure 15-4 explains the architecture of host-based mirroring.

Table 15-1 summarizes the pros and cons of array-based mirroring and host-based mirroring.

Challenges in Extended Clusters

Few challenges are normally seen in extended clusters that are not expected in normal clusters. The first important thing is the cost and complexity of the network connectivity between the nodes. The private interconnect plays a more important role in the extended clusters than normal clusters, as the distance between the nodes adds an important and expensive component to the overall performance—network latency. Network latency should be taken into consideration as every message or every block transfer includes this additional delta time.

The second important thing is the mirroring technique used for the storage replication. The choice of mirroring technique makes a difference, because from the application layer, the Oracle kernel should see the storage as a single storage and the abstraction should be provided from the lower layers. The choice of mirroring also plays an important role in manual restart during node failures.

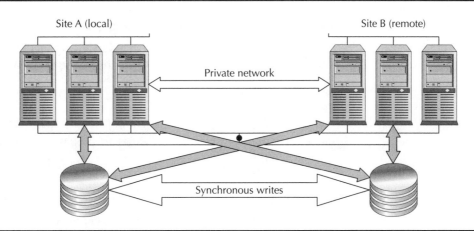

FIGURE 15-4. *Host-based mirroring*

The third important thing to be considered during the design is the quorum. A third site for the quorum device is recommended to maximize availability in an extended cluster environment. The third site acts as arbiter as to which site will survive during communication failures. This is worthwhile only when using third-party clusterware. Oracle's clusterware uses the quorum device during regular operations (versus only during a cluster reconfig event) and thus no advantage is gained by having it at a third location.

Normally, with the support of the mirrored voting disk, this problem can be overcome in the regular clusters. However, for the stretch clusters, another level of redundancy can be set up using a third site as a quorum site. This will enable the cluster to be functional if a disturbance occurs between the communications channels from the nodes. The choice of quorum plays an important role in tie-breaking during split-brain situations. The third site can be a simple workstation to act as an arbitrator in case of failures, as shown in Figure 15-5.

Extended RAC Limitations

RAC on extended clusters is a very specific solution for customers who want to build business applications on extended clusters. However, it does not work well for long distances. Extended clusters have not been tested for distances greater than 100 miles. If the distance between the nodes is greater than 100 miles, the system should be carefully tested and prototyped before being implemented.

Extended clusters *require* a dedicated point-to-point high-speed network. They cannot use the public network, and setting up a DWDM or dark fiber may cost hundreds of thousands of dollars. Extended RAC clusters are not suitable for unstable networks. A slight interruption in network service will cause node eviction and failures.

Description	Array-Based	Host-Based
Write propagation	Disk writes always sent to one site and changes are synchronously propagated to another node using disk mirroring techniques.	Writes are always sent to both nodes. Both nodes service user requests.
Primary/secondary setup	Requires primary/secondary site setup. If primary site fails, all access to primary disks is lost. An outage may be incurred before one can switch to secondary.	No primary/secondary required, as writes are propagated in both sides.
Support for additional software	Oracle Clusterware can be used.	Requires closely integrated clusterware and LVM, which does not exist with Oracle Clusterware at this time.
Storage appearance to the nodes	Storage system appears as two sets.	Storage is transparent to the application. The underlying storage structure is hidden by the OS, and application does not know the dual nature of the storage.
Failover during failures	Delay in recovery. Secondary site should be manually switched to active status during failures. This includes downtime.	Instant failure to surviving arrays. Surviving instance continues to run without downtime.
ASM support	Supported by ASM.	Not supported by ASM.
Requirement of third-party software	Not required. Oracle Clusterware can be used for basic clustering support.	Requires third-party software as Oracle Clusterware does not completely support mirroring of voting disk and OCR.
Advantage	Mirroring at the disk array level. Hence CPU not used from host nodes.	Both nodes can be used concurrently.
Disadvantage	Only one set of mirroring used at a time. Failover not instant.	Mirroring is done by the nodes and overhead is passed to the CPU.
Example	EMC (SDRF) Symmetric Remote Data Facility	HP open view storage mirroring, IBM HACMP

TABLE 15-1.   *Array-Based Mirroring vs. Host-Based Mirroring*

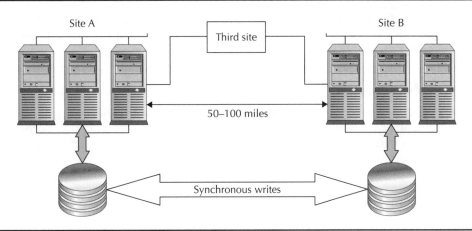

FIGURE 15-5. *Third site as quorum in a three-node structure*

Extended RAC vs. Data Guard

Extended RAC is a high availability solution that can be used as a limited disaster recovery solution. It does not replace the functionalities of Data Guard, which is a true disaster recovery solution. If you are looking for a true disaster recovery solution, Data Guard can be considered in conjunction with extended RAC. Data Guard can be used to overcome the intrinsic limitations imposed by the extended RAC and also offers the following advantages over extended RAC:

- **Network efficiency** Data Guard does not require expensive DWDM or dark fiber technologies for mirroring. It uses a normal TCP/IP for communication and does not require additional protocol converters. Data Guard transmits only redo data or incremental changes. It does not ship block images unless traditional hot backups are used.

- **No distance limitation** Fiber-based mirroring solutions have an intrinsic distance limitation and they cannot be deployed over thousands of miles. They also require additional protocol converters that indirectly add to cost, complexity, and latency.

- **Data protection** Data Guard protects from logical corruptions as the database is recovered from the primary. It validates the redo before applying to the secondary database. Both SQL apply and redo apply do not simply mirror the block images, thus providing a better protection against physical and logical corruptions.

- **Better flexibility and functionality** Data Guard uses commodity hardware and storage. It does not restrict you to specific storage vendors using proprietary mirroring technology. Remote mirroring solutions typically need identically configured storage from the same vendor. You cannot have a scaled-down version of the disaster recovery site. Data Guard can also be deployed in asynchronous mode. It provides a variety of protection methods and a graceful handling of network connectivity issues.

Deploying RAC on extended clusters requires careful architectural planning and deployment and can also be used as a disaster recovery solution. Oracle Data Guard and Oracle RAC are designed to protect different kind of failure scenarios. They do not compete with each other but complement each other when used correctly.

In a Nutshell

RAC on extended distance clusters is an attractive alternative architecture that allows scalability, rapid availability, and even some limited disaster recovery protection with all nodes fully active. This architecture can provide great value when used properly, but it is critical that its limitations are well understood.

CHAPTER
16

Developing Applications
for RAC

racle Real Application Clusters can be used for any kind of application—from custom to off-the-shelf. An application that runs on a single instance environment can be directly ported to the RAC platform without making any major architecture or code changes, and almost all packaged applications can be ported to RAC when scalability or availability of the application is in question.

In simplest terms, an application vendor could install Oracle RAC on a cluster, install the application on top of it, and run the application without any loss in business functionality due to changes in database status (single instance to multiple instances). That means that your Order Entry form or Balance Sheet report will not go missing from the application menu just because your database has been clustered.

It's not quite true to say that *any* application could be easily deployed (without modifications) on RAC. That might be true for well-designed and well-performing applications (on single instance as well as RAC), but while Oracle RAC is scalable, that's not necessarily the case for every application.

With this background, many technologists, architects, and managers *assumed* that RAC could solve all their scalability and performance problems. Suddenly, Oracle RAC was the much-anticipated panacea for a badly performing application on a single node. This created a large potential market for Oracle RAC, from small shops to large enterprises. What it also created, eventually, was much chagrin among users because RAC did not perform as it was "supposed" to. Like many new software products, RAC encountered many challenges in the beginning, but its technical prowess, robust features, and performance have always been its greatest strengths.

Oracle RAC is part of a high availability option that customers can exercise when maximum availability is a primary criteria. Using Oracle RAC for the sole purpose of improving system scalability and performance may or may not pay off, since such improvements depend on many factors. Key amongst these factors are application design and scalability.

NOTE
It is worth mentioning, at this point, the highly commendable work of many stalwarts in the field of performance and scalability of applications through education of the masses about the challenges, pitfalls, and techniques in achieving real-world scalability. Their books, whitepapers, articles, and web links are widely known in the Oracle world and a good scan of their repertoire is more than enough for Oracle users to help them through the maze of scalability and performance issues.

A well-designed and tuned database that services an equally well-designed application could scale admirably on RAC with multiple nodes, as compared to a single symmetric multiprocessing (SMP) box. This scalability in terms of number of concurrent users, workload achieved, and performance has been proven many times by hardware and application vendors on various platforms and different types of applications. Reliable figures and facts are available from individual companies and analysts to prove the scalability of RAC on multiple nodes. (For more information on the latest results, visit http://www.tpc.org. Oracle regularly publishes results of large TPC benchmarks on Oracle E-Business Suite and other well-known applications using Oracle RAC.)

Application performance in RAC depends on how well the application performs on a single instance. Even though no changes are required to run an application in RAC, specific issues must be considered when an application moves to RAC, as these issues could hinder the performance of the application or the overall system. More insight on these best practices are provided throughout this chapter.

Comparison of application and database scalability on single node SMP boxes versus scalability in clustered systems is tricky and sometimes inconclusive due to the complex nature of the various software layers involved and database/application characteristics. For example, a batch job to reconcile all accounts in a banking application may perform 25 transactions per second and consume 4,500 seconds to complete. Of the total 4,500 seconds, 4,000 seconds is CPU time on an 8-CPU box, at 90 percent utilization (7.2 CPUs fully utilized). For this example, consider the 500 seconds' worth of latency related issues such as I/O waits, locking, and so on. Also assume that no other job or process is running when this batch is executed.

If the job needs to be completed in half the time—2,250 seconds—then a generic solution would be to double the CPU capacity on the same box. Theoretically, a 16-CPU box should complete the same job in 2,250 seconds at 25 transactions per second and 90 percent utilization (14.5 CPUs fully utilized). This is assuming that nothing much can be done about reducing the wait time of 500 seconds and that the application is well tuned.

Without going deeper into any scalability formulas, queuing models, and theorems (which are critical, vital, and indispensable tools for architects, designers, and developers), and all the other technical complexities that accompany scalability challenges, can we provide a confident answer whether a single instance database with higher CPU capacity would scale? Is it possible to achieve the same scalability (completing the job in 2,250 seconds) if we deploy a 2-node RAC with 8 CPUs each?

A straightforward and simple answer would be difficult to provide without knowing factors such as these:

- How much time are we spending waiting on a single instance for I/O, locks, and so on? Can that be reduced?

- Can the application work exactly the same way, with the same throughput of 25 transactions per second, without modifications in RAC?

- Can the application perform the same without running into locking/concurrency issues when deployed on RAC?

- What would be the application throughput with lock mastering overhead when RAC is used?

- Do we have enough parallel streams/processes to take advantage of extra CPU resources?

- What about the cost factor? Which model is cheaper?

This is just the beginning of a long discussion that will take the consideration of many more factors before a useful answer results. All that could prove useless, however, if the application testing results on both single node and RAC are not considered.

Nevertheless, we have seen that with a given set of characteristics and metrics, significant trends can be observed and recorded in single node as well as RAC systems to provide effective and meaningful data for analysts and designers. This data can be used in conjunction with further testing results to make decisions or take positive actions. It would be rather naive to act solely upon individual data (such as just single node SMP results) to make a decision on the best model for scaling and achieving the required performance.

This chapter is by no means a complete lesson on application scalability and performance, how to achieve it, and how not to. The aim is to provide some best practice solutions and suggestions for an application running on an RAC database that can fit a wide variety of applications, from pure online transaction processing (OLTP) environments to a mix of data warehousing and online systems. Applications such as traditional enterprise resource planning, banking/insurance, general finance, customer relations, telecom billing, manufacturing, web applications, Internet stores, and data warehouses can apply these best practices according to their environments. As always, testing is mandatory since a generic recommendation that suits all requirements doesn't exist. The so-called "one size fits all" formula is a myth and fails more often than not.

These best practices and guidelines have been drawn from experience at various sites on different platforms and breeds of applications, from Oracle's own experiences and knowledge base, from debates and discussions with users, and from technologists and RAC enthusiasts across the globe. The guidelines are intended to reduce overall contention for resources such as data/index blocks, latches and locks, memory, and CPU cycles in an RAC environment.

Let's now examine some of the factors that affect application performance and scalability on an RAC database. No particular order of priority has been established, but they all deserve equal attention and probably more in certain situations, depending on the complexity and urgency of the problems/challenges being faced.

Even though this chapter is not an exhaustive list of all the factors that need careful consideration and analysis, it includes some of the most contentious issues that affect RAC databases of all versions and sizes.

Application Partitioning

To start, consider reading *Oracle 8i Parallel Server Administration, Deployment and Performance Release 2 (8.1.6) (Part No.A76970-01)*, available online on the Oracle Technology Network site at http://oraclesvca2.oracle.com/docs/cd/A87860_01/doc/paraserv.817/a76970.pdf. This manual is an excellent primer about the basic problems applications could face in a parallel server environment and the types of partitioning schemes that can be adopted to overcome them. Subsequent releases of Oracle documentation have eliminated much of this foundation material as they deem it unnecessary from Oracle 9i RAC onward. Yet a review of Chapters 5 and 6 in particular would do readers a lot of good, especially those who are new to RAC and its traditional problem areas.

In Oracle Parallel Server (OPS), application partitioning was necessary to scale applications. This scheme had to be adopted to avoid block pings across all participating instances in the parallel database. One of the stumbling blocks in OPS 8i in certain implementations was the disk pinging effect and its need for a *forced block write* of a dirty block to the disk by a holding instance when another instance requested the same block for modification. Remember that Cache Fusion I minimized the need to write blocks to disk even for a consistent read (CR) block. But when multiple instances required the same block for modification, application scalability was limited, since increased requests for the same block caused an increase in disk writes. This also increased global locking activity—interconnect traffic as well as heavy CPU usage. A lot of special care and attention was needed to tune such parameters as GC_FILES_TO_LOCK, which was almost the only way to control locking at the block level.

Contention occurs when the same application with the same transaction pattern is run on multiple nodes at the same time. Hence, the application needs the same set of blocks for Data Manipulation Language (DML) operations as they touch or operate on the same set of tables. This is called *table overlap* and occurs when the same table or set of tables are accessed by two or more application components concurrently. For example, a transaction table could be simultaneously used by both Receivables and Payments modules. This creates more chances of contention for a block or set of blocks, depending on the type of transaction.

A high INSERT rate into the same table from different nodes has the potential to cause contention for the block being affected and also for the bitmapped blocks (BMBs) (in the ASSM tablespace). If indexes are present for that table, this may also cause contention for the index branch/leaf blocks. The use of database sequences for generation of key values increases the chances of buffer contention.

In a freelist managed segment, the master freelist in the segment header block would come under tremendous pressure. Tuning experiences have shown that increasing FREELIST GROUPS and FREELISTS will help alleviate these issues. Large UPDATE requests on the same table, when submitted from two or more instances, can cause the same type of effect, though they may not necessarily fight for segment headers, but data block contention is quite possible. There may also be some enqueue problems that we won't discuss here.

In Oracle 9i and later, Cache Fusion II minimized some of the forced disk write effect by directly transmitting a copy of the current block across the high-speed interconnect to the requesting instance in some circumstances. So disk writes were reduced to an extent by the usage of the new past image (PI) blocks

Best Practice: Application Partitioning Schemes

To reduce these effects, application partitioning schemes were introduced in OPS 8i and continue to be used in Oracle 9i RAC installations. These schemes are definitely not obsolete in Oracle 10g and can still provide increased performance and scalability. However, application partitioning is not a requirement for RAC database installations, though many sites are known to use it effectively.

Application partitioning refers to the following:

■ Identification of the main functional business components of the application and segregation.

■ Scheduling an application or a component of the application to run on a specific node or nodes only, thereby restricting access to that application through a particular node(s).

For example, a production manufacturing application could run Inventory on node 1, BOM on node 2, Payments on node 3, and Receivables on node 4. It is rather difficult to avoid table overlaps in most of these types of applications, in which multiple modules share the same set of tables. By running an application module on a single node or a maximum of two, block pinging effects are minimized. This is a partial solution when tables cannot be split (so that each application module uses its own tables and indexes) and when data partitioning is not possible. In the next section, you'll see how data partitioning can be used to overcome this problem.

Application partitioning can reduce the chances of block pinging. The lesser the number of common tables across modules, the better the application performance. Oracle 10g RAC can also leverage from this basic type of partitioning, in OLTP as well as batch/decision support system (DSS) types of environments.

Data Partitioning

Partitioning has been available in Oracle since version 8. The benefits of data partitioning are well known to users, and many large databases have reaped rich rewards by implementing the many schemes introduced in each successive release of the Oracle server. (Note that partitioning requires an additional license fee.)

Partitioning data as well as indexes needs liberal consideration and a well-planned approach in RAC environments. Partitioning can help minimize a lot of contention for data and index blocks, provided the right partitioning strategy is chosen.

The type of environment/application is a crucial factor in choosing the type of partitions to create. This means that the application could be a straightforward OLTP system or a mix of OLTP and batch processing. Some environments are pure batch or DSS in nature, sometimes referred to as *data warehouses*. Each of these environments has a predominant "type" or "nature" of transaction. It could be INSERT intensive, UPDATE intensive, or SELECT intensive, or a mixture of these. It is common to see OLTP applications that do a lot of all three types of activities, including DELETEs. Some applications also have lots of DDL embedded in their systems. Transaction volume (rate of inserts, updates, and deletes) is another critical factor that needs to be considered while choosing the correct partitioning strategy.

Most of the discussion in data partitioning and buffer busy problems are restricted to large INSERT-related issues, since they are most common.

Best Practice: Guidance Systems

The data is guided or directed into each partition based on the data set that will be used for processing on that node/instance. This may also be broadly referred to as *workload characterization* and can be used in conjunction with application partitioning.

For example, the data is inserted using a guidance system to ensure that the data is processed from a particular node only. Assume a four-node RAC database with each node processing data for one region only. When data arrives for insert, the guidance system routes the data such that node 1 inserts Western region data only, node 2 inserts Eastern region data, and so on.

The guidance system can be application logic or a combination of software (for example Data Dependent Routing in Tuxedo) and intelligent devices with algorithms built in. Data is usually routed through these systems. Telecom applications make extensive use of guidance systems, though the usage is far more complicated and extensive.

In certain cases, the data arriving (from an external system, flat files, and so on) could be pre-sorted and guided to an instance such that no intelligence or guidance is required at the application end during the insert into a node. Once the data is in, the application on node 1 will process data from partition 1 to partition 25. Node 2 (running the same or another module) will process data from partition 26 to 50, and so on. User data is not shared between the nodes during processing except in certain unavoidable circumstances. This creates an affinity between nodes and data/index blocks. So the application is more likely to find a block or set of blocks in its local cache, thereby effectively reducing cross-instance communication and block transfers.

In typical OLTP environments, the number of blocks that are generally visited per query or DML operation is small. This is because data selection is driven mostly by primary or unique key lookups. Large-range scans are less likely, unless the application requires it, is not well designed, or suffers from various types of "over-indexing" and architectural issues.

In contrast, batch operations that select lots of data (data mining, reporting, DML) need hundreds of thousands of blocks to be visited to satisfy the query. Without partitioning and proper guidance, intense competition for data/index blocks among instances will cause block contention, which is visible as one or a combination of the following wait events:

```
'buffer busy waits',
'read by other session',
'global cache cr request',
'gc cr buffer busy',
'gc current block busy'
```

Application changes may be required to guide this data using a key value such as instance ID or the equivalent. Data structure changes are also required as a column will be added to the table(s). This column identifies the instance from which this row was inserted (or in some cases last updated). For example, if the table is to be range partitioned on `order_date`, the partition key can be `(order_date, instance_id)`. Some designers like to use a different column name that identifies each guided row and binds it to a particular instance or table partition. As mentioned before, guidance into each instance/partition is done using some predetermined algorithm. This column will also form a part of the partition key `(order_date, <column name>)`. Further, we could also have index partitions based on this column.

Using this key value, data is inserted or updated into the correct partition, which will later be processed by the application on a particular node only. This scheme can significantly reduce contention for data blocks, bitmap blocks, and index leaf blocks (when indexes are partitioned).

The following extract from Oracle documentation (Oracle 9i Real Application Clusters Deployment and Performance Release 2 (9.2) Part No. A96598-01) summarizes this strategy in a very lucid manner:

> Cache Fusion eliminates most of the costs associated with globally shared database partitions by efficiently synchronizing this data across the cluster. However, object partitioning, without changing your application, can sometimes improve performance for hot blocks in tables and indexes. This is done by re-creating objects as hash or composite partitioned objects.
>
> For example, consider a table that has a high insert rate which also uses a sequence number as the primary key of its index. All sessions on all nodes access the right-most index leaf block. Therefore, unavoidable index block splits can create a serialization point that results in a bottleneck. To resolve this, rebuild the table and its index, for example, as a 16-way hash partitioned object. This evenly distributes the load among 16 index leaf blocks.

Buffer Busy Waits/Block Contention

This particular subject has been covered extensively in almost every Oracle tuning book and in many articles and whitepapers since time immemorial. In Oracle 8i OPS days, reducing data block contention (mainly during inserts) was possible using FREELISTS and FREELIST GROUPS. If application designers, developers, and DBAs are able to work out the correct settings for these two parameters, it is still a valid and effective approach to reduce contention for data blocks significantly as well as segment header waits in RAC environments when concurrent inserts are used. Performance tests (9i and 10g) with large concurrent inserts have shown that using these parameters can provide the same or better benefits when compared to using ASSM tablespaces. Needless to say, end users would have to use locally managed tablespaces in Oracle 9i or 10g along with accurately sized extents and other segment management clauses. Free space management is done using FREELISTS and FREELIST GROUPS in manual segment

Hot Blocks and X$KSLHOT

In Oracle 10g, you no longer have to write multiple and repeated queries on V$BH or X$BH or dump data/index blocks to find hot blocks that are generally chased by applications. A new view called the X$KSLHOT has been added to simplify the identification of hot blocks. To use this feature, you need to set the little-known hidden parameter `_db_block_hot_tracking` to `true`.

This table has a sample of the RDBAs that are responsible for contention. The `kslhot_id` column is the RDBA and the `kslhot_ref` column is a count of the relative number of times it was encountered. A higher `kslhot_ref` implies the corresponding `kslhot_id` is a bright candidate for a hot buffer.

space management based tablespaces and using bitmap blocks in Automatic Segment Space Management (ASSM) tablespaces.

The segment header block can be a point of great contention between instances. Freelist groups alleviate the contention for the segment header block since they move the point of contention away from the segment header to dedicated blocks of master freelists. Each freelist group can be associated with an instance, provided the numbers of freelist groups are equal to or greater than the number of instances.

The `clustering_factor` is influenced by using multiple freelists (not freelist groups) as data gets scattered among more blocks.

Oracle 9i introduced ASSM, which is an effective "auto" method of reducing block contention, because it randomizes inserts by trying to pick a different block for insertion for each process. There is no guarantee that each time it will behave in the same way, but the chances that the same block will be picked by two or more inserting processes are low in ASSM. Hence this random factor tilts the balance in favor of ASSM, especially in RAC.

When the `FREELIST` parameter is used, Oracle maps a process to a freelist using the formula *mod(oracle process_id, no. of process freelists) + 1*. In ASSM, it uses the process ID to guide itself to a space map block, and even choosing a block is based on the process ID.

One of the key benefits of using ASSM tablespaces is that level 2 BMBs have an affinity to an instance. Hence, they are normally not sent across the interconnect. In addition, the blocks that they manage also have an affinity to the same instance as the level 2 BMBs.

Using ASSM can also have an extreme effect on the `clustering_factor` of an index (though it is not a symptom that is repeated every time), since the data is distributed across many blocks. Application development teams should test their applications on ASSM with high inserts and analyze the trend since no silver bullet solution exists for all situations. Also, using ASSM can cause performance problems during full table scans since the tables are generally larger than a non-ASSM table.

Index Partitioning

One of the most glaring mistakes at many sites is to partition the table and not partition related indexes. Index partitioning is equally or more important than table partitioning, as index blocks have a tendency to get hotter than the table blocks because of high concurrency at block level due to the smaller row length of index keys. The following techniques can be implemented to alleviate index block contention issues.

Buffer Busy Waits: Index Branch/Leaf Blocks Contention

In an application where the loading or batch processing of data is a dominant business function, there are more chances of performance issues affecting response times due to the overhead of index maintenance during large volume inserts. Depending on the access frequency and the number of processes concurrently inserting data, indexes can become hot spots and contention can be exacerbated by frequent leaf block splits, ordered and monotonically increasing key values in the index (usually generated using a sequence) and sometimes due to a low tree depth.

A leaf or branch block split can become an important serialization point if the particular leaf block or branch of the tree is concurrently accessed. The existence of the following wait events are typical indicators of this kind of block contention issue:

- `Enqueue Contention: TX`
- `gc buffer busy`
- `gc current block busy`
- `gc current split`

In an RAC environment, the transaction splitting a leaf block and the transactions waiting for the split to complete are affected if data required for the operation are not locally cached. Before and during a split operation, the transaction performing the split will have to execute a series of global locking operations before a pin is acquired on the target block. These operations are expensive, especially in RAC, where the latencies adversely affect application performance during large inserts. Blocking asynchronous trap (BAST) processing during a branch/leaf split has additional impact on the time taken to complete the split.

Note that periodic index rebuilding for so-called "performance improvement" in the RAC environment could be counterproductive. As a matter of fact, Oracle B-tree indexes are balanced by design, and under normal conditions, rebuilding the indexes at periodic intervals is not required. Rebuilding indexes makes the index blocks more compact and reduces the free space. In other words, we need to consider RAC implications not just for design or development issues, but for maintenance activities, too.

The challenge is to minimize the chances of multiple instance inserting (data and index) into the same block concurrently. This can be done by using hash or range partitions with appropriate changes in the application code or database structure. The partition scheme is dependent on the suitability to the application.

A right-growing index experiences increased contention for the leaf blocks mostly due to the fact that keys are generated in order of increasing sequence. Therefore the leaf blocks tend to heat up quite often. This is known as *buffer busy wait*. Moreover, frequent splitting of indexes may introduce further serialization points.

Distributing the access to the leaves over multiple index partitions alleviates the hot spots. Apart from a significant reduction of contention, local cache affinity improves because leaf blocks are retained in a local cache longer and are more available for local users.

Best Practice: Index Partitioning

Partitioning of indexes provides huge improvements in OLTP as well as batch type environments. The choice between local or global indexes is highly dependent on the application and how the data is queried, whether index lookups are unique key (or PK) based or index range scans. Partition maintenance and performance are also key points to consider while choosing an index partition type.

Global indexes are good for OLTP environments, where performance is generally high on the wish list, and for applications that like to perform unique key lookups. Oracle 10g supports hash partitioning of global indexes, which provides more flexibility for handling partitioned indexes.

In Oracle 9i, the only way to partition an index by hash was to partition the corresponding table as well. In Oracle 10g, it is possible to partition only the index independent of the table, and it becomes simpler if contention is limited to index blocks.

It is worth mentioning at this point, however redundant it might be, that SQL statements must make use of the partition key in their WHERE clause for partition elimination/pruning to happen. Note that partition elimination works only for range or list partitions. Index range scans can be disastrously slow without restrictive predicates based on partitioned and indexed columns. These columns should be the partition key or part of it to leverage on partition pruning. The type of predicate (=, >, <) has the potential to make or break the query.

Reducing Leaf Block Contention with Reverse Key Index

Some applications benefit from reverse key indexes (high INSERT environments) in terms of performance, but they are notorious for generating high I/O. Since the actual (non-reversed) values of the index are not stored sequentially in the index, index range scans cannot be performed. Generally, fetch-by-key and full index scans can be performed on a reverse key index. If the reverse key index is built on a single column, an index range scan will not be used by the Cost Based Optimizer (CBO). If the reverse key index is built on multiple columns, it will be used by CBO for a range scan operation when the equality predicate is used on the leading columns of the index.

Note that the `clustering_factor` of a reverse key index will incline more toward the number of rows since the index points to table rows that are scattered over different or many blocks. This will influence the CBO toward choosing an execution plan without the reverse key index.

Sometimes, a combination of reverse key indexes and an adequately cached database sequence that generates the key values can provide immense relief for databases with acute index leaf block contention.

You can attain great benefits (that are offset at times due to side effects) with the usage of reverse key indexes, but be careful while implementing reverse key indexes where the application performs index range scans. Designers and developers should also consider these options while choosing indexing and partitioning strategies.

One of the undesirable side effects of using reverse key indexes is that they must be constantly rebuilt with 50 percent or more free space to be beneficial, since a large number of block splits can and will take place in an active table.

Sorted Hash Clusters

Oracle offers several optional methods for storing table data, including clusters and hash clusters. Oracle 10g introduced new feature called *sorted hash clusters*, which is particularly suitable for systems requiring very high data insertion and retrieval rates.

This table structure better supports first-in first-out (FIFO) data processing applications, where data is processed in the order it was inserted. Such applications are typically found in the telecommunications and manufacturing environments. For example, consider a call detail record (CDR) data structure that is common in telecommunication environments. For billing and auditing purposes, each call is to be recorded and associated with its origin. Usually, calls are stored as they arrive from the switch. This data can be retrieved later in FIFO order or a customized order when customer bills are generated.

Though it is common practice to capture this data in two standard tables, a sorted hash cluster is a better solution as it allows inexpensive access to the sorted list of call records for any given subscriber and allows the billing application reading the call records to walk through the sorted list in a FIFO manner. Any application in which data is always consumed in the order in which it is inserted will see tremendous performance improvements by using this type of optimized table structure.

The key is to partition the data and indexes as required by the application. Store your data the way the application needs it and queries it. If the algorithm selects customers in a descending order, explore the possibilities of storing customers in a descending order and use an index created in descending order of customers. There might be potential overhead in using this method since it would require constant table/index rebuild, loading of data, and other associated administrative work. But with automated tasks, the benefits of using methods like these can sometimes outweigh the overhead.

In RAC environments, the application must build the intelligence to process data from a defined set of data/index partitions only. This reduces the chances of block contention and the "ping pong" effect of repeated blocks traveling between instances.

Working with Sequences

Database sequences are useful for generating numbers that grow or increase sequentially in an order that is configurable. Application designers need not use "home-grown" sequence generators using a database table and update it using local logic. Such sequences are not very scalable, especially in RAC environments with high inserts, when they are used with specific clauses. Yet, in certain cases, these customized and non-Oracle sequences are the only way to achieve certain goals that cannot be achieved using Oracle's own sequences.

A select from a sequence is an update to the data dictionary when it is not cached. So every select internally invokes a DML and commit, which is very expensive in RAC, since System Commit Numbers (SCNs) must be synchronized across the cluster when sequences are used extensively.

In RAC environments, performance degradation due to heavy (ab)use of sequences and a high insert rate can manifest in different ways:

- Contention for the SQ enqueue. If you see contention for SV enqueue, the problem is complicated and Oracle Support Services might be required.

- Buffer busy waits for various classes of blocks such as data, index leaves, or segment headers.

- TX enqueue waits on the index blocks may also be visible.

- In certain cases, ITL waits are also possible when a sufficient number of transaction slots is not reserved or available. This could be due to a very low setting for PCTFREE combined with a default value for INITRANS or artificially limiting transaction slots using MAXTRANS.

CACHE and NOORDER

The CACHE option speeds up selection and processing of sequences and minimizes the writes to SEQ$. Note that the CACHE option is usable only if an application is able to accept gaps in the sequence, irrespective of whether you use RAC.

From a performance and scalability perspective, the best way of using sequences is to use the CACHE and NOORDER options together. The CACHE option ensures that a distinct set of numbers are cached in each instance after the first use of the sequence. The NOORDER option specifies that the sequence numbers may not be in order. For applications that perform large concurrent inserts from multiple instances concurrently and a key value like the primary key is generated using the sequence, the NOORDER along with CACHE option provides the best throughput.

In a high insert environment, tables that have their key values generated from sequences tend to have hot blocks for both data and indexes, since the block where inserts are going is wanted by every instance. Without partitioning the table and the applicable indexes, these blocks would become a major point of contention. Hence, partitioning of data and indexes should be one of the first steps in reducing this type of contention. Along with partitioning, using an additional column along with the key value is critical to avoid contention.

These hot blocks are generally visible as buffer busy waits or read by other session depending on the mode waited for. There would also be an increase in the number of CR and CUR mode blocks transferred between instances, sometimes even with partitioning implemented.

One of the disadvantages of the NOORDER is that the key values may not be in order. So if an invoice number, customer number, or account number is generated using this sequence and regulatory norms require you to maintain the order of numbers, NOORDER cannot be used. An abnormal instance shutdown or a crash will introduce gaps in sequences. Cached sequences may be lost during a shared pool flush or rollback. Sequences do not support rollback as a sequence once fetched remains fetched and the number is deemed consumed forever.

CACHE and ORDER

If you need sequences for which the ordering of numbers needs to be guaranteed, the CACHE option with ORDER clause can be specified. This ensures the ordering of numbers, because each instance caches the same set of numbers unlike the NOORDER option.

Note that the Oracle documentation wrongly states that the CACHE and ORDER options do not work together. Both Oracle 9i and 10g RAC support this feature, however. These two options may not be as scalable as the CACHE and NOORDER method, but they ensure that sequences are in order, although gaps can still occur across instance startup and shutdown.

NOCACHE and ORDER

This option is used when an application requires all sequence values in an order and without gaps. Using NOCACHE and ORDER has the biggest performance impact on RAC environments, and designers must understand the inherent scalability limitations before choosing this model.

To overcome buffer busy waits for data blocks while using sequences to generate the key value, specify FREELISTS if segment management is manual or use ASSM tablespaces. In addition, the segment header block is also subject to heavy contention in RAC environments. To reduce that, use FREELIST GROUPS.

Best Practice: Use Different Sequences for Each Instance

A good practice in RAC is to use different sequences for each instance to avoid a single point of contention. Each inserting process on a particular node uses its own sequence to select monotonically increasing key values. Selecting from a different sequence for high inserts can be a great solution, but it needs a change in the application.

In RAC environments, to overcome buffer busy waits for index leaves where the key values are generated using sequences, do the following:

- Use ASSM tablespaces. Partition the table and its relevant indexes. Guide the data into the table partitions using additional columns, if necessary. Remember to analyze the effects on the `clustering_factor` of your indexes.

- `CACHE` large values of the sequence and use `NOORDER` if possible.

With caching, the difference between sequence values generated by different instances increases; thereby, newer index block splits would create an effect called an *instance affinity* to index leaf blocks. This seems to work only when `CACHE` and `NOORDER` are used together.

For example, if we use a sequence cache of 20, instance 1 would insert values 1, 2, 3, and so on, and instance 2 would concurrently insert 20, 21, 22, and so on. If the difference between the values is a lot smaller than the number of rows in the block, the two instances will continue to modify the same index block as sequence values increase.

If we set a value of 5000 for the sequence cache, instance 1 would insert values 1, 2, 3, and so on, while instance 2 concurrently inserts 5001, 5002, 5003, and so on. At the beginning of the inserts, both instances would write to the same leaf block, but subsequent block splits would cause the inserts to be distributed across different blocks since the difference in sequence values causes the inserts to map to different blocks.

There is no such thing as a best value for the `CACHE` option in sequences. Generally, developers should consider the rate of insert per second/per instance as a guide to setting the cache value. Sequences may not be the best scalable solution, especially when an instance is used for the generation of ordered and gapless sequence numbers at a very high rate.

Connection Management

Applications that do not use transaction monitors are generally guilty of poor database connection management. Efficient management of database connections is critical in single instance databases and in RAC databases.

Some applications disconnect from the database and then reconnect repeatedly. This is a common problem with stateless middleware applications such as Shell/Perl scripts and precompiler programs that exit on error and tend to use the `AUTO_CONNECT` option to re-establish the connection again. Even in precompiler programs such as Pro*C, application architecture and design would force an unnecessary "connection-disconnection-reconnection" to the database, impeding scalability and performance.

Connecting to the database incurs operating system costs associated with creating a new process or thread. Many recursive SQL statements also need to be executed during the process of establishing a new connection to the database. Because the session is new, these recursive SQL statements require a soft parse. This adds to the load on the library cache latches. Data file operations require operating system coordination, and this adds to the overhead of maintaining the process.

All these overheads can be avoided by retaining database connections as long as they are required. Usually, applications built with a transaction monitor such as BEA Tuxedo do not suffer from these issues since a database connection is maintained consistently.

Beginning Oracle 9i, the Pro*C/C++ Connection Pooling and OCI Session pooling features help maintain connections to the database. These features can be deployed in applications built using Pro*C/OCI and when transaction monitors such as BEA Tuxedo, CORBA, and WebSphere are not used. Stateless connection pooling improves the scalability of the mid-tier applications by multiplexing the connections.

Full Table Scans

Repetitive full table scans in RAC can impede performance and scalability as the private interconnect is used for transferring blocks, and that can eat into network bandwidth. This would cause a delay for other required and important blocks such as index blocks, undo blocks, header blocks, and any messages. The goal is to reduce interconnect traffic and bring down latency. With a lot of full table scans, interconnects could get overloaded, thereby flooding the private network.

Another very important factor to be considered with full table scans is an appropriate value for DB_FILE_MULTIBLOCK_READ_COUNT, also know as MBRC. Not only does this parameter have a charming influence on the optimizer to lean toward a full table scan (irrespective of RAC or non-RAC), but achieving interconnect saturation is easy if high values are used for this parameter.

Experience has shown that 16 can be a high MBRC value for an application such as Oracle E-Business Suite 11i. Many such systems experience severe performance degradation with a MBRC of 16 while running in RAC mode. Lowering the value to 8 immediately brings the performance back to acceptable or normal levels.

With a high MBRC in RAC, when Oracle performs multi-block reads and the data is transferred across instances, the interconnect tends to get flooded with large number of blocks flowing from one end to the other. Using a lower value for MBRC (8 or 4) is a good starting point for applications on RAC databases.

Full table scans are not necessarily evil, and in some cases they are the best data access method for a particular process. But they are a common issue in many RAC performance problems, especially with custom applications. You can easily identify the full table scans in the database using any of the following techniques.

Identifying Full Table Scans

Statspack (Automatic Workload Repository) is one of the most common tools used to monitor the most of the databases. You can easily spot and conclude from the top wait events whether full table scans are the problem. Existence of the db file scattered read wait event in the top five wait events is a quick and early indicator of a full table scan problem.

Other than Statspack, v$sysstat can be queried for the table scan statistic. You can run the following query on v$sysstat to check the number of times data is accessed using the full table scan method:

```
select name, value from v$sysstat
where name like 'table scan%'
```

A Statspack report quickly followed by the query on v$sysstat can confirm whether full table scans are a problem. Normally, performance monitoring tools or scripts built on using v$session_wait will quickly detect the full scans if they find the excessive waits on the db file scattered read. A db file scattered read wait event lists the *file#* and *block#* along with number of blocks it is reading (typically less than or equal to the MBRC value) during the full scan. These are displayed as p1, p2, and p3 values for the db file scattered read wait event. For known file#, block#, you can use the following query to get the name of the table that is being accessed via full table scans:

```
select distinct owner, segment_name,segment_type
from dba_extents where file_id=<file#> and
<block#> between  block_id and block_id+blocks -1;
```

Other than querying the v$sysstat or v$session_wait, you can implement numerous techniques to detect full table scans if you suspect they are a problem. For example, if the PHYSBLKRDS is significantly higher than the PHYRDS in the V$FILESTAT, there is a good chance of full scans on the segment residing in that data file. Also, blocks read by full table scans are not subject to normal LRU processing in the buffer cache. A special flag is set in the buffer cache (X$BH.FLAG), and if the state is 0×80000, you know the block is read using the full scans.

After identifying the table scans, you need to confirm whether they are expected or unreasonable. You can query either query the v$session_longops or the v$sql_plan to confirm that. Any of the following queries can be employed for this purposes, and using the hash_value the offending SQLs can be identified and tuned for efficiency:

```
select sid,username,opname,target,totalwork,sofar,sql_hash_value.
from v$session_longops
where opname='table scan'
and totalwork>sofar

select object_owner,object_name,hash_value
from v$sql_plan
where operation='TABLE ACCESS'
and options='FULL'
```

A distinct advantage of these views over the v$session_wait is the values are not quickly overwritten and they are cached for an extended period of time. You can even query at a later time and confirm the activity. The v$session_longops view is quite important here, as it also lists the other expensive operations in the database such as hash joins, sorting, and RMAN operations.

Interconnect Protocol

Choosing the appropriate protocol to carry your blocks across the high-speed interconnect is a crucial decision. So is the configuration and settings for the protocol.

Oracle 9i made the first definitive shift toward the User Datagram Protocol (UDP), a connectionless protocol. With 10g R1, Oracle has actively suggested the use of UDP on all platforms, even though hardware vendors have developed some exciting and lighting-fast technologies for transfer of data across high-speed interconnects. Prominent among them are Digital Equipment's (aka Compaq, aka HP) Reliable DataGram (RDG), HP's Hyper Messaging Protocol (HMP), and Veritas' Low Latency Transport (LLT).

Each of these protocols uses its own proprietary hardware interconnects based on fiber-optic or Gigabit Ethernet technology with very low network latency. Yet, each one of them has its own problems with RAC—except for RDG, which seems to perform and scale wonderfully well on Tru64 systems with minimal fuss.

What makes the crucial difference in interconnect performance (and subsequently application response time and scalability) is choosing the right values for the internal layers of each of these protocols, especially UDP. The receive and send buffer size is usually left at default values on many installation sites. The Oracle kernel uses its own default values (128K for UDP on all UNIX platforms). If the OS tunable parameters for UDP have been configured, the Oracle kernel uses those values to set its buffer sizes.

Default values are seldom adequate for applications that support hundreds or thousands of users. The number of connections and concurrent users may not always be a good yardstick for workload measurement. Some applications have less user count but a large transaction volume and cause lot of inter-node traffic. Using the default UDP settings, RAC databases/applications that tend to have highly active inter-node block transfers may not scale when the workload increases.

A value of 64K (65,536 bytes) for udp_sendspace can be used while tuning this layer. Any value above that is most likely useless since the lower layer (IP) cannot process more than 64K. A value that is 10 times that of udp_sendspace is a good setting for udp_recvspace. Usually, recommendations suggest setting both these parameters to 1MB each, which is also valid in many cases, yet 1MB is more of a generic tuning guideline as compared to the 64K practice, which is derived and calculated based on UDP and IP behavior.

An interesting relationship that UDP shares with FTS is that low or "untuned" values for UDP buffer sizes can cause timeouts when CR blocks are requested by remote instances. Timeouts are visible in the gc cr multi block wait event or in a trace file generated via SQL Trace or a 10046 event setting. A look into the V$SYSTEM_EVENT can provide the ratio of timeouts versus waits for the CR request event:

Event	Waits	Timeouts	Total Wait Time (s)	Avg wait (ms)	Waits /txn
gc cr multi block	12,852	**3,085**	612	47	3.6

A large value for MBRC can exacerbate the situation. Hence, proper care must be taken while choosing values for UDP buffers as well as MBRC.

Library Cache Effect in the Parsing

As in single instance environments, it is best to avoid excessive and unnecessary parsing of SQL statements and PL/SQL code in RAC. Additional overhead is incurred in Oracle RAC for parsing since many locks are now global. In old parlance, library cache related locks fall under the non-PCM locks category.

- Library cache load and pin lock acquisition on a library object such as a PL/SQL procedure, package, or function requires global coordination by Global Enqueue Services (GES).

- Though parsing of SELECT statesments do not require global lock coordination, data definition language (DDL) statements do need messages to be sent across to master nodes for synchronization and lock grants.

Note that if the same SQL statement is sent for parsing on all nodes, these statements are individually parsed and executed on each node and probably with different execution plans due to potentially varying init.ora or SPFILE parameters.

When many objects are compiled or parsed, even reparsed due to invalidations, it can give rise to delays and have significant impact on performance. Application developers must take care while using DDL statements including GRANT and REVOKE commands since these statements invalidate all objects that are referred to or by the PL/SQL object.

Repeated hard parsing and parse failures can severely limit scalability and harm the application performance. Tuning methodologies followed on single instance databases are also applicable in RAC and should be rigorously implemented.

Commit Frequency

Certain wait events have multiple effects in RAC. For example, a "log file sync" wait event is associated with excessive commits and application designers/developers usually are advised to reduce the frequency of their commits to reduce the burden on LGWR and reduce the number of LGWR writes to a log file. A close associate of "log file sync" is "log file parallel write."

In RAC environments, log file sync has more implications because each commit or rollback needs SCN propagation and global synchronization, and may also require controlfile synchronization. Hence, extra caution must be exercised in RAC environments when choosing a commit interval or frequency. Some business applications may need to commit more often than other applications require. Developers and users must be aware of the performance tradeoff that accompanies a high commit rate.

In a single instance database, when a user commits or rolls back a transaction, the process waits on log file sync and the background Oracle process (LGWR) will wait on a log file parallel write. On an RAC database, in addition to the latency created by these usual suspects, time consumed in SCN-related communication and control file writes will also need to be considered while calculating the cost of commit/rollback.

NOTE
Excessive cross-instance requests for changed or dirty blocks will cause more redo generation since all changes made to a block need to be written out before transferring a copy of the block across to the requesting instance. In this case, LMS initiates the log synchronization and waits on a log file sync. Once log writing is complete, LMS can go ahead and ship the copy of the block to the requestor.

Note that Oracle 10g R1 supports the Lamport scheme of SCN propagation (using MCPD) as well as Broadcast on Commit (BOC). In 10g R2, Oracle supports a single mechanism—BOC, the default on all platforms. MCPD is retained for backward compatibility and is not recommended by Oracle as a supported mechanism in Oracle 10g R2 onward.

There are some bugs in the later releases of Oracle—Bug 5360750 (9.2), Bug 5061068 (10.2.0.1), and Bug 5065930 (not RAC related)—that cause the log file sync to show excessive values in an RAC environment. Most of them are fixed in Oracle 10.2. A good scan of Metalink will provide enough clues. If you see a long wait for the log file sync in your database, it would be a good idea to check with Oracle Support whether it is a genuine application problem or bug.

In a Nutshell

As noted at the beginning of the book, RAC can be compared to a stereo amplifier. If the original music is good, you will hear good music with RAC. If the original music has a lot of noise, RAC will amplify that noise and the outcome is generally horrible. A well-performing application in a single instance environment will perform equally well or outperform when implemented on RAC.

Developing applications for RAC does not require any major changes other than the few considerations explained herein. Other than a few exceptions, all single instance application design best practices are applicable to RAC databases as well.

Good luck in designing and deploying a highly scalable application on RAC!

APPENDIX
A

RAC Reference

racle database is very rich in terms of providing diagnostic data and statistics. It provides an enormous amount of statistics about most of the internal operations, and they are exposed through a group of underlying views that are maintained by the database server. These views are normally accessible to the database administrator user *SYS*. They are called *dynamic performance views* because they are continuously updated while a database is open and in use, and their contents relate primarily to performance.

These views are built on the set of internal memory structures commonly known as *x$views*. These internal and undocumented views expose the runtime statistics of the relative data structures in a tabular format. Although these views appear to be regular database tables, they are not. You can select from these views, but you cannot update or alter them as the definitions are not stored in the dictionary.

The catalog.sql script (which is executed automatically by the Database Configuration Assistant during database creation) creates the public synonyms for the dynamic performance views. After installation, only user *SYS* or anyone with the DBA role has access to the dynamic performance tables.

In this appendix, we explore the important v$views that are used in Real Application Clusters for diagnostics and troubleshooting. These views contain the system-level statistics from the instance startup, and the contents are reset when the instance is shut down as the data structures containing the data are reset during the instance shutdown. All of the information is cached in the System Global Area (SGA) of the respective instances.

For clusterwide information, you can query GV$ views. For every v$view, a corresponding GV$ view exists. When you query the GV$ view, the data from other instances are retrieved by parallel query mechanisms and the initialization parameter `parallel_max_servers` should be set to a minimum of 2 for GV$ views to work.

Global Cache Services and Cache Fusion Diagnostics

The following views can be queried to get the details about the buffer cache contents and Global Cache Services (GCS) operations. Cache Fusion diagnostic information can also be obtained from these views.

V$CACHE

This view contains information about every cached block in the buffer cache. It also keeps the relevant details about the cached block to the database object. This view is a good source of information about cached blocks in local instances in RAC environments. Table A-1 shows information about columns and data types in this view.

Table A-2 shows block classes and descriptions. Table A-3 defines the buffer states.Table A-4 shows information about V$Cache_Transfer.

V$CACHE_TRANSFER

This RAC view is similar to V$CACHE, which contains information from block headers in SGA that have been pinged at least once of current instance relative to database object.

Column	Data Type	Description
FILE#	Number	Datafile ID (FILE# from V$DATAFILE or FILE_ID in DBA_DATA_FILES)
BLOCK#	Number	Block number of the cached block
CLASS#	Number	Class number (see Table A-2)
STATUS	Varchar2 (6)	Status of block in SGA (see Table A-3)
XNC	Number	Number of times PCM locks converted from X to null lock mode
FORCED_READS	Number	Number of times block was reread from cache as another instance forced it out by requesting this block in exclusive mode
FORCED_WRITES	Number	Number of times GCS had to write block to cache as this instance used block and another instance requested lock on block in conflicting mode
NAME	Varchar2 (30)	Name of database object to which block belongs
PARTITION_NAME	Varchar2 (30)	Name of partition; column null if object not partitioned
KIND	Varchar2 (15)	Type of object (table, view procedure, etc.)
OWNER#	Number	Number of owner
LOCK_ELEMENT_ADDR	Raw (4|8)	Address of lock element that contains PCM lock covering the buffer
LOCK_ELEMENT_NAME	Number	Name of lock element that contains PCM lock covering the buffer

TABLE A-1. *V$CACHE Information*

Class	Explanation
1	Data
2	Sort segment
3	Save undo block
4	Segment header
5	Save undo segment header
6	Freelist block
7	Extent map
8	Space management bitmap block
9	Space management index block

TABLE A-2. *Block Class and Descriptions*

State	Explanation
0	Buffer free, unused
1	Buffer current, locked in X mode
2	Buffer current, locked in S mode
3	Consistent read buffer
4	Buffer being read
5	Buffer under media recovery
6	Buffer under instance recovery
7	Write clone buffer
8	Past Image buffer

TABLE A-3. *Buffer States*

Column	Data Type	Description
FILE#	Number	Datafile ID. (FILE# from V$DATAFILE or FILE_ID in DBA_DATA_FILES
BLOCK#	Number	Block number
CLASS#	Number	Class number (see Table A-2)
STATUS	Varchar2 (6)	Status of block in SGA (see Table A-3)
XNC	Number	Number of times PCM locks converted from X to null lock mode
FORCED_READS	Number	Number of times block was reread from cache as another instance forced it out by requesting this block in exclusive mode
FORCED_WRITES	Number	Number of times GCS had to write this block to cache as this instance had used block and another instance had requested lock on block in a conflicting mode
NAME	Varchar2 (30)	Name of database object to which this block belongs
PARTITION_NAME	Varchar2 (30)	Name of partition; null if object is not partitioned
KIND	Varchar2 (15)	Type of object
OWNER#	Number	Owner number
GC_ELEMENT_ADDR	Raw (4|8)	Address of lock element containing PCM lock covering the buffer
GC_ELEMENT_NAME	Number	Name of lock element that contains PCM lock covering the buffer

TABLE A-4. *V$CACHE_TRANSFER Information*

V$INSTANCE_CACHE_TRANSFER

This view keeps information about the transfer of cache blocks through interconnect. These statistics can be used to find the number of blocks transferred from one instance to another instance using Cache Fusion. This view also shows how many block transfers incurred a delay or congestion (see Table A-5).

Column	Data Type	Description
INSTANCE	Number	Instance number transferring block
CLASS	Varchar2 (18)	Class of cache block being transferred
CR_BLOCK	Number	CR block transfers not affected by remote processing delays
CR_BUSY	Number	CR block transfers affected by remote contention
CR_CONGESTED	Number	CR blocks transfers affected by remote system load
CURRENT_BLOCK	Number	Current blocks transfers not affected by remote system delays
CURRENT_BUSY	Number	Current blocks transfers affected by remote contention
CURRENT_ CONGESTED		Current blocks transfers affected by remote system load

TABLE A-5. *V$INSTANCE_CACHE_TRANSFER Information*

V$CR_BLOCK_SERVER

This view keeps statistics about CR block transfer across the instances (Table A-6). Global Cache Service Process (LMS) from the holding instance constructs the CR block for the requesting instance and ships the CR version of the block using the interconnect. More discussion on CR building is discussed in Chapter 11.

Column	Data Type	Description
CR_REQUESTS	Number	Number of CR blocks served due to remote CR block requests
CURRENT_REQUEST	Number	Number of current blocks served due to remote CR block request
DATA_REQUEST	Number	Number of CR or current requests for data blocks
UNDO_REQUESTS	Number	Number of CR requests for undo blocks
TX_REQUESTS	Number	Number of CR request for undo segment header blocks. Total number of requests would be equal to sum of DATA_REQUEST, UNDO_REQUESTS, and TX_REQUESTS column
CURRENT_RESULTS	Number	Number of requests when no changes were rolled out of the block returned to requesting instance
PRIVATE_RESULTS	Number	Number of requests when changes were rolled out of the block returned to requesting instance and only the requesting transaction can use CR block
ZERO_RESULTS	Number	Number of requests when changes were rolled out of the block returned to requesting instance and only zero-XID transactions can use block
DISK_READ_RESULTS	Number	Number of requests when requesting instance had to read block from disk
FAIL_RESULTS	Number	Number of requests failed and requesting transaction reissued request
FAIRNESS_DOWN_CONVERTS	Number	Number of times instance receiving request has down-converted an X lock on a block because it was not modifying the block
FAIRNESS_CLEARS	Number	Number of times "fairness counter" was cleared. This counter tracks number of times block was modified after it was served
FREE_GC_ELEMENTS	Number	Number of times request was received from another instance and X lock had no buffers
FLUSHES	Number	Number of times LMS flushed the logs
FLUSHES_QUEUED	Number	Number of flushes queued by LMS
FLUSH_QUEUE_FULL	Number	Number of occasions flush queue was full
FLUSH_MAX_TIME	Number	Maximum flush time
LIGHT_WORKS	Number	Number of times lightwork rule was evoked (see Chapter 11)
ERRORS	Number	Number of occasions error signaled by LMS process

TABLE A-6. *V$CR_BLOCK_SERVER Information*

V$CURRENT_BLOCK_SERVER

This view keeps statistics about current block transfer across the instances (Table A-7). GCS Process (LMS) from the holding instance ships the current block to the requesting instance after flushing required recovery information to the redolog buffer. This view provides the most important information about how long the holding instance waited to flush the information before sending the block to the requestor.

Column	Data Type	Description
PIN1	Number	Number of pins taking less than 1ms
PIN10	Number	Number of pins taking 1ms to 10ms
PIN100	Number	Number of pins taking 10ms to 100ms
PIN1000	Number	Number of pins taking 100ms to 1000ms
PIN10000	Number	Number of pins taking 1000ms to 10000ms
FLUSH1	Number	Number of flush taking less than 1ms
FLUSH10	Number	Number of flush taking 1ms to 10ms
FLUSH100	Number	Number of flush taking 10ms to 100ms
FLUSH1000	Number	Number of flush taking 100ms to 1000ms
FLUSH10000	Number	Number of flush taking 1000ms to 10000ms
WRITE1	Number	Number of writes taking less than 1ms
WRITE10	Number	Number of writes taking 1ms to 10ms
WRITE100	Number	Number of writes taking 10ms to 100ms
WRITE1000	Number	Number of writes taking 100ms to 1000ms
WRITE10000	Number	Number of writes taking 1000ms to 10000ms

TABLE A-7.   *V$CURRENT_BLOCK_SERVER Information*

V$GC_ELEMENT

This view displays one-to-one information for each global cache resource used by the buffer cache (Table A-8). There is an entry for each global cache resource in this view, used by a buffer cache.

Column	Data Type	Description
GC_ELEMENT_ADDR	Raw (4|8)	Address of PCM lock element containing PCM lock covering buffer; if more than one buffer has same address, these buffers are covered by same PCM lock
INDX	Number	Platform-specific lock manager identifier; can be joined with V$CACHE_LOCK view
CLASS	Number	Platform-specific lock manager identifier; can be joined with V$CACHE_LOCK view
LOCK_ELEMENT_NAME	Number	Name of lock element that contains PCM lock covering buffer; if more than one buffer has same address, these buffers are covered by same PCM lock
MODE_HELD	Number	Value for lock mode held; often 3 for share and 5 for exclusive
BLOCK_COUNT	Number	Number of blocks covered by PCM lock
RELEASING	Number	Non-zero if PCM lock downgraded
AQUIRING	Number	Non-zero if PCM lock upgraded
INVALID	Number	Upon PCM lock failure would be non-zero
FLAGS	Number	Process level flags for lock element

TABLE A-8. *V$GC_ELEMENT Information*

Global Enqueue Services Diagnostics

The following views can be queried to get the details about statistics about Global Enqueue Services. Few of these views are extensively used in single instance environments to query enqueue statistics.

V$LOCK

This view maintains information about locks held within a database and outstanding requests for locks or latches (Table A-9). Table A-10 shows lock modes.

Column	Data Type	Description
ADDR	Raw (4 | 8)	Address of lock state object
KADDR	Raw (4 | 8)	Address of lock
SID	Number	Session identifier holding the lock
TYPE	Varchar2 (2)	Type of resource, which could be user or system type
ID1	Number	Resource identifier 1
ID2	Number	Resource identifier 2
LMODE	Number	Lock mode held (see Table A-10)
REQUEST	Number	Mode of lock requested (see Table A-10)
CTIME	Number	Time since current mode was granted
BLOCK	Number	1 if lock is blocking another lock, 0 otherwise

TABLE A-9. *V$LOCK Information*

Lock Mode	Description
0	none
1	null (NULL)
2	row-S (SS)
3	row-X (SX)
4	share (S)
5	S/row-X (SSX)
6	exclusive (X)

TABLE A-10. *Lock Modes*

V$GES_BLOCKING_ENQUEUE

This view maintains information about locks that are being blocked or blocking others and locks that are known to the lock manager (Table A-11). The content of this view is a subset of V$GES_ENQUEUE as this view maintains information only about blocked locks, whereas V$GES_ENQUEUE maintains all locks known to the lock manager.

Column	Data Type	Description
HANDLE	(Raw 4 | 8)	Pointer to lock
GRANT_LEVEL	Varchar2 (9)	Level granted to lock
REQUEST_LEVEL	Varchar2 (9)	Level requested for lock
RESOURCE_NAME1	Varchar2 (30)	Resource name of lock
RESOURCE_NAME2	Varchar2 (30)	Resource name of lock
PID	Number	Process identifier holding the lock
TRANSACTION_ID0	Number	Lower 4 bytes of transaction identifier the lock belongs
TRANSACTION_ID1	Number	Upper 4 bytes of transaction identifier the lock belongs
GROUP_ID	Number	Group identifier of lock
OPEN_OPT_DEADLOCK	Number	1 if DEADLOCK option is set, otherwise 0
OPEN_OPT_PERSISTENT	Number	1 if PERSISTENT option is set, otherwise 0
OPEN_OPT_PROCESS_OWNED	Number	1 if PROCESS_OWNED option is set, otherwise 0
OPEN_OPT_NO_XID	Number	1 if NO_XID option is set, otherwise 0
CONVERT_OPT_GETVALUE	Number	1 if GETVALUE convert option is set, otherwise 0
CONVERT_OPT_PUTVALUE	Number	1 if PUTVALUE convert option is set, otherwise 0
CONVERT_OPT_NOVALUE	Number	1 if NOVALUE convert option is set, otherwise 0
CONVERT_OPT_DUBVALUE	Number	1 if DUBVALUE convert option is set, otherwise 0
CONVERT_OPT_NOQUEUE	Number	1 if NOQUEUE convert option is set, otherwise 0
CONVERT_OPT_EXPRESS	Number	1 if EXPRESS convert option is set, otherwise 0
CONVERT_OPT_NODEADLOCKWAIT	Number	1 if NODEADLOCKWAIT convert option is set, otherwise 0
CONVERT_OPT_NODEADLOCKBLOCK	Number	1 if NODEADLOCKBLOCK convert option is set, otherwise 0
WHICH_QUEUE	Number	Which queue the lock is currently located, 0 if Null Queue; 1 for Granted Queue; 2 for Convert Queue
STATE	Varchar2 (64)	State of lock
AST_EVENT0	Number	Last know AST event
OWNED_NODE	Number	Node identifier owning the lock
BLOCKED	Number	1 if lock request is blocked by others, otherwise 0
BLOCKER	Number	1 if lock is blocking others, otherwise 0

TABLE A-11. *V$GES_BLOCKING_ENQUEUE Information*

V$ENQUEUE_STATISTICS

This view displays details about enqueue statistics in the instance (Table A-12). Most of the enqueues are global in nature and are visible across instances. Table A-13 shows enqueue types and descriptions.

Column	Data Type	Description
EQ_NAME	Varchar2 (64)	Name of enqueue request is for
EQ_TYPE	Varchae2 (2)	Type of enqueue (see Table A-13)
REQ_REASON	Varchar2 (64)	Reason for enqueue request
TOTAL_REQ#	Number	Total number of times enqueue requested or converted
TOTAL_WAIT#	Number	Number of times enqueue request or conversion resulted in wait
SUCC_REQ#	Number	Number of times enqueue request or conversion granted
FAILED_REQ#	Number	Number of times enqueue request or conversion failed
CUM_WAIT_TIME	Number	Amount of time in ms spent waiting for enqueue or conversion
REQ_DESCRIPTION	Varchar2 (4000)	Description of enqueue request
EVENT#	Number	Number for event

TABLE A-12.   *V$ENQUEUE_STATISTICS Information*

Enqueue Type	Description
enq: AD (allocate AU)	Synchronizes accesses to specific OSM (Oracle Software Manager) disk AU
enq: AD (deallocate AU)	Synchronizes accesses to a specific OSM disk AU
enq: AF (task serialization)	Serializes access to an advisor task
enq: AG (contention)	Synchronizes generation use of a particular workspace
enq: AO (contention)	Synchronizes access to objects and scalar variables
enq: AS (contention)	Synchronizes new service activation
enq: AT (contention)	Serializes 'alter tablespace' operations
enq: AW (AW$ table lock)	Global access synchronization to the AW$ table (analytical workplace table used in OLAP option)
enq: AW (AW generation lock)	In-use generation state for a particular workspace
enq: AW (user access for AW)	Synchronizes user accesses to a particular workspace
enq: AW (AW state lock)	Row lock synchronization for the AW$ table
enq: BR (file shrink)	Lock held to prevent file from decreasing in physical size during RMAN backup
enq: BR (proxy-copy)	Lock held to allow cleanup from backup mode during an RMAN proxy-copy backup
enq: CF (contention)	Synchronizes accesses to the control file
enq: CI (contention)	Coordinates cross-instance function invocations
enq: CL (drop label)	Synchronizes accesses to label cache when dropping a label
enq: CL (compare labels)	Synchronizes accesses to label cache for label comparison
enq: CM (gate)	Serializes access to instance enqueue
enq: CM (instance)	Indicates OSM disk group is mounted
enq: CT (global space management)	Lock held during change tracking space management operations that affect the entire change tracking file
enq: CT (state)	Lock held while enabling or disabling change tracking, to ensure that it is enabled or disabled by one user at a time
enq: CT (state change gate 2)	Lock held while enabling or disabling change tracking in RAC
enq: CT (reading)	Lock held to ensure that change tracking data remains in existence until a reader is done with it
enq: CT (CTWR process start/stop)	Lock held to ensure that only one CTWR (change tracking writer) process is started in a single instance CTWR. CTWR used to track block changes. Started with alter database enable block change tracking
enq: CT (tate change gate 1)	Lock held while enabling or disabling change tracking in RAC
enq: CT (change stream ownership)	Lock held by one instance while change tracking is enabled to guarantee access to thread-specific resources

TABLE A-13. *Enqueue Types and Descriptions*

Enqueue Type	Description
enq: CT (local space management)	Lock held during change tracking space management operations that affect data for one thread only
enq: CU (contention)	Recovers cursors in case of death while compiling
enq: DB (contention)	Synchronizes modification of database-wide supplemental logging attributes
enq: DD (contention)	Synchronizes local accesses to ASM disk groups
enq: DF (contention)	Enqueue held by foreground or DBWR when datafile is brought online in RAC
enq: DG (contention)	Synchronizes accesses to ASM disk groups
enq: DL (contention)	Lock to prevent index DDL during direct load
enq: DM (contention)	Held by foreground or DBWR to synchronize database mount/open with other operations
enq: DN (contention)	Serializes group number generations
enq: DP (contention)	Synchronizes access to LDAP parameters
enq: DR (contention)	Serializes the active distributed recovery operation
enq: DS (contention)	Prevents a database suspend during LMON reconfiguration
enq: DT (contention)	Serializes changing the default temporary table space and user creation
enq: DV (contention)	Synchronizes access to lower version DIANA (PL/SQL intermediate representation)
enq: DX (contention)	Serializes tightly coupled distributed transaction branches
enq: FA (access file)	Synchronizes accesses to open ASM files
enq: FB (contention)	Ensures that only one process can format data blocks in auto segment space managed tablespaces
enq: FC (open an ACD thread)	LGWR opens an ACD thread
enq: FC (recover an ACD thread)	SMON recovers an ACD thread
enq: FD (marker generation)	Synchronization
enq: FD (flashback coordinator)	Synchronization
enq: FD (tablespace flashback on/off)	Synchronization
enq: FD (flashback on/off)	Synchronization
enq: FG (serialize ACD relocate)	Only one process in the cluster may do ACD relocation in a disk group
enq: FG (LGWR redo generation enqueue race)	Resolves race condition to acquire Disk Group Redo Generation Enqueue
enq: FG (FG redo generation enqueue race)	Resolves race condition to acquire Disk Group Redo Generation Enqueue
enq: FL (flashback database log)	Synchronization

TABLE A-13. *Enqueue Types and Descriptions* (continued)

Enqueue Type	Description
enq: FL (flashback database command)	Synchronizes Flashback Database and deletion of flashback logs
enq: FM (contention)	Synchronizes access to global file mapping state
enq: FR (contention)	Begins recovery of disk group
enq: FS (contention)	Synchronizes recovery and file operations or synchronizes dictionary check
enq: FT (allow LGWR writes)	Allows LGWR to generate redo in this thread
enq: FT (disable LGWR writes)	Prevents LGWR from generating redo in this thread
enq: FU (contention)	Serializes the capture of the DB feature, usage, and high water mark statistics
enq: HD (contention)	Serializes accesses to ASM SGA data structures
enq: HP (contention)	Synchronizes accesses to queue pages
enq: HQ (contention)	Synchronizes the creation of new queue IDs
enq: HV (contention)	Lock used to broker the high water mark during parallel inserts
enq: HW (contention)	Lock used to broker the high water mark during parallel inserts
enq: ID (contention)	Lock held to prevent other processes from performing control file transaction while NID is running
enq: IL (contention)	Synchronizes accesses to internal label data structures
enq: IM (contention for blr)	Serializes block recovery for IMU transaction
enq: IR (contention)	Synchronizes instance recovery
enq: IR (ontention2)	Synchronizes parallel instance recovery and immediate shutdown
enq: IS (contention)	Synchronizes instance state changes
enq: IT (contention)	Synchronizes accesses to a temp object's metadata
enq: JD (contention)	Synchronizes dates between job queue coordinator and slave processes
enq: JI (contention)	Lock held during materialized view operations (such as refresh, alter) to prevent concurrent operations on the same materialized view
enq: JQ (contention)	Lock to prevent multiple instances from running a single job
enq: JS (contention)	Synchronizes accesses to the job cache
enq: JS (coord post lock)	Lock for coordinator posting
enq: JS (global wdw lock)	Lock acquired when doing WDW DDL
enq: JS (job chain evaluate lock)	Lock when job chain evaluated for steps to create
enq: JS (q mem clnup lck)	Lock obtained when cleaning up q memory

TABLE A-13. *Enqueue Types and Descriptions* (continued)

Enqueue Type	Description
enq: JS (slave enq get lock2)	Gets run info locks before slave object
enq: JS (slave enq get lock1)	Slave locks exec pre to session start
enq: JS (running job cnt lock3)	Lock to set running job count epost
enq: JS (running job cnt lock2)	Lock to set running job count epre
enq: JS (running job cnt lock)	Lock to get running job count
enq: JS (coord rcv lock)	Lock when coord receives message
enq: JS (queue lock)	Lock on internal scheduler queue
enq: JS (job run lock, synchronize)	Lock to prevent job from running elsewhere
enq: JS (job recov lock)	Lock to recover jobs running on crashed RAC instance
enq: KK (context)	Lock held by open redo thread, used by other instances to force a log switch
enq: KM (contention)	Synchronizes various Resource Manager operations
enq: KP (contention)	Synchronizes kupp process startup
enq: KT (contention)	Synchronizes accesses to the current Resource Manager plan
enq: MD (contention)	Lock held during materialized view log DDL statements
enq: MH (contention)	Lock used for recovery when setting Mail Host for AQ email notifications
enq: ML (contention)	Lock used for recovery when setting Mail Port for AQ email notifications
enq: MN (contention)	Synchronizes updates to the Log Miner dictionary and prevents multiple instances from preparing the same Log Miner session
enq: MR (contention)	Lock used to coordinate media recovery with other uses of data files
enq: MS (contention)	Lock held during materialized view refresh to set up MV log
enq: MW (contention)	Serializes calibration of manageability schedules with the Maintenance window
enq: OC (contention)	Synchronizes write accesses to the outline cache
enq: OL (contention)	Synchronizes accesses to particular outline name
enq: OQ (xsoqhiAlloc)	Synchronizes access to OLAPi history allocation
enq: OQ (xsoqhiClose)	Synchronizes access to OLAPi history closing
enq: OQ (xsoqhistrecb)	Synchronizes access to OLAPi history globals
enq: OQ (xsoqhiFlush)	Synchronizes access to OLAPi history flushing
enq: OQ (xsoq*histrecb)	Synchronizes access to OLAPi history parameter CB
enq: PD (contention)	Prevents others from updating the same property
enq: PE (contention)	Synchronizes system parameter updates
enq: PF (contention)	Synchronizes accesses to the password file

TABLE A-13. *Enqueue Types and Descriptions* (continued)

Enqueue Type	Description
enq: PG (contention)	Synchronizes global system parameter updates
enq: PH (contention)	Lock used for recovery when setting proxy for AQ HTTP notifications
enq: PI (contention)	Communicates remote Parallel Execution Server Process creation status
enq: PL (contention)	Coordinates plug-in operation of transportable tablespaces
enq: PR (contention)	Synchronizes process startup
enq: PS (contention)	Parallel Execution Server Process reservation and synchronization
enq: PT (contention)	Synchronizes access to ASM PST metadata
enq: PV (syncstart)	Synchronizes slave start shutdown
enq: PV (syncshut)	Synchronizes instance shutdown_slvstart
enq: PW (perwarm status in dbw0)	DBWR 0 holds enqueue indicating prewarmed buffers present in cache
enq: PW (flush prewarm buffers)	Direct Load needs to flush prewarmed buffers if DBWR 0 holds enqueue
enq: RB (contention)	Serializes OSM rollback recovery operations
enq: RF (synch: per-SGA Broker metadata)	Ensures R/W atomicity of DG configuration metadata per unique SGA
enq: RF (synchronization: critical AI)	Synchronizes critical apply instance among primary instances
enq: RF (new AI)	Synchronizes selection of the new apply instance
enq: RF (synchronization: chief)	Anoints 1 instance's Dataguard Broker Monitor (DMON) as chief to other instances' DMONs
enq: RF (synchronization: HC master)	Anoints 1 instance's DMON as health check master
enq: RF (synchronization: aifo master)	Synchronizes apply instance failure detection and failover operation
enq: RF (atomicity)	Ensures atomicity of log transport setup
enq: RN (contention)	Coordinates NAB computations of online logs during recovery
enq: RO (contention)	Coordinates flushing of multiple objects
enq: RO (fast object reuse)	Coordinates fast object reuse
enq: RP (contention)	Indicates resilvering is needed or data block is repaired from mirror
enq: RS (file delete)	Lock held to prevent file from accessing during space reclamation
enq: RS (persist alert level)	Lock held to make alert level persistent
enq: RS (write alert level)	Lock held to write alert level
enq: RS (read alert level)	Lock held to read alert level

TABLE A-13. *Enqueue Types and Descriptions* (continued)

Enqueue Type	Description
enq: RS (prevent aging list update)	Lock held to prevent aging list update
enq: RS (record reuse)	Lock held to prevent file from accessing while reusing circular record
enq: RS (prevent file delete)	Lock held to prevent deleting file to reclaim space
enq: RT (contention)	Thread locks held by LGWR, DBW0, and Recovery Writer (RVWR, used in Flashback Database operations) to indicate mounted or open status
enq: SB - contention	Synchronizes Logical Standby metadata operations
enq: SF (contention)	Lock used for recovery when setting sender for AQ email notifications
enq: SH (contention)	Should seldom see this contention as this enqueue is always acquired in no-wait mode
enq: SI (contention)	Prevents multiple streams table instantiations
enq: SK (contention)	Serializes shrink of a segment
enq: SQ (contention)	Lock to ensure that only one process can replenish the sequence cache
enq: SR (contention)	Coordinates replication/streams operations
enq: SS (contention)	Ensures that sort segments created during parallel DML operations aren't prematurely cleaned up
enq: ST (contention)	Synchronizes space management activities in dictionary-managed tablespaces
enq: SU (ontention)	Serializes access to Save Undo segment
enq: SW (contention)	Coordinates the 'alter system suspend' operation
enq: TA (contention)	Serializes operations on undo segments and undo tablespaces
enq: TB (SQL Tuning Base Cache Update)	Synchronizes writes to the SQL Tuning Base Existence Cache
enq: TB (SQL Tuning Base Cache Load)	Synchronizes writes to the SQL Tuning Base Existence Cache
enq: TC (contention)	Lock held to guarantee uniqueness of a tablespace checkpoint
enq: TC (contention2)	Lock of setup of a unique tablespace checkpoint in null mode
enq: TD (KTF dump entries)	KTF dumping time/SCN mappings in SMON_SCN_TIME table
enq: TE (KTF broadcast)	KTF broadcasting
enq: TF (contention)	Serializes dropping of temporary file
enq: TL (contention)	Serializes threshold log table read and update
enq: TM (contention)	Synchronizes accesses to object
enq: TO (contention)	Synchronizes DDL and DML operations on temp object
enq: TQ (TM contention)	TM access to queue table
enq: TQ (DDL contention)	TM access to queue table

TABLE A-13. *Enqueue Types and Descriptions* (continued)

Enqueue Type	Description
enq: TQ (INI contention)	TM access to queue table
enq: TS (contention)	Serializes accesses to temp segments
enq: TT (contention)	Serializes DDL operations on tablespaces
enq: TW (contention)	Lock held by one instance to wait for transactions on all instances to finish
enq: TX (contention)	Lock held by transaction to allow other transactions to wait for it
enq: TX (row lock contention)	Lock held on particular row by transaction to prevent other transactions from modifying it
enq: TX (allocate ITL entry)	Allocating an ITL entry to begin transaction
enq: TX (index contention)	Lock held on index during a split to prevent other operations on it
enq: UL (contention)	Lock used by user applications
enq: US (contention)	Lock held to perform DDL on undo segment
enq: WA (contention)	Lock used for recovery when setting watermark for memory usage in AQ notifications
enq: WF (contention)	Serializes the flushing of snapshots
enq: WL (contention)	Coordinates access to redolog files and archive logs
enq: WP (contention)	Handles concurrency between purging and baselines
enq: XH (contention)	Lock used for recovery when setting No Proxy Domains for AQ HTTP notifications
enq: XR (quiesce database)	Lock held during database quiesce
enq: XR (database force logging)	Lock held during database force logging mode
enq: XY (contention)	Lock used for internal testing

TABLE A-13. *Enqueue Types and Descriptions* (continued)

V$LOCKED_OBJECT

This view displays information about DML locks acquired by different transactions in databases with their mode held (Table A-14). It also keeps the transaction ID of the transaction (transaction ID is XIDUSN.XIDSLOT.XIDSQN).

Column	Data Type	Description
XIDUSN	Number	Number of undo segment
XIDSLOT	Number	Number of slot
XIDSQN	Number	Sequence number of transaction
OBJECT_ID	Number	ID of object being locked by this transaction
SESSION_ID	Number	Session ID responsible for this transaction and lock hold
ORACLE_USERNAME	Varchar2 (30)	Oracle user name
OS_USER_NAME	Varchar2 (30)	OS user name
PROCESS	Varchar2 (14)	OS process ID
LOCKED_MODE	Number	Lock mode; same as LMODE column of V$LOCK

TABLE A-14.   *V$LOCKED_OBJECT Information*

V$GES_STATISTICS

This view displays miscellaneous statistics for GES (Table A-15).

Column	Data Type	Description
STATISTIC#	Number	Statistic ID
NAME	Varchar2 (64)	Name of statistic
VALUE	Number	Value attached with this statistic

TABLE A-15.   *V$GES_STATISTICS Information*

V$GES_ENQUEUE

This view displays information about all locks known to the Lock Manager (Table A-16). It also keeps the grant level and request level and other related information.

Column	Data Type	Description
HANDLE	(Raw 4 | 8)	Pointer to lock
GRANT_LEVEL	Varchar2 (9)	Level granted to lock
REQUEST_LEVEL	Varchar2 (9)	Level requested for lock
RESOURCE_NAME1	Varchar2 (30)	Resource name of lock
RESOURCE_NAME2	Varchar2 (30)	Resource name of lock
PID	Number	Process ID holding the lock
TRANSACTION_ID0	Number	Lower 4 bytes of transaction ID to which lock belongs
TRANSACTION_ID1	Number	Upper 4 bytes of transaction ID to which lock belongs
GROUP_ID	Number	Group ID of lock
OPEN_OPT_DEADLOCK	Number	1 if DEADLOCK option is set, otherwise 0
OPEN_OPT_PERSISTENT	Number	1 if PERSISTENT option is set, otherwise 0
OPEN_OPT_PROCESS_OWNED	Number	1 if PROCESS_OWNED option is set, otherwise 0
OPEN_OPT_NO_XID	Number	1 if NO_XID option is set, otherwise 0
CONVERT_OPT_GETVALUE	Number	1 if GETVALUE convert option is set, otherwise 0
CONVERT_OPT_PUTVALUE	Number	1 if PUTVALUE convert option is set, otherwise 0
CONVERT_OPT_NOVALUE	Number	1 if NOVALUE convert option is set, otherwise 0
CONVERT_OPT_DUBVALUE	Number	1 if DUBVALUE convert option is set, otherwise 0
CONVERT_OPT_NOQUEUE	Number	1 if NOQUEUE convert option is set, otherwise 0
CONVERT_OPT_EXPRESS	Number	1 if EXPRESS convert option is set, otherwise 0
CONVERT_OPT_NODEADLOCKWAIT	Number	1 if NODEADLOCKWAIT convert option is set, otherwise 0
CONVERT_OPT_NODEADLOCKBLOCK	Number	1 if NODEADLOCKBLOCK convert option is set, otherwise 0
WHICH_QUEUE	Number	Tells which queue the lock is currently located, 0 if Null Queue; 1 for Granted Queue; 2 for Convert Queue
STATE	Varchar2 (64)	State of lock
AST_EVENT0	Number	Last know AST event
OWNED_NODE	Number	Node ID owning the lock
BLOCKED	Number	1 if lock request is blocked by others, otherwise 0
BLOCKER	Number	1 if lock is blocking others, otherwise 0

TABLE A-16. *V$GES_ENQUEUE Information*

V$GES_CONVERT_LOCAL

This view maintains information about all local GES operations (Table A-17). It displays such information as average convert time, count, and number of conversions.

Column	Data Type	Description
INST_ID	Number	Instance ID
CONVERT_TYPE	Varchar2 (64)	Conversion type
AVERAGE_CONVERT_TIME	Number	Average conversion time for each lock in hundredths of a second
CONVERT_COUNT	Number	Number of conversions

TABLE A-17.   *V$GES_CONVERT_LOCAL Information*

V$GES_CONVERT_REMOTE

This view maintains information about all remote GES operations (Table A-18). It displays such information as average convert time, count, and number of conversions.

Column	Data Type	Description
INST_ID	Number	Instance ID
CONVERT_TYPE	Varchar2 (64)	Conversion type
AVERAGE_CONVERT_TIME	Number	Average conversion time for each lock in hundredths of a second
CONVERT_COUNT	Number	Number of conversions

TABLE A-18.   *V$GES_CONVERT_REMOTE Information*

V$GES_RESOURCE

This view maintains information about all resources known to lock manager (Table A-19). It keeps the information about the master node for that particular resource.

Column	Data Type	Description
RESP	Raw (4 | 8)	Pointer to resource
RESOURCE_NAME	Varchar2 (30)	Resource name in hexadecimal format for the lock
ON_CONVERT_Q	Number	1 if on convert queue, otherwise 0
ON_GRANT_Q	Number	1 if on convert queue, otherwise 0
PERSISTENT_RESOURCE	Number	1 if it is a persistent resource, otherwise 0
RDOMAIN_NAME	Varchar2 (25)	Recovery domain name
RDOMAINP	Raw (4 | 8)	Pointer to recovery domain
MASTER_NODE	Number	Node ID mastering this resource
NEXT_CVT_LEVEL	Varchar2 (9)	Next lock level to be converted on global convert queue
VALUE_BLK_STATE	Varchae2 (32)	State of value block
VALUE_BLK	Varchar2 (64)	First 64 bytes of value block

TABLE A-19. *V$GES_RESOURCE Information*

Dynamic Resource Remastering Diagnostics

Dynamic resource remastering is a key feature of Oracle RAC that masters the frequently accessed resources to the local node. More information on dynamic remastering is available in Chapter 11.

V$HVMASTER_INFO

This view maintains information about current and previous master instances of GES resources in relation to hash value ID of resource (Table A-20).

Column	Data Type	Description
HV_ID	Number	Hash value ID of resource
CURRENT_MASTER	Number	Instance currently mastering the resource
PREVIOUS_MASTER	Number	Previous instance that mastered this resource
REMASTER_CNT	Number	Number of times this resource has remastered

TABLE A-20. *V$HVMASTER_INFO Information*

V$GCSHVMASTER_INFO

This view displays the same kind of information for GCS resources that V$HVMASTER_INFO displays for GES resources (Table A-21). Both views display information about the number of times remastering has occurred for resources. This view does not display information about resources belonging to files mapped to a particular master.

Column	Data Type	Description
HV_ID	Number	Hash value ID of resource
CURRENT_MASTER	Number	Instance currently mastering this PCM resource
PREVIOUS_MASTER	Number	Previous instance that mastered this PCM resource
REMASTER_CNT	Number	Number of times this resource has remastered

TABLE A-21.   *V$GCSHVMASTER_INFO Information*

V$GCSPFMASTER_INFO

This view displays information of current and previous masters about GCS resources belonging to files mapped to a particular master, including the number of times the resource has remastered (Table A-22). File based remastering was available in Oracle 10g R1; starting with Oracle 10g R2, remastering is done by object level, which allows fine grained remastering.

Column	Data Type	Description
FILE_ID	Number	File ID
CURRENT_MASTER	Number	Instance currently mastering this file
PREVIOUS_MASTER	Number	Previous instance that mastered this file
REMASTER_CNT	Number	Number of times this file has remastered

TABLE A-22.   *V$GCSPFMASTER_INFO Information*

Cluster Interconnect Diagnostics

Starting from Oracle 10g, the cluster interconnect information is available from the v$views. In previous versions, you had to query the alert log or invoke a IPC dump to get details about the interconnects used. The following views provide information about the interconnects configured and used in RAC.

V$CLUSTER_INTERCONNECTS

This view displays information about interconnects being used for cluster communication (Table A-23). This view also lists details about the source of the information as interconnect information is also stored in the Oracle Cluster Registry (OCR) and can be configured using the initialization parameter.

Column	Data Type	Description
NAME	Varchar2 (15)	Name of interconnec—eth0, eth1, etc.
IP_ADDRESS	Varchar2 (16)	IP address of interconnect
IS_PUBLIC	Varchar2 (4)	Yes if interconnect is public, No if interconnect is private; could be null if type of interconnect is unknown to cluster
SOURCE	Varchar2 (31)	Indicate where interconnect was picked up; interconnect information available from OCR, OSD software, or from CLUSTER_INTERCONNECTS parameter

TABLE A-23. *V$CLUSTER_INTERCONNECTS Information*

V$CONFIGURED_INTERCONNECTS

This view's display is same as V$CLUSTER_INTERCONNECTS, but this view displays information for all configured interconnects of which Oracle is aware, instead of those being used (Table A-24).

Column	Data Type	Description
NAME	Varchar2 (15)	Name of interconnect—eth0, eth1, etc.
IP_ADDRESS	Varchar2 (16)	IP address of interconnect
IS_PUBLIC	Varchar2 (4)	Yes if interconnect is public, No if interconnect is private; could be null if type of interconnect is unknowsn to cluster
SOURCE	Varchar2 (31)	Indicates where interconnect was picked up

TABLE A-24. *V$CONFIGURED_INTERCONNECTS Information*

APPENDIX
B

Adding and Removing Cluster Nodes

ne of the most common requirements in the data center environment is the need to add and remove nodes dynamically when the demand spikes. Oracle 10g RAC extends the capacity to add and remove the cluster nodes online. Nodes should be homogeneous and should have the same computing capacity. Though adding a node with higher or lower capacity than the members is technically possible, it is usually not recommended as it creates a logical imbalance between the nodes.

Adding a Node

Adding a node to an existing cluster is similar to the installing the RAC environment. You must prepare the new hardware for the new node, and the new node should have the same directory structure and user equivalences as the existing nodes. The new node should be able to access the voting disk and Oracle Cluster Registry as do existing nodes. If you are going to use ASMLib for the ASM instance, the ASM library should be preinstalled and the disks should be discovered before starting the installation. In addition, the required network configuration files should be updated and shared across the cluster.

In the following example, we add a new node to the cluster ORARAC, which has three nodes: RAC1, RAC2, and RAC3. The Oracle instance on each node will be called ORARAC1, ORARAC2, and ORARAC3. The newly added node will be called RAC4, and the Oracle instance on it will be named ORARAC4. The following walkthrough shows the process of adding the node RAC4 to the cluster ORARAC.

Pre-install Checking

The Cluster Verification utility can be used to verify that the system has been configured properly for the Oracle clusterware. The following command can be used to verify the readiness of the new node. The Cluster Verification utility can be run either from the staging directory or from any of the existing nodes. The following command in the node RAC1 invokes the Cluster Verification utility from the staging directory:

```
$ /staging/Disk1/cluvfy/runcluvfy.sh  stage - pre crsinst -n rac1,rac2,rac3
,rac4 -r 10gR2
```

Alternatively, the following command runs the Cluster Verification utility from the existing nodes:

```
$ cluvfy stage - pre crsinst -n rac1,rac2,rac3,rac4 -r 10gR2
```

The Cluster Verification utility should be successful before installation begins. If any error is reported during the verification, it must be fixed before proceeding with the Cluster Ready Services installation.

NOTE
It is generally considered that the UNIX user oracle is the owner of the Oracle software (ORACLE_HOME) and CRS software (ORA_CRS_ HOME). It is common for users to use different names as the owner of Oracle software. Any reference in this chapter to the user oracle is specifically meant to denote the owner of ORACLE_HOME and/or ORA_CRS_HOME.

Installing Cluster Ready Services

Oracle Cluster Ready Services (CRS) should be installed in the new node before installing any Oracle software in the new node. Installation of CRS for the new node can be started from any existing node. The following example shows adding a node from ORARAC1.

1. Log in as *oracle* (or the owner ORA_CRS_HOME) user in any of the existing cluster nodes and run the addNode.sh script. In this example, we log in to the node RAC1. The addNode.sh script is available in the $ORA_CRS_HOME/oui/bin.

   ```
   $ ./addNode.sh
   ```

   This script invokes the Oracle Universal Installer (OUI) and opens the OUI Welcome screen.

   OUI recognizes that the installation is part of a cluster (when CRS is running) and populates the screen with the existing cluster nodes.

2. In the Specify Cluster Nodes to Add to Installation screen, enter the name of the new names for the Public, Private, and virtual host interfaces.

3. Click Next to see the summary page. Here you can verify the entries and optionally go back to the previous screens should any changes be required.

4. If you are satisfied with the configuration, click Install. The installer will copy the files from the existing nodes to the new node via remote copy mechanisms. The installer will also create an Oracle inventory in the new node similar to the existing nodes. Once all the files are copied to the target node, the installer will ask you to run orainstRoot.sh and root.sh.

5. Run orainstRoot.sh and root.sh in the new nodes and rootaddnode.sh in the node from the node on which you invoked the installer. The first script, orainstRoot.sh, sets the Oracle inventory in the new node and sets the ownership and permissions to the inventory. The second script, rootaddnode.sh, configures the Oracle Cluster Registry (OCR) to include the new node as part of the cluster. The third script, root.sh, checks whether the Oracle CRS stack is already configured in the new node. It also creates the /etc/oracle directory and adds the relevant OCR keys to the cluster registry, and it adds the daemons to CRS and starts CRS in the new node.

6. After the scripts are finished, click Next to complete the installation. Now you have successfully installed the CRS in the new node. Now you need to configure Oracle Notification Services (ONS). The port for ONS can be identified by the following command. The configuration file is located in the $ORA_CRS_HOME/opmn/conf directory.

   ```
   cat ons.config
   ```

7. Now run the ONS utility (RACGONS) by supplying the <remote_port> number obtained from the previous command:

   ```
   ./racgons add_config node2:<remote_port>
   ```

Installing Oracle Database Software

After you have installed the Oracle Clusterware, you can install the Oracle software. Installation of the Oracle database software can also occur from any of the existing nodes. The shell script addNode.sh in the $ORACLE_HOME/oui/bin calls the OUI and copies the software to the new node. The following process installs the Oracle software to the newly added node.

1. Log in as the *oracle* user on any of the cluster nodes and set the environment variables. Invoke addNode.sh from $ORACLE_HOME/oui/bin:

   ```
   $ ./addNode.sh
   ```

2. Click Next on the Welcome screen to open the the Specify Cluster Nodes to Add to Installation screen. This screen lists the nodes in the existing cluster and allows you to select the new node. If you want to install the software for more than one node, you can select this here. Select the new node and click Next.

3. In the Summary page, you can verify the summary and click Install to start the installation of the Oracle database software to the new node.

4. The installer will copy the database software to new node and ask you to run root.sh at the end. Run the script on the newly added node as specified. Click OK in the dialog box.

The End of Installation screen tells you that you have successfully installed the Oracle database software in the new node.

Configuring the Listener

After the database software is installed in the new node, follow these steps to configure the listener in the new node.

1. Log in as the *oracle* user and set the environment to the database home. Remember to set the DISPLAY environment variable and export it.

   ```
   $ORACLE_HOME/bin/netca
   ```

2. Choose Cluster Management.

3. Choose Listener.

4. Choose ADD.

5. Choose the name as LISTENER.

These steps will add a listener on RAC4 with the name LISTENER_rac4.

Creating a Database Instance

Now follow these steps on first node to create the database instance in the new node.

1. Log in as the user *oracle* on RAC4, set the environment to database home, and invoke the database creation assistant (DBCA):

   ```
   $ORACLE_HOME/bin/dbca
   ```

2. In the Welcome screen, choose Oracle Real Application Clusters Database to create the instance and click Next.

3. Choose Instance Management and click Next.

4. Choose Add Instance and click Next.

5. Select ORARAC (or the cluster database name you have set up) as the database and enter the SYSDBA username and password at the bottom of the screen. Then click Next.

6. You will see a list of the existing instances. Click Next, and on the following screen enter **ORARAC4** as the instance name and choose RAC4 as the node name.

7. This will create a database instance ORARAC4 (on RAC4). Click Next in the Database Storage screen. During creation, you will be asked whether the ASM instance should be extended to RAC4. Choose Yes.

Removing a Node

Removing an RAC node includes similar steps—such as adding the node—but the process is done in reverse order:

1. Delete the instance on the node to be deleted.

2. Clean up the ASM.

3. Remove the listener from the node to be deleted.

4. Remove the node from the database.

5. Remove the node from the clusterware.

Deleting the Instance on the Node to Be Deleted

You can delete the instance using the database creation assistant (DBCA) ($ORACLE_HOME/ bin/dbca). Invoke the DBCA and choose the RAC database. In this screen, choose Instance Management, and then choose Delete Instance. You will see a screen with the database name. At the bottom of the screen, enter the SYSDBA user and password. Then choose the instance to delete and confirm the deletion.

Clean up the ASM

If your database is running on ASM, follow these steps to clean up ASM on RAC4. If the database is not running on ASM, you can skip this section. (Most of the steps can also be done from any node, as OraInventory is present in all the nodes; however, we suggest executing from the first node, where the original installation started.) Run the following from node1:

```
$ srvctl  stop asm -n rac4

$ srvctl  remove asm -n rac4
```

Run the following from RAC4:

```
$cd    $ORACLE_HOME/admin

$rm  -rf  +ASM

$cd  $ORACLE_HOME/dbs

$rm -f  *ASM*
```

You may also have to edit the /etc/oratab file and remove entries beginning with *+ASM* to remove the references of the ASM instance in the node.

Remove the Listener from Node to Be Deleted

Do the following from RAC4 to remove the listener:

1. Log in as the *oracle* user and set the ORACLE_HOME to database home:

   ```
   $ORACLE_HOME/bin/netca
   ```

2. Choose Cluster Management.
3. Choose Listener.
4. Choose Remove.
5. Confirm deletion of LISTENER.

Removing the Node from the Database

Do the following to remove the node from the database.

1. Run this script from RAC4:

   ```
   $ cd   $ORACLE_HOME/oui/bin
   $ ./runInstaller  -updateNodeList ORACLE_HOME=$ORACLE_HOME
   "CLUSTER_NODES={rac4}" -local
   $ ./runInstaller
   ```

2. Choose to deinstall products and select the dbhome. This will remove the database home software and leave behind only some files and directories.

3. Run the following from RAC1:

   ```
   cd   $ORACLE_HOME/oui/bin

        ./runInstaller  -updateNodeList ORACLE_HOME=$ORACLE_HOME
   "CLUSTER_NODES={rac1,rac2,rac3}"
   ```

Removing RAC4 from the Clusterware

Do the following to remove the RAC4 node from the clusterware.

1. Run the following from RAC1:

   ```
   $CRS_HOME/bin/racgons remove_config  rac4:6200
   ```

   (Replace port 6200 in this command with the port number that you get in the remoteport section of the ons.config file found in the $ORA_CRS_HOME/opmn/conf directory.)

2. Run the following from RAC4. This should be done as user *root* as the clusterware is run as user *root*.

   ```
   cd  $CRS_HOME/install
   #./rootdelete.sh
   ```

3. Upon successful completion of the rootdelete.sh script, run the following from RAC1 as *root*:

    ```
    $CRS_HOME/bin/olsnodes -n
    ```

    This command's output will provide the node number for RAC4 (which is 4):

    ```
    cd  $CRS_HOME/install
    ./rootdeletenode.sh  rac4,4
    ```

4. Run the following from RAC4 as user *oracle*:

    ```
    cd  $CRS_HOME/oui/bin
    ./runInstaller  -updateNodeList ORACLE_HOME=$CRS_HOME
    "CLUSTER_NODES={rac4}"   CRS=TRUE -local
    ./runInstaller
    ```

5. Choose Deinstall Software and remove the CRSHOME.

6. Run the following from RAC1. First log in as the *oracle* user.

    ```
    cd  $CRS_HOME/oui/bin

    ./runInstaller -updateNodeList  ORACLE_HOME=$CRS_HOME
    "CLUSTER_NODES={rac1,rac2,rac3}" CRS=TRUE
    ```

To verify the removal of the RAC4 from the cluster, run the following commands.

1. First, run the following from RAC1:

    ```
    srvctl  status nodeapps -n rac4
    ```

    You should see a message saying "Invalid node."

2. Now run the following:

    ```
    crs_stat| grep -i rac4
    ```

    You should not see any output for this command.

    ```
    olsnodes -n
    ```

    You should see the present node list without the deleted node(s) (that is, RAC1, RAC2, and RAC3 only).

APPENDIX
C

References

e made every effort to provide you with a list of all the materials we have used as references for this book. Any omission from this list is purely unintentional.

Chapter 1

Dictionary.com. http:/www.dictionary.com

Peterson, Erik. "RAC at a Distance." Oracle OpenWorld conference, San Francisco, 2005.

Oracle Database High Availability Overview 10g Release 2 (10.2). Part Number B14210-02.

Oracle Database High Availability Best Practices 10g Release 2 (10.2). Part Number B25159-01

"Implementing HA with Oracle Real Application Clusters," Oracle World Presentation, 2005.

Oracle Database New Features Guide 10g Release 2 (10.2). Part Number B14214-02

Chapter 2

Pfister, Gregory F. *In Search of Clusters*, 2nd ed. Prentice Hall PTR, 1997.

Slee, Roland. "Oracle RAC 10g Value Proposition." October 2004. http://www.oracleracsig.org.

Oracle8i Parallel Server Concepts and Administration Release 8.1.5. Part Number A67778-01.

Oracle8i Parallel Server Setup and Configuration Guide Release 8.1.5. Part Number A67439-01.

Oracle9i Real Application Clusters Administration Release 2 (9.2). Part Number A96596-01.

Oracle Database New Features Guide 10g Release 2 (10.2). Part Number B14214-02.

Chapter 3

Oracle Corporation. Metalink forum and support notes. http://metalink.oracle.com.

Vaidyanatha, Gaja Krishna, Kirtikumar Deshpande, and John A. Kostelac. *Oracle Performance Tuning 101*. Osborne/Mc Graw-Hill, 2001.

Oracle9i Real Application Clusters Concepts Release 2 (9.2). Part Number A96597-01.

Oracle Database Reference 10g Release 1 (10.1). Part Number B10755-01.

Oracle Database Concepts 10g Release 2 (10.2)Part Number B14220-02.

Oracle Database Oracle Clusterware and Oracle Real Application Clusters Installation Guide 10g Release 2 (10.2) for hp Tru64. Part Number B14206-01.

Oracle Database Oracle Clusterware and Oracle Real Application Clusters Installation Guide 10g Release 2 (10.2) for Linux. Part Number B14203-07.

Oracle Database Oracle Clusterware and Oracle Real Application Clusters Administration and Deployment Guide 10g Release 2 (10.2). Part Number B14197-03.

Oracle Database Patch Set Notes 10g Release 1 (10.1.0.4). Patch Set 2 for Linux x86.

Chapter 4

Gopalakrishnan, K. "Tracing Universal Installer." *SELECT Journal.* Quarter 4, 2005.

Oracle Database Oracle Clusterware and Oracle Real Application Clusters Installation Guide 10g Release 2 (10.2) for Linux. Part Number B14203-07.

Oracle Database Oracle Clusterware and Oracle Real Application Clusters Administration and Deployment Guide 10g Release 2 (10.2). Part Number B14197-03.

Oracle Database Patch Set Notes 10g Release 1 (10.1.0.4), Patch Set 2 for Linux x86.

Oracle Database New Features Guide 10g Release 2 (10.2). Part Number B14214-02.

Chapter 5

Oracle Corporation. Metalink forum and support notes. http://metalink.oracle.com.

Oracle Database Oracle Clusterware and Oracle Real Application Clusters Installation Guide 10g Release 2 (10.2) for Linux. Part Number B14203-07.

Oracle Database Oracle Clusterware and Oracle Real Application Clusters Administration and Deployment Guide 10g Release 2 (10.2). Part Number B14197-03.

Oracle Database Patch Set Notes 10g Release 1 (10.1.0.4) Patch Set 2 for Linux x86.

Oracle Database New Features Guide 10g Release 2 (10.2). Part Number B14214-02.

Chapter 6

Oracle Corporation. Metalink forum and support notes. http://metalink.oracle.com.

Oracle Database Oracle Clusterware and Oracle Real Application Clusters Installation Guide 10g Release 2 (10.2) for Linux. Part Number B14203-07.

Oracle Database Oracle Clusterware and Oracle Real Application Clusters Administration and Deployment Guide 10g Release 2 (10.2). Part Number B14197-03.

Oracle Database Patch Set Notes 10g Release 1 (10.1.0.4) Patch Set 2 for Linux x86.

Oracle Database Administrator's Guide 10g Release 2 (10.2). Part Number B14231-02.

Oracle Database New Features Guide 10g Release 2 (10.2). Part Number B14214-02.

Chapter 7

Oracle Database Concepts 10g Release 2 (10.2). Part Number B14220-02.

Oracle Database Oracle Clusterware and Oracle Real Application Clusters Administration and Deployment Guide 10g Release 2 (10.2). Part Number B14197-01.

Oracle Database Administrator's Guide 10g Release 2 (10.2). Part Number B14231-02.

Oracle Database New Features Guide 10g Release 2 (10.2). Part Number B14214-02.

Oracle Database Reference 10g Release 1 (10.1). Part Number B10755-01.

Chapter 8

Oracle Database Oracle Clusterware and Oracle Real Application Clusters Administration and Deployment Guide 10g Release 2 (10.2). Part Number B14197-01.

Oracle Database Net Services Administrator's Guide 10g Release 2 (10.2). Part Number B14212-01.

Oracle Database Reference 10g Release 1 (10.1). Part Number B10755-01.

Oracle Database Application Developer's Guide: Fundamentals 10g Release 2 (10.2). Chapter 15. Part Number B14251-01.

Oracle Database PL/SQL Packages and Types Reference 10g Release 2 (10.2). Part Number B14258-01.

Oracle Database Patch Set Notes 10g Release 1 (10.1.0.4), Patch Set 2 for Linux x86.

Chapter 9

Oracle Database Backup and Recovery Basics 10g Release 2 (10.2). Part Number B14192-03.

Oracle Database Oracle Clusterware and Oracle Real Application Clusters Installation Guide 10g Release 2 (10.2) for hp Tru64. Part Number B14206-01.

Oracle Database Backup and Recovery Advanced User's Guide 10g Release 2 (10.2). Part Number B14191-02.

Oracle Database New Features Guide 10g Release 2 (10.2). Part Number B14214-02.

Oracle Database Concepts 10g Release 2 (10.2). Part Number B14220-02.

Oracle9i Real Application Clusters Administration Release 2 (9.2). Part Number A96596-01.

Oracle9i Real Application Clusters Real Application Clusters Guard I: Concepts and Administration Release 2 (9.2). Part Number A96601-01.

Oracle9i Real Application Clusters Setup and Configuration Release 2 (9.2). Part Number A96600-02.

Oracle8i Parallel Server Concepts and Administration Release 8.1.5 A67778-01.

Oracle9i Real Application Clusters Concepts Release 2 (9.2). Part Number A96597-01.

Oracle Database Oracle Clusterware and Oracle Real Application Clusters Installation Guide 10g Release 2 (10.2) for Linux. Part Number B14203-07.

Oracle Database Oracle Clusterware and Oracle Real Application Clusters Administration and Deployment Guide 10g Release 2 (10.2). Part Number B14197-03.

Chapter 10

Deshpande, Kirtikumar, Richmond Shee, and K. Gopalakrishnan. *Oracle Wait Interface: A Practical Guide to Performance Diagnostics & Tuning.* Osborne/Mc-Graw Hill, 2004.

Oracle Database Performance Tuning Guide 10g Release 2 (10.2). Part Number B14211-01.

Oracle Database New Features Guide 10g Release 2 (10.2). Part Number B14214-02.

Oracle Database Concepts 10g Release 2 (10.2). Part Number B14220-02.

Oracle9i Real Application Clusters Administration Release 2 (9.2). Part Number A96596-01.

Oracle8i Parallel Server Concepts and Administration Release 8.1.5 A67778-01.

Oracle9i Real Application Clusters Concepts Release 2 (9.2). Part Number A96597-01.

Chapter 11

Deshpande, Kirtikumar, Richmond Shee, and K. Gopalakrishnan. *Oracle Wait Interface: A Practical Guide to Performance Diagnostics & Tuning.* Osborne/Mc-Graw Hill. 2004.

E-mail discussions in comp.databases.oracle.server and oracle-l mailing lists.

Oracle Database Concepts 10g Release 2 (10.2). Part Number B14220-02.

Oracle9i Real Application Clusters Real Application Clusters Guard I - Concepts and Administration Release 2 (9.2). Part Number A96601-01.

Oracle8i Parallel Server Concepts and Administration Release 8.1.5 A67778-01.

Oracle9i Real Application Clusters Concepts Release 2 (9.2). Part Number A96597-01.

Chapter 12

Demel, Sohan. "Oracle Real Application Clusters: Cache Fusion Delivers Scalability." Oracle whitepaper. February 2002.

E-mail discussions in comp.databases.oracle.server and oracle-l mailing lists.

Oracle Database Concepts 10g Release 2 (10.2). Part Number B14220-02.

Oracle9i Real Application Clusters Real Application Clusters Guard I: Concepts and Administration Release 2 (9.2). Part Number A96601-01.

Oracle8i Parallel Server Concepts and Administration Release 8.1.5 A67778-01.

Oracle9i Real Application Clusters Concepts Release 2 (9.2). Part Number A96597-01.

Chapter 13

E-mail discussions in comp.databases.oracle.server and oracle-l mailing lists.

Oracle Database Net Services Administrator's Guide 10g Release 2 (10.2). Part Number B14212-02.

Oracle Database Net Services Reference 10g Release 2 (10.2). Part Number B14213-01.

Oracle9i Real Application Clusters Real Application Clusters Guard I - Concepts and Administration Release 2 (9.2). Part Number A96601-01.

Oracle8i Parallel Server Concepts and Administration Release 8.1.5 A67778-01.

Oracle9i Real Application Clusters Concepts Release 2 (9.2). Part Number A96597-01.

Chapter 14

E-mail discussions in comp.databases.oracle.server and oracle-l mailing lists.

Oracle Database Concepts 10g Release 2 (10.2). Part Number B14220-02.

Oracle9i Real Application Clusters Real Application Clusters Guard I: Concepts and Administration Release 2 (9.2). Part Number A96601-01.

Oracle8i Parallel Server Concepts and Administration Release 8.1.5 A67778-01.

Oracle9i Real Application Clusters Concepts Release 2 (9.2). Part Number A96597-01.

Chapter 15

Peterson, Erik. "RAC at a Distance." Oracle OpenWorld Conference, San Francisco, 2005.

E-mail discussion in Oracle-l mailing list.

E-mail discussions in comp.databases.oracle.server and oracle-l mailing lists.

HP/Oracle CTC Webpage. http://www.hporaclectc.com.

Oracle Maximum Availability Architecture (MAA). http://www.oracle.com/technology/deploy/availability/htdocs/maa.htm.

Chapter 16

E-mail discussions in comp.databases.oracle.server and oracle-l mailing lists.

Oracle Database Concepts 10g Release 2 (10.2). Part Number B14220-02.

Oracle Database Application Developer's Guide: Fundamentals 10g Release 2 (10.2)Part Number B14251-01.

Oracle8i Parallel Server Concepts and Administration Release 8.1.5 A67778-01.

Oracle9i Real Application Clusters Concepts Release 2 (9.2). Part Number A96597-01.

Index

GET YOUR FREE SUBSCRIPTION
TO ORACLE MAGAZINE

Oracle Magazine is essential gear for today's information technology professionals. Stay informed and increase your productivity with every issue of *Oracle Magazine*. Inside each free bimonthly issue you'll get:

- Up-to-date information on Oracle Database, Oracle Application Server, Web development, enterprise grid computing, database technology, and business trends
- Third-party vendor news and announcements
- Technical articles on Oracle and partner products, technologies, and operating environments
- Development and administration tips
- Real-world customer stories

IF THERE ARE OTHER ORACLE USERS AT YOUR LOCATION WHO WOULD LIKE TO RECEIVE THEIR OWN SUB-SCRIPTION TO ORACLE MAGAZINE, PLEASE PHOTOCOPY THIS FORM AND PASS IT ALONG.

Three easy ways to subscribe:

① Web
Visit our Web site at otn.oracle.com/oraclemagazine.
You'll find a subscription form there, plus much more!

② Fax
Complete the questionnaire on the back of this card and fax the questionnaire side only to +1.847.763.9638.

③ Mail
Complete the questionnaire on the back of this card and mail it to P.O. Box 1263, Skokie, IL 60076-8263

ORACLE

FREE SUBSCRIPTION

○ **Yes, please send me a FREE subscription to *Oracle Magazine*.**   ○ **NO**

To receive a free subscription to *Oracle Magazine*, you must fill out the entire card, sign it, and date it (incomplete cards cannot be processed or acknowledged). You can also fax your application to +1.847.763.9638.
Or subscribe at our Web site at otn.oracle.com/oraclemagazine

○ From time to time, Oracle Publishing allows our partners exclusive access to our e-mail addresses for special promotions and announcements. To be included in this program, please check this circle.

○ Oracle Publishing allows sharing of our mailing list with selected third parties. If you prefer your mailing address not to be included in this program, please check here. If at any time you would like to be removed from this mailing list, please contact Customer Service at +1.847.647.9630 or send an e-mail to oracle@halldata.com.

signature (required) _____   date _____

X

name _____   title _____

company _____   e-mail address _____

street/p.o. box _____

city/state/zip or postal code _____   telephone _____

country _____   fax _____

YOU MUST ANSWER ALL TEN QUESTIONS BELOW.

① WHAT IS THE PRIMARY BUSINESS ACTIVITY OF YOUR FIRM AT THIS LOCATION? (check one only)
- □ 01 Aerospace and Defense Manufacturing
- □ 02 Application Service Provider
- □ 03 Automotive Manufacturing
- □ 04 Chemicals, Oil and Gas
- □ 05 Communications and Media
- □ 06 Construction/Engineering
- □ 07 Consumer Sector/Consumer Packaged Goods
- □ 08 Education
- □ 09 Financial Services/Insurance
- □ 10 Government (civil)
- □ 11 Government (military)
- □ 12 Healthcare
- □ 13 High Technology Manufacturing, OEM
- □ 14 Integrated Software Vendor
- □ 15 Life Sciences (Biotech, Pharmaceuticals)
- □ 16 Mining
- □ 17 Retail/Wholesale/Distribution
- □ 18 Systems Integrator, VAR/VAD
- □ 19 Telecommunications
- □ 20 Travel and Transportation
- □ 21 Utilities (electric, gas, sanitation, water)
- □ 98 Other Business and Services

② WHICH OF THE FOLLOWING BEST DESCRIBES YOUR PRIMARY JOB FUNCTION? (check one only)
Corporate Management/Staff
- □ 01 Executive Management (President, Chair, CEO, CFO, Owner, Partner, Principal)
- □ 02 Finance/Administrative Management (VP/Director/ Manager/Controller, Purchasing, Administration)
- □ 03 Sales/Marketing Management (VP/Director/Manager)
- □ 04 Computer Systems/Operations Management (CIO/VP/Director/ Manager MIS, Operations)
IS/IT Staff
- □ 05 Systems Development/ Programming Management
- □ 06 Systems Development/ Programming Staff
- □ 07 Consulting
- □ 08 DBA/Systems Administrator
- □ 09 Education/Training
- □ 10 Technical Support Director/Manager
- □ 11 Other Technical Management/Staff
- □ 98 Other

③ WHAT IS YOUR CURRENT PRIMARY OPERATING PLATFORM? (select all that apply)
- □ 01 Digital Equipment UNIX
- □ 02 Digital Equipment VAX VMS
- □ 03 HP UNIX
- □ 04 IBM AIX
- □ 05 IBM UNIX
- □ 06 Java
- □ 07 Linux
- □ 08 Macintosh
- □ 09 MS-DOS
- □ 10 MVS
- □ 11 NetWare
- □ 12 Network Computing
- □ 13 OpenVMS
- □ 14 SCO UNIX
- □ 15 Sequent DYNIX/ptx
- □ 16 Sun Solaris/SunOS
- □ 17 SVR4
- □ 18 UnixWare
- □ 19 Windows
- □ 20 Windows NT
- □ 21 Other UNIX
- □ 98 Other
- 99 □ None of the above

④ DO YOU EVALUATE, SPECIFY, RECOMMEND, OR AUTHORIZE THE PURCHASE OF ANY OF THE FOLLOWING? (check all that apply)
- □ 01 Hardware
- □ 02 Software
- □ 03 Application Development Tools
- □ 04 Database Products
- □ 05 Internet or Intranet Products
- 99 □ None of the above

⑤ IN YOUR JOB, DO YOU USE OR PLAN TO PURCHASE ANY OF THE FOLLOWING PRODUCTS? (check all that apply)
Software
- □ 01 Business Graphics
- □ 02 CAD/CAE/CAM
- □ 03 CASE
- □ 04 Communications
- □ 05 Database Management
- □ 06 File Management
- □ 07 Finance
- □ 08 Java
- □ 09 Materials Resource Planning
- □ 10 Multimedia Authoring
- □ 11 Networking
- □ 12 Office Automation
- □ 13 Order Entry/Inventory Control
- □ 14 Programming
- □ 15 Project Management
- □ 16 Scientific and Engineering
- □ 17 Spreadsheets
- □ 18 Systems Management
- □ 19 Workflow

Hardware
- □ 20 Macintosh
- □ 21 Mainframe
- □ 22 Massively Parallel Processing
- □ 23 Minicomputer
- □ 24 PC
- □ 25 Network Computer
- □ 26 Symmetric Multiprocessing
- □ 27 Workstation
Peripherals
- □ 28 Bridges/Routers/Hubs/Gateways
- □ 29 CD-ROM Drives
- □ 30 Disk Drives/Subsystems
- □ 31 Modems
- □ 32 Tape Drives/Subsystems
- □ 33 Video Boards/Multimedia
Services
- □ 34 Application Service Provider
- □ 35 Consulting
- □ 36 Education/Training
- □ 37 Maintenance
- □ 38 Online Database Services
- □ 39 Support
- □ 40 Technology-Based Training
- □ 98 Other
- 99 □ None of the above

⑥ WHAT ORACLE PRODUCTS ARE IN USE AT YOUR SITE? (check all that apply)
Oracle E-Business Suite
- □ 01 Oracle Marketing
- □ 02 Oracle Sales
- □ 03 Oracle Order Fulfillment
- □ 04 Oracle Supply Chain Management
- □ 05 Oracle Procurement
- □ 06 Oracle Manufacturing
- □ 07 Oracle Maintenance Management
- □ 08 Oracle Service
- □ 09 Oracle Contracts
- □ 10 Oracle Projects
- □ 11 Oracle Financials
- □ 12 Oracle Human Resources
- □ 13 Oracle Interaction Center
- □ 14 Oracle Communications/Utilities (modules)
- □ 15 Oracle Public Sector/University (modules)
- □ 16 Oracle Financial Services (modules)
Server/Software
- □ 17 Oracle9*i*
- □ 18 Oracle9*i* Lite
- □ 19 Oracle8*i*
- □ 20 Other Oracle database
- □ 21 Oracle9*i* Application Server
- □ 22 Oracle9*i* Application Server Wireless
- □ 23 Oracle Small Business Suite

Tools
- □ 24 Oracle Developer Suite
- □ 25 Oracle Discoverer
- □ 26 Oracle JDeveloper
- □ 27 Oracle Migration Workbench
- □ 28 Oracle9*i* AS Portal
- □ 29 Oracle Warehouse Builder
Oracle Services
- □ 30 Oracle Outsourcing
- □ 31 Oracle Consulting
- □ 32 Oracle Education
- □ 33 Oracle Support
- □ 98 Other
- 99 □ None of the above

⑦ WHAT OTHER DATABASE PRODUCTS ARE IN USE AT YOUR SITE? (check all that apply)
- □ 01 Access
- □ 02 Baan
- □ 03 dbase
- □ 04 Gupta
- □ 05 IBM DB2
- □ 06 Informix
- □ 07 Ingres
- □ 08 Microsoft Access
- □ 09 Microsoft SQL Server
- □ 10 PeopleSoft
- □ 11 Progress
- □ 12 SAP
- □ 13 Sybase
- □ 14 VSAM
- □ 98 Other
- 99 □ None of the above

⑧ WHAT OTHER APPLICATION SERVER PRODUCTS ARE IN USE AT YOUR SITE? (check all that apply)
- □ 01 BEA
- □ 02 IBM
- □ 03 Sybase
- □ 04 Sun
- □ 05 Other

⑨ DURING THE NEXT 12 MONTHS, HOW MUCH DO YOU ANTICIPATE YOUR ORGANIZATION WILL SPEND ON COMPUTER HARDWARE, SOFTWARE, PERIPHERALS, AND SERVICES FOR YOUR LOCATION? (check only one)
- □ 01 Less than $10,000
- □ 02 $10,000 to $49,999
- □ 03 $50,000 to $99,999
- □ 04 $100,000 to $499,999
- □ 05 $500,000 to $999,999
- □ 06 $1,000,000 and over

⑩ WHAT IS YOUR COMPANY'S YEARLY SALES REVENUE? (please choose one)
- □ 01 $500, 000, 000 and above
- □ 02 $100, 000, 000 to $500, 000, 000
- □ 03 $50, 000, 000 to $100, 000, 000
- □ 04 $5, 000, 000 to $50, 000, 000
- □ 05 $1, 000, 000 to $5, 000, 000

100103